Traumatic Affect

Traumatic Affect

Edited by

Meera Atkinson and Michael Richardson

CAMBRIDGE
SCHOLARS

PUBLISHING

Traumatic Affect,
Edited by Meera Atkinson and Michael Richardson

This book first published 2013

Cambridge Scholars Publishing

12 Back Chapman Street, Newcastle upon Tyne, NE6 2XX, UK

British Library Cataloguing in Publication Data
A catalogue record for this book is available from the British Library

ISBN (10): 1-4438-4867-0, ISBN (13): 978-1-4438-4867-1

TABLE OF CONTENTS

Part III: Mediatized

Part IV: Embodied

ACKNOWLEDGMENTS

Traumatic Affect, a collection of essays from contributors around the world, was conceived and developed within the Writing and Society Research Centre at the University of Western Sydney, Australia. The Centre hosted a public symposium on "Trauma: Writing, Art and Affect" in April 2011, which we convened, and has since supported the production of this book. We owe thanks to Anthony Uhlman, Ivor Indyk, our invaluable copyeditor and indexer Melinda Jewell, and all those in the Centre who pitched in along the way. We also wish to thank the participants and attendees of the 2011 symposium, several of whom appear in this volume, who helped begin the dialogue of which *Traumatic Affect* is the result. We would like to extend a special thanks to Anna Gibbs, Magdalena Zolkos, Deborah Staines and Catherine Camden-Pratt for their encouragement and assistance, and we are indebted to Kylie Boxall for her striking work on the cover image. Last but certainly not least, we thank the contributors to this collection who have so generously participated in this project, delivering powerful essays on the nexus of trauma and affect.

Shoshana Felman's essay "Benjamin's Silence" was previously published in *Critical Inquiry* Vol. 25 No. 2 (1999).

Jennifer L. Biddle's chapter "Radical Realism and Other Possibilities in Contemporary Intercultural Indigenous Australian Cinema" was developed from an essay written for the Sydney *Un_imaginable* exhibition catalogue, published in-house by Ivan-Dougherty Gallery (2008).

INTRODUCTION

AT THE NEXUS

MEERA ATKINSON
AND MICHAEL RICHARDSON

> The story of trauma [. . .] as the narrative of a belated experience, far from telling of an escape from reality—the escape from a death, or from its referential force—rather attests to its endless impact on a life.
>
> —Cathy Caruth, *Unclaimed Experience*, 7.

> Affect is an impingement or extrusion of a momentary or sometimes more sustained state of relation *as well as* the passage (and the duration of passage) of forces or intensities. That is, affect is found in those intensities that pass body to body (human, nonhuman, part-body, and otherwise), in those resonances that circulate about, between, and sometimes stick to bodies and worlds, *and* in their very passages or variations between these intensities and resonances themselves.
>
> —Melissa Gregg & Gregory Seigworth, *The Affect Theory Reader*, 1.

These quotes gesture towards the heart of this collection: the question of how trauma might be approached with respect for, and recognition of, its existence, recurrence, and lived presence as an "impossible event," while nonetheless examining the form, substance and dynamics of that impossibility in new ways. How might we recognize the continuum between personal and collective, without collapsing them into dichotomy? How can we think about trauma in terms of present relation rather than absence or disconnection? How would we re-imagine the transmission of trauma between bodies? How might we acknowledge, and even intervene upon, the cycle of affect and effect between individual and collective, familial and national? It is the contention of this volume that thinking trauma in terms of affect offers enormous promise. In what follows, we aim to set out a theoretical topology of the intersection of trauma and affect. Our intent here is not to provide a complete account of either field, but rather to establish those dynamics and relations of theory upon which these essays intervene.

Traumas

Trauma is inescapable. Inevitable. It is not rare, but common. The word "trauma" comes with innumerable connotations: hysteria, suffering, damage, and catastrophe, to name a few. What is catastrophic or exceptional for some—rape, war, torture—might constitute the everyday for others. Distinctions such as "everyday" and "extraordinary" between certain traumas are a useful shorthand, but prone to collapse all too readily. Trauma occurs on a relational spectrum—it is impossible to divorce it from context, whether personal or collective. Thus while it is crucial to address, theoretically and therapeutically, those most violent traumas, it is equally necessary to recognize those "lesser" shatterings that nonetheless shake not the world, but the inner workings of an individual body and psyche, or the dynamics and trajectory of a family or a group of friends, co-workers, neighbors or strangers. These are often the hidden sites of trauma: cyber bullying, porn culture, sexual harassment, violent video games, anorexia chat rooms, work and exercise addictions, just to name a few.

Globalized technology and the Internet have ushered in an era of unprecedented trans-national communication, transmitting information and affect in ways, at speeds, and across distances previously impossible. The question of what this means for the proliferation of trauma is an urgent one. Turn on the television, open a newspaper, click on a news site: disaster, death, loss, grief and pain in images of accidents, violent crime, children disappeared, rivers dried up, freak storms, refugees drowning in sinking boats, exported sheep slaughtered un-stunned and fighting for life in foreign harbors. That the world has always been a place of trauma is a given, but in our age we are implicated and confronted with it on a newly grand scale; we are thoroughly bound up with its endless mutations, complexities and ubiquity. A horror film shot in HD video can be edited on home computers and released to the world. Photographs of starving children and cats being experimented upon in a university laboratory go viral in Facebook newsfeeds. Adam Lanza kills 26 children and adults at Sandy Hook Elementary School in Newtown, Connecticut, and within hours a town's trauma is known to the world through cable news, web sites, amateur video. Our exposure to different and multiple traumatic events occurs in new modes and practices, proliferating at a pace our understanding and nervous systems struggle to keep up and cope with.

Faced with mounting trauma, either face to face or via media networks, many of us wish to close our eyes, to refuse the overwhelming onslaught from without and, often enough, from within. There is comfort in doing so; in staying within the safe bounds of knowing, recognizing trauma at a distance—as if through fog—but declining to draw closer. But at what cost? Even when the knowledge of trauma is refused, justified, minimized, or rationalized, can anyone ever hope to escape the affect that often generates it, and is generated by it? One option is to accumulate one's own traumas, attempting to keep them at arm's length and hoping to be spared that of others. To do so may well be the most common mode of existence in contemporary society. Yet to turn away from trauma is also to fail a crucial test of humanity. It might be that being open to one's own trauma is necessary in order to be open to that of another, and conversely opening to the trauma of others facilitates opening to one's own; a kind of Levinasian "responsibility to the Other."[1] There may be no more urgent necessity than this—to the degree that in denying one's own trauma, the other is exposed to the consequences of trauma and its affect. And by the same token, the trauma of others, irresponsibly unacknowledged, has a way of making itself known in the form of damaging effects. In this way, a dangerous cycle is perpetrated, a cycle in which everyone is affected and implicated.

Being implicated in complex and enduring trauma is something that we, as non-indigenous writers and editors working in the "Great Southern Land" of Australia, must acknowledge. We view the devastating and egregious post-colonial, post-traumatic cycle of denial around the trans-generational suffering of the Indigenous peoples of Australia[2] to be one of the most pressing concerns, in practical and ethical terms, of our nation. The telling of Aboriginal stories is critical to addressing, and intervening in this cycle, yet working in tension to this is the notorious difficulty of speaking trauma, especially trauma of a profound and intergenerational nature. The question of traumatic representation and embodiment is particularly interesting in the Indigenous context since traditionally Indigenous storytelling takes place through song, dance, body art and ceremony. Despite such tensions, Indigenous stories—traditional and traumatic—feature not only in the unique visual art now heartily embraced by the International art community, but also in a rich canon of

[1] Emmanuel Levinas, *Time and the Other*, trans. Richard A. Cohen (Pittsburgh: Duquesne University Press, 1987). 104., for example.

[2] This is discussed in the UN Committee on the Elimination of Racial Discrimination's "Concluding Observations of the Committee on the Elimination of Racial Discrimination (Australia)," (United Nations, 2010).

contemporary, diverse and emergent Indigenous textuality. Writers like Lionel Fogarty and Tara June Winch, who appeared in the *Macquarie PEN Anthology of Aboriginal Literature*[3] and Alexis Wright, whose novel *Carpentaria* won the 2007 Miles Franklin Award[4]—offer insights into Aboriginal experience. Film is another medium in which Indigenous stories are shining and surprising. *Samson and Delilah,*[5] director Warwick Thornton's indomitable and poignant portrayal of a young couple up against the odds, competed in and then won the Un Certain Regard section of the Caméra d'Or ("Gold Camera Award" for best first feature film). It was also nominated in the Academy Awards best foreign language film category and was critically acclaimed around the world. Rachel Perkin's feature film, *Bran Neu Dae,*[6] was a radically different and paradoxical take on collective trauma with its ironic employment of the soap and musical comedy genres and plot in which "everyone turns out to be related to everyone else to ameliorate traumatic loss by laughter, possibly because the effects of forcible separation touch almost everyone in that community."[7] Though the tunes are cheery, the deadly serious trauma at the heart of the film cannot be mistaken in lyrics like "There's nothing I would rather be than to be an Aborigine and watch you take my precious land away." The ground breaking six-part drama series *Redfern Now,*[8] produced by Blackfella Films in association with ABC TV, tells the stories of six inner-city households living in one street in the infamous Sydney suburb of Redfern. In each, the complexity of urban Indigenous life is conveyed with extraordinary skill. At every turn trauma intertwines with the remarkable spirit, resilience and resourcefulness of this community to yield stories with as much courage as heart; uncompromisingly honest and smart, these are not just stories by Indigenous people for Indigenous people: they even demand the attention of those who would not readily give it, commanding witness, engagement, ethical response.

From the macro world of geopolitics to the micro of familial relations, the recognition of trauma as trauma is crucial because it gives name and shape to a form of experience that is a rupturing of the capacity to make sense of the world; it recognizes the impossible event as existing, lived in

---

[3] Anita Heiss and Peter Minter eds., *Macquarie PEN Anthology of Aboriginal Literature*, NSW: Allen & Unwin, 2008.
[4] Alexis Wright, *Carpentaria*, Sydney: Giramondo Publishing, 2006.
[5] *Samson and Delilah*, dir. Warwick Thornton, Australia: Madman Entertainment, 2009.
[6] *Bran Neu Dae*, dir. Rachel Perkins, Australia: Roadshow Films, 2009.
[7] Anna Gibbs in a private conversation in December 2012.
[8] *Redfern Now*, Blackfella Films and ABC TV, 2012.

the catastrophic, the everyday and every gradation between. But to name something trauma is also to inscribe it within the discourses and definitions of clinical trauma studies and literary trauma theory. Trauma has its scientific meaning, particularly within medicine, and is also a deeply loaded psychological and psychoanalytic term. It is the latter understanding that has gained common currency in political, cultural, and social uses of the word. By the end of the 20th century trauma theory had emerged from its origins in psychoanalysis and the experience of listening to the testimony of Holocaust survivors to deepen understandings of violence and vulnerability. Theorists such as Nicolas Abraham and Maria Torok, Shoshana Felman and Dori Laub, Dominick LaCapra, and Cathy Caruth brought this emergent interest in trauma to bear on literature in ways that expanded understanding of the operations of both.[9] While their work is varied in focus and sensibility, in broad terms it views trauma as the delayed manifestation of a psychic wound sustained during an experience that has happened too quickly to allow registration and processing of the event at the time of its occurrence. To study trauma in literary or cultural terms, then, is to be concerned with the tension between what is known and what is not known, and with the impact and dynamics of the woundedness and machinations of trauma—not only its purely physical instantiation, but in all its reverberations. This is what brings the study of trauma to the uncertainty of truth, the impossibility of bearing absolute witness to catastrophe, the multiplicity of historical narratives.

If one were to imagine what comes after the ground-breaking work of the aforementioned scholars, it is surely not an effort to resolve the dilemmas outlined with such elegance and perspicacity by such thinkers. Rather, it would be to seek to understand the relationality of trauma. This relationality applies to the traumatic event itself—to the dynamic between knowing and not, between body and event, between event and memory. It is hardly surprising that during the 20th century, with its two world wars

---

[9] Nicolas Abraham and Maria Torok, *The Shell and the Kernel*, trans. Nicholas T. Rand, vol. 1 (Chicago: University of Chicago Press, 1994); Shoshana Felman and Dori Laub, *Testimony: Crises of Witnessing in Literature, Psychoanalysis, and History* (New York: Routledge, 1992); Dominick LaCapra, *Writing History, Writing Trauma* (Baltimore: The Johns Hopkins University Press, 2001); Cathy Caruth, *Unclaimed Experience: Trauma, Narrative, and History* (Baltimore: Johns Hopkins University Press, 1996); Cathy Caruth, *Trauma: Explorations in Memory* (Baltimore: The Johns Hopkins University Press, 1995); Dominick LaCapra, *Representing the Holocaust: History, Theory, Trauma* (Ithaca, NY: Cornell University Press, 1994); Dominick LaCapra, *History and Memory after Auschwitz* (Ithaca, NY: Cornell University Press, 1998).

and countless other conflicts, genocidal hot spots, and forging and crumbling of empires, trauma and its testimony became something of a norm. As Felman has noted, testimony is the literary mode of our times, and "our era can precisely be defined as the age of testimony."[10] Not only is trauma central to life in our age, it increasingly takes new forms, is transmitted in new ways, and has new effects. We need to consider what advanced dimensions might be brought to our understanding of trauma, and what those fresh understandings might produce.

When trauma theory emerged as a distinct mode of literary and cultural analysis in the 1990s, Felman and Laub, Caruth, LaCapra, and others drew extensively on poststructuralism and deconstruction, the dominant theoretical discourses of the time. Re-thinking psychoanalytic models of trauma through a poststructural lens enabled texts—literature, cinema, art—to be read as structurally and linguistically traumatized, rather than simply describing, directly or thematically, the experience of trauma. Arguably, it was this linking of theoretical modes that facilitated the establishment of trauma theory as a field in and of itself, emerging as a coherent critical practice grounded in the key thought of the day. Since the turn of the century, poststructuralism, while still a productive and useful mode of analysis, has ceded ground in the academy to a renewed materialism. At the forefront of this new materialism is the revitalized study of affect. This volume contends that affect theory offers productive possibilities for thinking differently about trauma.

Affects

For much of the 20th century, mainstream literary criticism in the west was dominated by "New Criticism," which held that literature was to be "examined with exclusive attention to the facts of the work undistorted by the reader's personal encounter with it."[11] Likewise, the poststructural revolution was concerned solely with the pure text, but this time in terms of instabilities, linguistic play, and structures of meaning. Fragmentation, decentered narratives, disrupted binaries, marginalized terms—these and other entities made their way into the light in deconstructive analysis. Singular truth claims no longer stood, felled by the end of metanarratives —an event that found its political mirror in the collapse of the Soviet Union. But where poststructuralism reached its theoretical limit was in the

[10] Felman and Laub, *Testimony,* 5.

[11] Alice Brand, "Hot Cognition: Emotions and Writing Behavior," *Journal of Advanced Composition* 6 (1985-6): 7.

experience of the body, the singularity within the multiplicity that is moved by an encounter—with a text, with an other, with art or culture, politics or experience. For example, Paul de Man's *Allegories of Reading*,[12] for all its analytic brilliance and persuasive force, leaves the encounter of body and text in the wake of his deconstructive philosophy of textual referentiality.

It is exactly this question of encounter the "affective turn"[13] addresses. As Melissa Gregg and Gregory J. Seigworth write, "Affect is in many ways synonymous with *force* or *forces of encounter*."[14] Affect is always about moving or being moved. Affect theory—and emotions studies[15]—also challenges the assumptions of both traditional psychoanalysis and certain central tenets of poststructuralism, in particular its tendency toward abstraction. Feminist and critical race theorists have long been at the forefront of challenges to such assumptions and abstractions in championing focus on the body, on specific bodies, and in particular on those bodies most ignored, maligned and exploited, whether in social, political or theoretical realms. Elaborated through the study of film, art, literature, and the everyday, affect theory has been concerned with a steadfast refusal to establish homogeneity. "Affect theory" is, in this sense, a misnomer. Not singular, it is rather a complex, and often contradictory, jostling of theoretical approaches, some of which existed well before the term "affect theory" gained currency. [16] If trauma theory is rooted in

---

[12] Paul de Man, *Allegories of Reading* (New Haven: Yale University Press, 1979).

[13] Patricia Ticiento Clough, "Introduction," in *The Affective Turn: Theorizing the Social*, ed. Patricia Ticiento Clough (Durham: Duke University Press, 2007).

[14] Melissa Gregg and Gregory J. Seigworth, "An Inventory of Shimmers," in *The Affect Theory Reader*, ed. Melissa Gregg and Gregory J. Seigworth (Durham, NC: Duke University Press, 2010), 2.

[15] For an account of the study of both affect and emotion in relation to politics, culture and the everyday, see Sara Ahmed, *The Cultural Politics of Emotion* (New York: Routledge, 2004).

[16] To cite just a handful of influential texts, Gilles Deleuze and Felix Guattari, *A Thousand Plateaus: Capitalism and Schizophrenia*, trans. Brian Massumi (Minneapolis: University of Minnesota Press, 1987); Gilles Deleuze and Felix Guattari, *What Is Philosophy?*, trans. Hugh Tomlinson and Graham Burchell (New York: Columbia University Press, 1994); Brian Massumi, *Parables for the Virtual: Movement, Affect, Sensation*, Post-Contemporary Interventions (Durham: Duke University Press, 2002); Eve Kosofsky Sedgwick, *Touching Feeling: Affect, Pedagogy, Performativity* (Durham & London: Duke University Press, 2003); Teresa Brennan, *The Transmission of Affect* (Ithaca: Cornell University Press, 2004); Silvan S. Tomkins, *Affect, Imagery, Consciousness*, 4 vols. (New York &

diverse locations, spanning industrial accidents, psychiatric interest in sexuality, the psychology of war and more, and generating a range of proto-traumatic ideas such as shell shock and railway spine syndrome, affect theory similarly boasts a multifaceted conceptual genealogy. As Gregg and Seigworth show in the introduction to *The Affect Theory Reader*, there are at least eight recognizable strands of affect, but we share their view that the two most significant are "Silvan Tomkins's psychobiology of differential affects and Gilles Deleuze's Spinozist ethology of bodily capacities."[17] While the former rebels against traditional psychoanalytic thinking in establishing an alternative framework for thinking about human development and interaction, the latter focuses on the visceral and autonomic forces and capacities that constitute and transform bodies and the relations between them.[18] Broadly speaking, the essays in this volume work with understandings of affect that draw from one or both of these strands. As such, these two approaches deserve some explication.

On the first page of *The Affective Turn*, Michael Hardt names 17th century scholar Baruch Spinoza as the "philosopher who has advanced furthest the theory of the affects and whose thought is the source, either directly or indirectly, of most of the contemporary work in this field."[19] He goes on to identify Spinoza's challenge to the Cartesian mind/body split by way of his theory of the affects, which, in effect, posits affect as straddling the relationship between mind and body in what amounts to an affect-ethic.[20] Spinoza's ethics refers to the increase or decrease of the power, or being-ness, of a being—that which increases being-ness is ethical; that which decreases it is unethical. Spinoza cites affect as the capacity to

---

London: Springer & Tavistock, 1963-1992). Of course, further works by these and other authors could be readily added to this list.

[17] Gregg and Seigworth, "An Inventory of Shimmers," 5. Key texts in these two strands include Eve Kosofsky Sedgwick and Adam Frank, *Shame and Its Sisters: A Silvan Tomkins Reader* (Durham: Duke University Press, 1995); Tomkins, *Affect, Imagery, Consciousness*; as well as Brian Massumi, "The Autonomy of Affect," in *Deleuze: A Critical Reader*, ed. Paul Patton (Cambridge, MA: Blackwell, 1996); and Gilles Deleuze, *Spinoza: Practical Philosophy*, trans. Robert Hurley (San Francisco: City Lights Books, 1988).

[18] For more detailed discussion on these and other approaches to affect, see Gregg and Seigworth, "An Inventory of Shimmers," and Patricia Clough's introduction to her edited collection *The Affective Turn: Theorizing the Social* (Durham: Duke University Press, 2007).

[19] Michael Hardt, "Foreward," in *The Affective Turn: Theorizing the Social*, ed. Patricia Ticiento Clough (Durham: Duke University Press, 2007), ix.

[20] Ibid., x.

increase being-ness through its facilitation of perception leading to understanding and reason. Whatever decreases this capacity is unethical. He states:

> Whatever so disposes the human body that it can be affected in a great many ways, or renders it capable of affecting external bodies in a great many ways, is useful to man; the more it renders the body capable of being affected in a great many ways, or of affecting other bodies, the more useful it is; on the other hand, what renders the body less capable of these things is harmful.[21]

This combination of ethics and affectivity, or bodily capacity, deeply influences Deleuze's conception of affect. For Deleuze, affect is constitutive of the body, which is the "capacity for affecting and being affected."[22] In his works on cinema, for example, Deleuze emphasizes the necessity of considering cultural artifacts in terms of encounter. The there-ness of the cinematic image—its sheer existence without the scaffolding of words—demands attention.[23] One must view it and view it over time. Which is to say, one must encounter it bodily, affectively. Deleuze, along with Felix Guattari, influences the work of Brian Massumi, author of the influential essay "The Autonomy of Affect."[24] Here affect is also termed "intensity" and is considered operative as virtual. It is, writes Massumi, "something that happens too quickly to have happened."[25] Massumi defines *affect* as "unqualified. As such, it is not ownable or recognizable,"[26] whereas *emotion* is "subjective content," "qualified intensity" that is "owned and recognized."[27] Massumi declares that affect is "resistant to critique," pointing out that: "It is not that there are no

---

[21] Baruch Spinoza, *The Ethics and Selected Letters*, trans. Samuel Shirley (London: Hackett Publishing Company, 1982), 137.
[22] Gilles Deleuze, "Ethology: Spinoza and Us," in *Incorporations*, ed. Jonathan Crary and Sanford Kwinter (New York: Zone, 1992), 626.
[23] Gilles Deleuze, *Cinema 1: The Movement-Image*, trans. Hugh Tomlinson and Barbara Habberjam (London: Continuum, 2005).
[24] Massumi, "The Autonomy of Affect." Gregg and Seigworth, "Shimmers," 5, attest to the importance of this essay, as well as that of Sedgwick and Frank on Silvan Tomkins, in defining these two approaches to affect. Eve Kosofsky Sedgwick and Adam Frank, "Shame in the Cybernetic Fold: Reading Silvan Tomkins," in *Shame and Its Sisters: A Silvan Tomkins Reader* (Durham: Duke University Press, 1995).
[25] Massumi, "The Autonomy of Affect," 224.
[26] Ibid., 222.
[27] Ibid., 221.

philosophical antecedents to draw on. It is just that they aren't the usual ones for literary and cultural studies."[28] Viewing affect in this way is to view existence as a continuum, clusters of intensity within a swirling world of changing bodies.

This neo-Spinozan view of affect as an autonomous force or intensity of relation has its counter-point in those affect theorists whose work was rooted in the study of emotions, and who responded not to the linguistic turn of deconstruction but to Freudian psychoanalysis. While the modern study of emotions might be said to begin with Charles Darwin's *The Expression of the Emotions in Man and Animals*[29] and be developed further by William James,[30] it was Freud's linking of affect to instinct and the unconscious that brought forth the concept of an autonomic bodily force within the purview of psychoanalysis. In the 1960s Silvan Tomkins re-cast affects as "the primary motivational system in human beings" and "the primitive gods within the individual."[31] While some echoed these ideas in academic contexts, such as Daniel N. Stern with his work on infant psychology, numerous authors adopted them for the bourgeoning market of pop psychology, which gave rise to the proto-affective idea of "toxic shame" so prevalent in the self-help annals of the 1980s and 1990s. This trend spawned a trove of titles, and was epitomized by the John Bradshaw best-seller, *Healing the Shame That Binds You*, a book Amazon.com refers to as a "Recovery Classic."[32]

Teresa Brennan, in her innovative work *The Transmission of Affect*, writes that "The term 'affect' is one translation of the Latin *affectus*, which can be translated as 'passion' or 'emotion.'"[33] For Brennan, then, affects "are material, physiological things" that "may be felt and taken on board by the other, depending on circumstances."[34] In this, Brennan follows Silvan Tomkins,[35] who put forth a model of affect/feeling/emotion that

---

[28] Ibid., 222.

[29] Charles Darwin, *The Expression of the Emotions in Man and Animals*, ed. F. Darwin (London: John Murray, 1904).

[30] Interestingly, James's philosophy of perception has also significantly influenced the recent work of Massumi, further pointing to the productive dynamics to be found between differing approaches to affect and emotion. Brian Massumi, *Semblance and Event: Activist Philosophy and the Occurrent Arts* (Cambridge, Mass: The MIT Press, 2011).

[31] Sedgwick and Frank, *Shame and Its Sisters*, 57.

[32] John Bradshaw, *Healing the Shame That Binds You* (Florida: Health Communications, Inc, 1988).

[33] Brennan, *The Transmission of Affect*, 3.

[34] Ibid., 6.

[35] Tomkins, *Affect, Imagery, Consciousness*.

views affect as a distinct biological, innate response to stimulus (biology/trans-cultural); while feeling is the awareness of the affect and the ability to comprehend it (psychology/subjective) and emotion is the affect/feeling filed away as memory (biography/individual history). There is a subtle distinction here between the conceptions of affect, sensation and emotion offered by Massumi, but, as a number of works in this volume demonstrate, productive possibility resides in working with both understandings of affect (and emotion). The work of Tomkins and Brennan show that affect is both specific and lived. Diverse thinkers such as Elspeth Probyn, Anna Gibbs, and Sara Ahmed[36] tease out the more material conception of affect espoused by Tomkins in different ways, often inflecting their work with Deleuzian notions of flux in their application of theory to lived experience and real-world situations. Affect, then, is concerned with what occurs in the currents and exchanges between bodies, not just what happens within them. It is this that gives it so much potential to deepen and widen our understanding of trauma.

Traumatic Affect

Thinking trauma in terms of affect is not without risk. The danger of doing so lies in either translating bodily experience to whole societies and cultures on the one hand, or on the other slipping into an endless field of Deleuzian multiplicities that coalesce, cohere, then erupt, decay or drift apart. The works collected here avoid these problems by grounding both affect and trauma within specific cultural, literary, cinematic, artistic and political milieus. Each asks questions at the intersection of trauma and diverse fields and forms of affect. In terms of methodology, specific chapters tend to focus on cultural works, but the stakes are higher: such analysis works through new thinking and is rarely the limit of the possible applications of each chapter.

---

[36] Ahmed, *The Cultural Politics of Emotion*; Anna Gibbs, "Contagious Feelings: Pauline Hanson and the Epidemiology of Affect," *Australian Humanities Review* 25 (2002) http://www.australianhumanitiesreview.org/archive/Issue-December-2001/gibbs.html; Anna Gibbs, "Panic! Affect Contagion, Mimesis and Suggestion in the Social Field," *Cultural Studies Review* 14, no. 2 (2008); Anna Gibbs, "After Affect: Sympathy, Synchrony and Mimetic Communication," in *The Affect Theory Reader*, ed. Melissa Gregg and Gregory J. Seigworth (Durham, NC: Duke University Press, 2010); Eslpeth Probyn, *Blush: Faces of Shame* (Sydney: UNSW Press, 2005); Sara Ahmed, *The Promise of Happiness* (Durham: Duke University Press, 2010).

Shoshana Felman's 1999 essay, "Benjamin's Silence,"[37] published just as the wave of affect theory was gathering strength, foreshadows the nexus of trauma and affect with which this collection is concerned. We are proud to be able to include this essay here. It is the first in this collection and the only reprint. "Benjamin's Silence" foreshadowed the nexus of trauma and affect the other contributors take up. As such, it is something of a foundation for the chapters that follow. For Felman, Benjamin is "a thinker, a philosopher, and a narrator of the wars and revolutions of the twentieth century." His life and writing are bound up with not only collective trauma, but also his own, particularly that which struck him silent in the wake of both the First World War and the suicide of his best friend Fritz Heinle, and of Heinle's girlfriend. According to Felman, "Benjamin's whole writing could be read as work of mourning, structured by a mute address to the dead face and the lost voice of the young friend who took his own life in desperate protest in the first days of the First World War." Although she does not use the term affect explicitly, Felman reveals how Benjamin's writings evoke trauma's affective resonances and forces within his silences. Felman's essay, then, prefigures the interrelation of affect and trauma with which this volume is concerned.

It is at this nexus of affect and trauma that we locate our vision of traumatic affect. There is no unitary definition of traumatic affect that can do justice to the varied approaches taken in this volume, or to the multiplicity of experiences of traumatic affect. Traumatic affect can, however, be understood as the mode, substance and dynamics of relation through which trauma is experienced, transmitted, conveyed, and represented. Traumatic affect crosses boundaries, between personal and political, text and body, screen and audience, philosophy and culture. It is not a prescriptive and contained concept, but an open one. Rather than narrowing the meaning of its constitutive terms, traumatic affect brings them into relation in dynamic and surprising ways, sometimes discovering spaces in between that refuse to conform to either.

Anna Gibbs's essay does more than discover surprising spaces of traumatic affect; it performs them in the affective resonance between apparently unrelated events. Over the past decade, Gibbs has written compellingly on affective contagion and the notion that "bodies can catch feelings as easily as catch fire."[38] While productive work no doubt needs to be done in considering trauma in such terms, in this volume Gibbs pushes her thinking on affect in exciting new directions when she speaks to the *concatenation* of traumatic affect in the everyday, from European

---

[37] Shoshana Felman, "Benjamin's Silence," *Critical Inquiry*, 25 no. 2 (1999).
[38] Gibbs, "Contagious Feelings," n.p.

cinema to a university environment in Australia. Concatenation: a term borrowed from formal language theory and computer programing, a word with a connection to circuitry, evoking linkages, patterns, a chain, and chain-reactions. Resonating between personal narrative and theory, Gibbs's "Apparently Unrelated: Affective Resonance, Concatenation and Traumatic Circuitry in the Terrain of the Everyday" asks that we re-imagine what constitutes traumatic relations. Conceiving of trauma as a shattering of the complex structure of the self, something that while not ubiquitous occurs across a range of spectrums and in numerous circumstances, Gibbs explores that which is inherent to the viewing of images, the way in which *something* is communicated before being cognitively grasped, as a structure analogous to trauma itself. Her text enacts and evokes this affectivity, not just in moving from unrecognized affect to grasped concept but with intensities spilling over, outside the words, remaining purely affective. Chantal Akerman's film *D'Est*, shot in 1991 in Paris, resonates with a traumatic academic institution, and with the act of writing her text for this collection—apparently unrelated traumas in circuit, affectively experienced.

Circuitries of trauma and affect are at the heart of Ben O'Loughlin's careful consideration of the complex ways in which we are at once increasingly subject to the gaze of the media and more empowered as media agents. "The Mediatization of Trauma and the Trauma of Mediatization: Benjamin, Tulloch, and the Struggle to Speak" asks how the traumatic event might be brought to a new audience. O'Loughlin "explores the ways in which trauma becomes publicly present in a mediatized environment but also examines the trauma of finding oneself mediatized." There is, he shows, an inherent tension between the news media paradigm of "stories" and the breaking of narrative that occurs in the traumatic event. After reading Benjamin's writings on history against the contemporary media environment, O'Loughlin draws on the case of John Tulloch, communications professor and survivor of the 7/7 London bombings, to explore the process of being traumatized by mediatization, as well as how such an experience can be worked through, and agency regained. Significantly, O'Loughlin argues that "the breakdown of distinctions between mass and personal communication and between public and private creates new opportunities for ordinary citizens to mediatize trauma on their own terms."

If the media environments of the 21st century present new challenges for both the understanding and experience of trauma, the catastrophic collective traumas of the 20th century—it's two world wars, multiple genocides, and the struggle against colonial empires, to name a few—

presented their own distinct problems for processing trauma through visual media. While in the west Godzilla is more pop icon than serious metaphor, Aaron Kerner shows how Gojira (a closer transliteration of the Japanese name) is a crucial response to Japan's national trauma following both the bombing of Hiroshima and Nagasaki, and collapse of empire and ensuing military emasculation. In "Gojira's Bones: The Monster as a Vessel of Affective Energy," Aaron Kerner traces traumatized Japanese nationalism's through the Gojira series of films, which are "a complex matrix of highly fluid historical and socio-cultural concerns." Kerner shows how Gojira represents "the traumatic experience the Japanese people endured." The monster, who must return to the ocean, enacts "an expulsion of what is impure, what is abject." As the "visible manifestation of social anxiety in the face of the stranger within the national-self," Gojira functions as an affective vessel for the "national(ist) trauma" of post-war Japan. Kerner's careful analysis reveals how identity itself can become traumatized, and how the affects of that trauma are taken up and given shape and intensity by the Gojira series, which not only dramatizes this process, but asks viewers to experience it affectively.

Jennifer Biddle, visual anthropologist of Aboriginal art, explores this territory in relation to the Indigenous nations of Australia. In "Radical Realism and Other Possibilities in Contemporary Intercultural Indigenous Australian Cinema" Biddle takes a sharply critical look at the post-colonial establishment. Turning her attention from the central desert art so globally celebrated and coveted in recent decades, to the under-rated, under-the-radar, yet essential and vital medium of short film, Biddle shows that such films, only minutes long, "shock, stun; they hurt, humiliate; they tantalize, delight and tickle." She adds that, "Their effectiveness / affectiveness resides in their very troubling of the supposed distinction between the drama taking place on the screen and the experience incited in viewer response." Drawing on Laura Marks's conception of "intercultural cinema," Biddle teases the political out of the personal in four short films that straddle worlds black and white and in-between. These celluloid snapshots of traumatic affect stretch across generations, harking back to pre-invasion bonds and traditions while simultaneously portraying present-day realities, both fractured and cunning. And in the background of these films and Biddle's analysis of them looms the "Apology," the history that gave rise to it, and the policies and practices currently part of the Northern Territory Intervention for which, perhaps, some as-yet-unknown Prime Minister of the future may be called upon to apologize.

An in-depth consideration of traumatic affect asks questions such as: what are the affective operations, aftershocks and echoes of a traumatic encounter? What implications and potential does affect have for our understanding of trauma as a social force? What are its limitations? Where does a radical revisioning of the substance of social relations leave us? What is trauma in a poststructural world? What recourse is there from the failure of language, when language is everything? Affect allows exploration of the prospect that trauma may not be inherently, or merely, a discreet subjective experience, but rather it might primarily be a cultural and transgenerational operation. Exploration at the nexus of trauma and affect is nothing less than an attempt to guide trauma theory into brave new territory, territory that makes it possible to consider trauma beyond cognition and language, beyond the individual and the collective, and even beyond the human.

Several chapters in this volume stretch the nexus in each of these ways, among them Jonathan L. Knapp's "Where the Buffalo No Longer Roam: Affect and Allegory in *The Last Hunt* and *The Last Buffalo Hunt*." Rarely does writing on trauma consider the non-human, and in his bid to do so Knapp examines the interplay of affect and allegory in depictions of animal death in the American west. Both films use footage of real buffalo slaughters, serving "to elicit affect and to allegorize the traumatic history of violence—against animals, Native Americans, and the land itself—that haunts the Western landscape." Drawing on both Benjamin and Deleuze, Knapp shows how the doubling layers of allegories are given an affective intensity by time-images of death, decay, and meat, and holds the attention of the audience such that "the viewer *feels* the suffering of the animal and reacts to it viscerally—with shudders of physical disgust, flashes of rage and agony, and waves of grief." Histories of trauma—the death and dispossession of native populations, the slaughter of buffalo, the reshaping of landscapes—are affectively allegorized. Watching, we cannot help but be both implicated in trauma, and made viscerally aware of our mortality.

Intricate relations between natural disaster, philosophy, literature, and individual experience are the subject of Karyn Ball's contribution to this volume, "The Earthquake after Kant's Lisbon: 'Visceral Reason' in Kleist's Precarious Modernity." Ball shows how trauma is not limited in transmission between individuals or within collectives. Rather, trauma can be affectively charged across events and texts, philosophies and experiences, fiction and theory. Where the Lisbon earthquake had rocked the metaphysical world of Kant and his generation, Kleist felt its aftershock within philosophy and the revolutionary upheavals of his time. In Ball's reading, trauma ripples affectively through texts and bodies and societies, manifesting in the visceral, over-spilling reason that dooms social relations in Kleist's novellas. As Ball shows, "Kleistean violence attests to an *inescapably volatile affective economy*, which pre-empts a social contract that enlists emotional control while ensnaring Kleist's rationalistic protagonists in nasty, brutish, and foreshortened fates." Tracing the web of relations between Kantian philosophy, the Lisbon earthquake, social contract theory, and Kleist's own trauma, Ball finds in his fiction a visceral awareness of the fragile existence that derives from trust in the habits and conventions of both the state and civility.

Meera Atkinson also addresses political, historical, and textual movements across time, space and spheres in her examination of trauma via theories of "hauntology." In her account of a poetics that reaches past cognition, the individual, and the human, Atkinson argues that texts and practices of writing can be spooked by the traumas of previous generations and specifically what she calls "trans-trauma"—the transgenerational transmission of trauma—can thereby stand as testimony beyond subjective trauma. Reflecting on her own creative practice in her essay "Channeling the Specter and Translating Phantoms: Hauntology and the Spooked Text," Atkinson shows how such writing is "not simply about trauma, but rather it is writing that embodies its subjective and cultural processes." Following Derrida, Atkinson argues that traumatic affect—particularly grief and shame—can be brought to consciousness through an active process of textual engagement, one that renders the neither-past-nor-present quality constitutive of trauma into literature. She performs "a Derridean inflected reading of the psychoanalytic phantom that subverts the impulse toward interrogation in favor of a kind of experiential witnessing" which, she claims, is a central objective of the poetics of trans-trauma. In this sense, embodied affect is what enables that quality of trauma that remains unknowable and outside language to be spectrally evoked within the haunted text.

Traumatic affect thus encompasses the rich and dense territory between trauma and affect and the potential of as yet untapped discoveries, as well as the productive tensions between trauma and affect theories. But traumatic affect opens up more portals than those in the study of literature, cinema, and culture. What we need—and what this collection proposes—are ways of thinking about trauma that work with the uncertainty and instability inherent in the contemporary fluidity and proliferation of trauma, rather than looking for fixity or cohesive, cognitive representation. Clearly, there are no easy answers, yet grapple with these questions we must, not just in the journals of academic publications and the arts, but in countless everyday situations and in the streets.

Ricardo Mbarkho's chapter, "Trauma Stimulated Art, or the Embodiment of Affect in Lebanon: An Allegory," departs from academic discourse to offer a glimpse into life on one such avenue. Mbarkho's depiction of Beirut's bustling and conflicted art community grounds the nexus of trauma and affect in lived experience and in the daily lives of traumatized and affected societies. It is, as the title suggests, an allegorical exploration of trauma, art and affect in post-civil war Lebanon. Through two figures symbolic of the deeply entrenched political tensions in the Lebanese art world, Mbarkho meditates on the complex interplay of art, funding, cultural politics, and societal and personal trauma. Mbarkho describes the Beirut art world as occupying a difficult liminal space: of necessity concerned with the traumatic aftermath of war, but at risk of being co-opted as political propaganda. This tricky position means that "for art to negotiate trauma it sometimes needs to mutate into other kinds of art that can exist in a traumatized society without compromise." That project has led to art that embodies "the residual traumatic affect" of the country's violent histories.

Writing traumatic violence also presents distinct challenges to creative practice, particularly when that violence is torture, the pain of which is frequently understood as not simply beyond language, but destroying language. Michael Richardson's speculative essay, "Torturous Affect: Writing and the Problem of Pain," contemplates how affect theory might open new ways of understanding the relationship between pain, language, and the act of writing. Bringing the work of Massumi and Tomkins on affect into dialogue with trauma theory, Richardson suggests that the temporal aspect of trauma, both the latency inherent in the traumatic event itself and the passing of time in its aftermath, provide a way of writing pain beyond language. Writing to evoke an affective semblance rather than direct representation might enable fiction to gesture past the page and, in doing so, to express both the instance and aftermath of world-destroying pain.

Another way to think about the communication of trauma beyond language (indeed at the point of language's very failure) is to consider the body itself and in particular its gestures from within silence. In her chapter "'Un Petit Geste': Affect and Silence in Claude Lanzmann's *Shoah*" Magdalena Zolkos brings the corporeality of affect to bear on one of the most oft-analyzed traumatic representations, Lanzmann's epic film about the Holocaust. Focusing on the single scene in which the hairdresser Bomba tells his story, Zolkos shows how existing interpretations tend to "either overlook the rich non-verbal semiotics of Bomba's testimony's, which include silence, gesturality, movement, and other forms of bodily expression, or to regard them as indicative of trauma's non-representability and as the breakdown of meaning." Drawing on Giorgio

Agamben's essays on gesture, Zolkos shows that what occurs within silence and narrative collapse is not so much un-representable, as outside language. It is, in a word, affective. Zolkos proposes the notion of "testimonial gesturality" as a response to the apparently unbridgeable divide between knowing and not. When language fails for Bomba, gesture both performs that failure and compensates for the "unavailability or inaccessibility of traumatic memories, and the aporias of narrativization and recollection."

Anne Rutherford engages a similar problematic in her consideration of the "enunciative present," when she seeks to "understand filmic affect in trauma-related work within an ethics of address." Where Zolkos is concerned with gesture and affect as a way of understanding "unspeaking" or "un-narratable" silences, in "Film, Trauma and the Enunciative Present" Rutherford is interested in the complex affectivity of witnessing trauma, particularly from a position removed from the experience itself. Identifying intensities of affect and narrative, or somatics and semantics, "as dimensions of film through which affect can draw spectators into a heightened sensory-affective engagement can enable ways to explore how these elements are deployed across a range of film genres that address experiences of trauma." Elaborating her theoretical propositions through analysis of *Bashu*, an Iranian drama, and *A Poet: Unconcealed Poetry*, an Indonesian film, Rutherford calls for an ethical approach to the act of translating trauma into language, whether visual or verbal.

As even this brief movement through the essays collected here reveals, this volume does not pretend to offer a cohesive approach to traumatic affect. Far from it. Their diverse approaches to both affect and trauma, the degree to which their theorizing is implicit or explicit, conceptualized or allegorized, speaks to the multiplicities to which trauma is open, both inside the clinic and beyond it. The scholars gathered together in this volume grapple in diverse ways with the intersection of two theoretical fields, between subject, image, and text, in considering whether affect theory can account for, or move beyond, the unrepresentability of the traumatic event. They consider circuitries within and between affect and trauma, suggesting previously uncharted ways of thinking about testimony and witnessing and asking how trauma and affect might offer insight into creative practice. They question how the anti-essentialist currents in affect theory and their conception of a relational subject might potentially undermine certain presuppositions of trauma theory and how the ethical imperatives of trauma might require a rethinking of aspects of affect theory.

These essays, almost all original, are interdisciplinary in their theoretical positioning and range of topics. The collection's contributions come from Canada, the United States, the United Kingdom, Lebanon and Australia. Its contributors are writers and artists, curators and political theorists, film critics and art theorists. As such, we trust that this book will interest scholars and students studying affect and trauma theory, as well as researchers of trauma in creative practice, cinema, art, literature and philosophy at both undergraduate and post-graduate levels. At "Trauma: Writing, Art, and Affect," a public symposium we convened in Sydney in April 2011, we were inspired by the enthusiastic engagement of the multi-disciplinary and diverse audience, which included psychotherapists and a refugee caseworker. Judging by the keen interest expressed by these front liners of trauma, we expect that the volume may also prove useful for therapists and others working with traumatized people, particularly those professionals with an interest in trauma in relation to the creative arts. As creative practitioners ourselves, we believe firmly in theory and philosophy having an impact on both life and art. Our passion for this volume arose from the productive possibilities we each encountered in the harnessing of trauma and affect theory in our own creative practice. It is our hope that others might find a similar utility of this collection of essays—some way of bringing the insights of theory to life as artists and perhaps even in creative ways in non-artistic contexts.

Traumatic Affect is an exploration of the impact of trauma upon lives at all strata of society. The following chapters consider the productive and problematic tensions at the nexus of the fields of affect and trauma, and their interest in irreducible experience, embodiment, and events. While trauma and affect continues to independently offer crucial insights into both individual and collective experience, an exploration of the productive tension between these two fields develops new textual analyses and theoretical approaches that are both timely and necessary.

PART I:

SILENCE

CHAPTER ONE

BENJAMIN'S SILENCE

SHOSHANA FELMAN

Nothing more desolating than his acolytes, nothing more godforsaken than his adversaries. No name that would be more fittingly honored by silence.

—Walter Benjamin, "One-Way Street"[1]

"Expect from me no word of my own. Nor should I be capable of saying anything new; for in the room where someone writes the noise is so great. … Let him who has something to say step forward and be silent!"

—Karl Krauss, quoted by Walter Benjamin[2]

Conversation strives toward silence, and the listener is really the silent partner. The speaker receives meaning from him; the silent one is the unappropriated source of meaning.

—Walter Benjamin, "The Metaphysics of Youth"[3]

 Originally published as "Benjamin's Silence" in *Critical Inquiry*, Vol. 25 no. 2 (1999): 201-234. A modified, extended version of this text constitutes part of the opening chapter on Benjamin in Shoshana Felman's book, *The Juridical Unconscious: Trials and Traumas in the Twentieth Century* (Cambridge, MA and London, UK: Harvard University Press, 2002). The related chapter is entitled, "The Storyteller's Silence: Walter Benjamin's Dilemma of Justice."

[1] Walter Benjamin, "One-Way Street," trans. Edmund Jephcott, *Selected Writings, 1913-1926,* ed. Marcus Bullock and Michael W. Jennings (Cambridge, MA: Harvard University Press, 1996), 469, from a section written in commemoration of Karl Krauss entitled "Monument to a Warrior."

[2] Benjamin, "Karl Krauss," *Reflections: Essays, Aphorisms, Autobiographical Writings*, trans. Jephcott, ed. P. Demetz, (New York: Harcourt Brace, 1986), 243.

[3] Benjamin, "The Metaphysics of Youth," trans. Rodney Livingstone, *Selected Writings,* 6; hereafter abbreviated as "MY."

I propose here to address—and listen to—that element in Benjamin's language and writing that specifically, decisively remains beyond communication. "In all language and linguistic creations," Benjamin has said, "there remains in addition to what can be conveyed something that cannot be communicated. … It is the task of the translator to release in his own language that pure language which is exiled among alien tongues, to liberate the language imprisoned in a work." In Benjamin's own work, in his abbreviated, cryptic style and in the essentially elliptical articulation of his thought, a surcharge of meaning is quite literally "imprisoned" in instances of silence. It is the task of the translator of Benjamin's own work to listen to these instances of silence, whose implications, I will try to show, are at once stylistic, philosophical, historical, and autobiographical. "Midway between poetry and theory," my critical amplification and interpretation of this silence—my own translation of the language that is still "imprisoned" in Benjamin's work—will thus focus on what Benjamin himself has underscored but what remains unheard, unheeded in the critically repetitive mechanical reproduction of his work: "that element in a translation that goes beyond transmittal of subject matter."[4]

1. Wars and Revolutions

It is customary to view Benjamin essentially as an abstract philosopher, a critic and a thinker of modernity (and/or of postmodernity) in culture and in art. In contradistinction to this dominant approach, I propose to look at Benjamin far more specifically and more concretely as a thinker, a philosopher, and a narrator of the wars and revolutions of the twentieth century. "Wars and revolutions," writes Hannah Arendt, "have thus far determined the physiognomy of the twentieth century. And as distinguished from the nineteenth century ideologies—such as nationalism and internationalism, capitalism and imperialism, socialism and communism, which, though still invoked by many as justifying causes, have lost contact with the major realities of our world—war and revolution … have outlived all their ideological justifications."[5]

> The seeds of total war developed as early as the First World War, when the distinction between soldiers and civilians was no longer respected because it was inconsistent with the new weapons then used. … The magnitude of

---

[4] Benjamin, "The Task of the Translator," trans. Harry Zohn, *Selected Writings*, 261, 259, 257.

[5] Hannah Arendt, *On Revolution* (Harmondsworth: Penguin, 1990), 11; hereafter abbreviated *OR*.

> the violence let loose in the First World War might indeed have been enough to cause revolutions in its aftermath even without any revolutionary tradition and even if no revolution had ever occurred before.
>
> To be sure, not even wars, let alone revolutions, are ever completely determined by violence. Where violence rules absolutely, … everything and everybody must fall silent. [*OR*, 14, 18]

In my reading, Walter Benjamin's life work bears witness to the ways in which events outlive their ideologies and consummate, dissolve the grounding discourse of their nineteenth century historic and utopian meanings. Benjamin's texts play out, thus, one against the other and one through the other, both the "constellation that poses the threat of total annihilation through war against the hope for the emancipation of all mankind through revolution" (*OR*, 11), and the deadly succession of historical convulsions through which culture—in the voice of Benjamin who is its most profound witness—must fall silent.

Theory and Autobiography

Silence can be either the outside of language or a position inside language, a state of noiselessness or wordlessness. Falling silent is, however, not a state but an event. It is the significance of the event that I will try to understand and think through in the present essay. What does it mean that culture—in the voice of its most profound witness—must fall silent? What does it mean for culture? What does it mean for Benjamin? How does Benjamin come to represent and to incorporate concretely, personally, the physiognomy of the twentieth century? And how in turn is this physiognomy reflected, concretized, in Benjamin's own face?

In searching for answers to these questions, I will juxtapose and grasp together theoretical and autobiographical texts. Benjamin's own work includes a singular record of an autobiographical event that, to my mind, is crucial to the author's theories as much as to his destiny (although critics usually neglect it). Benjamin narrates this event in one of his rare moments of personal directness, in the (lyrical) autobiographical text entitled "A Berlin Chronicle." I will interpret this event together with, and through, two central theoretical essays that constitute the cornerstones of Benjamin's late work: "The Storyteller" and "Theses on the Philosophy of History." In reading the most personal, the most idiosyncratic autobiographical notations through the most far reaching, groundbreaking theoretical constructions, my effort will be to give Benjamin's theory a face.[6] The conceptual question that will override and guide this effort will be, What is the relation between the theory and the event (and what, in general, is the relationship between events and theories)? How does the theory arise out of the concrete drama of an event? How does the concrete drama of an event become theory? And how do both event and theory relate to silence (and to Benjamin's embodiment of silence)?

2. Theories of Silence

Because my sense is that in Benjamin, the theory is (paradoxically) far less obscure than the autobiography, I will start by reflecting on the two theoretical essays—perhaps Benjamin's best known abstract texts—of which I propose to underscore the common theoretical stakes. I will argue that both "The Storyteller" and the "Theses on the Philosophy of History" can be construed as two theories of silence derived from, and related to, the two world wars: "The Storyteller," written in 1936, is retrospectively, explicitly connected with the First World War; "Theses on the Philosophy of History," written shortly before Benjamin's death in 1940, represent his ultimate rethinking of the nature of historical events and of the task of historiography in the face of the developments of the beginning of the Second World War.

I will suggest that these two texts are in effect tied up together. I propose to read them one against the other and one through the other, as two stages in a larger philosophical and existential picture, and as two variations of a global Benjaminian theory of wars and silence. I argue therefore that "The Storyteller" and "Theses" can be viewed as two theoretical variations of the same profound underlying text. My methodology is here inspired by the way in which Benjamin himself discusses—in his youth—"Two Poems by Friedrich Hölderlin," in analyzing in the two texts (as he puts it) "not … their likeness which is nonexistent" but their "'comparativeness,'" and in treating them—despite

---

[6] This textual juxtaposition of the theory and the autobiography will be illuminated, in its turn, by Benjamin's work as a literary critic, especially in the early literary essays on Hölderlin, on Dostoyevsky, and on Goethe's *Elective Affinities*. I will thus borrow metaphors from Benjamin's own literary criticism and will in turn use them as interpretive tools and as evocative stylistic echoes. My methodology will be attentive, therefore, to three distinct levels of the text that the analysis will grasp together: the conceptual level of the theory, the narrative level of the autobiography, and the figurative level of the literary criticism.

their distance—as two "versions" (or two transformations) of the same profound text.[7]

The End of Storytelling

"The Storyteller" is presented as a literary study of the nineteenth-century Russian writer Nikolai Leskov and of his striking art of storytelling. But the essay's main concern is in depicting storytelling as a *lost art*: the achievements of the nineteenth-century model serve as the background for a differential diagnosis of the ways in which *storytelling is lost to the twentieth century*. Something happened, Benjamin suggests, that has brought about the death—the agony—of storytelling, both as a literary genre and as a discursive mode in daily life. Benjamin announces thus a historical drama of "the end of storytelling"—or an innovative cultural theory of the collapse of narration—as a critical and theoretical appraisal (through Leskov) of a general historical state of affairs.

The theory, thereby, is Benjamin's way of grasping and of bringing into consciousness an unconscious cultural phenomenon and an imperceptible historical process that has taken place outside anyone's awareness and that can therefore be deciphered, understood, and noticed only retrospectively, in its effects (its symptoms). The effects, says Benjamin, are that today, quite symptomatically, *it has become impossible to tell a story*. The art of storytelling has been lost along with the ability to share experiences.

> Less and less frequently do we encounter people with the ability to tell a tale properly. … It is as if something that seemed inalienable to us … were taken from us: the ability to exchange experiences.[8]

Among the reasons Benjamin gives for this loss—the rise of capitalism, the sterilization of life through bourgeois values, the decline of craftsmanship, the growing influence of the media and the press—the first and most dramatic is that people have been struck dumb by the First World War. From ravaged battlefields, they have returned mute to a wrecked world in which nothing has remained the same except the sky. This vivid and dramatic explanation is placed right away at the beginning of the text,

---

[7] Benjamin, "Two Poems by Friedrich Hölderlin," trans. Stanley Corngold, *Selected Writings*, 33.

[8] Benjamin, "The Storyteller: Reflections on the Work of Nikolai Leskov," *Illuminations: Essays and Reflections*, trans. Zohn, ed. Arendt, (New York: Schocken, 1969), 83; hereafter abbreviated "S."

like an explosive opening argument or an initial shock or blast inflicted on the reader and with whose force of shock the whole remainder of the text will have to cope and to catch up. The opening is, indeed, as forceful as it is ungraspable. The text itself does not quite process it; nor does it truly integrate it with the arguments that follow. And this ungraspability or unintegratability of the beginning is not a mere coincidence; it duplicates and illustrates the point of the text, that the war has left an impact that has struck dumb its survivors, with the effect of interrupting now the continuity of telling and of understanding. The utterance repeats in act the content of the statement: it must remain somewhat unassimilable.

In Benjamin, however, it is productive to retain what cannot be assimilated. And it is crucially important in my view that what cannot be assimilated crystallizes around a date. Before it can be understood, the loss of narrative is *dated*. Its process is traced back to the collective, massive trauma of First World War.

> With the [First] World War a process began to become apparent which has not halted since then. Was it not noticeable at the end of the war that men returned from the battlefield grown silent—not richer, but poorer in communicable experience? What ten years later was poured out in the flood of war books was anything but experience that goes from mouth to mouth. And there was nothing remarkable about that. For never has experience been contradicted more thoroughly than strategic experience by tactical warfare, economic experience by inflation, bodily experience by mechanical warfare, moral experience by those in power. A generation that had gone to school on a horse-drawn streetcar now stood under the open sky in a countryside in which nothing remained unchanged but the clouds, and beneath these clouds, in a field of force of destructive torrents and explosions, was the tiny, fragile human body. ["S," 84]

Thus, narration was reduced to silence by the First World War. What has emerged from the destructive torrents—from the noise of the explosions—was only the muteness of the body in its absolutely helpless, shelterless vulnerability. Resonating to this dumbness of the body is the storyteller's dumbness.

But this fall to silence of narration is contrasted with, and covered by, the new loudness, the emerging noise of information—"journalism being clearly … the expression of the changed function of language in the world of high capitalism."[9]

---

[9] Benjamin, "Karl Krauss," 242. Compare "S," 88-91. Information and narration are not simply two competing modes of discourse (two functions of language). They are in fact two strategies of living and communicating, two levels of

In a world in which public discourse is usurped by the commercial aims and by the noise of information, soldiers returning from the First World War can find no social or collective space in which to integrate their death experience. Their trauma must remain a private matter that cannot be symbolized collectively. It cannot be exchanged, it must fall silent.

The Unforgettable

Gone are the days when dying was "a public process in the life of an individual and a most exemplary one" ("S," 93). Irrespective of the battlefield experience, mortality is self-deceptively denied in sterilized bourgeois life, which strives to keep death out of sight symbolically and literally.[10]

Narration was, however, born from the pathos of an ultimate exchange between the dying and the living. Medieval paintings represent the origin of storytelling: they show the archetypal or inaugural site of narration to be the deathbed, in which the dying man (or the original narrator) reviews his life (evokes his memories) and thus addresses the events and lessons of his past to those surrounding him. A dying speaker is a naturally authoritative storyteller; he borrows his authority from death.[11]

Today, however, agonizers die in private and without authority. They are attended by no listeners. They tell no stories. And there is no authority—and certainly no wisdom—that has survived the war. "We have no counsel either for ourselves or for others. After all, counsel is less an

---

existence within culture. Narration seeks a listener, information, a consumer. Narration is addressed to a community, information is directed toward a market. Insofar as listening is an integral part of narration, while marketing is always part of information, narration is attentive and imaginatively productive (in its concern for the singularity, the unintelligibility of the event), while information is mechanical and reproductive (in its concern for the event's exchangeability, explainability, and reproducibility).

Benjamin was concerned not only with communication but (implicitly, essentially) with education. Educationally, these two modes conflict not only as two separate roles or institutions. They wage a battle *within* every institution and *within* every discipline of knowledge. They are in conflict, in effect, *within* every pedagogy. They struggle (to this day) within every university.

[10] "Today people live in rooms that have never been touched by death and … when their end approaches they are stowed away in sanatoria or hospitals by their heirs" ("S," 94).

[11] "Death is the sanction of everything the storyteller has to tell. He has borrowed his authority from death," ("S," 94).

answer to a question than a proposal concerning the continuation of a story which is just unfolding" ("S," 86).

It is not simply that there is no longer a proposal for historical or narrative continuation. The First World War is *the first war that can no longer be narrated*. Its witnesses and its participants have lost their stories. The sole signification which "The Storyteller" can henceforth articulate is that of mankind's double loss: a loss of the capacity to symbolize; a loss of the capacity to moralize.[12]

A Philosophy of History

The outburst of the Second World War in 1939 (three years after the publication of "The Storyteller") brings Benjamin to write, in 1940—in the months that were to be the last ones of his life—what I have called his second theory of silence, entitled "Theses on the Philosophy of History." At first, this text seems altogether different from "The Storyteller." Its topic is not literature but history, of which the essay offers not a diagnosis but a theory. The theory is programmatic: its tone is not descriptive but prescriptive. The "theses" are audaciously abbreviated and provocatively dogmatized. They do not explicitly reflect on silence. The essay focuses rather on (scholarly and scientific) *discourses* on history. The word *silence* does not figure in the text.

And, yet, speechlessness is at the very heart of the reflection and of the situation of the writer. Like the storyteller who falls silent or returns mute from the First World War, the historian or the theorist of history facing the conflagration of the Second World War is equally *reduced to speechlessness*: no ready-made conceptual or discursive tool, no discourse about history turns out to be sufficient to explain the nature of this war; no available conceptual framework in which history is customarily perceived proves adequate or satisfactory to understand or to explain current historical developments. Vis-à-vis the undreamt-of events, what is called for, Benjamin suggests, is a *radical displacement of our frames of reference*, a radical transvaluation of our methods and of our philosophies of history.

---

[12] Since the storyteller (in Leskov and his tradition) is "a righteous man," a "teacher" and a "sage" ("S," 108), what now falls to muteness is the very possibility of righteousness. Similarly, literature as teacher of humanity (in the manner of Leskov) has lost its voice. In the collapse of narrative as a generic, literary mode of discourse, literature as ethics—"counsel," education—is thus inherently historically and philosophically reduced to silence.

> The current amazement that the things we are experiencing are "still" possible in the twentieth century is *not* philosophical. This amazement is not the beginning of knowledge—unless it is the knowledge that the view of history which gives rise to it is untenable.[13]

History is now the property and the propriety of Nazis (of those who can control it and manipulate its discourse). It is by virtue of a loyalty to history that Hitler is proposing to avenge Germany from its defeat and its humiliation in the First World War. All the existing discourses on history have proven ineffective either to predict or to counteract the regime and the phenomenon of Hitler.[14]

History in Nazi Germany is Fascist. Fascism legitimates itself in the name of national identity on the basis of a unity and of a continuity of history. The philosophical tenets of this view are inherited from nineteenth-century historicism, which has equated temporality with progress, in presupposing time as an entity of natural development, progressively enhancing maturation and advancing toward a betterment as time (and history) go by. Benjamin rejects this view, which has become untenable vis-à-vis the traumas of the twentieth century.

It is the victor who forever represents the present conquest or the present victory as an improvement in relation to the past. But the reality of history is that of the traumatized by history, the materialist reality of those who are oppressed by the new victory. Historicism is, however, based on an unconscious identification with the discourse of the victor and thus on an uncritical espousal of the victor's narrative perspective. "If one asks with whom the adherents of historicism actually empathize," Benjamin writes,

> the answer is inevitable: with the victor. ... Empathy with the victor inevitably benefits the ruler. Historical materialists know what that means. Whoever has emerged victorious participates to this day in the triumphal procession in which the present rulers step over those who are lying prostrate. According to traditional practice, the spoils are carried along in the procession. They are called cultural treasures, and a historical materialist views them with cautious detachment. For without exception the cultural treasures he surveys have an origin which he cannot contemplate without horror. They owe their existence not only to the

[13] Benjamin, "Theses on the Philosophy of History," *Illuminations*, 257; hereafter abbreviated "TPH."

[14] Among the theories of history that Benjamin critiques and "deconstructs" are pure theology (religion), pure historicism (positivism), pure liberalism (idealism), and pure Marxism (uncritical historical materialism).

> efforts of the great minds and talents who have created them, but also to the anonymous toil of their contemporaries. There is no document of civilization which is not at the same time a document of barbarism. And just as a document is not free of barbarism, barbarism taints also the manner in which it was transmitted from one owner to another. ["TPH," 256]

Historicism is thus based on a perception of history as victory. But it is blind to this presupposition. So blind that it does not see the irony with which this axiom has been borrowed—taken to extremes—by the discourses of Fascism. Fascism is, indeed, quite literally, a *philosophy of history as victory*. Unlike historicism, it is not unconscious of this prejudice; it is grounded in a cynical and conscious *claim* of this philosophy of history.[15]

Historicism is then based on a confusion between truth and power. Real history is, on the contrary, the ineluctable discrepancy between the two.[16] History is the perennial conflictual arena in which collective memory is named as a *constitutive dissociation* between truth and power.

What, then, is the relation between history and silence? In a (conscious or unconscious) historical philosophy of power, the powerless (the persecuted) are constitutionally deprived of voice.

Because official history is based on the perspective of the victor, the voice with which it speaks authoritatively is *deafening*; it makes us unaware of the fact that there remains in history a claim, a discourse which we *do not hear*. And in relation to this act of deafening, the rulers of the moment are the heirs of the rulers of the past. History transmits, ironically enough, a legacy of deafness in which historicists unwittingly share. What is called progress, and what Benjamin sees only as a piling of catastrophe upon catastrophe, is therefore the transmission of historical discourse from ruler to ruler, from one historical instance of power to another. This transmission is constitutive of what is (misguidedly) perceived as

---

[15] Compare Hitler's harangue to his top civilians and military officials in 1939, on the occasion of the invasion of Poland: "Destruction of Poland is in the background. The aim is elimination of living forces, not the arrival at a certain line … I shall give a propagandistic cause for starting the war,—never mind whether it be plausible or not. The victor shall not be asked later on whether we told the truth or not. In starting and making a war, not the right is what matters but victory" (quoted by Robert Jackson, introduction to Whitney Harris, *Tyranny On Trial: The Evidence at Nuremberg* [New York: Barnes & Noble, 1954], xxxi).

[16] In this conception, Benjamin is the interpreter—the synthesizer—of the diverse legacies of Nietzsche, Marx, and Freud.

continuity in history. "The continuum of history is that of the oppressors." "The history of the oppressed is a discontinuum."[17]

If history, despite its spectacular triumphal time, is thus barbarically, constitutively conflict ridden, the historian is not in possession of a space in which to be removed, detached, "objective"; the philosopher of history cannot be an outsider to the conflict. In the face of the deafening appropriation of historical philosophy by Fascism; in the face of the Nazi use of the most *civilized* tools of technology and law for a most barbaric racist persecution, "objectivity" does not exist. A historical articulation proceeds not from an epistemological "detachment" but, on the contrary, from the historian's sense of urgency and of emergency.[18]

> The tradition of the oppressed teaches us that the "state of emergency" in which we live is not the exception but the rule. We must attain to a conception of history that is in keeping with this insight. Then we shall clearly realize that it is our task to bring about a real state of emergency, and this will improve our position in the struggle against Fascism. ["TPH," 257]

The theory of history is thus itself an *intervention in the conflict*; it is itself historical. In the middle of a cataclysmic world war that shifts the grounds from under our very feet, danger, Benjamin implies, is what triggers the most lucid and the most clairvoyant *grasp* of history. Historical insight strikes surprisingly and unexpectedly in "moments of sudden illumination" in which "we are beside ourselves."[19] Danger and emergency illuminate themselves as the conditions both of history (of life) and of its theory (its knowledge). New, innovative theories of history (such that enable a displacement of official history) come into being only under duress.

> To articulate the past historically does not mean to recognize it "the way it really was" (Ranke). It means to seize hold of a memory as it flashes up at

---

[17] Benjamin, "Paralipomènes et variantes des *Thèses 'Sur le concept de l'histoire*,'" *Écrits français*, ed. Jean-Maurice Monnoyer (Paris: Gallimard, 1991), 352; my trans.

[18] The reality of history is grasped (articulated) when the historian *recognizes* a historical *state of emergency* that is, precisely, *not* the one the ruler has declared or that (in Hobbes's tradition, in Carl Schmitt's words) is "decided by the sovereign" (Carl Schmitt, *Politische Theologie* [Munich: Duncker & Humblot, 1922], a work cited and discussed by Benjamin in his *The Origin of German Tragic Drama*, trans. John Osbourne [1928; London: NLB, 1977] 65, 74, 239 nn. 14-17; hereafter abbreviated *OG*.)

[19] Benjamin, "A Berlin Chronicle," *Reflections*, 56, 57; hereafter abbreviated "BC."

> a moment of danger. Historical materialism wishes to retain that image of the past which unexpectedly appears to man singled out by history at a moment of danger. ["TPH," 255]

In Benjamin's own view, history—a line of catastrophe—is not a movement toward progress but a movement toward (what Benjamin calls enigmatically) redemption. Redemption—what historical struggles (and political revolutions) are about—should be understood as both materialist (Marxist, political, interhistorical) and theological (suprahistorical, transcendent). Redemption is discontinuity, disruption. It names the constant need to catch up with the hidden reality of history that always remains a debt to the oppressed, a debt to the dead of history, a claim the past has on the present.

Redemption is the allegory of a future state of freedom, justice, happiness, and recovery of meaning. History should be assessed only *in reference* to this state that is its goal. Historical action should take place as though this goal were not utopian but pragmatic. Yet it can never be decided by a mortal if redemption, ultimately, can be immanent to history or if it is doomed to remain transcendental, beyond history. "This world," Benjamin has written elsewhere, "remains a mute world, from which music will never ring out. Yet to what is it dedicated if not redemption?"[20]

Dedicated to Redemption

When, therefore, will redemption come? Will there be a redemption after the Second World War? Will there ever be redemption *from* the Second World War? Benjamin foresees the task of the historian of the future.

He will be sad. His history will be the product of his sadness.

> Flaubert, who was familiar with [the "cause of sadness"], wrote: *"Peu de gens devineront combien il a fallu être triste pour resusciter Carthage"* ["Few will be able to guess how sad one had to be in order to resuscitate Carthage"]. ["TPH," 256]

---

[20] Benjamin, "Goethe's Elective Affinities," trans. Corngold, *Selective Writings* 355; hereafter abbreviated "GEA." Redemption seems, therefore, to be linked to the moment of illumination which suddenly and unexpectedly gives us the capacity to *hear the silence*—to *tune into* the unarticulated and to *hear* what is in history deprived of words. Redemption starts by redeeming history from deafness.

Before the fact, Benjamin foresees that history will know a holocaust. After the war, the historian's task will be not only to "resuscitate Carthage" or to *narrate extermination*, but paradoxically, to *save the dead*:

> Nothing that has ever happened should be regarded as lost to history. ["TPH," 254]

> Only that historian will have the gift of fanning the spark of hope in the past who is firmly convinced that *even the dead* will not be safe from the enemy if he wins. ["TPH," 255; emphasis mine; Benjamin's italics]

Thus, the historian of the Second World War will be sad. Beyond sadness, he will have to be intently vigilant. In this war particularly, the conceptual question of the historian's identification with the victor inadvertently evolves into a graver, far more serious question of political complicity.

The task of the historian of today is to *avoid collaboration* with a criminal regime and with the discourses of fascism. Similarly, the historian of tomorrow will have to be watchful to avoid complicity with history's barbarism and with culture's latent (and now patent) crimes. Benjamin's text, I argue, is the beginning of the critical awareness of the treacherous questions of collaboration that so obsessively preoccupy us to this day. It is still early in the war. Benjamin intuitively senses the importance of this question, as it will arise precisely, later, *out of* the Second World War. The historian, Benjamin suggests, must be revolutionary lest he be unwittingly complicit. And complicity, for Benjamin, is a graver danger, a worse punishment than death.

> Historical materialism wishes to retain the image of the past which unexpectedly appears to man singled out by history at a moment of danger. The danger affects both the content of the tradition and its receivers. The same threat hangs over both: that of becoming a tool of the ruling classes. In every era the attempt must be made to wrest tradition away from a conformism that is about to overpower it. ["TPH," 255]

The historian, paradoxically, has no choice but to be a revolutionary if he does not want to be a collaborator.[21]

---

[21] For a historiography free of complicity, we must disassociate ourselves from our accustomed thinking:

> Thinking involves not only the flow of thoughts, but their arrest as well. Where thinking suddenly stops in a configuration pregnant with tensions, it gives that configuration a shock, by which it crystallizes into a monad. A

History and Speechlessness

Benjamin advances, thus, a theory of history as trauma—and a correlative theory of the historical conversion of trauma into insight. History consists in chains of traumatic interruptions rather than in sequences of rational causalities. But the traumatized—the subjects of history—are deprived of a language in which to speak of their victimization. The relation between history and trauma is speechless. Traditional theories of history tend to neglect this speechlessness of trauma: by definition, speechlessness is what remains out of the record. But it is specifically to this speechless connection between history and trauma that Benjamin's own theory of history intends now to give voice.

He does so by showing how the very discipline, the very "concept of history" is constituted by what it excludes (and fails to grasp).[22] History (to sum up) is thus inhabited by an historical unconscious related to—and founded on—a double silence: the silence of "the tradition of the oppressed," who are by definition deprived of voice and whose story (or whose narrative perspective) is always systematically reduced to silence; and the silence of official history—the victor's history—with respect to the tradition of the oppressed. According to Benjamin, the hidden theoretical centrality of this double silence defines historiography as such. This in general is the way in which history is told, or, rather, this is in general the way in which history is silenced. The triumph of Fascism and the outbreak of the Second World War constitute only the most climactic demonstration, the most aberrant materialization or realization of this historiography.

Whereas the task of the philosopher of history is thus to take apart "the concept of history" by showing its deceptive continuity to be in fact a process of silencing, the task of the historian is to reconstruct what history has silenced, to give voice to the dead and to the vanquished and to resuscitate the unrecorded, silenced, hidden story of the oppressed.

---

historical materialist approaches a historical subject only where he encounters it as a monad. In this structure he recognizes a sign for a Messianic cessation of happening, or, put differently, *a revolutionary chance* in the fight for the oppressed past. ["TPH," 262-63, emphasis mine]

[22] The original and current German title of the essay is, precisely, "On the Concept of History" ("Über den Begriff der Geschichte").

3. The Event

I would like now to look backward from the theory to the autobiography and to try to reach the roots of Benjamin's conceptual insights in an original event whose theoretical and autobiographical significance remains totally ungrasped in the voluminous critical literature on Benjamin. The event takes place at the outbreak of the First World War. It consists in the conjunction of the German invasion of Belgium on 4 August 1914 with the joint suicide, four days later, of Benjamin's best friend, Fritz Heinle, and of Heinle's girlfriend. A farewell express letter of the now-dead friend informs Benjamin where to find the bodies. This shared readiness to die and this joint act of self-inflicted violence is interpreted by Benjamin and his friends as a symbolic gesture of protest against the war. For Benjamin, the event is therefore one of loss, of shock, of disillusionment, and of awakening to a reality of an inexorable, tragic historical connection between youth and death. For the world, it is the outbreak of the First World War.

The impact of this event marks a dramatic turning point in Benjamin's life and in his thought. Before this event, Benjamin is involved in political activism in the youth movement, working to revolutionize German society and culture through a radical reform of education. In the youth groups supporting this reform, he holds a position of strong leadership as president of the Berlin Free Students' Union. After the event, he abdicates his leadership and turns away from political activity. He gives up any public role along with the belief that language can directly become action. He breaks with his admired teacher, Wyneken, of whose ideas he has been both the disciple and the ardent follower. Because this former mentor now guides youth toward the war, Benjamin realizes that philosophy has failed and that authority can no longer be relied on: "*theoria* in you has been blinded," he writes to Wyneken, in severing his links with him.[23]

In the duplicity of governments, in the duplicity of teachers, and in the isolated words of the letter of a dead youth telling Benjamin—the friend, the leader, the collaborator—where to find the bodies, language has betrayed. But the betrayal constitutes precisely the event; the betrayal is precisely history. "Midway through its journey," Benjamin will write, "nature finds itself betrayed by language, and that powerful blocking of feeling turns to sorrow. Thus, with the ambiguity of the word, its *signifying*

[23] Quoted in "Chronology, 1892-1926," in *Selected Writings*, 499.

power, language falters. … History becomes equal to signification in human language; this language is frozen in signification."[24]

Refusing to participate in the betrayal of language and in the madness of the war, Benjamin leaves Germany for Switzerland and resorts to a silence that will last six years, until 1920.[25] During these years, he does not publish anything. He writes and circulates among close friends a text on Hölderlin in which he meditates on the nature of the lyric and its relation to the poet's death. The poet's death relates to Heinle's death. Heinle also has left poems, which Benjamin reads and rereads in an attempt to deepen his acquaintance with the dead. It is, indeed, as a dead poet that he now comes to know his friend. But Benjamin vows to give the dead poet immortality: to save Heinle from oblivion, to save the suicide from its meaninglessness, by publishing his friend's poetic work. This hope will never be relinquished. In the years of silence following the suicide, he edits Heinle's manuscripts. Benjamin's own text on Hölderlin and on the nature of the lyric is also an implicit dialogue with Heinle's work, a dialogue with Heinle's writing as well as with his life and with his death. Hence, Benjamin's specific interest in two poems by Hölderlin, "The Poet's Courage" and "Timidity," which designate the difference between Heinle's (suicidal) courage and the timidity of Benjamin's own (condemnation to) survival: suicide or survival—two existential stances between which Benjamin no doubt has oscillated but that he declares to be, surprisingly and paradoxically, two "versions" of the same profound text, deeply comparable or similar despite their difference.[26]

Belated Understanding

This drama and this suicide are narrated (among other things) in Benjamin's most personal autobiography, "A Berlin Chronicle." I will argue that for Benjamin, this autobiographical narrative becomes an allegory of the ungrasped impact of the First World War.

But "A Berlin Chronicle" is written eighteen years later, in 1932. The direct result of the events of the war at the time of their ungraspable occurrence is that Benjamin quite literally falls silent. And especially, quite literally and strictly silent, speechless about the subject of the war: as though by oath of loyalty to the dead friend; as though his own speech, or

---

[24] Benjamin, "The Role of Language in Trauerspiel and Tragedy," *Selected Writings,* 60.
[25] Compare Momme Brodersen, *Walter Benjamin: A Biography*, trans. Malcolm R. Green and Ingrida Ligers, ed. Martina Dervis (London: Verso, 1996), 118.
[26] Benjamin, "Two Poems by Friedrich Hölderlin," 33.

the language of youth they shared, had equally committed suicide. Something within himself has died as well. The traumatic (and, belatedly, theoretical) significance of this silence remains equally ungrasped by critics, who keep expressing their politically correct critique of it and their amazement at this eccentricity of Benjamin. Nor does anybody grasp the profound connection of this early silence to the later, much admired classic essays, "The Storyteller" and the "Theses on the Philosophy of History." Benjamin's early experience is, thus, on the contrary, separated from his later theory and is at once dismissed and trivialized: "Silence as an expression of inner protest at contemporary events: little doubt was cast on the legitimacy of such a stance at the time," the latest biographer Momme Brodersen historicizes.[27] The editors of the Harvard volume, more tuned in, feel equally compelled to mark a pious reservation: "Remarkably enough, Benjamin's letters … focus exclusively on personal issues. … There is rarely mention of the war, and no direct consideration of it or of his attitude toward it. It is as if Benjamin's injunction against political activity at the time also precluded cognizance of the most difficult events of the day."[28] What critics fail to see is how Benjamin's own narration of his war experience in "A Berlin Chronicle" is precisely, quintessentially, an autobiographical (and theoretical) *account of the meaning of his silence.*

4. The Subject Represented by the "I"

Eleven pages into "A Berlin Chronicle," Benjamin begins the narration of his war experience by insisting on his reluctance to say "I":

> If I write better German than most writers of my generation, it is thanks largely to twenty years' observance of one little rule: never use the word "I" except in letters. ["BC," 15]

However, Benjamin adds ironically, in this solicited piece he has accepted not just to say "I" but to be paid for it; if, therefore, these subjective notes have become longer than he had intended, it is not only because the subject, "accustomed for years to waiting in the wings, would not so easily be summoned to the limelight" but also because, metaphorically and literally, "the precaution of the subject represented by the 'I' … is entitled not to be sold cheap" ("BC,"15-16).

The autobiographical impulse is therefore in conflict with a speechlessness, a muteness of the "I" that constantly defeats narration

[27] Brodersen, *Walter Benjamin,* 89.
[28] "Chronology, 1892-1926," 502.

from inside. And, yet, the text originates in an imperative to tell, in a symbolic debt that goes beyond the personal and that makes narration unavoidable and indispensable. What is at stake, says Benjamin, are "deep and harrowing experiences" that constitute "the most important memories in one's life" ("BC," 16). Of these experiences, all the other witnesses are now dead: "I alone remain" ("BC," 17). The ethical impetus of the narration stems from this aloneness and from this necessity: since the narrator is the last surviving witness, history must be told despite the narrator's muteness. The narrator sees himself surrounded by dead doubles, younger than himself or of his age, dead witnesses who, had they been alive, might have helped him to cross the difficult thresholds of memory but whose dead faces now appear to him "only as an answer to the question whether forty [Benjamin's age at the time of writing] is not too young an age at which to evoke the most important memories of one's life" ("BC," 16). "A Berlin Chronicle" implicitly announces, thus, the author's fortieth birthday, with which its writing coincides. The autobiographer celebrates his birthday by mourning for the death of his contemporaries. From the start, death and birth are juxtaposed. "Berlin" is the name for this juxtaposition.

Prosopopeia

Longing for the complementary narration of his dead doubles and identified with their eternal silence, the speaker in fact writes an epitaph much more than a biography. "A Berlin Chronicle" is an autobiography that is inherently, profoundly epitaphic and that seeks, thus, not expression but precisely "the expressionless": the moment in which life is "petrified, as if spellbound in a single moment" ("GEA," 340). In line with Benjamin's analysis of "the expressionless," the writing possesses a "critical violence" that interrupts expression, with which "every expression simultaneously comes to a standstill" with the abruptness of "a moral dictum" ("GEA," 340, 341, 340). "Only the expressionless completes the work, by shattering it into a thing of shards, into a fragment of the true world, into the torso of a symbol" ("GEA," 340). To use the terminology of Paul de Man, we might say that in "A Berlin Chronicle" "autobiography veils a defacement of the mind of which it is itself the cause."[29] De Man's rhetorical analysis is here particularly pertinent: "the dominant figure of the epitaphic or autobiographical discourse is … the prosopopeia," "the fiction of an

---

[29] Paul de Man, "Autobiography as De-Facement," *The Rhetoric of Romanticism* (New York: Columbia University Press, 1984), 81.

apostrophe to an absent, deceased or voiceless entity, which posits the possibility of the latter's reply and confers upon it the power of speech."[30]

I would suggest, indeed, that an implicit figure of prosopopeia structures not just Benjamin's autobiography but his entire work; the underlying, understated evocation of the dead is present and can be deciphered everywhere. Benjamin's whole writing could be read as work of mourning, structured by a mute address to the dead face and the lost voice of the young friend who took his own life in a desperate protest in the first days of the First World War.

> In all mourning there is the deepest inclination to speechlessness, which is infinitely more than the inability or disinclination to communicate.[31]

All of Benjamin's evolving subjects, I will argue, are implicitly determined by the conceptual implications of the underlying autobiographical prosopopeia, or the mute address to the dead friend: lyric ("Heinle was a poet" ["BC," 17]), language ("Because she is mute, nature mourns"), *Trauerspiel* (the corpse is the sole bearer of signification), and, finally, history itself:

> In allegory the observer is confronted with the *facies hippocratica* [agonizer's face] of history as a petrified, primordial landscape. Everything about history that, from the very beginning, has been untimely, sorrowful, unsuccessful, is expressed in a face—or rather in a death's head. [*OG*, 166]

A Lecture on the Nature of the Lyric, or The Face of History (A Primal Scene)

It is precisely as a metaphor for his entire work as inarticulate prosopopeia that Benjamin describes the lecture on Hölderlin and on "the nature of the lyric" that, after Heinle's suicide, he struggled to articulate in memory of his deceased friend.

It is significant that "A Berlin Chronicle"'s narration of the war events and of its "harrowing experiences" starts (disorientingly, hermetically) by

---

[30] Ibid., 77, 75-76.

[31] Benjamin, "On Language as Such and On the Language of Man," trans. Jephcott, *Selected Writings*, 73: "Even where there is only a rustling of plants, there is always a lament. Because she is mute, nature mourns. Yet the inversion of this proposition leads even further into the essence of nature; the sadness of nature makes her mute" (ibid.).

the description of this lecture—by the mediation, that is, of the trauma by the work, by the translation of the lived event into *a thought on literature*. "A Berlin Chronicle" cannot go directly either to the proper name of the dead friend or to the actual story of his death. Temporally as well as spatially, the story keeps moving in circles, as though around an empty, silent center. The word suicide does not figure in the text. Heinle's name is introduced as though in passing: it vanishes as soon as it is mentioned; and so does the event. Throughout the text, the name and the event keep vanishing.

> It was in Heidelberg, during what was doubtless self-forgetful work, that I tried to summon up, in a meditation on the nature of the lyric, the figure of my friend Fritz Heinle, around whom all the happenings in the Meeting House arrange themselves and with who they vanish. Fritz Heinle was a poet, and the only one of them all whom I met not "in real life" but in his work. He died at nineteen, and could be known in no other way. All the same, this first attempt to evoke the sphere of his life through that of poetry was unsuccessful, and the immediacy of the experience that gave rise to my lecture asserted itself in the incomprehension and snobbery of the audience. ["BC," 17][32]

In a roundabout way, what Benjamin is trying to evoke is not Hölderlin but history: an original historical event that has remained completely untranslatable. History is "the original," the writings, its translations. The task of the translator is the witness's task. The lecture tried, but failed, to translate the impact of the event. Nevertheless, the lecture gives a sense of the remoteness, of the unapproachability of the historical event. Behind this failed translation of the lecture on Hölderlin and on the nature of the lyric, the untranslatable historical original—the lived experience of the outbreak of the war—constitutes for Benjamin a veritable intellectual and existential *primal scene*.

The Meeting House (*Das Heim*)

What, then, is the core of the historical event that cannot be approached but must be distanced even in the very act of bearing witness to it? What is the meaning of the story that the text cannot arrive at, cannot reach, cannot

---

[32] The incomprehension of the audience then could ironically today stand for the incomprehension of Benjamin's contemporary critics with respect to the significance of the event (and of its subsequent inscription as a silence) in Benjamin's life and in his work.

begin except through what has followed, the lecture that attempted to translate it—unsuccessfully?

It is the story of a death without signification, though pregnant with sense, with life and with emotion. It is the story of a meeting and of a Meeting House that turns out to be, ironically, the house of an encounter with a corpse, the posthumous symbol of a lost community and of the loss of language as communal, and the empty center of the space of the remembrance of so many missed encounters: a missed encounter with the audience of the lecture; a missed encounter with the war; a missed encounter with the friend who, dying so young, dies before he could be truly met. "Fritz Heinle was a poet, and the only one of them all whom I met not 'in real life' but in his work. He died at nineteen, and could be known in no other way." It is the story of a war, and of its casualties that history does not narrate and does not count. It is the story of a letter doubled by a corpse that has become the bearer of a meaning it cannot deliver:

> No matter how much memory has subsequently paled, or how indistinctly I can now give an account of the rooms in the Meeting House, it nevertheless seems to me today more legitimate to delineate the outward space the dead man inhabited, indeed the rooms where he was "announced," than the inner space in which he created. But perhaps this is only because, in this last and most crucial year of his life, he traversed the space in which I was born. Heinle's Berlin was the Berlin of the Meeting House. … I once visited him … after a long separation resulting from a serious dissention between us. But even today I remember the smile that lifted the whole weight of these weeks of separation, that turned a probably insignificant phrase into a magic formula that healed the wound. Later, after the morning when an express letter awoke me with the words, "You will find us lying in the Meeting House"—when Heinle and his girlfriend were dead—this district remained for a period the central meeting place of the living. ["BC," 17-18]

The Letter and the Corpse

The unnamed suicide takes place in the blank, the interval between a future—"you will find us"—and a past: "were dead." The corpse has left an urgent letter which awakens Benjamin in shock. But the letter does not speak, it tells no story. It does not explain the motivation of the suicide or its grounds; it does not *narrate* anything other than the utter muteness of the body—of the corpse: "You will find us lying in the Meeting House." What remains of Heinle now are only words. Words of poetry, which Benjamin preserves and hopes to publish. Words of an unintelligible letter.

"Just as a certain kind of significant dream"—Benjamin writes—"survives awakening in the form of words when all the rest of the dream content has vanished, here isolated words have remained in place as marks of catastrophic encounters" ("BC," 14).

Heinle at nineteen, Benjamin at twenty-two have come to the end of the experience that enables telling, or that makes narration possible. In 1936, in "The Storyteller," Benjamin will write that people have returned mute from the battlefields of the First World War. Benjamin himself falls silent not at the war's end but before the war, at the beginning of the war, because he grasps before the others its significance in history and its senseless violence, because he sees ahead of time the consequences of the war. The meaning of the war reveals itself to him in one stroke, in an obscure illumination or in the shock of an epiphany of darkness, in the image of the suicide and in the vision of the combination of the private trauma and of the collective one.

> It was in this café that we sat together in those very first August days, choosing among the barracks that were being stormed by the onrush of volunteers. We decided on the cavalry of Belle-Alliance Strasse, where I duly appeared on one of the following days, no spark of martial fervor in my breast; yet however reserved I may have been in my thoughts, which were concerned only with securing a place among friends in the inevitable conscription, one of the bodies jammed in front of the barrack gates was mine. Admittedly only for two days: on August 8 came the event that was to banish for long after both the city and the war from my mind. ["BC," 21]

"Autobiography"—said de Man—"veils a defacement of the mind of which it is itself the cause." The "place among friends" Benjamin tries to "secure" in "the inevitable conscription" turns out to be a place among corpses. "A Berlin Chronicle" is an autobiography of trauma. The event consists in an erasure: an erasure of Berlin and of the war out of the map of consciousness; an erasure of the self—its transformation into an automaton or a half-corpse, a body dispossessed of consciousness. "One of the bodies jammed in front of the barrack gates was mine," says Benjamin. The war, the shock against the mass of bodies replicated, two days later, by the shock of the discovery of two dead bodies, strips the self of "I": "It is to this immolation of our deepest self in shock that our memory owes its most indelible images" ("BC," 57).

Unspeakable Youth, or Living Outside Experience

Benjamin mourns thus his own lost youthful self, for which Fritz Heinle has become the metaphor: he grieves at the same time over Heinle's and his own lost youth. "The medium in which the pure melody of his youth would swell was destroyed. … In despair, he thus recalls his childhood. In those days there was time without flight and an 'I' without death. … Finally, he is redeemed by losing his comprehension. Amid such obliviousness … he begins the diary. It is the unfathomable document of a life never lived" ("MY," 11).

The suicide represents, however, not simply death but a refusal to compromise with life. Benjamin loves deeply Heinle's absolute commitment to a youth that, unlike Benjamin, he refuses to survive. "Never in any other work," Benjamin will say of Goethe, "did he give to youth what he granted it in Ottilie: the whole of life, in the way that, from its own duration, it has its own death" ("GEA," 353). This description equally applies to Heinle. Paradoxically, Heinle's suicide comes to represent not death but, on the contrary, vitality of life: "The pure word for life in its immortality is 'youth,'" writes Benjamin, in analyzing traumatized youth in Dostoyevsky's *The Idiot*: "This young generation suffers from a damaged childhood."[33]

Unexpectedly, trauma meets youth precisely in its absence—its erasure—of experience: "we have not yet experienced anything," said Benjamin

---

[33] Benjamin, "Dostoyevsky's *The Idiot*," trans. Livingstone, *Selected Writings*, 80-81; hereafter abbreviated "DI." Paradoxically, traumatized youth embodies both a principle of life (an everlasting youth) and a concurrent principle of the survival within language of a childish inarticulateness. Benjamin's interpretation of this wounded generation pursues one principle (life, youth) into the other (speechlessness, deficient language): "The pure word for life in its immortality is 'youth.' Dostoyevsky's great act of lamentation in this novel is for the failure of the youth movement. Its life remains immortal, but the 'idiot' is obscured by his own brightness. … *This young generation suffers from a damaged childhood. … The child's inability to express itself continues to have a crippling effect on the speech* of Dostoyevsky's characters" (ibid.; emphasis mine). Damaged youth is marked, thus, at once by a fixated condensation of vitality ("immortal life," eternal youth) and by a speechless inarticulateness (a damaged, "crippled," silent language). A traumatized language is for Benjamin the sign of a traumatized (an overwhelming) youth. This analysis applies to Benjamin as well (as will be demonstrated and elucidated by what follows). In childhood, life itself is a prisoner of silence (etymologically, an "infant" means "unable to speak"). Language develops with experience. But youth eternalized in death remains forever a prisoner of muteness.

at twenty-one, speaking for youth.[34] At twenty-two, the trauma as erasure—"the event that was to banish for long after both the city and the war from my mind"—equally remains outside experience.[35]

> In spite—or perhaps because—of this … the city of Berlin was never again to impinge so forcefully on my existence as it did in that epoch when we believed we could leave it untouched, only improving its schools, only breaking the inhumanity of their inmates' parents, only making a place in it for the words of Hölderlin or George. It was a final, heroic attempt to change the attitudes of people without changing their circumstances. We did not know that it was bound to fail, but there was hardly one of us whose resolve such knowledge could have altered. And today, as clearly as at that time, even if on the basis of an entirely different reasoning, I understand that the "language of youth" had to stand at the center of our associations. ["BC," 18]

Benjamin pledges fidelity to the "language of youth" the war has erased and which his subsequent work has struck dumb and reduced to silence. But "A Berlin Chronicle" narrates the way in which what is erased—the war, the corpse—remains precisely at the center. The center will thus be a silence. What is erased, what falls to silence at the outbreak of the war, is youth. But youth can have an unexpected afterlife. Heinle's youth lives on in Benjamin. And Benjamin's own silenced youth still speaks in interrupted lyric intervals that have become expressionless through Benjamin's own silence. "Fidelity shall be maintained, even if no one has done so yet," wrote Benjamin at twenty-one, signing "Ardor."[36] Grown mute, the aged writer still asserts: "And today, as clearly as at that time …

---

[34] Benjamin, "Experience," trans. Lloyd Spencer and Stefan Jost, *Selected Writings*, 3.

[35] "The greater the share of the shock value in particular impressions …, the less do these impressions enter experience *[Erfahrung]*," Benjamin will later write in his essay on Baudelaire (Benjamin, "On Some Motifs in Baudelaire," *Illuminations*, 163; hereafter abbreviated "B"). As Freud explained in *Beyond the Pleasure Principle*, memory fragments "are 'often the most enduring when the incident which left them behind was one that never entered consciousness'" (quoted in "B," 160) "Put in Proustian terms this means that only *what has not been experienced explicitly and consciously*, what has not happened to the subject as an experience, can become the object of the *mémoire involontaire*" ("B," 160-161; emphasis mine). "Perhaps the special achievement of shock defense may be seen in its function of assigning to an incident *a precise point in time at the cost of the integrity of its content*" ("B," 163; emphasis mine). The *integrity of content* of the war experience—the integrity of its narration—is thus lost to consciousness and lost to language.

[36] Benjamin, "Experience," 4.

I understand that the 'language of youth' had to stand at the center of our associations."

"Death," Benjamin discovers, "has the power to lay bare like love." "The human being appears to us as a corpse. ... The human body lays itself bare" ("GEA," 353). In a shocking, unnarratable epiphany of darkness, the war lays bare the body, in suddenly revealing youth as corpse.

The Burial

But the most traumatic memory that Benjamin keeps from the war is not simply this unnarratable epiphany—this sudden overwhelming revelation of youth as a corpse—but the added insult, the accompanying shame of the impossibility of giving the beloved corpse a proper burial, the shame of the incapability of taking leave of the dead bodies by giving them the final honor of a proper grave. It is because the bodies cannot be appropriately buried that the corpse of youth becomes a ghost that never will find peace. The grave, symbolically, cannot be closed. The event cannot be laid to rest.

> And when, finally, after August 8, 1914, the days came when those among us who were closest to the dead couple did not want to part from them until they were buried, we felt the limits in the shame of being able to find refuge only in a seedy railway hotel on Stuttgart Square. Even the graveyard demonstrated the boundaries set by the city to all that filled out hearts: it was impossible to procure for the pair who died together graves in one and the same cemetery. But those were days that ripened a realization that was to come later, and that planted in me the conviction that the city of Berlin would also not be spared the scars of the struggle for a better order. If I chance today to pass through the streets of the quarter, I set foot in them with the same uneasiness that one feels when entering an attic unvisited for years. Valuable things may be lying around, but nobody remembers where. ["BC," 20]

The graveyard stands for space in culture and in history: a grave materializes the survival of a name in the deterioration of the corpse. Symbolically, however, these casualties of war remain outside the map of history. The corpse of youth must remain nameless. "Valuable things may be lying around, but nobody remembers where."

The trauma, therefore, is not simply that a capitalist society and a capitalist war have killed youth and have taken *life* away. The real trauma is that they have taken *death* away, that they have robbed youth even from the possibility of mourning. In a world which has condemned youth to die at the war or from the war and in which even a burial is unaffordable; in a society in which even a grave is a commodity that needs to be bought and that can therefore be afforded only by the fortunate, youth, lacking proper funds, are subject—literally and metaphorically—to *a grief beyond their means*: "It was impossible to *procure* for the couple who died together graves in one and the same cemetery."[37]

The Lesson of the War

The mourning will thus be transformed into shame. And it is the lesson of this shame, the moral of this shame, that will enable the autobiographer to say "I" despite his reluctance, as long as he is sufficiently paid,[38] and that will, on the other hand, give the narrator insight into the historical relation between war and revolution: "But those were days that ripened a realization that was to come later … that the city of Berlin would also not be spared the scars of the struggle for a better order." The lesson of the war is revolutionary, as history has demonstrated, in effect, in giving rise to the Russian revolution in the wake of and as a major consequence of the First World War. Benjamin will come both to endorse and to support this revolutionary logic that leads from war to revolution. If history has once revealed youth as a corpse, and if historically youth means "the existence of a beginning that is separated from everything following it as though by an unbridgeable chasm" (*OR*, 20), only the new rupture of a revolution—only a new radical historical beginning—might perhaps one day redeem the corpse of youth or mean a possible return of youth in history. The loyalty to youth is henceforth revolutionary: it looks not to the past, but to the future. "Fidelity shall be maintained. …" "And today, as clearly as at that time, *even if on the basis of an entirely different reasoning*, I understand that the 'language of youth' had to stand at the center of our associations."

[37] There may have been additional reasons for the impossibility of giving the suicidal couple a proper burial: religious reasons (since Heinle's girlfriend was Jewish; Jewish communities had their separate communal graveyards) and sociological reasons (middle class families owned large familial burial sites potentially sufficient for the accommodation of their entire family; but the couple obviously did not qualify to be buried as family members by either family). The Selikson family (the wealthier of the two) would have probably accused Heinle of having dragged their daughter to suicide.

[38] To overcome, that is, ironically and lengthily "the precaution of the subject represented by the 'I,' which is entitled not to be sold cheap."

Written For A Child

To whom, however, is this revolutionary lesson of a corpse passed on? To whom does Benjamin address the message of the "I," this tale of the divorce between words, deeds, motivation, understanding, that is called history? For whom does Benjamin defeat "the precaution of the 'I'" that is "entitled not to be sold cheap"? The dedication of "A Berlin Chronicle" reads: "For my dear Stefan." Stefan is Benjamin's only son, then fourteen years old. This unnarratable narration of a war, this horrifying, baffling story of a suicide and of the absence of a grave is, paradoxically, surprisingly, itself *addressed precisely to a child.*[39]

What Benjamin attempts, in other words, is to *transmit* the story that cannot be told and to become himself the storyteller that cannot be one but that is one—the last narrator or the post-narrator. The trauma—or the breakdown of the story and of memory, the fragmentation of remembrance and the rupture of the chain or of the web of stories—is itself passed on to the next generation as a testament, a final gift.

> *Memory* creates the chain of tradition which passes a happening on from generation to generation. … It starts the web which all stories form in the end. One ties on to the next, as the great storytellers … have always readily shown. ["S," 98]

"A Berlin Chronicle," much like "The Storyteller," is about transmission and about a breakdown of transmission. But this rupture is itself materialized now in the drama—in the image—of the suicide's corpse. What the corpse cannot tell will become the torso of a symbol.

> The images, severed from all earlier associations, … stand—like precious fragments or torsos in a collector's gallery—in the prosaic rooms of our later understanding. ["BC," 26]

---

[39] "For childhood, knowing no preconceived opinions, has none about life. It is as dearly attached … to the realm of the dead, where it juts into that of the living, as to life itself" ("BC," 28). Compare, toward the very end of "A Berlin Chronicle," Benjamin's own childish memory of having been the addressee of a paternal narrative of death. "So the room in which I slept at the age of six would have been forgotten had not my father come in one night—I was already in bed—with the news of a death. It was not, really, the news itself that so affected me. … But in the way in which my father told me, there lay [text breaks off]" ("BC," 57).

> Reminiscences ... do not always amount to an autobiography. And these quite certainly do not. ... For autobiography has to do with time, with sequence and what makes up the continuous flow of life. Here, I am talking of a space, of moments and discontinuities. ["BC," 28]

Benjamin knows that "the flood of war books" published in the aftermath of the First World War cannot bridge over this gap in experience. Like Freud, Benjamin has therefore understood that the impact of the break will be belated and that the real problem of the trauma will be that of the second generation. This is why the post-narrator wants to reestablish the transmissibility of his experience and to transmit the happening that cannot be told—to transmit the war, the corpse, the suicide—to his son.

> It is not the object of the story to convey a happening *per se*, which is the purpose of information; rather, it embeds it in the life of the storyteller in order to pass it on as experience to those listening. ["B," 159]

> Where there is experience in the strict sense of the word, certain contents of the individual past combine with material from the collective past. ["B," 159]

"Seen in this way," Benjamin himself, much like the storyteller, "joins the ranks of the teachers and sages" ("S," 108).[40]

5. The Angel of History

In "A Berlin Chronicle" (1932), Benjamin speaks of the First World War in facing Hitler's rise to power. In "The Storyteller" (1936), Benjamin speaks of the First World War because he foresees already the unavoidability of the outbreak of the Second World War. "At the door awaits the economic crisis, and the shadow of the next war is right behind," he writes in 1933. "In [the] buildings, in [the] paintings and in [the] stories

---

[40] In addressing his impossible narration to a child, Benjamin returns to his original (early) concern with pedagogy and with education, a concern that in turn has been struck by silence but that he has never in effect abandoned. "But who would trust a cane wielder who proclaimed the mastery of children by adults to be the purpose of education? *Is not education, above all, the indispensable ordering of the relationship between generations* and therefore mastery ... of that relationship and not of children? (Benjamin, "One Way Street," 487; emphasis mine).

[of those who have made the radically new their concern], humanity prepares itself to survive culture, if there is no choice."[41]

The traumatic repetition of the war will make Benjamin fall silent a second time, this time definitively.

Before this final fall to silence, in the second winter of the war, Benjamin will write, however, the "Theses on the Philosophy of History" (1940), in which the story of the silence of narration—the story of the First World War—is again narrated but this time interpreted as a theory of history. Again, Benjamin sees ahead of time the consequences of the war. The theory of history names the constellation of the two world wars—the past one and the present one—envisioned one against the other and one through the other. "One ought to speak of events that reach us like an echo awakened by a call," wrote Benjamin in "A Berlin Chronicle" ("BC," 59). It is therefore through the repetition of the trauma that the historian will read history and that the theorist will theorize it; it is from the repetition of the trauma that Benjamin derives his crucial insight into the "philosophy" of history as a constitutive process of silencing, a discourse covering the muteness of the victims and drowning in its own noise the real happenings of their repeated fall to silence.

Thus, the angel of history is mute: his mouth is speechlessly open, as he is helplessly *pushed back toward the future*, pushed back from the Second World War to the speechless experience of the First.[42] The invasion of France in May 1940 repeats the invasion of Belgium twenty six years earlier, on 4 August 1914, an invasion that was to be followed, four days later, by the double suicide.

---

[41] Benjamin, "Erfahrung und Armut," *Gesammelte Schriften*, ed. Hermann Schweppenhäuser and Rolf Tiedemann, 7 vols. in 14 (Frankfurt am Main: Suhrkamp, 1972-89), 2:1:219.

[42] Compare "TPH":

> A Klee painting named "Angelus Novus" shows an angel looking as though he is about to move away from something he is fixedly contemplating. His eyes are staring, his mouth is open, his wings are spread. This is how one pictures the angel of history. His face is turned toward the past. Where we perceive a chain of events, he sees one single catastrophe which keeps piling wreckage upon wreckage and hurls it in front of his feet. The angel would like to stay, awaken the dead, and make whole what has been smashed. But a storm is blowing from Paradise; it has got caught in his wings with such violence that the angel can no longer close them. This storm irresistibly propels him into the future to which his back is turned, while the pile of debris before him grows skyward. This storm is what we call progress. ["TPH," 257-258]

Benjamin is trapped in what has now become occupied France. He plans to escape, to cross the Franco-Spanish border in the hope of ultimately reaching the United States, not so much because he wants to save his life as because he wishes to transmit a manuscript to the free world, because he wishes to *transmit*, that is, beyond the silence—and beyond the silencing—to the next generation. He carries this manuscript precisely on his body. Ironically, it is not known today what was this manuscript. Materially, the manuscript has not survived. It is presumed that this manuscript was indeed the very essay on history, of which copies were preserved elsewhere. But we cannot be sure. The title of the manuscript that Benjamin transported on his body will remain forever shrouded in silence.

"The Time of Death Is Our Own"

Arrested at the border and informed that he will be handed over, the next day, to the Gestapo, Benjamin will end his story by a final suicide. His own suicide will repeat, therefore, and mirror, the suicide of his younger friend, his alter ego, at the outbreak of the First World War.

What is highly ironic is that history repeats also the story of the absence of a grave—for lack of proper funds. The money left in Benjamin's pocket at his death turned out, apparently, to be sufficient only for the "rental" of a grave. After a while, the body was disinterred and the remains were moved to a nameless collective grave of those with no possessions. History repeats itself at once intentionally (suicide) and intentionlessly (absence of a burial). "The language of the intentionless truth … possesses authority," Benjamin has written; "this authority stands in opposition to the conventional concept of objectivity because its validity, that of the intentionless truth, is historical."43 After the fact, "A Berlin Chronicle" sounds almost like a prophecy: "Valuable things are lying around," Benjamin insisted, "but nobody remembers where." Benjamin, writes Demetz, "is buried in Port Bou, but nobody knows where, and when visitors come …, the guardians of the cemetery lead them to a place that they say is his grave, respectfully accepting a tip."[44] For a long time, there was in that Spanish cemetery "neither monument nor flower." In 1992, a

[43] Benjamin, "On the Topic of Individual Disciplines and Philosophy," trans. Livinstone, *Selected Writings*, 404.

[44] Demetz, introduction to Benjamin, *Reflections*, xv.

monument was built.[45] But Benjamin's body is not in the grave where the monument now stands.

"For storytelling is always the art of repeating stories," Benjamin has written in "The Storyteller" ("S," 91). Benjamin's own suicide will ironically and tragically repeat, thus, both the story of the suicide of his youth and the shameful story of the absence of a burial. By asserting his own choice of death and by taking his own life, Benjamin repeats as well, from Heinle's story, *the message of the corps*: the posthumous, mute message of the suicide as a symbolic gesture of protest against the war and as the autonomous assertion of an uncoerced and uncoercible will in the face of the overpowering spread of world violence.

In repeating Heinle's suicide at the threshold of the First World War and in reactivating his symbolic message of resistance to the war, Benjamin's own rush to suicide in the early stages of the Second World War will achieve, thus, a definitive reunion with the cruelly lost friend.

> It was after a long separation. … But even today I remember the smile that lifted the whole weight of these weeks of separation.

Benjamin has always known—since the trauma of the First World War and the example of the suicide of his friend—that "the cowardice of the living" (the survivor's timidity that paralleled "The Poet's Courage" or the poet's death) "must ultimately become unbearable" ("MY," 14). Already at the age of twenty-one, he writes prophetically, as though in premonition of his future suicide:

> The diary writes the story of our greatness from the vantage point of our death …
>
> In death we befall ourselves. … And the time of death is our own. Redeemed, we become aware of the fulfillment of the game. … The vocation that we proudly dismissed in our youth takes us by surprise. Yet it is nothing but a call to immortality. ["MY," 15]

A Signature (A Call to Immortality)

Framed as it is by Benjamin's own texts, prefigured by his life and central to the processes of his entire thought, the suicide therefore is not just an act of weariness and abdication, a mere untimely gesture of fatigue

---

[45] The monument (sponsored by the German Government) was planned and built by the "Arbeitskreis selbständiger Kulturinstitut" (ASKI).

and of despair—as Hannah Arendt has quite famously depicted it (and mourned it) in underscoring its essential feature as "bad luck."[46] Beyond

[46] There is … another … element … which is involved in the life of those "who have won victory in death." It is *the element of bad luck*, and this factor, very prominent in Benjamin's life, cannot be ignored here because he himself … was so extraordinarily aware of it. In his writing and also in conversation he used to speak about "the little hunchback," … a German fairy-tale figure … out of … German folk poetry. The hunchback was an early acquaintance of Benjamin. … His mother … used to say, "Mr. Bungle sends his regards" … whenever one of the countless little catastrophes of childhood had taken place. … The mother referred to "the little hunchback," who caused the objects to play their mischievous tricks upon children. … (*With a precision suggesting a sleepwalker [Benjamin's] clumsiness invariably guided him to the very center of misfortune.*). … Wherever one looks in Benjamin's life, one will find the little hunchback. …

On September 26, 1940, Walter Benjamin, who was about to emigrate to America, took his life at the Franco-Spanish border. There were various reasons for this. The Gestapo had confiscated his Paris apartment, which contained his library … and many of his manuscripts. … Besides, nothing drew him to America, where, as he used to say, people would probably find no other use for him than to cart him up and down the country to exhibit him as "the last European." *But the immediate occasion for Benjamin's suicide was an uncommon stroke of bad luck.* Through the armistice agreement between Vichy France and the Third Reich, refugees from Hitler Germany … were in danger of being shipped back to Germany. … To save this category of refugees … the United States had distributed a certain number of emergency visas through its consulates in unoccupied Europe. Thanks to the efforts of the Institute in New York, Benjamin was among the first to receive such a visa in Marseilles. Also, he quickly obtained a Spanish transit visa to enable him to get to Lisbon and board a ship there. However, he did not have a French exit visa … which the French government, eager to please the Gestapo, invariably denied the German refugees. In general this presented no great difficulty, since a relatively short and none too arduous road to be covered by foot over the mountains to Port Bou was well known and was not guarded by the French border police. Still, for Benjamin apparently suffering from cardiac condition … even the shortest walk was a great exertion, and he must have arrived in a state of serious exhaustion. The small group of refugees that he had joined reached the Spanish border town only to learn that Spain had closed the border that same day and that the border officials did not honor visas made out in Marseilles. The refugees were supposed to return to France by the same route the next day. During the night Benjamin took his life, whereupon the border officials, upon whom this suicide had made an impression, allowed his companions to proceed to Portugal. A few weeks the irony of fate, beyond misfortune, the suicide makes of death a sign. In desperation, dying becomes a language. It makes a point. It is not only a decision to stop suffering and to lapse into protective and forgetful sleep. It is—across the gap of two world wars—a knocking at the doors of history. It is the punctuation of a life of writing that, by a final, willful act of silence, leaves behind *its signature*: a signature of desperate but absolutely *unconditional refusal of complicity and of collaboration* with the coercive tyranny of world wars.

> Yet tragic silence … must not be thought of as being dominated by defiance alone. Rather, this defiance is every bit as much a consequence of the experience of speechlessness as a factor which intensifies the condition. The content of the hero's achievements belongs to the community, as does speech. Since the community … denies these achievements, they remain unarticulated in the hero. And he must therefore all the more forcefully enclose within the confines of his physical self every action and every item of knowledge the greater and the more potentially effective it is. It is the achievement of his *physis* alone, not of language, if he is able to hold fast to his cause, and he must therefore do so in death. [*OG*, 108]

Projected into his own words, Benjamin's own suicide can be read as "the attempt of moral man, still dumb, still inarticulate … to raise himself up amid the agitation of that painful world" (*OG*, 110). Benjamin himself embodies, thus, in his own concept but with the "authority of … the intentionless truth," the "paradox of the birth of the genius in moral speechlessness" (*OG*, 110). His death gives his posterity a language; it endows the future with a yet unborn word.

The repetition of the suicide recovers the collective meaning that was lost to death both in the battlefields—and in the suicide—of the First World War. "The voice of the anonymous storyteller" ("S," 107) recovers "a collective experience to which even the deepest shock of every individual experience, death, constitutes no impediment or barrier" ("S," 102).[47]

> later the embargo on visas was lifted again. One day earlier Benjamin would have got through without any trouble; one day later the people in Marseilles would have known that for the time being it was impossible to pass through Spain. Only on that particular day was the catastrophe possible. [Arendt, introduction to Benjamin, *Illuminations*, 5-18; emphasis mine]

[47] Benjamin in this way reenacts, beyond the moral speechlessness of Heinle's story, a more effective transformation of the corpse into a message. If "storytelling

> One can … ask oneself whether the relationship of the storyteller to his material, human life, his own and that of others, is not itself a craftsman's relationship, whether it is not his very task to fashion the raw material of experience, his own and that of others, in a solid, useful, and unique way … exemplified by the proverb if one thinks of it as an ideogram of a story. A proverb, one might say, is a ruin which stands on the site of an old story and in which a moral twines about a happening like an ivy around a wall. ["S," 108]

Through his death, Benjamin converts, thus, his own life into a proverb.

The Will (A Posthumous Narration)

Scholem tells us that the idea of suicide was not new to Benjamin, who was close to suicide several times throughout his life. Particularly, Scholem has learnt after the fact that, upon writing "A Berlin Chronicle," Benjamin had an imminent suicide plan in mind, a plan that unpredictably was changed at the last moment. This is why, as a correlative or counterpart to the autobiographical "A Berlin Chronicle," Benjamin has also left a will, a will that he "did not destroy when his will to live gained the upper hand at the eleventh hour," and that after his death was found in his documents. The will reads:

> All the manuscripts in my estate—both my own writings and those of others—shall go to Dr. Gerhard Scholem, Abyssinian Road, Jerusalem. My entire estate contains in addition to my own writings the works of the brothers Fritz and Wolf Heinle. It would be in accordance with my wishes if their writings could be preserved in the university library in Jerusalem or in the Prussian State Library. These comprise not only Heinle's manuscripts but also my edited handwritten copies of their works. As regards my own

---

is always the art of repeating stories," it goes without saying that *not every repetition is an art*. In "the age of mechanical reproduction," not every reiteration is endowed with what "The Storyteller" calls "the gift of retelling" ("S," 91), a gift which is specifically, says Benjamin, *a listener's gift*—an insight born out of the capacity for silent listening. Benjamin's "gift of retelling" is both autobiographical and theoretical: it is at once a literary gift and a historical force of perception; it is compellingly subjective (it pays the ultimate subjective price) and compellingly objective (it speaks with the intentionless authority of history). There are various ways of "repeating stories"—with or without historical surprises, with or without new meaning, with or without historical authority. Benjamin's historical retelling of the story of the suicide is authoritative, because it makes *transmissible* what it repeats, because it rescues the past suicide from its meaninglessness and from its original forgettability, in endowing it with a transmissible historical intelligibility.

> works, it would be in accordance with my wishes if the University Library in Jerusalem provided space for some of them. Should Dr. Gerhard Scholem publish a posthumous selection of my writings ..., it would be in accordance with my wishes if he sent a certain portion of the net profits from that edition—about 40-60% after deducting his expenses—to my son Stephan.[48]

In the enclosed farewell letter to his cousin Egon Wissing, the executor of his will, Benjamin declared:

> I think it would be nice if the manuscript department of the library of the University of Jerusalem accepted the posthumous papers of two non-Jews from the hands of two Jews—Scholem's and mine.[49]

As posthumous narration, the will insures transmission of the story of the other. Beyond its author's death, it must secure, safeguard, the other's immortality. It is in thus resisting another's loss of life and another's loss of meaning that Benjamin in death recovers, for himself and for his friend, what Heinle in his suicide lost precisely: the "'narrator's stance.'"

> With this comes to light the innermost basis for the "narrator's stance." *It is he alone who, in the feeling of hope, can fulfill the meaning of the event. ...* Thus, hope finally wrests itself from it ... like a trembling question. ... This hope is the sole justification of the faith in immortality, which must never be kindled from one's own existence. ["GEA," 355; emphasis mine]

Immortality takes from the other. Life can become immortal only insofar as it is linked to others' lives. What is immortal is the other, not the self. What is immortal is, in other words, not the narrator but the very story of the repetition, a story that, repeated at least twice, is not simply individual. And the transmission must go on.

In the "trembling question" of a hope, Benjamin assigns to Scholem the task of continuing the story: the task of duplicating now, in Scholem's own life, the prosopopeia to the dead; the task of inheriting and of continuing the *Story of a Friendship*. Scholem will fulfill this task. Benjamin has proven thus that "not only a man's knowledge or wisdom,"

> but above all his real life—and this is the stuff that stories are made of—first assumes transmissible form at the moment of his death. Just as a

---

[48] Quoted in Gershom Scholem, *Walter Benjamin: The Story of a Friendship*, trans. Zohn (New York: Schocken, 1988), 187-88.
[49] Quoted in ibid., 188.

sequence of images is set in motion inside a man as his life comes to an end—unfolding the views of himself under which he has encountered himself without being aware of it—suddenly in his expressions and looks the unforgettable emerges and imparts to everything that concerned him that authority which even the poorest wretch in dying possesses for the living around him. This authority is at the very source of the story. ["S," 94]

Textual Authority

Authority is what commends a text (a life) to memory, what makes it unforgettable. What Benjamin—prophetically again—says of Prince Myshkin—the protagonist of Dostoyevsky's *The Idiot*—can equally account for his own effect and for the literary impact of his own textual authority:

> Immortal life is unforgettable. ... *It is the life that is not to be forgotten, even though it has no monument or memorial.* ... And "unforgettable" does not just mean that we cannot forget it. It points to something in the nature of the unforgettable itself, something that makes it unforgettable. ["DI," 80]

What is the secret of Myshkin's charisma? "His individuality," says Benjamin, "is secondary to his life" ("DI," 80). Like Myshkin, Benjamin is unforgettable because his individuality (including his own death, his suicide) is subordinated to his life.

Like the storyteller, Benjamin has "borrowed his authority from death." But the authority he has borrowed from death is none other than the storyteller's power to transmit, to *take across a limit*, the *uniqueness of a life*. It is life that, over and beyond the author's death, has been preserved in the texts of Benjamin. It is life that, over and beyond the Second World War, still reaches out to us and touches us and teaches us in the words of Benjamin and in his silence. It is the textual authority of Benjamin's life that has claimed Scholem and that has compelled him to repeat the story and to continue in his own way Benjamin's prosopopeia to the dead.

In "The metaphysics of Youth," when he was still himself a very young man, Benjamin wrote:

> Conversation strives toward silence, and the listener is really the silent partner. The speaker receives meaning from him; the silent one is the unappropriated source of meaning.

Benjamin was a good listener, because he was always faithful to the silent one.

I would suggest that the task of criticism today is not to drown Benjamin's texts in an ever growing critical noise, but to return to Benjamin his silence.

CHAPTER TWO

"UN PETIT GESTE": AFFECT AND SILENCE IN CLAUDE LANZMANN'S *SHOAH*

MAGDALENA ZOLKOS

Introduction

This essay focuses on a single scene in Claude Lanzmann's 1985 film *Shoah*, where one of the first-hand witnesses of the mass murder of European Jews in the gas chamber of the Treblinka extermination camp, Abraham Bomba, gives account of his traumatic experiences. The purpose of the essay is to engage with selected academic analyses of that scene (from the vast body of scholarship that has been produced about Lanzmann's film), in order to suggest that, while often highly insightful and constructive, many of the existing interpretations have tended to equate testimony with its narrative dimensions. In result, the dominant tendency of the existing interpretations has been to either overlook the rich non-verbal semiotics of Bomba's testimony's, which include silence, gesturality, movement, and other forms of bodily expression, or to regard them as indicative of trauma's non-representability and as the breakdown of meaning.

The significance of the non-verbal aspects of traumatic testimony requires a re-framing of the existing conceptions of the testimonial subject, beyond the oralist interpretations of meaning-making. This essay aims to achieve such a re-framing in an alternative reading of Bomba's testimony from the perspective of "affect" evidenced and generated by the non-oral expressions. The notion of affect in this essay will traverse two of its definitions: affect as the emotional and visceral dimension of the inner life of the subject, and affect as a shift in the bodily capacity for action. The suggestion is that at stake in an "affective" interpretation of the scene of Bomba's testimony is the questioning of the dualist or binary conceptualizations of speech and silence in mass murder testimony, as well as a recognition of the complexity of gesturality and silence in the literary procedures of traumatic memory beyond the tradition of the "negative sublime."[1]

The essay starts with contextualizing the testimonial scene with Abraham Bomba in relation to some of the theoretical considerations that have been raised by the critical scholarship on *Shoah*, in particular in regard to how the witnessing subject is constituted, and comes into being, through the interpellative chain of what Karyn Ball has called "the confessional effect" in the literature of mass murder testimony.[2] Drawing on Foucauldian insights and on the psychoanalytic trauma theory, Ball offers critical insights into the importance of the categories of confessionality and intimate disclosure for the contemporary literature of historical trauma. The scene with Abraham Bomba, and in particular Claude Lanzmann's controversial role in what has been regarded as a staged bodily re-enactment of memory, rather than creation of a recollective space,[3] illustrates poignantly the "disciplinary structure of a testimonial transmission of traumatic knowledge."[4]

Next, the essay turns to an examination of those moments in Bomba's testimony that seem saturated with non-verbal forms of communication. It draws on the deconstructionist view that asserts the non-oppositionality and non-binarity of the relation between speech and silence. By focusing on two dimensions of the non-oralist expression in the testimony (Bomba's hand and facial gestures and the extended moments of silence), and by tracing their affective movements in constituting spaces of traumatic memory, I seek to demonstrate that the space of non-verbality holds a potential for reframing the witnessing subject in terms of her/his resistance against the confessional interpellations. Finally, the essay turns to the political philosophy of Giorgio Agamben and, more specifically, his two essays on gesture in order to pull out the possible political dimension

---

[1] Theodor W. Adorno's conceptualization of the "sublime" remains indebted to the Kantian nexus of the sublime (as a "negative pleasure" or "indirect pleasure" and terror, which arises in the human encounter with nature. However, Adorno radically reframes the sublime in relation to the power and terror of the state, capable of genocidal violence. See discussion of the "negative sublime" in Karyn Ball, *Disciplining the Holocaust: Traumatic History as Object of Inquiry and Desire* (New York: SUNY Press, 2008), 83-86.

[2] Ball, *Disciplining*, 201.

[3] See for example Marianne Hirsch and Leo Spitzer, "The Witness in the Archive. Holocaust Studies / Memory Studies," in *Memory. Histories, Theories, Debates,* eds. Susannah Radstone and Bill Schwartz, 396-398 (New York: Fordham University Press, 2010).

[4] Ball, *Disciplining,* 201.

of thinking about testimony and memory in terms of embodied affectivities that "testimonial gestures" frame and reside in.

1. Shoah as The Odyssey: Home-return, Involuntary Memory, and Mirrors

One of the most widely discussed and undoubtedly most haunting scenes in Lanzmann's *Shoah* takes place in the suburbs of Tel Aviv in a barbershop. It involves Abraham Bomba, who was an inmate of the Treblinka extermination camp in 1942-1943. Born in an orthodox Jewish family in 1913 in Beuthen in the German Schlesien (currently Bytom in Poland), Bomba was forced into a residence in the Czestochowa ghetto in 1941, where he worked as a barber. In September 1943, Bomba, his wife Reizl and infant son Berl were deported to Treblinka extermination camp. Bomba's wife and son were killed on arrival. Abraham Bomba was forcibly recruited into the labor unit *Sonderkommando,* where he worked in a clothes-sorting group. As a barber, he was also forced to cut the hair of children and women at their entry into the gas chambers. Bomba managed to escape the Treblinka camp in January 1943. He returned to the Czestochowa ghetto and became involved in the activities of the Jewish Combat Organization, until, together with his second wife, Regina, Bomba was deported to the Tschenstochau camp in June 1943, which they escaped together just before the camp's liberation by the Soviet Army in January 1945.[5]

Claude Lanzmann met Abraham Bomba in New York,[6] and filmed the interviews with him, including the momentous scene in a rented barbershop in Holon, in the autumn of 1979/1980. Surrounded by the local Israeli barbers and their clients, Bomba gives his testimony while cutting the hair of a male friend. In a discussion at Yale University following the screening of the film, Lanzmann commented extensively on the choice of the location, emphasizing in particular the objectives in finding a setting

---

[5] "Abraham Bomba," Visual History Biographic Profiles, USC Shoah Foundation Institute, http://tc.usc.edu/vhiechoes/bios/Bomba.Abraham.pdf (accessed March 16, 2012). Abraham and Regina survived the war, and in 1951 moved to the United States, where he worked as a barber. In 1964-1965 and 1970 Bomba served as a witness at the Treblinka Trials in Düsseldorf. A detailed testimony of Bomba was recorded in 1996 by Louise Bobrow in Montello, and is available at: "Interview with Abraham Bomba," 14.08.1996; USC Shoah Foundation Institute, http://tc.usc.edu/vhiechoes/video.aspx?testimonyid=19398 (accessed March 20, 2012).

[6] See Claude Lanzmann, *Le lièvre de Patagonie* (Paris: Gallimard, 2009), 614-619.

that remained in a relation of both "distance and closeness" to Bomba's experiences in the camp. In contrast to the female victims of the Treblinka gas chamber, and the hasty pace at which their hair was removed, here there is only one person—a man—and the scene extends over twenty minutes. Lanzmann has also reflected on the gendered dimension of that scene, arguing that to film it with female extras, or in a women's barbershop, would have been "unbearable and obscene [*insupportable et obscène*]."[7] This is because the gendered "mourned object" in the film (for Bomba as much as for other male witnesses in *Shoah,* who had survived the women, or "left [them] behind") remains coded through her absences, or, paradoxically, through the erasure of gender differentiation.[8]

Margaret Olin suggests that at work in Bomba's testimonial scene in the barbershop is a topographically elicited *disjunctive effect,* which results from the contrast between the places and spatial arrangement where the survivors give their testimonies, and the places "where the Holocaust occurred."[9] Specifically, Lanzmann elicits this effect by mounting a contrast between the bustling barbershop in Holon and the death site of the gas chamber in Treblinka. This dissonance is perhaps even more striking in the preceding scenes with Bomba, which are filmed on a sunny terrace in Jaffa with a background view of sea and yachts. Notably, Olin translates this disjunctive rhetoric from spatial into temporal terms, by emphasizing that at play in *Shoah*'s testimonial scenes is a staged contrast between "past and present." Accordingly, Olin juxtaposes this effect of *temporal disjointedness* or *temporal discontinuity* with Lanzmann's investment in showing "the continuity of the survivors' memories."[10]

An important difference between the gas chamber and the barbershop is the absence of mirrors in the chamber, and their proliferation in the décor of the shop. Lanzmann asks Bomba explicitly: "Were there mirrors [in the gas chamber]?" even though he admits to the ridiculousness of this question, having seen the "bare walls […] of the gas chambers in Auschwitz

---

[7] Lanzmann, *Le lièvre*, 621. See also Claude Lanzmann, Ruth Larson and David Rodowick, "Seminar With Claude Lanzmann 11 April 1990," *Yale French Studies* 79 (1991): 98.

[8] For a critique of *Shoah* from a feminist perspective, see Marianne Hirsch and Leo Spitzer, "Gendered Translations: Claude Lanzmann's *Shoah*," in *Claude Lanzmann's* Shoah. *Key Essays,* ed. Stuart Liebman, (Oxford: Oxford University Press, 2007).

[9] Margaret Olin, "Lanzmann's *Shoah* and the Topography of the Holocaust Film," *Representations* 57 (1997): 4.

[10] Ibid., 4.

and in Majdanek."[11] In contrast, "the barbershop is lined with mirrors, which *reflect* [Bomba's and the barbers'] *gestures into infinity*."[12]

This multiplication and dispersion of gestures of the witness (and others) suggests that the performative aspect of gesturality in *Shoah* situates it beyond the register of what is proper to, and contained by, individual agency. One of *Shoah*'s commentators, Stuart Liebman, argues that:

> in this Tel Aviv barber shop, so far removed from wartime Poland, the people reflected and refracted in the complicated, unstable spaces of the facing mirrors invoke invisible spectral presences that haunt Bomba's—and our—present.[13]

The significance of the mirrors in the testimonial scene lies in the metaphorical connotation between the reflections, refractions and reduplications of the witness's gestures on the one hand, and the question about the ethical status of traumatic memory on the other. The gestural proliferations "*into infinity*" in the barbershop suggest that the testimonial expressions extend beyond the dominant narrative framework inscribed in the dual relation of the director's questions and the witness's answers, as well as beyond the temporal framing of the interview in the present, or even beyond the level of oral communication. This requires that the recipient of the testimony takes into account the psychic and somatic dynamics of *transmission* and *transference* in the process of mnemonic articulations, which, in addition to the narrative elements, structure the embodied, affective, apophatic—and, undoubtedly, cinematic—dimensions of Bomba's testimony.

Importantly, the contrast between "past and present," as analyzed by Olin, extends not only to the analysis of the scene, but to the subject formation of the witness. Not only is Bomba "inserted" by Lanzmann into the serene and luxurious environment of the Jaffa apartment, but also in the barbershop's setting, Bomba—speaking English and wearing a bright yellow uniform from the barbershop at Grand Central Station in New York where he had worked prior to his retirement—differs strikingly from the other barbers. That contextual dissonance is evocative of a *hauntological trait* at work in the testimonial scenes in *Shoah* (in relation to Bomba and

---

[11] Lanzmann, *Le lièvre*, 623.

[12] Ibid., *emphasis mine*.

[13] Stuart Liebman, "Introduction," in *Claude Lanzmann's* Shoah. *Key Essays,* ed. Stuart Liebman, 16 (Oxford: Oxford University Press, 2007).

to others).[14] The haunting effect of the scene is elicited, *inter alia*, by the aforementioned reflections of human faces in the barbershop mirrors, or by a blurred photo of a woman hanging on the wall.

In the analyzed scene the epistemological order of witnessing defies the chronological and binary arrangement of the past and present in accordance with the logic of trauma.[15] Also, and perhaps more importantly, it reflects Lanzmann's association of the figure of the witness with (what is termed here as) "thanatic proximities," that is the remnants in the testimonial subject formation of the propinquity to the gas chamber as the site of death.[16] The witness's survival of mass murder is understood in terms of "spectral" or "ghostly" modalities of subjective being. As Friedland puts it poetically, surviving approximates "living-on that is not (or not-quite) living."[17] Further, in his critique of Lanzmann's emphasis on the acting-out of past trauma as the substructure of witnessing, Dominick LaCapra points out that *Shoah* features primarily "figures who are closest to death, who have an eschatological significance in that they bring together two ultimate singularities: the absolute beginning and the final end."[18] This reflects Lanzmann's own *thanatic obsessions* ("affect and phantasms")[19] in the making of the film.[20]

---

[14] For example, Lanzmann explicitly refers to the two survivors of the Chelmno mass murder of Jews, Michael Podchlebnik and Szymon Srebrnik, as "ghosts" (*revenants*). See Lanzmann, *Le lièvre*, 626.

[15] See for example Petar Ramadanovic, "In the Future… On Trauma and Literature," in *Topologies of Trauma. Essays on the Limit of Knowledge and Memory,* eds. Linda Belau and Petar Ramadanovic (New York: Other Press, 2002); Ulrich Baer, *Spectral Evidence: The Photography of Trauma* (Cambridge, MA: MIT Press, 2005); Susannah Radstone, "Trauma Theory: Context, Politics, Ethics," *Paragraph* 30, no.1 (2007): 9–29.

[16] Numerous engagements in continental philosophy with the testimonial genre have understood survival of mass murder in terms of a liminal condition of a subject that collapses any binary and oppositional constructions of life and death. For example, Jacques Derrida writes that "to survive, in the usual sense of the word, is to continue to live, but also to live after death. […] Benjamin underlines the distinction between *überleben*, to live after death, as a book can survive the death of its author or the child the death of parents, and *fortleben*, to continue to live." Jacques Derrida and Jean Birnbaum, *Learning to Live Finally: The Last Interview* (New York: Studio Visit, 2004).

[17] Amos Friedland, *Forgiveness, Reconciliation, and the Remains of Resentment* (PhD Thesis, The New School, New York, 2002).

[18] Dominick LaCapra, "Lanzmann's 'Shoah': 'Here There Is No Why'," *Critical Inquiry* 23, no.2 (1997): 255.

[19] Ibid., 266.

Numerous commentators have also suggested that the location of Bomba's testimonial speech at the barbershop (*while* cutting hair) indicates that Lanzmann represents witnessing as radically different from the practice of giving a narrative account of past experiences.[21] Instead, witnessing in *Shoah* involves a staged *return* to the traumatic events and their emotional and sentient reliving, or "acting out."[22] Witnessing is thus, primarily, a bodily and affective act, rather than a narrative and recollective practice. This line of affective inquiry into the vicissitudes of witnessing has been pursued, *inter alia*, by Kelly Oliver who (drawing on Teresa Brennan's theory of affect) has written about the affect-based economies of testimony.[23] According to Oliver, the extent to which "the emphatic witness" is involved in a process of working-through of the past trauma in the act of giving testimony is closely related to symbolization of affects and drives. However, while the testimonial act endows the traumatic affects with meaning, the symbolization does not exhaust its operations or effects, insofar as testimony also constitutes a setting of "affective mobility" at the level of "both subjective and political life."[24] This concept of witnessing is highly influenced by Brennan's notion of affect, understood not as a matter of "private or personal" impression or sensation, but, rather, as "a silent or barely articulated experience of

---

[20] Lanzmann reminisces in his autobiography: "I was obsessed with the last moments of the victims [*des condamnés*], or […] the first moments of their arrival to the camp, such as the thirst and the cold—what does it mean, for example, to wait naked in the minus twenty degrees for one's turn to enter and die in the gas chambers in Treblinka or in Sobibor." And, further, reflecting on his participation in an academic conference on the Holocaust, "The participants of the conference, many of them established authorities in the area, were striking in their merriment. […] I was so filled with and haunted by death that I couldn't understand the academics' insouciance. […] I was thinking about [death] more and more, […] to the extent that I imagined that the whole world was dead, the victims as well as the murderers. Whenever I found a survivor [*un vivant*], my astonishment was absolute, I felt as if it was an archeological exhumation, and my find appeared like a sign and a vestige of an enormous catastrophe" Lanzmann, *Le lièvre,* 611 & 614.

[21] See Gerturd Koch, "The Aesthetic Transformation of the Image of the Unimaginable: Notes on Claude Lanzmann's 'Shoah'," *October* 28 (1989): 20.

[22] See LaCapra, "Lanzmann's 'Shoah'," 255-257. See also Sami Naïr, "Shoah, une leçon d'humanité," in *Au sujet de Shoah: Le Film de Claude Lanzmann,* ed. Michel Deguy, (Paris: Belin, 1990),172-174.

[23] Kelly Oliver, *Witnessing: Beyond Recognition* (Minneapolis: University of Minnesota Press, 2001).

[24] Charles Shepherdson, "Emotion, Affect, Drive," in *Living Attention. On Theresa Brennan,* eds. Alice A. Jardine, Shannon Lundeen, and Kelly Oliver, (New York: SUNY Press, 2007), 69.

exhaustion or incapacity, […] distributed unevenly in the social sphere." The distinctive feature of affect is that "it always circulates […] sometimes in the service of vitality, and sometimes as the mark of forgotten conflict."[25]

Notably, in his explanation of the choice of a barbershop as the setting for Bomba's testimony, Lanzmann pays attention to the embodied mnemonic connections between Bomba's experiences in Treblinka and his testimonial "return" (or a "home-coming"), which takes place in Holon. For Lanzmann, these gestural and affective connections conditions the possibility of (what Karyn Ball calls) "[the] testimonial transmission of traumatic knowledge." [26] Without naming explicitly his conceptual apparatus, the filmmaker uses here a mnemonic category of affective associations. Following either the Freudian psychoanalytic nexus of memory and affect, or the neuroscientific tradition of Bessel van der Kolk and others, trauma theorists have referred to these associations between the mnemonic and affect as "body memory" or "pain memory." [27] This conceptualization relies on the idea of memory, which is placed beyond "our capability to remember certain events of our past, or to retain and retrieve data and knowledge." [28] Also, it is linked to those forms of embodiment and gesturality that retain, store and transmit traumatic content "outside of conscious recollections."[29]

Lanzmann reflects:

> Why a barbershop? I thought that *the same gestures* could provide a support for the feelings [*la béquille des sentiments*], and that it would make it easier for [Bomba] to both speak and demonstrate in front of the camera. Of course, these were not *the same gestures*: the barbershop is not a gas chamber. […]
>
> During the shooting I asked Abraham to *show me those gestures*, and he, holding the scissors in an extended hand, […] showed me how he did [the cutting of women's hair] and in what pace. […] Without the scissors, that scene would have been hundred times less evocative, hundred times

---

[25] Ibid., 68 and 69.

[26] Ball, *Disciplining*, 201.

[27] Felicity Callard and Constantina Papoulias, "Affect and Embodiment," in *Memory. Histories, Theories, Debates,* eds. Susannah Radstone and Bill Schwarz, (New York: Fordham University Press, 2010).

[28] Thomas Fuchs, "The Phenomenology of Body Memory," in *Body Memory, Metaphor and Movement,* eds. Sabine C. Koch, Thomas Fuchs, Michela Summa, and Cornelia Müller, (Amsterdam: John Benjamins Publishing, 2004), 10.

[29] Ibid., 10.

> weaker. And perhaps it would not have taken place at all; the scissors allowed [Bomba] at the same time to embody his story and to […] regain his breath and his strength, since what he had to say was both incredible and exhausting.[30]

On the one hand Lanzmann upholds the metaphoric construction of Bomba's Treblinka experiences and the staged testimonial act, through the trope of "embodied" or "incarnated" (*incarné*) return. The witness's professional gestures and presence of material objects such as hair and scissors operate as *triggers of involuntary memory* (perhaps not unlike Proust's madeleines). The aim is to *access* and *unlock* the realm of repressed, or blocked out, memories, which, according to the psychoanalytic trauma theory, had resulted from the overwhelmed ego defenses. Lanzmann is strongly invested in establishing the relationship of resemblance between these the two events—haircutting in the gas chamber and in the Israeli barbershop—that allegedly condition the possibility of the experiential transmission of the witness's traumatic knowledge. In contrast to the Proustian "episode of the madeleine," at stake is not an experience of a deep, almost ecstatic pleasure that the author of *In Search of Lost Time* undergoes at the access to his involuntary and sensuous childhood memories. Rather, what occurs is an unbearable ordeal or even a risk of re-traumatizing the witness.[31]

On the other hand, Lanzmann recognizes the futility and impossibility, perhaps even impudence, of these attempts: "the same gestures [performed by Bomba in Holon], […] these were not the same gestures" (*"[l]es memes gestes […] ce n'étaient pas les memes gestes*"). In other words, while Lanzmann expresses his aspiration to "place [Bomba] once again in a situation where his *gestures* would be identical,"[32] as part of his strategy of "interpolating blocks of [the witness's] imagery,"[33] this project is subsequently rendered futile and inoperative by Lanzmann's own admittance of the aporetic nature of these odyssean desires and ambitions.

Lanzmann asks Bomba to demonstrate, or, rather, to "redo," the gesture of cutting the hair of women in the gas chamber (*refaire les gestes*), and Bomba complies, using his fictitious client's hair. The demonstration is inscribed within a spectacle of traumatic repetition that relies strongly

---

[30] Lanzmann, *Le lièvre*, 622-623, *emphasis mine*.
[31] See LaCapra, "Lanzmann's 'Shoah'," 255.
[32] Claude Lanzmann in Marc Chevrie and Hervé Le Roux, "Site and Speech. An Interview with Clause Lanzmann about *Shoah*," in *Claude Lanzmann's* Shoah. *Key Essays*. Ed. Stuart Liebman, (Oxford: Oxford University Press, 2007), 41.
[33] Liebman, "Introduction," 17.

on the Freudian trope of *uncanniness* (*das Unheimliche*), which has to do with a certain emotional impulse, or sensation, of the "strangely familiar," inscribed within the structure of the testimonial reception.[34] For example, Liebman refers to the uncanny effect of the image of a short-haired woman, which hangs on the wall of the Tel Aviv barbershop during Bomba's testimony. Barely perceptible "in the illusory depths of the frame," the image "makes the presence of women who died [in the gas chamber] uncannily palpable." [35] The unsettling and disorienting effect of the "repetition of the same thing"—the cutting of the hair in the camp and in the bustling Israeli barbershop—thus seeks to evoke strong affective, imaginary and sensuous resonances not only in the witness, but also in the audience. This resonates with Lanzmann's claim that in the barbershop scene "[e]very expression of feeling demonstrates something, and conversely, every proof of this sort is itself a form of emotion."[36]

Lanzmann's Proustian impulse to invoke and operationalize the bodily gesture of the witness as an automatic memory trigger suggests a level of epistemic involuntariness and viscerality in the testimonial production(s) in *Shoah.* Karyn Ball has critiqued these productions for building on a "confessional effect." Ball has argued that Lanzmann "clearly operates on the assumption that the more personally devastating it is for the witness to recall an incident, the more profound the nature of the evil displayed." Accordingly:

> [l]earning this unbearable 'lesson' firsthand is important, but it comes to us by means of a confession employed as a disciplinary technology to ferret out a 'hidden truth' rendered more valuable by virtue of the painful reluctance that surrounds it and the labor of mining it.[37]

When approached from the perspective of affect theory, the proliferating silences and evocative gestures in Bomba's testimony can be interpreted as a subjective resistance to such "confessional effect," as they mark, potentially, constitution of the recalcitrant witness.

---

[34] For a discussion of the aesthetic and psychoanalytic notions of the uncanny see for example Nicholas Royle, *The Uncanny* (Manchester: Manchester University Press, 2011) and Anneleen Masschelein, *The Unconcept: The Freudian Uncanny in Late-Twentieth-Century Theory* (New York: SUNY Press, 2011).

[35] Liebman, "Introduction," 16.

[36] Lanzmann in Chevrie and Le Roux, "Site and Speech," 41.

[37] Ball, *Disciplining*, 201 and 202.

2: Testimonial Silence beyond the Figure of the Mute Witness

A pivotal moment in Bomba's testimony comes after Lanzmann asks, repetitively, about Bomba's emotional response to seeing the victims as they entered the gas chamber:

> Claude Lanzmann [CL]: But I asked you and you didn't answer: What was your impression the first time you saw these naked women arriving with children? What did you feel?
>
> Abraham Bomba [AB]: I tell you something. To have a feeling about that [...] it was very hard to feel anything, because working there day and night between dead people, between bodies, your feeling disappeared, you were dead. You had no feeling at all. As a matter of fact, I want to tell you something that happened. At the gas chamber, when I was chosen to work there as a barber, some of the women that came in on a transport from my town of Czestochowa, I knew a lot of them. I knew them; I lived with them in my town. I lived with them in my street, and some of them were my close friends. And when they saw me, they started asking me, Abe this and Abe that—'What's going to happen to us?' What could you tell them? What could you tell?
>
> A friend of mine worked as a barber—he was a good barber in my hometown—when his wife and his sister came into the gas chamber [...] I can't. It's too horrible. Please.
>
> CL: We have to do it. You know it.
>
> AB: I won't be able to do it.
>
> CL: You have to do it. I know it's very hard. I know and I apologize.
>
> AB: Don't make me go on.
>
> CL: Please. We must go on.[38]

What is not recorded in the transcript of Bomba's testimony is an extended moment of silence that cleaves the witness's speech and precedes his account of the abysmal encounter in the gas chamber between one of the barbers and his female family members.

---

[38] Claude Lanzmann, *Shoah. The Complete Text of the Acclaimed Film* (New York: Da Capo Press, 1995), 107-108.

Lanzmann describes the events accompanying the filming of that scene:

> In the beginning of his story, Abraham adopts a neutral, objective, and detached tone, as if his narrative did not concern him, as if these horrors could be generated [*s'engendre*] without his input, almost harmoniously. […] I ask incongruous, absurd questions. […] They help me to recreate the place and the situation with precision, but they also facilitate transition to the most difficult question: 'What did you feel that first time when you saw these naked women and these children entering the gas chamber?' Abraham avoids the question, changes the subject. […]
>
> It was in that moment […] that I saw something alarming in Abraham's face, […] in the tone of his voice, in the silence that separated his words. There was a visible, palpable, tension in the room, […] I wasn't sure, but I had the feeling that an important event might materialize. […]
>
> In this moment [Bomba] became overwhelmed with feeling so powerful [*le sentiment avec une violance*] that he wasn't able to continue, he only made a small hand gesture [*un petit geste*], which meant that it was futile and impossible to continue the narration, and […] that it was impossible and in vain to understand. This is a famous scene, Abraham is wiping the tears […], he is silent, he continues to maneuver with the scissors around his friend's head, and […] trying to regain his strength, he whispers something confidentially in Yiddish to his friend. [39]

These extended moments of silence mark distinctive prosodic units in Bomba's testimony where, according to Shoshana Felman's influential essay on *Shoah*, that silence coincides with a powerful re-enactment of traumatic memory. It marks a "return" of something that evades narrative language and individual capacity of enunciation.[40] What unfolds here is emergence of the subject position of a "mute witness," whereby signification of Bomba's silence becomes irreducible to its subsequent overcoming by speech (to which Bomba is prompted by the director). Lanzmann's notion of a "powerful feeling," or a "violent feeling" (*le sentiment avec une violence*), suggests a close alignment of the subjective position of a "mute witness" with an affective shift. This affective shift in the testimonial scene seems to operate (in accordance with recent theorizations of affect) as a "visceral force, […] other than conscious knowing" that drives the subject "toward movement, toward thought and

---

[39] Lanzmann, *Le lièvre*, 623-624, *emphasis mine*.

[40] Shoshana Felman, "In an Era of Testimony: Claude Lanzmann's *Shoah,*" *Yale French Studies* 97 (2000).

extension, that can likewise suspend [the subject] (as if in neutral) across a barely registering accretion of force-relations."[41]

Lanzmann's interference into the prolonged moments of silence and his relentless insistence that Bomba continues the verbalization of his experiences has been interpreted by many as a highly problematic, if not utterly violent or even sadistic, move.[42] This is in spite of the fact that according to the director it expressed "a paradigm of love" (*le paradigm de la piété*).[43] Furthermore, the suggestion has been that Lanzmann's interventions should be read not only in terms of his commitment to recording Bomba's unique insights, but also as integral to the objective of exploring the limits and thresholds of Holocaust representation. Lanzmann critically engages here with the interpretation of the mass murder of European Jews within the apophatic tradition, which aligns the Holocaust with the "negative sublime,"[44] and where testimonial silence figures as the "dialectic of unspeakability."[45] In her discussion of Felman's establishment of the idea of trauma as anti-narrativity, Ball points out that within the "rhetoric of unrepresentability [...] the principal sign of the Holocaust is the proliferation of silences." This is because:

> such an event not only drastically wounds those witnesses it did not physically destroy, but also remains in abeyance—in spaces where inadequate responses, disbelief, or prurient fascination exacerbate the isolating experience of traumatic degradation and loss.[46]

---

[41] Gregory J. Seigworth and Melissa Gregg, "An Inventory of Shimmers," in *The Affect Theory Reader*, eds. Gregory J. Seigworth and Melissa Gregg,(Durham: Duke University Press, 2012), 1.

[42] See for example Hirsch and Spitzer, "The Witness," 396-397.

[43] Lanzmann's commentary on the scene: "Some [viewers] interpreted this dangerous scene as a manifestation of sadism on my part, but, on the contrary, I see it as a paradigm of love, which does not retreat at the sight of another's suffering, but which, above all, obeys the categorical imperative to search and disseminate truth." Lanzmann, *Le lièvre*, 625.

[44] For an extensive discussion of this issue see Ball, *Disciplining*.

[45] This phrase is taken from a text by Peter Haidu, who, however, interprets unspeakability in a very different context than survivors' testimony, namely Himmler's 1943 Posen Speech. See: Peter Haidu, "The Dialectics of Unspeakability: Language, Silence, and the Narratives of Desubjectification," in *Probing the Limits of Representation. Nazism and the "Final Solution,"* ed. Saul Friedlander (Boston: Harvard University Press, 1992).

[46] Ball, *Disciplining*, 140.

Felman argues that Lanzmann refuses to forge an "alliance with the silence of the witness […] the kind of emphatic and benevolent alliance through which interviewer and interviewee often implicitly concur, and work together, for the mutual comfort of an avoidance of the truth."[47] At play here is the depiction of a morphological connection between silence, understood as one of the manifestations or materializations of trauma's unspeakability, and trauma as a death-like experience.[48] Consequently, "in order to revive the Holocaust and to rewrite the event-without-a-witness into witnessing, and into history," Lanzmann takes upon himself the task of breaking the silence of the witness. Lanzmann's softly whispered, yet not less forceful, interpellations ("please […] we must go on"), which ultimately blur the distinction between plea and coercion, exceeds in Felman's interpretation the appeal to simply narrate what is emotionally painful and unbearable. Rather, the director insists on the breaking of the witness's silence in order for the witness "to replicate the past [through speech], […] to replicate [the subject's] own survival." The figure of the "mute witness," prevalent in the contemporary literary theory of trauma, provides an evocative illustration of what "remains beyond communication."[49] As an event that reduces narrative to a "state of noiselessness or wordlessness," the silence of the witness, Felman argues in the reference to Walter Benjamin's writings, marks "a radical displacement of our frames of reference."[50]

Rather than signify the testimonial silence of Bomba, and perhaps others in *Shoah*, as either the "antiworld of speech,"[51] or as synonymous with the violence *being silenced*,[52] this essay proposes an interpretative engagement with silence as a "metaphor for communication,"[53] which plays out at multiple levels: linguistic, visual, affective, kinetic and gestural. As such, it challenges the implicit privileging of oralism in the testimonial culture and theorizing. The suggestion is that this alternative thinking about non-verbal witnessing helps to recognize the "formal and

---

[47] Felman, "The Return," 220.

[48] For discussion of silence as a metaphor of death see Adam Jaworski, "Introduction: An Overview," in *Silence. Interdisciplinary Perspectives,* ed. Adam Jaworski (Berlin: Mouton de Gruyter, 1997), 29.

[49] Shoshana Felman, "Benjamin's Silence," *Critical Inquiry* 25, no.2 (1999): 201 / 23 in this volume.

[50] Ibid., 208 / 30.

[51] Haidu, "The Dialectics," 278.

[52] See for example Gabriele Schwab, *Haunting Legacies: Violent Histories and Transgenerational Trauma* (New York: Columbia University Press, 2010).

[53] Jaworski, "Introduction," 3.

semantic richness of silence"[54] in the testimonial genre that marks silence as irreducible to identifications of apophatic discourse of the negative sublime and to questions of (un)representability. In order to uncover what Jay Winter calls the "hidden deposits" of silence in mass murder testimony, it is thus necessary to trouble and complicate the binary equation of "silence [with] the space of forgetting and [of] speech [with the space of] remembrance."[55]

Drawing on the conceptual register of the deconstructionist approaches to language and speech, this essay suggests that aphasia and apophasis in witnessing be approached as not simply a question of a difficulty or a hardship *of oral expressions* (which would leave testimonial speech vulnerable to psychological reductionism). Rather, they are linked to the undecidable or unstable relation between (testimonial) verbalization and (testimonial) silence. Jacques Derrida, writing in a different context, points out that the "undecidable" operates not as a "mere oscillation between two significations," as if silence were equatable to the non-presence or non-occurrence of speech. The logocentric investment in the "metaphysics of presence" of speech and the verbal sign, masks a desire for a "transcendental signifier" (where orality is imagined as transcending the order of silence), which Derrida famously deconstructs by the use of the notion of the "trace."[56] Accordingly, rather than equate speech with the mastery of overcoming or transcending silence induced by trauma, testimonial speech appears as marked, constitutively, by traces of silence. The deconstructive reading reveals the privileged category of orality as internally incongruous and non-binary in its relation to non-orality.

From this perspective silence is radically different from a "wholly negative disposition toward life with others," and a token of withdrawal, disengagement, or obscurity. Rather, silence appears as a form of signification and affective mobility, which, at the same time, points to the thresholds in the task of testimonial signification. The relationship

---

[54] Ibid., 32.

[55] Jay Winter, "Thinking About Silence," in *Shadows of War. A Social History of Silence in the Twentieth Century,* eds. Efrat Ben-Ze'ev, Ruth Ginio and Jay Winter, (Cambridge: Cambridge University Press, 2012), 3 and 4.

[56] The Derridean notion of the "trace" has been discussed at length in secondary literature (see for example Paola Marrati, *Genesis and Trace* (Stanford: Stanford University Press, 2004)). It belongs to a deconstructionist index of terms that have as their aim to indicate that any dualist and/or oppositional terminology is always already "impure" (dislodged, disrupted and inconsistent). A deconstructionist reading reveals the existence of "traces" within the allegedly oppositional binaries inasmuch as they appear reciprocally contaminated and incongruous.

between silence and verbalization in testimony is conceptualized as not only non-oppositional, but also as mutually indebted, reciprocal and cross-contaminated.

What follows is that in the scene of Bomba's witnessing silence is not isolatable to specific moments of speech interruption. Rather, it infiltrates and interpenetrates Bomba's narrative, while it is itself permeated and marked by diverse forms of the witness's bodily and sonic expression: jerks, gesticulations, grunts, and whispers. This further questions the idea that testimony contains two oppositional categories: the "public" speech and the "non-public" silence and gesturality—incommunicable and incomprehensible—which are to be either ignored as insignificant, or re-worked into meaningful forms of expression. In contrast to such a binary perspective, the deconstructionist view troubles the essentialism of thinking about both non-verbality and verbality as pure categories. Both non-verbality and verbality form repository spaces of testimonial signification—and both resist reducibility to such signification through the play of polysemy, ambiguity and prevarication.

Finally, the proliferations of non-verbality (silence and gestures) in Bomba's testimony have no clearly delineated temporality. Instead, they seem to operate affectively in constant movements of emergence, extension and intensification. While the testimonial theory that equates witnessing with speech and utterance tends to dismiss the bodily, sonic and mute occurrences as interruptions, or speech intervals, which are themselves devoid of meaning and hence not subject to symbolization (as a form of an "ambient and unintentional noise"[57]), the approach proposed here is in line with the theory of testimonial subjectivity, which conceives of its foundations and its "sources of meaning" in "non-subjective terms."[58]

As such, the non-verbal forms of testimonial expression are not conceived of as (volitional or non-volitional) properties of the individual subject, but as unfolding within the plan of affective mobility. This is not to say that either silence or gesturality figure as "pre-linguistic" or "pre-discursive," insofar as, according to Shepherdson, one does not take affect to designate "a biological energy that, if not symbolically contained or conscripted into signification, overflows into its […] recipients."[59] Rather, as markers of affective circulation, silence or gesturality are "effect[s] of symbolization, and thus an abyss in the field of meaning," or, put in

[57] Joseph Branden, "John Cage and the Architecture of Silence," *October* (1997): 80-104.
[58] Teresa Brennan, *History After Lacan* (London: Routledge, 1993), 16.
[59] Shepherdson, "Emotion," 69.

Lacanian vernacular, "a product of the Other."[60] This follows an approach proposed by Anna Gibbs, which recognizes different forms of gesturality (movement, sound, and rhythm) as "anterior to symbolic verbal communication," and as its "prototype," insofar as "verbal communication," and, one would want to add, other forms of narrativity, "is formally predicated on the rhythms of nonverbal behavior, which it does not ever entirely replace or supersede."[61]

3. Gesture, Gag—At Loss In Language

In her reflections on the figure of silence in art, Susan Sontag has argued for an understanding of silence as neither "the experience of the audience" nor "a property of an artwork."[62] Instead of a "raw and achieved silence, one finds various moves in the direction of *an ever receding horizon of silence*."[63] In Bomba's barbershop testimony, just as the witness's speech is at once interrupted and connected, or *seamed*, by silence, so is Bomba's falling into muteness "impure" and "contaminated" by the sounds of the clipping scissors, whispers, groans, sighs and, not least, the proliferating hand gestures, facial expressions, body position, and expressive gaze. What needs to be considered at the background of the proposed irreducibility of testimonial silence to the absence or postponement of speech, or as manifestation of the inexpressibility (or unrepresentability) of trauma, is what this essay proposes to call "testimonial gesturality." It will be understood as a space of appearance, or initiation, of the subjective position of a witness, beyond her/his submission to the "confessional effect" of the testimonial model embraced and practiced by Lanzmann.

The significance of the gesture for subjective emergence has been brought to the fore in recent interpretations of the political thought of Giorgio Agamben. In the texts "Kommerell, or On Gesture" and "Notes on Gesture," Agamben attributes gesture to the "stratum of language that is not exhausted in communication," and that is "more originary than

---

[60] Ibid., 69.

[61] Anna Gibbs, "After Affect: Sympathy, Synchrony, and Mimetic Communication," in *The Affect Theory Reader*, eds. Gregory J. Seigworth and Melissa Gregg, (Durham: Duke University Press, 2012), 199.

[62] Susan Sontag, "The Aesthetic of Silence," in *Styles of Radical Will,* Susan Sontag, (New York: Delta Publishing, 1969), 9.

[63] Ibid., 10, *emphasis mine*.

conceptual expression."[64] The context for Agamben's theorization of gesturality is the thesis of the "loss of gesture" in the modern (Western) world. He draws from the differentiation between "acting" and "doing" in Varro's *De lingua latina,* which is in turn indebted to the Aristotelian distinction between *praxis* and *poiesis.*[65] This allows Agamben to define gesturality in terms of *neither action nor production*, but as an expression of supporting, sustaining and enduring, which, he argues, is liberated from the binary structure of "ends" and "means."[66]

Gesture indicates a different form of being in the world than either acting or doing: "if doing is a means in sight of an end and praxis [action] is an end without means, gesture breaks the false alternative between ends and means that paralyzes morality."[67] Subsequently, for Agamben gesture "presents means which, *as such*, are removed from the sphere of mediation without thereby becoming ends."[68] He illustrates the undertaking of gesture by a reference to bodily movement in dance and its "aesthetic dimension," as opposed to the activity of walking, where the body aims to cover a given spatial distance. In contrast to walking dance *has no ends*; it is "nothing but the physical tolerance of bodily movements and the display of their mediating nature."[69]

Elsewhere, Agamben names the work of one of the key precursors of modern dance, Isadora Duncan, and the founder of the Ballets Russes, Sergei Diaghilev, as an attempt to counter the loss of gesturality in the late 19th century. In addition to dance, one could give examples of other forms of expression that in the positive psychology of Mihály Csíkszentmihályi (admittedly a very different tradition of thought than the Agambenian philosophy of gesture) have been classified as "flow experiences." They include such activities as martial arts, yoga, and mountain climbing etc. When approached from the perspective of the subjective immersion in

---

64 Giorgio Agamben, "Kommerell, or On Gesture," in *Potentialities. Collected Essays in Philosophy,* Giorgio Agamben, (Stanford: Stanford University Press, 1999), 77.

65 Aristotle differentiates action (*praxis*) from production (*poiesis*) in *The Nicomachean Ethics*: "[P]roduction aims at an end other than itself; but this is impossible in the case of action, because the end is merely to do what is right." Quoted in Giorgio Agamben, "Notes on Gesture," in *Infancy and History. On the Destruction of Experience,* Giorgio Agamben (London: Verso, 2007), 154.

66 Agamben, "Notes," 154.

67 Ibid., 154-155.

68 Ibid., 155, *emphasis in original.*

69 Ibid. Also, see Barbara Formis, "Dismantling Theatricality: Aesthetics of Bare Life," in *The Work of Giorgio Agamben: Law, Literature, Life,* eds. Justin Clemens, Nicholas Heron and Alex Murray (Edinburgh: Edinburgh University Press, 2011).

these bodily undertakings, these activities not only have no orientation towards an external goal, but reveal the very notion of "ends" as nugatory and hollow.

Similarly to the deconstructionist approach to language and silence, on which this essay has drawn for its interpretation of the non-verbal expression in testimony in the previous section, Agamben rejects nonlinguistic conceptualizations of gesturality. Taking his lead from the German literary historian and critic in the interwar period, Max Kommerell, Agamben approximates gesture as "a forceful presence in language itself, one that is older and more originary than conceptual expression."[70] As such, at issue in gesture is "not so much prelinguistic content as […] *the other side of language*, the muteness inherent in humankind's very capacity for language."[71] It is a "state of speechlessness in language," which in Kommerell's writings plays out, first, within the plane of "the enigma (*Rätsel*), in which the more the speaker tries to express himself in words, the more he makes himself incomprehensible"; next, within the plane of "the secret (*Geheimnis*), which remains unsaid in the enigma and is nothing other than the Being of human beings insofar as they live the truth of language"; and, finally, within the plane of "the secret (*Mysterium*), which is the mimed performance of the secret."[72] Non-orality in Bomba's testimony (both as silence and as gesture) plays out, and is interpretable, at all three levels: as enigma, secret, and as mystery.

Furthermore, as "movement[s] of [the] human body that are […] removed from the relation to an end or goal,"[73] gestures—transitory, fleeting and non-intentional as they might appear—have crucial significance for Agamben's theorizing of (what he terms) the politics of "pure means" or "pure mediality" as a sphere of human experience that centers on communicating nothing else but *potential of communicability itself.* As Catherine Mills puts it, in Agamben's philosophy gesturality becomes "the name for the sheer communicability of language, or speech that has nothing to say or express other than the taking place of language itself."[74] However, at the same time as the gesture shows "being-in-language of human beings as a pure potential for mediation," it ultimately also expresses non-communicability, that is the "non-making of sense in

---

[70] Agamben, "Kommerell," 77.

[71] Ibid., 78, *emphasis mine.*

[72] Ibid., 78.

[73] Catherine Mills, *The Philosophy of Giorgio Agamben* (Montreal: McGill / Queen's University Press, 2008), 130.

[74] Ibid, 53.

language."[75] Thus, just as in the proposed deconstructionist reading of Abraham Bomba's testimony speech and silence are cross-contaminating and cross-fertilizing registers of meaning, the gesture is a marker of the non-oppositional relationship between communicability and non-communicability of language.

The relevance of Agamben's theory of gesturality for interpreting non-verbal expressions in Abraham Bomba's testimony in *Shoah* is particularly apparent in Agamben's juxtaposition of gesture and the notion of a "gag." A gag means, firstly, "something that is put in the mouth to hinder speech, and [secondly] the actor's improvisation to make up for a memory lapse or some impossibility of speech."[76] In Bomba's performance, the category of "testimonial gesturality" acquires the dual (and ambiguous) status of a "gag." First, it hinders or prevents speech, while, in the trauma theoretical perspectives, it at the same time comes *prior to* and *conditions* speech. Second, it is a performative act that compensates for, or offsets, the unavailability or inaccessibility of traumatic memories, and the aporias of narrativization and recollection.

To conclude, I refer again to Susan Sontag's essay on the aesthetic of silence in artwork, and, in particular, Sontag's emphasis on the a-symmetrical relation between the self and the other in silence. While Sontag's reflections are firmly grounded in a humanist position (and thus exist in some conflict with the post-humanist view of the subject espoused in this essay), the significance of her intervention is precisely that Sontag represents silence as a mimetic procedure that situates the subject vis-à-vis the "enigma" of the other. This is insofar as, Sontag argues, "a person who becomes silent becomes opaque for the other." Consequently, "somebody's silence opens up an array of possibilities for interpreting that silence, for imputing speech to it."[77] The latter is subject to a critique of violence (as the discussions of Lanzmann's position in his film have demonstrated), but what it more important for the argument pursued in this essay is that the spaces of testimonial silence and gesturality are potentially also sites of resistance (and, perhaps, recalcitrance) of the witnessing subject against the "confessional effect." Their affective reading as sites that require particular "atunement," "synchrony," or "entrainment"[78] of the subject in the reading of testimonies, leaves us with a question about the prospects for developing testimonial critique and interpretation beyond the epistemic privilege of verbality and dominance

[75] Agamben, "Notes," 156.
[76] Ibid., 156.
[77] Sontag, "Silence," 16.
[78] Gibbs, "After," 197.

of oralism. What has been attempted in the offered interpretation of silence and gesturality as testimonial practices, was not a utopian attempt of reaching into the realm of pre-discursivity, or a play with "the inexpressible," but, on the contrary, an engagement with the complexity of verbal and non-verbal traces and manifestations of alterity in traumatic memory.

CHAPTER THREE

FILM, TRAUMA AND THE ENUNCIATIVE PRESENT

ANNE RUTHERFORD

Prologue: Silence and Speech

Two tendencies—apparently similar but in fact quite contradictory—run like an undercurrent through trauma studies. The first is a compulsion to repeat; the second a compulsion to recount.

The compulsion to repeat is an often-documented aftermath of trauma—the survivor of trauma going over and over in minute detail the events of the traumatic situation. Tied to the vivid nature of traumatic memory, itself a correlate of the extraordinary quality of present-ness of survival situations, and no doubt biologically wired in by the endocrinal responses of the adrenaline cycle, the compulsion to repeat has at its heart an awareness of failure. Preoccupied with the details of an event, the gap between the details and what actually happened haunts these attempts to somehow, through repetition, understand the nature of the fracturing that occurred in the traumatic moment and to somehow repair it.[1] At the heart of this repetition is a silence.

The compulsion to recount, found in those one step removed from trauma and trying to understand it, is plagued by a similar failure, but here the failure comes not from the knowledge that the recitation never quite grasps the nature of trauma, but from an expectation that coming face-to-face with the "facts of the case" will provide such an understanding. In these accounts, there is often a focus on the importance of testimony, on laying out, blow-by-blow in intimate detail, the horrors that were enacted.

A paradox underlies these contradictory impulses, one closely tied to the question of knowledge. A pivotal aspect of major trauma, and the

[1] This is in no way to discount experiences of dissociation; these are two sides of the same coin. The psychic mechanism that takes over to produce dissociation signals to the intolerability of such acute presentness.

"unspeakability" of it, is that the survivor has knowledge of something that nobody should know—a knowledge that potentially tears at the social fabric and ruptures the fundamental existential ground of existence in one's own body. Traumatic events that assault the integrity of this existence in the body fracture something that we do not even know we have until it is gone. Trauma ruptures something that is so fundamental to our existence as human subjects that we don't even begin to grasp it until we lose it.[2] To try to describe this encounter with one's own annihilation is to come up against the limitations of our conceptual vocabulary in thinking about who and what we are to start with. We could try to describe this as facing an existential abyss, but the existential is a philosophical concept that in most articulations does not encompass the fully somatic depth of experience.[3]

The paradox, given this knowledge that no human should know, is the attempt among those one step removed but committed, for ethical and political reasons, to understanding trauma, to try to know it. And perhaps this intolerable knowledge is at the core of the "unspeakability" of trauma.[4] Indeed, this raises the question—if the searchers truly understood,

---

[2] This claim is a complex one. How does it accommodate the increasingly widespread nature of trauma? Is this to proclaim the tragedy of some kind of lost innocence, which is more a privilege than a norm, and how then can we define human subjectivities marked by trauma? Any ethical work on trauma must acknowledge and respect the resilience, resourcefulness and courage of "survivors." On the other hand, unless a politics of trauma can fully grasp and articulate what the damage is and why it is so unacceptable—in other words, unless it takes the benchmark of the non-traumatised subject as a measure, it will have no way to conceptualise what atrocity is and why it must be unveiled and prevented.

[3] Clearly there are many different types of trauma. The term "trauma" encompasses both "threshold" survival experiences and experiences that do not necessarily stem from atrocity or extremity. While the inclusiveness of the term is important to theorising the nature of trauma, to some extent it precludes discussions that recognise different degrees of traumatisation. I find Dominick La Capra's suggestion that the term be reserved for experiences above a certain threshold a very useful one to allow for meaningful distinctions to be made between liminal experiences that threaten either physical or psychic disintegration and more common "quotidian" forms of traumatic experience that may be accrued during a lifetime. The "threat of one's own annihilation" here refers more to these forms of extreme trauma. Dominick LaCapra, *Writing History, Writing Trauma.* (Baltimore: Johns Hopkins University Press, 2001).

[4] For Herman, "unspeakability" is a primary characteristic of trauma; this is a contested claim in the literature, but one that I agree with. Judith Herman, *Trauma and Recovery: from Domestic Abuse to Political Terror* (London: Pandora, 1994).

in a fully embodied way, what is at the heart of trauma, would this not initiate them into its wraith-like embrace?

This silence is often theorized as shame. Certainly shame may be in the mix—like the layers of an onion, trauma becomes compounded, overlaid with social dimensions and the difficult associations that memory accrues. Like peeling back the layers of an onion, one can work back through these accumulated resonances, but it may never release the stranglehold of the initial shattering. If trauma is understood as a kind of "piercing of the psychic shield," then the impact of major trauma is in the Humpty Dumpty-like inability to put the pieces back together.[5] This is not to say that they cannot be re-integrated, but surely this must be central to the goal of any trauma studies: the hope that, through adequately conceptualizing the nature of the shattering, it would be possible to find a pathway through the damage toward healing and equilibrium. This is what is at stake in the theorization of trauma. At the sharp edge of the failure to understand this is the wreckage of individuals, communities and indeed whole nations battling it out with only their survival instincts available, or perhaps worse, having given up after repeated ineffectual professional attempts at "resolution" of the trauma.

The silence itself is complex and may involve as much a refusal to talk as an impossibility. Firstly, there is a desire to protect the listener; to tell can feel like smearing the listener with faeces, and this is where disgust comes into play—a sense of taboo, of defilement. The refusal to tell can also involve a refusal to take into oneself the image of the traumatic event, as if to tell is to own or identify with an image of oneself that is incompatible with psychic survival, and to provide the listener with such images may feel like inviting them to view the teller in this frame. This is where shame is paramount, and insulating such images, keeping them at a distance, is a defense against this. A third factor is the ever-present question of re-traumatization. This is the danger of proximity, and fear is its characteristic—as speech comes closer to the core of the trauma, anxiety increases exponentially in the face of the threat of reviving the original presentness. Laura Marks has written of a language that comes close enough to the event to "ignite [...in a] flash of embodied meaning."[6] In the context of aesthetics, this is the aspiration that animates the work, the Holy Grail of an affective art practice. In the context of trauma, it is the black hole that threatens to suck the teller into it.

---

[5] I am grateful to Magdalena Zolkos for this phrase.

[6] Laura Marks, *The Skin of the Film* (Durham & London: Duke University Press, 2000), 141. Marks here refers to the ideas of both Walter Benjamin and Maurice Merleau-Ponty.

This is the paradox of silence. In a sense, this silence at the heart of trauma also sacralizes the event, rendering it inaccessible and protecting it from any scrutiny that might unravel the tight knots that wrap around it like a protective cocoon.

1. A Question of Enunciation

Underlying these issues is a question of the relationship between language and experience. These are two parallel lines, or at best an asymptote.[7] A fuller recognition of this disparity would fundamentally shift the understanding of trauma. In particular, this raises the question of the complex nature of the enunciative acts that underpin trauma studies as a practice: who speaks, who listens, and how is the speech act formulated?

Despite the existence of foundational primary texts written or spoken by those whom Dominick LaCapra refers to as "primary witnesses"—those who speak *as* the victim/survivor—much of the discourse is presented from the perspective of the "secondary witness."[8] Despite LaCapra's injunction against the assumption that a secondary witness can "inhabit" the experience of the traumatised,[9] much of this work takes the form of speaking *for* the victim. In some cases this may be mandated, as it may involve an ethical commitment to the dead, but it may also adopt a relatively unreflective position of speaking for the other, who may be assumed to be absent but still living. In some of the literature on trauma this position is a self-reflexive one. Ann Kaplan writes that, "most of us most of the time experience trauma in the 'secondary' rather than direct position."[10] At least this account of the vicarious encounter with trauma acknowledges its assumptions, albeit speaking for and to an "us" that by its nature excludes the survivor from the community of listeners/viewers (and speakers).[11]

This assumption that the "we" who speak and listen are secondary or tertiary witnesses insulates the discourse from a primary point of reference, for an acknowledgement that survivors may be among those who speak,

---

[7] Converging lines that never meet.

[8] Dominick LaCapra, "Lanzmann's 'Shoah': 'Here There is No Why'," *Critical Inquiry* 23, no. 2 (Winter 1997).

[9] LaCapra himself cites Shoshana Felman as exemplary of this tendency. Shoshana Felman and Dori Laub, *Testimony: Crises in Witnessing in Literature, Psychoanalysis, and History* (New York: Routledge, 1992).

[10] E. Anna Kaplan, *Trauma Culture: the Politics of Terror and Loss in Media and Literature* (New Brunswick, NJ: Rutgers University Press, 2005), 39.

[11] Kaplan does spell out the differences between these differences.

listen and have a stake in the discourse automatically raises the bar of accountability. On the one hand, they may serve as an arbiter of the kind of knowledge or understanding claimed by the speaker. On the other hand, the presence of survivors among an audience demands that an ethically committed speaker be aware of the dynamics of his/her own speech.

When detailed accounts of atrocity are not simply presented as sensationalist exploitation pieces, as is common in media/journalistic work, the ethics of the accounts are most often articulated as the importance of "bearing witness," a sense of solidarity with victims/survivors and the courage to face up to the evidence of atrocity. In attempts of secondary witnesses to convey this to listeners/readers, description—the blow-by-blow recounting of facts, details, specifics—comes to the fore as a rhetorical strategy for rendering unthinkable events concrete and affective, in order to bring the trauma alive to the secondary listener. Conversely, this very strategy can meet an entirely different reception among survivors. These detailed accounts, in themselves, can be potent triggers of traumatic associations in survivors.[12]

On one level, no analysis of language or the image itself can address this dynamic, as this is about particular subjects, configurations of trauma and the variability of memory. No one can predict the sense memory that may trigger a breakthrough of traumatic memory into the present. It may be a piece of music, a gesture, a smell, a word, water, darkness, a story, a doorway, fire, a helicopter… This is a key feature of what LaCapra calls the "afterlife of trauma." On another level, despite this unpredictability one can assume that direct accounts of atrocity can be especially disturbing to some trauma survivors. The way this process plays out in mediatized culture is especially complex, and the omnipresence of mediated images and accounts of war and sexual violence can play a potent role in reinscribing, on a daily basis, the memory of trauma in those who have experienced it.[13]

---

[12] The ambivalence around this bearing witness has been explored in depth in the context of photojournalism. See, for example, Susan Sontag, *Regarding the Pain of Others* (London: Penguin, 2003).

[13]This is not to imply that survivors live in a constant state of victimhood, but their resilience can be assaulted in ways that bring trauma to the fore in the present. Bennett cites the artist Charlotte Delbo who talks of having different selves—her present-day self and her "Auschwitz self." Both co-exist like layers but the "Auschwitz self" can re-emerge painfully into the present under certain conditions. Jill Bennett, *Empathic Vision: Affect, Trauma, and Contemporary Art* (Stanford, Calif. : Stanford University Press, 2005), 25.

Censorship cannot provide an answer to this dilemma, but an inclusive ethics of address alert to this dynamic and recognizing the diversity of listeners would mandate a very different approach. This might start from the recognition that atrocity is an act; trauma is an experience. While acts may be described, the experience of trauma may be "unshareable even when communicated." [14] Detailed accounts of atrocity conflate the experience with the act, as if the act can explain/stand in for the experience, but there is no way it can do that. No amount of detail can lead someone to an understanding of something that is totally outside the range of anything they have ever experienced. This demands an acknowledgement of what cannot be said—of the gaps, elisions and impossibilities of speech, the partial nature of it. This defies the assumption that what can be said in language can engender a knowledge, can render the experience available to the listener/spectator. As Susan Sontag writes of the experience of primary witnesses:

> We—this we is everyone who has never experienced anything like what [survivors] went through—don't understand. We don't get it. We truly can't imagine what it was like. We can't imagine how dreadful, how terrifying it was; and how normal it becomes. Can't understand, can't imagine. That's what every soldier, and every journalist and aid worker and independent observer who has put in time under fire, and had the luck to elude the death that struck down others nearby, stubbornly feels. And they are right.[15]

Miriam Marquez, a survivor of torture at the hands of the Pinochet regime, explicitly links her experience as a witness to a question of an unfathomable knowledge:

> It's completely foreign, it's completely impossible to adjust what you are and what you have learned to the world you know…Everything you could imagine of my world…was burnt in that moment.[16]

---

[14] Ibid., 6.

[15] Sontag, *Regarding the Pain,* 125.

[16] Alejandra Canales, *A Silence Full of Things,* 2005, http://vimeo.com/3504830 (accessed June 22, 2012). Recent work on mirror neurons provides a neurological basis to understand this differential quality in spectators' experience of images of torture. In Canales' film, the image does not attempt to represent the trauma, does not assume to be able to bridge the gap between the said and the known. There is a voice that gives a scanty account of the events but the images are only small fragments—hands, feet, piss. It is Marquez who is present, who speaks—not an assumed encounter with her traumatic experience. The film recognizes Marquez as the subject who has lived these atrocities and their aftermath. The spectator has a

How much more unknowable is the experience of survivors, such as Marquez, who are not just witnesses to the violation of others, but whose own bodies have been the target of the violation? How much more profound is the "piercing of the psychic shield" when even one's own body is not a refuge, a base, a carapace for a fragile subjectivity?[17] Why would we assume that language has the capacity to communicate the experience of an assault on the body that can produce a fragmentation or disintegration of subjectivity?

Many survivors are quite capable of talking about the events they have experienced. There is often a toughness, a resilience, a kind of grim frankness with each other in the face of the knowledge that has been thrust upon them. But, as Jill Bennett points out, this knowledge has an "inside" and an "outside."[18] It may be possible to talk about the outer shell that comprises facts, events, details, as if an external witness, but the inside is a different matter. For Bennett, one of the goals of trauma-related artwork is to "put insides and outsides into contact."[19] This project of "speaking from the inside" is an entirely different one to the project of a trauma studies articulated from and for the position of the "secondary witness."

In his penetrating analysis of Claude Lanzmann's epic documentary, *Shoah*, Dominick LaCapra unveils the dynamic of eliciting details from a survivor in order to produce an affective experience for the spectator, to instigate knowledge and empathy in the secondary or tertiary witness.[20] In a scene in which a barber, Abraham Bomba, tells of his experience in Auschwitz, Lanzmann prods the survivor to speak to the point at which the possibility of detached discourse breaks down and the presentness of traumatic memory erupts through the surface of the discourse. Here testimony serves the interests of history, rather than those of the survivor. What was the aftermath of this interview for Bomba and how would other survivors respond to witnessing this intrusive style of interview? This

connection with her, and a sense of the transgressive/fracturing nature of trauma but no sense of fullness, no illusion of having lived through it.

[17] This is not to claim a "hierarchy" of trauma, but a specificity of certain kinds of trauma.

[18] Bennett, *Empathic Vision*, 22 and following pages.

[19] ibid., 45.

[20] LaCapra is careful to qualify this critique, declaring his respect for Lanzmann's fim, which he describes as a "masterpiece."

question does not arise in the construction of testimony that is aimed to produce an empathetic engagement in viewers as "secondary witnesses."[21]

In the context of the image, debates around the ethics of representation have been most commonly articulated in terms of the question of "showing or not showing."[22] These debates have been well rehearsed in both studies and documentary theory.[23] Where the discussion shifts the debate away from representation per se to consider the relation between representation and spectatorship, to consider dynamics of watching or receiving mediated accounts or images of trauma, it has often focused on the idea of "secondary traumatization," particularly in attempts to differentiate the experience of "empathic trauma" from that of survivors.[24] The work on reception has also considered the complex and ambivalent dynamics of witnessing—what it means to be an ethical spectator, what an empathic witness can do with the information and affect that images of atrocity convey and the work of meaning-making that needs to be done to process these images.[25] My concern here is not with the image per se, or the showing/not showing binary, but to understand filmic affect in trauma-related work within an ethics of address.

Speech and Affect

A woman speaks to an interviewer of the experience of finding her son hanging from a tree.[26] As her account approaches the moment of trauma, her voice drops to a raspy whisper, the sentences cryptic, her body very

---

[21] In so far as LaCapra focuses on this process of triggering a traumatic reliving, his focus is on the production of the film, not its reception, and in so far as he considers the question of spectatorship, the spectator is not a survivor.

[22] Miriam Hansen, "*Schindler's List* is not *Shoah*: the Second Commandment, Popular Modernism and Public Memory," *Critical Inquiry* 22 (Winter 1996), 302.

[23] See, for example, ibid., 301 on the un-representability of horror; also Sontag, *Regarding the Pain*; and Georges Didi-Huberman, *Images Malgré Tout* (Paris: Éditions de Minuit, 2003).

[24] Bennett gives a brief resume of this debate, citing Geoffrey Hartmann's discussion of so-called "secondary traumatisation." Bennett, *Empathic Vision*, 35. See also Kaplan, *Trauma Culture.*

[25] See, Anna Gibbs, "Horrified: Embodied Vision, Media Affect And The Images," in *Interrogating the War on Terror*, ed. Deborah Staines (London: Cambridge Scholars Publishing, 2007). Gibbs specifically addresses questions around photography and the images of torture at Abu Ghraib prison.

[26] I do not have any details of this interview, seen on Australian television some time in 2010/11. It was this moment that made an impact, registered in the affective memory, and all other details have receded.

still. Whatever it takes for her to speak these words, it is not a detached translation of trauma into language. The words are just a cipher that catches at the moment, suggests it and drops it into the space between the woman and the interviewer. Many viewers may be insensitive to this moment, but for viewers attuned to the dynamics of trauma, this moment can prompt recognition of the intensities that surround speech. The communication takes place across a gap that can be an abyss of understanding. The gulf between the spoken word and the embodied memory has a palpable presence here. The affective contagion that passes across that gap and across the screen to the viewer happens not through the words but through the silences that inhabit them and through the non-verbal registers of voice, eye and gesture. Writing these words, I am aware that I could be describing a performance, a stylized rendition of traumatic memory staged for the camera, but this is no such staging. This is not merely a question of recourse to the performative codes of affective presence.

In a sense, language meets a taboo, a sense of boundaries that should not be crossed. This signals to the complex duality of language. As re-presentation, language stands in for that which is absent: it marks a gap. As enunciation, language can carry an unbearable presence, can assume a plenitude, marked by an affective undercurrent that presses up from below, threatening to break through the controlled structures of language or narrative. This is the contradictory dialectic of language.

Speech that is not marked by affect, not riven through with the intensities of the act of enunciation, in a sense lets the listener off the hook. Speech that is marked by dissociation—the repression or protective blocking of affect—can strike the sensitive listener/viewer with a sense of that absence—of the sucking in of energy around the abyss. But the depersonalized speech that characterizes so much of academic work, based as it is on an assumed faith in the significatory power of words, the linear unfolding of a discourse, the dispassionate theorization of trauma as historical or socio/psychic phenomenon, is often founded not on this energetic dynamic but on its absence, as if speech and listening are buttoned up and don't reverberate into the affective bodily memory of the listener.

Not only does this lack of understanding let the listener off the hook; it also lets the speaker off the hook: she/he who can speak without awareness that words can unleash these undercurrents, who can move on to the next thing unscathed. It is as if anything can be said with impunity.

In a public lecture, in the interests of restoring the historical record, a speaker tells of a terrible atrocity committed on a child.[27] No detail is spared. She speaks with gravitas, holding the audience in the moment. And yet, she segues, apparently effortlessly, onto the next point. In the space of barely five minutes she is jocular, loquacious. How is this possible? This is what Bennett describes as a "failure to witness."[28] The speaker has lost a sense that some things exist in another register and this should be respected. Approaching them in a pedestrian way—in a "normal" register of discourse—implies acceptability, negating the special care with which they need to be treated.

In a therapeutic context, the "existential engagement"[29] of the therapeutic relationship is paramount in attempts to provide a space to close the gap between affect and enunciation. As the discourse of trauma moves out of the clinical context and into concerns with history and public memory, this fundamental awareness of an ethics of care around speech and its reception loses its primacy.[30]

Facts can vibrate; they can give off colors, sounds, smells, images. To talk of these facts with no recognition of this is to lack any awareness of the act of enunciation, of the gaps between language and experience and the unpredictable ways that sparks can break out of language, leap across the gap and ignite the tinderbox of traumatic memory.

An insect buzzing around a flower sees colors, shades and contrasts completely invisible to the human eye. Only with ultraviolet light can we humans simulate the perceptual experience of an insect. Like the insect attuned to a differently-marked perceptual world, the trauma survivor picks up resonances imperceptible to the unaffected, their residue reverberating through the fractures in the psychic shield.

In Alejandra Canales' documentary film, *A Silence Full of Things,* trauma survivor Miriam Marquez encapsulates this understanding:

> People who don't know about torture can look at the Iraqi man with a hood on his head and his arms outstretched and be completely insensitive to that

[27] The speaker, who shall remain anonymous, was talking of events in early colonial Australian history.
[28] Bennett writes, "a kind of failure to witness can result from viewing disturbing images under conditions that precisely don't compel one's continued involvement." Bennett, *Empathic Vision*, 64.
[29] Herman, *Trauma and Recovery,* 147.
[30] This disparity highlights a significant fault-line in trauma studies as an interdisciplinary field.

image because people don't know the noise, the smells of that image. Who can imagine this horror? No one can imagine this horror.[31]

2. Affect, Aesthetics and Trauma

In her consideration of the nexus between trauma and aesthetic practice, Jill Bennett shifts the focus from traumatic event to the nature of post-traumatic memory.[32] Drawing on Bessel van der Kolk's assertion that "traumatic memory is of a 'non-declarative' type, involving bodily responses that lie outside verbal-semantic-linguistic representation," Bennett argues the limitations of both narrative and documentary film, on the grounds that both assume the primacy of signification and the importance of identification with character.[33] Narrative film, she argues, relies on a realist interpretation based on characterization, and in documentary, character "can be said to interpellate witnesses into a particular kind of sympathetic relationship."[34]

Following Bertolt Brecht and trauma theorists such as LaCapra, Bennett argues against a "'crude empathy'"[35] that blurs the boundaries between the experience of the trauma survivor and the sympathetic engagement of viewers. She cites LaCapra's call for a more nuanced, self-reflexive form of empathy that recognizes and maintains the differentiation between "the trauma that resists representation" and the experience of spectators—one that avoids the "assimilation of the other's experience to the self."[36] Bennett herself takes a different tack. In her account, the absence of character or direct reference prevents any recourse to crude empathy, and she privileges forms of experimental contemporary art that "[bear] the imprint of trauma" but eschew both the politics of testimony and the realist assumption that art can "capture and transmit" the experience of trauma.[37] This imprint, she argues, resides in the non-significatory affective charge of the work:

---

[31] Canales, *Silence*.

[32] Bennett writes that "the art of sense memory […] does not make a claim to represent originary trauma—the cause of the feeling—but to enact state or experience of post-traumatic memory." Bennett, *Empathic Vision*, 40.

[33] Ibid., 23.

[34] Ibid., 8.

[35] Ibid., 10. Bennett cites Brecht.

[36] Ibid., 23.

[37] Ibid., 23; 3. Bennett does not proscribe character altogether, giving credence to artworks that present "character as flow," rather than as narrativised objects of empathetic identification.

> Affect in art does not operate at the level of arousing sympathy for predefined characters; it has a force of its own [...] it goes beyond reinforcing the moral emotions that shape responses to a particular narrative scenario.[38]

Bennett works with a Deleuzian-inflected concept of affect as intensity aroused by sensation and she emphasizes the need to resist art that produces "meaning rather than body."[39] Bennett claims that this sensory intensity elicits thought, leading to a critical engagement with the material that is "more complex and considered than a purely emotional or sentimental reaction."[40] She describes this critical aesthetic engagement as "empathic vision."[41] Bennett argues that:

> the value of Deleuze's notion that affect is produced as intensity by formal means rather than by narrative is that it allows us to understand affect as something other than an emotional response to character and thus to address the limitations of a narrative organization that contains affect within certain corporeal and moral boundaries.[42]

Bennett argues persuasively that experimental art can produce an affective encounter, a somatic experience of something that is not named but registers the "force of trauma."[43] She describes this evocatively as "transactive rather than communicative."[44] However, the argument that our response to narrative is necessarily subsumed or contained into moral emotions connected to character relies on a very limited model of narrative and an assumption that narrative film is univocal. Whereas both narrative and documentary have the potential to submerge affective experience within narrativized renditions of character and emotion, they also have the potential to work in much more flexible ways than this, and recognizing this opens up more generative ways of thinking about how different types of film can engage with traumatic affect.

This narrow way of understanding narrative film is not an uncommon one; indeed, an emphasis on the pivotal role of character and plot is central to the key paradigm of "classical narrative cinema" that held primacy in film studies for several decades. This paradigm rests on an assumed

---

[38] Ibid., 50.
[39] Ibid., 7; 10. Bennett cites Maurice Blanchot.
[40] Ibid., 24.
[41] Ibid., 21.
[42] Ibid., 31.
[43] Ibid., 46 and following pages.
[44] Ibid., 7.

hierarchy in which all aesthetic and affective dimensions of the film serve to bolster the causal chain of narrative events driven by character goals. Similarly, conventional theoretical models of documentary film have privileged the production of meaning and marginalized the operations of affect. However, both of these truisms have sustained widespread challenges over several decades of film theory that has argued that cinema has a body and cinematic experience is embodied.[45]

In a summation of a broad-ranging rethinking of the nature of narrative cinema, that inverts this assumed hierarchy, Miriam Hansen draws sensory-affective experience into center stage in the understanding of film narrative. Hansen argues that what has become known as "classical narrative cinema" in fact operates as "a scaffold, matrix, or web that allows for a wide range of aesthetic effects and experiences."[46] Similarly, the understanding of documentary as a "discourse of sobriety," in which affect is anathema to the desire for knowledge, has been systematically challenged by both new forms of "performative documentary" and emerging discourses around the role of affect and embodied spectatorship in documentary cinema.[47] Understanding the experience of cinema as intrinsically embodied and affective opens up a more flexible way of thinking about how film can engage with trauma. Hansen moves away from questions of representation tied up with the image to approach film as a fully "aesthetic" medium, that is, a medium that works with all of the senses and sensory experience.[48] Affect depends on the viewer: if we understand affect as a relation, then we need to consider that relation with a fully embodied spectator.

---

[45] See for example, Marks, *The Skin*, Vivien Sobchack, *The Addres of the Eye: A Phenomenology of Film Experience* (Princeton: Princeton University Press, 1992); and Anne Rutherford, *"What Makes a Film Tick?": Cinematic Affect, Materiality and Mimetic Innervation* (Bern: Peter Lang, 2011).

[46] Miriam Hansen, "The Mass Production of the Senses: Classical Cinema as Vernacular Modernism," in *Reinventing Film Studies*, eds. Christine Gledhill and Linda Williams (London: Arnold, 2000), 339.

[47] The term "performative documentary" comes from Bill Nichols, *Blurred Boundaries: Questions of Meaning in Contemporary Culture* (Bloomington & Indianapolis: Indiana University Press, 1994). For an extended discussion of these debates in documentary, see Anne Rutherford, "The Poetics of a Potato: Documentary that Gets Under the Skin," *Metro* 137 (2003). The term "discourse of sobriety" comes from influential early documentary theorist and practitioner, John Grierson.

[48] Hansen refers here to Walter Benjamin's definition of aisthitikos, from the Greek, as "a discourse of the body."

Explorations of the materiality of cinematic experience, which argue the embodied basis of cinematic experience, open up more generative understandings of how film can awaken that "tactile, sensuous mode of perception" central to what Walter Benjamin calls mimetic experience.[49] For early film theorist Siegfried Kracauer, film constantly hooks into or "pushes downwards"[50] into embodied experience. For many contemporary film theorists this capacity to awaken a heightened embodied experience is at the core of how film works to draw the spectator into an affective mimetic engagement with film, whether narrative, documentary or experimental.

Film is polyvocal. The enunciative strategies of film are complex: they are dispersed across all the embodied dimensions of sound, image, movement, rhythm, pace and color that make up the polyvocal medium of cinema. If we understand narrative as a "scaffold," we can begin to identify the pulse of narrative film that constantly dips down into the materiality of embodied experience. If we explore the movement back and forward between body and narrative, between materiality and the virtuality of story, we can start to understand another layer of how both narrative and documentary film can engage the spectator that cannot be reduced to mechanisms of characterization. These are embodied but uncodified intensities that run as undercurrents, parallel streams, interwoven voices that drive the oscillatory dynamics of narrative. They are the same dimensions that drive experimental work in its evocation of traumatic affect. Both narrative and documentary have the potential to engage with the experience of trauma and post-traumatic memory in ways that deploy all of these polyvocal dimensions. To accept that affect cannot be reduced to representation does not mean that it is incompatible with representation or narrative; it is just of a different order.

Rather than a simple binary—narrative *or* affect; semantics *or* somatics—identifying these intensities as dimensions of film through which affect can draw spectators into a heightened sensory-affective engagement can enable ways to explore how these elements are deployed

---

[49] Miriam Hansen, "Benjamin and Cinema: Not a One-Way Street," *Critical Inquiry* 25, no. 2 (Winter 1999), no page. Hansen writes that Benjamin's use of the term dissociates those understandings of mimesis associated with verisimilitude: "beyond naturalist or realist norms of representation and a particular relation (copy, reflection, semblance) of the representation to reality, the mimetic is invoked as a kind of practice that transcends the traditional subject-object dichotomy [...] a mode of cognition involving sensuous, somatic, and tactile forms of perception."

[50] Miriam Hansen, "'With Skin and Hair': Kracauer's Theory of Film, Marseille 1940," *Critical Inquiry* 19 (Spring 1993), 447.

across a range of film genres that address experiences of trauma. What does it mean to have these affective elements nested in a scaffold of situational context? If narrative gives a frame for that affective dimension to emerge, what is the relationship between content-driven character-dependent emotional engagement and this more amorphous, fluid, material affect?

Brian Massumi's work on affect can be productive for understanding the relations between significatory elements and these material, embodied dimensions.[51] Massumi makes an essential distinction between affect, which he describes as a logic of intensity, and the conventional content-dependent semantic coding of emotion. Massumi argues that affect is "outside this loop [... it is] unassimilable"[52] to this content. However, Massumi suggests a more complex relationship between affect and semantic content, not an either/or: "language is not simply in opposition to intensity"; they are not incompatible—while linguistic expression can "dampen intensity,"[53] it can also resonate with or amplify the affect of the image. This implies that narrative structures do not necessarily annihilate affect. It opens up a sense of two relatively autonomous spheres that can interact with each other, rather than a hierarchy in which one overrides the other.

Rather than a simple equation of affect with sensation, Massumi writes of affect as the perception of one's own vitality, one's own aliveness. As a dimension of experience that is always present in different degrees, this model allows us to think about affect and signification as a "co-presence," to envisage a dialectical tension between the two.

This concept of co-existing but disparate layers provides a framework to think about ways that film registers on many levels operating simultaneously.

When we think about the implications of this for understanding film spectatorship, we need to recognize that a film can produce different kinds of experience: it can be an amalgam of elements that work in different ways and to different ends. Macro models that argue from genre—such as categorical thinking about narrative or documentary—cannot address the subtle and fluid dynamics of how this dialectical tension works in film spectatorship and therefore cannot reveal much about how film can engage with traumatic experience.

---

[51] Brian Massumi, "The Autonomy of Affect," in *Deleuze: A Critical Reader*, ed. Paul Patton (Oxford & Cambridge, Massachusetts: Blackwell, 1996).
[52] Ibid., 219-221.
[53] Ibid., 219.

Film can contain different kinds of temporality.[54] Spectators can be split, pulled in different directions. A spectator may be engaged in the linear, causal temporality of the represented diegetic world, but they are drawn into a film moment by moment. This is a very live process constructed in the performative presence of the moment. This can unfold on the micro level of a sound, a camera movement, a space, and it can work with or against narrative dimensions. Embodied experience here is a different kind of knowing.[55] Elements of a film that privilege either affect or narrative may be sequential, alternating as the film dips into the material building blocks of spectator engagement and harvests that sensory-affective richness back into the narrative. They can also be simultaneous, in complex ways. Intensity and the significatory dimensions of a scenario may contradict each other or they may resonate with each other. Gradations of affect may vary at different points through a film. We need to see films on a continuum with the most prosaic or univocal forms at one end—be they documentary, narrative or experimental—and the most sensorially and corporeally rich, aesthetically expansive and polyvocal at the other.

Bennett calls for attention to specificity in the ways that art can "embody and register trauma."[56] Equally, we need to explore the unique capacities of embodied, sensory forms of narrativized film to engage traumatic experience. We need to look to more flexible and subtle frameworks to analyze how film can work with affect and how it can be deployed in the engagement with trauma. Rather than a prescriptive approach, it is more productive to see this as a process of experimentation and to look at how diverse films have done this, and what we can learn from them.

Affect and Performativity in Film

Two films—one narrative, one documentary—offer ways of working with the polyvocal dimensions of film to engage with experiences of trauma. Both films work with an inclusive ethics of address to take up the experience of survivors and the dynamics of post-traumatic memory, but each works with testimony in an oblique way, using the performative register to shake loose the realist faith in language and representation and

---

[54] These can include narrative time, screen time and duration.

[55] In Bennett's model, sensory intensity *leads to* thought. I am suggesting here, rather, a concept of "animate thought"—intrinsic to the experience, not subsequent to it.

[56] Bennett, *Empathic Vision*, 4.

to provoke an affective embodied engagement with spectators. Each film eschews a matter-of-fact recounting of traumatic event and raises questions about the affective dynamics of testimony for both survivor and spectator.

Bahram Beyzai's film *Bashu* (*The Little Stranger*)[57] deploys the phenomenological capacities of cinema to invoke an understanding of the nature of post-traumatic experience. As a fiction film, *Bashu* stands out for the clarity of its understanding of the nature of traumatic memory—its intrusive quality and its eruption across somatic registers. The film is set during the 1980s Iran-Iraq war. Articulated through the figure of an Iranian child, the film has no place for a distanced reflection on the events or a matter-of-fact telling of what happened. The prologue of the film shows the events of the child's family disappearing into the earth under fire from Iraqi bombs, but these are brief fragments, which become inseparable from the child's experience of them. The trauma exists here in its residue in the child, triggered by the sound of explosions, the sight of flames and gestural traces that bring forward flashes of his lost family. Bashu is unable to speak at all through the first part of the film. He is a kinetic figure, running, flailing, cowering, a streak of dark skin against the yellow corn, a tiny body in a vast expanse of green fields. When his mute presence finally breaks out into speech, it is not an objective account of facts that breaks forth, but a bodily torrent that comes pouring out of him in words and gestures. In the turning point of the film, that seems to flick a switch in Bashu and open up the possibility of his reintegration, this torrent is released kinetically in a frenzied body percussion, infinitely more eloquent than words could be. The sound and rhythm give the moment an overwhelming affect.

Bashu narrativizes this through the catharsis of the body but the film allows a space for intensities that cannot be expressed in the same way through narrative. When Bashu finally speaks, his expression defies any linguistic/bodily or cognitive/affective separation, as if this is the condition of speech. His performance draws spectators into a heightened somatic engagement. A conventional narrative approach might argue that this engenders a closer, fuller embodied engagement with character, thereby enhancing the mechanisms of identification, but it is the performative energy of gesture and percussion that is at stake here. The moment unleashes an affective excess that lodges this moment "under the skin," in the embodied memory of spectators, in ways that resist easy assimilation to the diegesis. It breaks through into the present of spectator experience.

[57] Bahram Beyzai *Bashu,* dir. (*The Little Stranger*), 1986.

This is not to say that all filmic images of the body in the grips of a somatic release would function in this way, rather than being rendered simply as spectacle. In *Bashu*, the energetic economy of the film, particularly the mute, kinetic figuring of Bashu, builds to this moment in such a way that the spectator is engaged with the bodily release. It operates both on the cognitive level of narrative and in the affective, energetic dynamics of the spectator.[58]

This is a film that is about much more than trauma: it is equally about difference, prejudice and the redemptive power of emotional bonding. Bashu is persecuted by the petty-minded bigots of the village he winds up in, but is fiercely defended by Naii, the woman who takes him in. These aspects work clearly on emotional identification with character. The issue of discrimination is explored overtly through dialogue, but the rural village setting of the film opens up the possibility of another level, written into the script, but taking form in the film through the "enunciative present" of sound and gesture rather than speech.[59] Bashu's protector, Naii, lives in an almost animistic exchange with the birds and wild animals of her fields. This exchange is articulated in a heightened awareness of animal presence—an ability to sniff the animals out—and a communication with them through cries, grunts and growls. There is much in the film that remains a riddle, not least this porous boundary between the somatic communication of the animal world and the human. To some extent, the somatic and vocal expression of Bashu is nested in this broader aesthetic economy of the film that renders many elements inaccessible to language and gives space to intensities that are not clearly defined and find no equivalent in verbal language enunciation.[60]

---

[58] The response of spectators to this moment will vary, depending on their prior experience: it speaks in a voice that allows a point of entry to those who know the afterlife of trauma, even as it constructs a scenario for those who do not.

[59] The framing of this essay within questions of enunciation has been influenced by Raquel Schefer's very interesting discussion of the "enunciative present" in Ruy Guerra's film, *Mueda: Memory and Massacre*. Raquel Schefer, "Re-constitutions. On "Mueda, Memória e Massacre" ("Mueda, Memory and Massacre"), by Ruy Guerra," *Le Journal de La Triennale* 4 (May 18, 2012), http://www.latriennale.org/en/lejournal/you-do-not-stand-one-place-watch-masquerade/re-constitutions-mueda-memoria-e-massacre (accessed November 1, 2012).

[60] Negar Mottahedeh situates Bashu in the context of the tradition of Ta'ziyeh , a form of ritual Persian theatre. Negar Mottahedeh, "Bahram Bayzai," in *Life and Art: the New Iranian Cinema*, eds. Rose Issa and Sheila Whitaker (London: National Film Theatre, 1999). According to Peter Chelkowski, in the history of Ta'ziyeh, text was added last: in the traditional form, drama is conveyed wholly or predominantly through music and singing. This contextualisation suggests the

Bashu's location in a village with remnants of folk culture and myth, and its narrative focus on a child, all facilitate the recourse to non-linguistic tropes in a way that is not generalizable into other narrative contexts. However, the film suggests that an expanded narrative repertoire—one which explores more fully all the performative registers of kinetic, vocal, rhythmic, sensory and narrative expression, and their capacity to evoke that which cannot easily be rendered into language—may be a richer seam to mine than more prosaic modes. These registers offer ways of working phenomenologically with film that situates trauma within a narrative context, opening up a recognition of the dynamics of post-traumatic memory at the same time as it signals the unassimilable nature of traumatic experience, thereby opening up a place in the text that addresses the spectator-survivor.

The significance of the performative register also emerges in the Indonesian film, *A Poet*, a stylized documentary re-enactment that commemorates the 1965 massacre of supposed Communist sympathizers that erupted across the Indonesian archipelago.[61] The film is structured around the memories of Acehnese survivor, Ibrahim Kadir, who was accused of being a communist and imprisoned. Kadir is the leader of a didong troupe—a group that performs a traditional communal form of sung performance poetry. While a commitment to public memory is paramount here, director Garin Nugroho eschews the disembodied voice of history, choosing to work instead with the emotional registers of the oral tradition of didong.[62] The film starts and ends with the rhythmic pounding and singing of didong and didong provides a rhythmic current that weaves in and out through the film like a structure of call and response. The film moves back and forth between dramatic sections of recitation or dialogue and musical sections of singing, dancing and clapping.

This is a very hybrid film. To be sure, it works at points specifically to establish identification with character, but there are many more layers to

---

influence of the performance tradition on this somatic and rhythmic narrative economy of Bashu. Peter Chelkowski, *Ritual and Drama in Iran* (New York: New York University Press, 1979), http://worldcinemadirectory.co.uk/component/film/?id=986 (accessed November 25, 2012).

[61] dir Garin Nugroho, *A Poet: Unconcealed Poetry (Puisi Tak Terkuburkan)* (1999). For details of the purge, in which up to two million people were killed, see Dierdre Griswold, *Indonesia 1965: The Second Greatest Crime of the Century* (New York: World View Publishers, 1979).

[62] For a detailed analysis of the use of didong and the formal strategies of the film, see Rutherford, "Poetics and Politics."

this film that build an affective register that complicates the experience of spectators, at times unsettling an identificatory position as well as affirming it. The film unfolds entirely in the space of two cells and much of it is about the fear of prisoners waiting, listening, being led out to execution. Through the microcosm of one prison cell, the film provides both recognition of what was a communal trauma on a massive scale and empathy with the individual prisoners. At times it slides toward sentimentality and a cello provides mood music. However, *A Poet* draws on a theatrical performance tradition that enhances awareness that this is a staging: a self-reflexive structure dispersed across several interlacing strands of drama, performance and music; a highly stylized use of a restless mobile camera; and a dense and stylized soundscape.[63] Theatricality tempers identification. At times the cello is more like a self-conscious mode of punctuation than a parallel to emotional content. The film moves through a set of structured repetitions that enhance an awareness of the structure. Low resolution video adds to the layers that pull the viewer away from a naturalistic viewing.

The performance of Kadir similarly slides across registers. There is a duality at play, as Kadir is both performer and witness/survivor together. At times he is a character in the cell; at times he steps out and becomes himself. Framed alone in a black space, in these few brief moments Kadir gives his testimony. His memories emerge in the film not as facts but as bodily memory–the "crak, crak, crak" sound of bodies being severed by the short sword, and the gesture of the hand that slices head from body. We see just a sliver of his shadowed face through a hole in the wall as his hands repeatedly enact the strike of the sword. In another brief fragment, Kadir asks what it means to be decapitated, enacting the severing of head from body with his hands and breaking down in a kind of crazy laughing, before the film takes us back into the respite of song. Back in the black space of testimony again, he tells of a woman murdered with her baby, and as the memory becomes overwhelming, Kadir enacts the movement of her body rolling, turns his back to the camera, and slides into the performative poetic mode. These ruptures register the impossibility of rendering memory into the standard forms of linguistic discourse or a one-dimensional narrative account. Kadir's performance through gesture and the shift in registers carries the viewer affectively into an engagement with the embodied quality of memory, even as it maintains an awareness of the duality at play, of Kadir as both performer and subject, both inside and outside the role. Proximity and distance co-exist.

---

[63] The actors in the film are both professional members of a theatre troupe and local Acehnese villagers.

There is an ethics underlying this film which is an ethics of care for the survivor, a concern to honor the experience of the survivor—in its fullness—and also a recognition that the film stages the aftermath of a communal trauma shared by many of the viewers. The filmmakers are sensitive to the need to approach trauma with integrity, but without doing violence to the post-traumatic vulnerabilities of viewers. Theirs is not an attempt to spell out all the details of murder and mayhem. The film takes an integrative, healing approach to the trauma, rather than a historical one. Kadir has agency here: rather than prodding and poking him to spell out facts and details, the film allows him to speak selectively and on his own terms, in his own idiom. The performative dimension allows a space to work with the many possible voices of film. There is a recognition of the limited capacity of language to translate or encompass affective traumatic experience, and the staging facilitates an embodied audience engagement with testimony but does not simulate plenitude or completeness in the telling. [64]

An Ethical Practice

Bennett argues that there is a "temporal collapse" in artworks and discourse that focus on the "reduction of trauma to the shock-inducing signifier," rather than on the duration of post-traumatic memory.[65] For Bennett, it is crucial to recognize that trauma is not relegated to the past but has an ongoing constitutive role in the present.[66] While this recognition of the persistence of traumatic effects is of course pivotal, LaCapra's description of these experiences as the "afterlife of trauma" allows for a more accurate understanding of the fact that trauma can happen in an instant—the moment in which something breaks through the "psychic shield"— *and* its effects can continue indefinitely. Trauma is both event and condition. At the same time, it is a mistake to assume that the recitation of events can provide an understanding of the individual effects of traumatic experience. Bennett's focus on art gives another discursive space for a "commitment to registering a sense of the lived experience of traumatic events as a counterbalance to the necessary production of common memory."[67]

---

[64] Accounts of the production tell of a process of filming marked by tears and grieving. SAPFF, (Sydney Asia Pacific Film Festival) 2001 press kit for *A Poet.*
[65] Bennett, *Empathic Vision*, 65.
[66] Ibid., 40.
[67] Ibid., 58. Bennett here is writing of the work of artist, Charlotte Delbo.

In so far as trauma theory aims in part to articulate the ethical, political dimensions of trauma—to understand it as a communal problem and not merely an individual (pathological) one—this focus on testimony and documentation is important, particularly in lifting the burden of shame off an individual and providing a screen on which to project an understanding of larger social and political forces within which the individual has been entrapped. However, despite the explicit ethical commitment of much of this work, the very terms of the discourse can itself lead to an unknowing.

Concepts of discrete affects of guilt, shame and fear open a pathway into understanding emotion and thereby the processes of empathetic identification, and some of the components that may feed into a potentially traumatic situation; but they cannot address the affective "piercing of the psychic shield" that is constitutive of trauma. This term in itself, for all its specificity, does not encompass the embodied ground of "psychic integrity." We need more flexible, non-categorical ways of thinking about affect and embodied experience to approach this.

By the same token, if we believe that language can encapsulate or express trauma, then it makes sense that the aim of an ethical practice—in discourse or in artwork—is to document events, that this is what bearing witness demands. If we shift attention from representation to the act of enunciation, we can begin to recognize that enunciation is something that is, in itself, fraught. These accounts lodge into a complex mesh of knowledge and memory. If we work backwards from examples of artistic production that acknowledges this, even partially, we can see how opposing assumptions inform other attempts to bear witness to trauma. What would a film look like that is informed by this recognition? If one of the aims of trauma studies is to integrate recognition of atrocity into the public memory, then it must be acknowledged that that public is a plural one that includes both survivors and others. If we start from film and discourse that works with an inclusive ethics of address, it becomes clear how other approaches can unwittingly marginalize survivors in their mode of address. It is when we see an inclusive approach that we can identify the lack in other work.

If we believe that traumatic memory and experience can be translated into language, then that process of representation becomes a desirable one and the normalization of speech around the trauma—the rendering into normal quotidian discourse—is understood as a redemptive process. If, however, we don't accept this translatability—if we believe that there is a core that eludes representation—then an ethical approach must be entirely different and must involve awareness of the affective dynamics of the enunciative act. This is not prescriptive but suggests certain principles for an ethical practice. Such dynamics are not specific to the image or to artwork—they are relevant to all discourses of trauma. As much as specific questions about visual culture are pertinent here, the debate must go beyond the question of images to a broader ethics of address.

PART II:

CULTURES

CHAPTER FOUR

THE EARTHQUAKE AFTER KANT'S LISBON: "VISCERAL REASON" IN KLEIST'S PRECARIOUS MODERNITY

KARYN BALL

Secondary criticism on Heinrich von Kleist has, perhaps, too frequently identified his so-called "Kant crisis" [*Kanterlebnis*], documented in letters written in 1801, as the spur of a dazzling literary talent that the writer himself abruptly snuffed out in 1811, at the age of 34, when he fulfilled his suicide pact with the terminally ill Henriette Vogel. D.F.S. Scott speculates on a Fichtean incentive for the legendary crisis, attributed to Kleist's stark realization that truth is merely a personal creation and does not outlive our existence in the world.[1] More recently, James Philips has intimated that Kant's emphasis in *The Critique of Pure Reason* on the *a priori* conditions of experience that foreclose unmediated access to the Thing-in-itself[2] ostensibly derailed Kleist's belief in transcendent truths

[1] Scott reconsiders Ernst Cassirer's hypothesis in *Idee und Gestalt* (1921) that Kleist's crisis was precipitated, not by Kant's writings, but by Fichte's *Die Bestimmung des Menschen* published in 1800. After a variety of acrobatic qualifications and insinuations about the chain of influence, Scott arrives at the conclusion that it was, rather, Fichte's *Sonnenklarer Bericht* of 1801 that provoked Kleist's "cry of pain to Ulrike" in the famous letter of March 23, 1801 to the effect that truth is as fleeting as existence itself. D.F.S. Scott, "Heinrich von Kleist's Kant Crisis," *The Modern Language Review* 42, no. 4 (1947): 480.

[2] Desmond Hogan cites Kant's claim from the *Transcendental Analytic* that "fundamental concepts or 'categories' including cause-and-effect and substance-and-accident are not themselves derived from experience, and are implicated in all of our knowledge of analytic necessities." These concepts serve as "'first sources of our cognition,' which 'contain the grounds of the possibility of all experience in general from the side of the understanding.'" The transcendental is, accordingly, defined by Kant's stipulation that the application of these *a priori* categories is limited to appearances (phenomena) and cannot pertain to "things in themselves"

along with the sentimental residues of Leibniz's rational optimism.[3] Similarly, Tim Mehigan reiterates a widely-held perception that Kleist's "early letters reveal that his entire worldview was thrown over as a result of his encounter with Kant," while stressing the wider implications of this turnabout: that Kleist's stories, essays and plays pursue a philosophical inquiry about whether "the data of self-consciousness can be enlisted in the service of a theory of knowledge, whether self-consciousness and knowledge are fundamentally of a piece (and if they are, what this would mean for ordinary living)."[4]

In Mehigan's assessment, "Kleist's Kant crisis demonstrates with exceptional force the sense of shock accompanying the fundamental alteration of thinking that occurred at the threshold of the modern era. The crisis of consciousness arising from this shock," Mehigan stresses, "was to cast its shadow over Kleist's entire literary production."[5] Mehigan's vision of a Kleistean oeuvre written "beguilingly" in Kant's shadow epitomizes a fascination with psychological causality that has propelled scholars throughout the decades to look for the repercussions of the writer's crisis in his literary work. Even when critics do not sidestep counter evidence that Kleist was probably inclining in this direction without any specifically Kantian duress, they cannot resist the insinuation that Kleist felt *betrayed* by Kant's delineation of the transcendental limits of cognition and then descended into writing to work through this "trauma."

There is no need to psychologize "Kleist" (or even to take the writer himself at his own word) to recognize that five of the eight *Novellen* chart the devastating progressions of betrayal. Kleist's principal post-Kantian issue, in Mehigan's interpretation, is how ordinary life can be sustained in

---

(*noumena*) (Hogan 27 citing Kant's *Critique of Pure Reason* B 167-8). In *A Kant Dictionary*, Howard Caygill notes that what Kant's *thing-in-itself* shares with noumena and transcendent ideas is "the negative quality of limiting the employment of the understanding and reason to what can be an object of intuition, and the positive quality of denoting a problematic space beyond these limits. Thus the thing-in-itself cannot be known since knowledge is limited to possible experience, but it can be thought, provided that it satisfies the condition of a possible thought which is not to be self-contradictory" (393). In his entry on *thing in itself*, Caygill cites the *Prolegomena to Any Future Metaphysics that will be able to come forward as Science* §29 and the *Critique of Pure* Reason B xx, A 30/B45 and B xxvi.

[3] James Philips, *The Equivocation of Reason: Kleist Reading Kant* (Stanford: Stanford University Press, 2007).

[4] Tim Mehigan, *Heinrich von Kleist: Writing after Kant* (Rochester, NY: Camden House, 2011), vii, 5.

[5] Ibid., 16.

the absence of epistemological certainty. This question receives a melancholic answer, I contend, in plots that orchestrate the irreversible damage that faithlessness leaves in its wake while gesturing awkwardly toward a tragic solace for those surviving characters that carry on as if they might look forward to a prospective renewal of communal ties. More prominently, however, Kleist's plots besiege us with the pessimistic presentiment that, in a world wherein humans cannot see beyond appearances, those naïve enough to misinterpret signs as augurs of redemption will be obliterated. Knowledge for these protagonists always comes too late, converting their torpid reverence for rationality, integrity, and solicitude into the reader's somber afterthoughts, pathetic ruins of what might have been.

Kleist's betrayal motif, I will argue, compels his readers to confront a profound anxiety about our ability to survive after the illusion of a tacit truce to protect vulnerable life has been laid unequivocally to rest. In reflecting on the dynamics of self-preservative anxiety as a "visceral" (survival-laden) affect, the following reading of Kleist's betrayal scenarios will foreground three "lessons" for studies of the imaginative economies that bring about violence: First, Kleistean betrayal unbearably confirms the paranoid's commonplace that the other (no matter how familiar or familial) is out to get me, or, in any case, is not what he or she purports to be, and that his or her treachery is always imminent if not already actual. Second, the frequency of Kleist's betrayal scenarios attests to a foreboding that a whole-scale collapse of solidarity haunts every community, placing every member at risk of sudden and potentially lethal ostracism. Third, to the extent that these scenarios foreground precariousness at the expense of quasi-contractual social causalities, the violence that punctuates Kleist's literary writings figures as the last recourse of the disenchanted once they have given up on the agency of reason to serve the interests of collective survival; it retrieves the force of a warning against the façade of an affectively deracinated civility.

1. After Kant's Lisbon

While the Lisbon earthquake that shook Kant's generation occurred 22 years before Kleist was born, his youthful trajectory nevertheless reels from the aftershocks of the revolutions in France and Haiti, among other tumultuous events. Kleist himself was promoted to the rank of Sergeant in the fight against Napoleon, and rumor has it that, in 1807, he landed in the same Fort du Joux cell previously occupied by Toussaint l'Ouverture, the leader of the Haitian Revolution (1791-1804).[6] The March 1801 Kant crisis that added grist to Kleist's short-lived literary career transpires at the fault lines of "world historical" upheavals, nearly three quarters of a century before the unification of the German state.

Despite his critics' tendency to treat the first *Critique* as the centrifuge of Kleist's *Götterdämmerung*, Mehigan notes that the writer never specifies any of Kant's writings apart from the *Critique of Judgment* in a short review from 1810 on a play by Voß.[7] Of course, the dating of this review cannot tell us when Kleist, if ever, actually read the third *Critique*. It remains, nevertheless, compelling to consider the figurative language he employs in his letters to his half sister Ulrike and his fiancée Wilhelmine von Zenge to depict the extremity of his Kant-induced disorientation, language that often seems to echo the philosopher's use of earthquake imagery to characterize the sublime.

In the famous letter to Ulrike, dated March 23, 1801, Kleist lays bare his anguished thought "that what we call Truth has quite another name after death, and that therefore all attempts to win a possession that goes with us to our grave are quite in vain and fruitless." It is this thought that "has *shaken* [Kleist] in the innermost sanctum of [his] soul" ["*dieser Gedanke hat mich in dem Heiligtum meiner Seele erschüttert*"].[8] Notably, Kleist's language here recycles figures he previously deployed in his March 22, 1801 letter to his fiancée Wilhelmine von Zenge, where he

---

[6] Sander Gilman (1975) cites Kurt Günther as a source of this connection. See Günther's "Die Konzeption von Kleists 'Die Verlobung in Santo Domingo.'" *Euphorion* 17 (1910): 68-95, 313-331.

[7] Mehigan, *After Kant*, 40-1.

[8] Philip B. Miller ed., *An Abyss Deep Enough: Letters of Heinrich von Kleist* (New York: E.P. Dutton), 98, *emphasis mine*; Heinrich von Kleist, *Sämtliche Werke und Briefe, Münchner Ausgabe Band II: Erzählungen Prosa Gedichte Briefe*, (Munich: Deutscher Taschenbuchverlag, 2011), 714, hereafter *Sämtliche Werke.* In his letter to Ulrike, dated 23 March 1801, Kleist writes: "Der Gedanke, daß wir hienieden von der Wahrheit nichts, gar nichts, wissen, daß das was wir hier Wahrheit nennen, nach dem Tode ganz anders heißt, und daß folglich das Bestreben, sich ein Eigenthum zu erwerben, das uns auch in das Grab folgt, ganz vergebich und fruchtlos ist, dieser Gedanke hat mich in dem Heiligtum meiner Seele erschüttert – Mein *einziges* und *höchstes* Ziel ist gesunken, ich habe keines mehr" (*Sämtliche Werke* 714). Translation: "The thought that we here on earth may know nothing, nothing at all of Truth, and that what we call Truth has quite another name after death, and that therefore all attempts to win a possession that goes with us to our grave are quite in vain and fruitless: this thought has shattered me in the innermost sanctum of my soul. – My *single* and *highest* goal is sunk from sight, [and] I have no other" (Miller, *Abyss*, 97-98; translation modified).

describes the soul-wrenching impact of relinquishing access to the *Ding an sich* [thing-in-itself], "after Kant," as a shattering convulsion or *Erschütterung.*[9]

Kleist's repeated recourse to earthquake figures to characterize the traumatic aftereffects of Kantian skepticism encourages my longing to see his betrayal motif answer to Adorno. Though Adorno's shudder aesthetics privileges modernist art, the Kantian lineage of his language for the sublime, as Gene Ray has argued, connects *Erschütterung* back to the Lisbon earthquake of November 1, 1755.[10] Reiterating the commonplace that the calamity in Lisbon confronted the 18th-century philosophers "with some very troubling counter-evidence to the intuitive endorsement of metaphysical optimism," [11] Ray records a temptation to understand Kant's transcendental idealism as his endeavor to counter pessimism after the earthquake by refuting "both skepticism and unbound metaphysical speculation," or, in short, both Hume and Leibniz at once.[12] Moving beyond textbook causalities, Ray discovers traces of Lisbon's impact in the Prussian philosopher's early elaborations on the sublime.

In contrast to the harmonizing effects of the beautiful, Kant's emplotment of the sublime produces an "indirect" or "negative" pleasure, which, as Ray paraphrases it, compensates "for the pain [the mind] feels when the imagination reaches its limits" before the "magnitude" of rude nature (the mathematical sublime) or the expression of nature's "violent

---

[9] Earthquake imagery also inflects Kleist's letter to Wilhelmine von Zenge, dated July 21, 1801, where he writes, without reference to Kant, of "trembling" before annihilation: "[…] der Wille, der über uns waltet!—dieses räthselhafte Ding […] sind wir nicht durch ein Naturgesetz gezwungen es zu lieben? Wir müssen vor der Vernichtung *beben* [tremble], die doch nicht so qualvoll sein kann als oft das Dasein, und indessen Mancher das traurige Geschenk des Lebens beweint, muß er es durch Essen und Trinken ernähren und die Flamme vor dem Erlöschen hüten, die ihn weder erleuchtet noch erwärmt" (*Sämtliche Werke*, 751; my emphasis). Translation: "O, how incomprehensible the will that rules over us! This enigmatic thing […] . are we not obligated by Nature to love it? We must tremble at annihilation, which could not be the torment that existence often is; and while many a man bewails this sad gift of life, he must nourish it with food and drink, and protect the flame, although it affords him neither heat nor light" (Miller, *Abyss*, 115).

[10] Gene Ray, "Reading the Lisbon Earthquake: Adorno, Lyotard, and the Contemporary Sublime," *The Yale Journal of Criticism* 17, no. 1 (2004).

[11] Ray cites the Voltaire scholar Theodore Besterman to the effect that "the Lisbon earthquake was nothing less than 'the death of optimism'" (Ibid., 8 citing Theodore Besterman, *Voltaire* (Oxford: Blackwell, 1976), 365).

[12] Ibid., 10.

power" (the dynamic sublime).[13] Ray spotlights a passage from Kant's explication of the dynamic sublime in which the "textual effects of the Lisbon earthquake first become legible":

> In presenting the sublime in nature the mind feels *agitated* [*bewegt*], while in an aesthetic judgment about the beautiful in nature it is in *restful* contemplation. This agitation (above all at its inception) can be compared with a tremor [*Erschütterung*: a shuddering vibration, disruption, blow, shock, trauma], i.e., with a rapidly alternating [*schnellwechselnden*] repulsion from and attraction to the same object. For the imagination (driven to such agitation as it apprehends some object in intuition), this gushing and effusing [*das Überschwengliche*] is, as it were, an abyss [*Abgrund*] in which it fears to lose itself. Yet at the same time, from the perspective of reason's idea of the supersensible, this object does not gush or effuse at all; rather, it conforms to reason's law for the imagination to strive in this way. Thus, the object is now attractive to the same degree to which, before, it was repulsive to mere sensibility.[14]

It is, of course, not coincidental to my analysis that the word *Erschütterung* in this passage surfaces so pivotally, not only in Kleist's epistolary announcements about his Kant crisis, but in the *Aesthetic Theory* where Adorno's language seems to reverberate with the traumatic aftershocks of the Lisbon earthquake as mediated by the Kantian sublime. Adorno stresses the *involuntary* disposition of the "moment of being shaken" by a modernist artwork – a response "colored by fear of the overwhelming" to the objectivity of the work irrupting "into subjective consciousness."[15] In the "Art Beauty" chapter of *Aesthetic Theory* he insists that, "[i]n the artifact, the shudder is freed from the mythical deception of being-in-itself, without however the work's being reduced to subjective spirit."[16] He subsequently links the shudder with an unanticipated and unmollifiable experience of otherness, in which "recipients lose their footing" as "the possibility of truth, embodied in the aesthetic image, becomes tangible."[17] If Adorno has his way, then the modernist sublime "quakes" the narcissistic ground of self-rationalization: it conjures a delirious feeling of vanishing into the artwork as the *Ich* "becomes aware, in real terms, of the

---

[13] Ibid., 9.

[14] Ibid., 9-10 citing Kant, *Kritk der Urteilskraft*, 181-182; *Critique of Judgment,* 115, translation modified.

[15] Theodor W. Adorno, *Aesthetic Theory*, trans. Robert Hullot-Kentor (Minneapolis: University of Minnesota Press, 1997), 245.

[16] Ibid., 80.

[17] Ibid., 244.

possibility of letting self-preservation fall away," without actually "realizing this possibility."[18]

J.M. Bernstein endows Adorno's shudder with a *memorial* agency: the shock of the modernist artwork *reminds* the spectator of primal terror—the terror and awe before nature's power that our technological civilization has buried. In *Erschütterung*, the object's form materially overwhelms a rational ego that would imaginatively unify and subjectively aggrandize every phenomenon in converting it into a familiar, self-affirming theme. The resurgence of this disavowed dread is what bestows Adorno's negative revision of the Kantian sublime with its uncanny fault line as once familiar "pre-rational" fears about our vulnerability before unruly nature return in an unfamiliar scene.[19]

A crucial dimension of "truth" in Adorno's aesthetics might be figured as the underbelly of autonomous art: an unintelligibly "sensuous particular" in the artist's formation of materials *refracts* the forces of domination that modern subjects internalize as we numb ourselves toward the other and thereby discipline aggressive survival instincts. If "the work of art's detachment from empirical reality is at the same time mediated by that reality," Adorno writes, then art's possibility is negatively determined by an encounter with the materiality of domination itself, which artistic form simultaneously recapitulates and resists.[20]

At the seething heart of Adorno's shifting remarks on the (impossible) conditions of lyric poetry, art, metaphysics, and even criticism "after Auschwitz" is the contention that any seemingly pure or hermetically-sealed expression of subjectivity attests to a longing for spontaneity, freedom and real solidarity that inversely mirrors and thus determinately negates the cold recourses of bourgeois survival at the expense of more precarious lives. Subjectivity petrifies through self-hardening adaptations against witnessing and protecting the vulnerable, the very patterns of foreclosure that laid the tracks into Auschwitz.[21] The affective crux of Adorno's "after Auschwitz" writings is an acrid feeling of betrayal: it reactivates the traumatic knowledge that Germans and collaborators watched and rarely protested when their Jewish acquaintances, friends,

---

[18] Ibid., 245.

[19] "Once upon a time," Ray declares, "encounters with the power or size of nature defeated the imagination and moved us to terror and awe" (Ray, "Reading," 1).

[20] Theodor W. Adorno, "On Lyric Poetry and Society," in *Notes to Literature, Volume One*, trans. Shierry Weber Nicholson (New York: Columbia University Press), 33.

[21] Theodor W. Adorno, *Negative Dialectics,* trans. E.B. Ashton (New York: Continuum, 1996), 50.

neighbors, and co-workers were incrementally dehumanized, marked out with yellow stars, publicly beaten or shot on the street, and rounded up for deportation. Moreover, even if they were not, themselves, active participants in the deportations and mass murders, law-abiding Germans turned their backs simply because it was more convenient or lucrative to do so, opportunistically disavowing the evidence of their Jewish neighbors' fate while looting newly *Judenfrei* apartments following the round-ups.

The Frankfurt School critic's "after Auschwitz" pronouncements convulse with a kind of post-traumatic outrage about the grotesque magnitude and grisly consequences of this betrayal. This is to suggest, with Ray, that Adorno's shudder aesthetics not only bears the poetic traces of Kant's Lisbon, but also voices his historically tortured awareness that solidarity based on the intimacies of everyday life will not protect us from a self-rationalizing majority whose members *enjoy* believing the worst about "the others." In a sense, as Ray remarks, what the Lisbon earthquake was to Kant, "Auschwitz" was to Adorno: "After this history," Ray proclaims, "human-inflected disaster will remain more threatening, more sublime, than any natural disaster."[22]

Kleist's dramatization of moral disorientation "at the threshold of the modern era," to borrow from Mehigan, foreshadows Adorno's post-Auschwitz contention that a shared interest in survival will not save us once the optimistic ground of species solidarity falls away.[23] In contending that Kleist's betrayal motif anticipates Adorno's shudder aesthetics, I am stressing a convergence between these writers in a fully justifiable (and modern) paranoia about the shallowness of this very guarantee.

To crystallize this intersection between Kleist and Adorno after Kant (and Lisbon), I want to introduce the oxymoronic term *visceral reason* to delineate the affective *ratio* of an adrenalized poetics that unmasks the shameful fragility of safety nets and of the law that *should* (but doesn't) shore up vital protections when they go awry. The emplotment of a Kleistean protagonist's enraged disillusion shares the sublimely-uncanny signature of Adorno's conception of *Erschütterung* [the shudder]: shocking eruptions of instinctual aggression—when what should remain deep "inside" or "underneath" gurgles forth—recall a once familiar yet discarded terror of "primal nature" in the unfamiliar space of a supposedly civilized society. Resurgent "first nature" so defined pierces the deadened

---

[22] Ray, "Reading," 1. Ray subsequently writes: "The compensatory, second-stage pleasure of the traditional sublime, anchored in metaphysical optimism, is no longer possible: after the industrialized genocide of the camps, all we are left with is the anguish of the imagination and a desolated human dignity" (Ibid., 12).
[23] Mehigan, *After Kant*, 16.

cortical layers of "second nature," or reified conformity in Frankfurt School terms. Kleist's novellas unleash this "primordial" affect in the course of obliterating a naively rationalistic belief in an unspoken guarantee that family members, lovers, and community can be trusted to step in to protect us if we are singled out for arbitrary or excessive cruelty, including the state's. Robbed of this trust, Kleist's viscerally reasoning characters bear the potential to ignite a first-natural *Angst* in second-natured readers.

Perhaps one of the most literal inscriptions of Adorno's shudder aesthetics transpires in Kleist's "The Earthquake in Chili" (alluding to the catastrophe of 1647). The novella opens with the full-scale condemnation of Doña Josefa Asterón, the daughter of "one of the richest nobleman of [Santiago]," and Jéronimo Rugera, her tutor, after her pregnancy is discovered while she is interned in Our Lady of the Mountain convent. As Jéronimo paces his prison cell, Josefa proceeds to her beheading, a sentence which, with prototypical Kleistean sarcasm, has been commuted from burning at the stake. The third person narrator makes sure to inform us that her march toward execution inspires *Schadenfreude* instead of compassion among "the pious daughters of the city [who] invited their female friends to witness with them, in sisterly companionship, this spectacle about to be offered to divine vengeance."[24]

The earthquake that thwarts Santiago's lust for "divine vengeance" initially assumes the appearance of a cosmic intervention that annihilates the current order, recalling both the biblical flood and the destruction of Sodom. Jéronimo finds opportunity in heaving ground and cracking walls to slide down the sloping floor through a gap that opens as the prison edifice crashes into the opposite house (53). The course of his escape is, at once, miraculous and surreal: compelled by circumstances to flee the frying pan by jumping into the fire, Jéronimo is chased by demonically personified "flames flashing through clouds of smoke, [that] were licking out of every gable," even as the Mapocho river "overflow[s] its banks" and "roll[s] roaring after him." Kleist's deictics anchor the roaming shots of destruction in Jéronimo's fleeting observations:

> Here lay a heap of corpses, there a voice still moaned under the rubble, here people were screaming on burning house-tops, there men and animals were struggling in the floodwater, here a brave rescuer tried to help and there stood another man, pale as death, speechlessly extending his

---

[24] Heinrich von Kleist, *The Marquise of O—and Other Stories*, trans. David Luke and Nigel Reeves (New York: Penguin, 1978), 52. Hereafter, all page references to Kleist's novellas will be made in parentheses in the text.

trembling hands to heaven. When Jéronimo had reached the gate and climbed a hill beyond it, he fell down at the top in a dead faint. (53)

Kleist's crescendo of grammatically and semantically parallel elements configures the mathematical with the dynamic sublime in telescopically detailing the earthquake's devastation. Jéronimo's "dead faint" thus provides the coda to a vertiginous oscillation between fire and flood as the narration rises to the rooftops and descends into the flooding streets, reaches heavenwards, only to plummet again as Jéronimo falls.[25] The parallel structure of the oppositional elements in this description endows it with a fairy tale tone that formally links this passage to a subsequent list depicting class-transcending camaraderie among the earthquake's survivors.

> And indeed, in the midst of this horrifying time in which all the earthly possessions of men were perishing and all nature was in danger of being engulfed, the human spirit itself seemed to unfold like the fairest of flowers. In the fields, as far as the eye could see, men and women of every social station could be seen lying side by side, princes and beggars, ladies and peasant women, government officials and day laborers, friars and nuns: pitying one another, helping one another, gladly sharing anything they had saved to keep themselves alive, as if the general disaster had united all its survivors into a single family. (60)

The suspended animation of this idyllic solidarity contrasts dramatically with the stunning pace of the story's opening, which moves with cataclysmic alacrity from a rehearsal of the most pertinent details about Josefa and Jéronimo on the cusp of execution into an onslaught of Armageddon imagery that illustrates the earthquake. The blissful reunion in the valley, followed by the picturesque harmonization of class opposites depicted above, evoke, "with one eye cast to Rousseau," the archetypal comfort of paradise regained; these scenes seem to comfort us with the thought that the saved have also been redeemed.[26] In addition, the syntax heightens the fable force of Paradise restored through its concatenation of parallel elements—a list of high-low couplings that convey the dispersal of class hierarchies.

---

[25] Steven R. Huff in *Heinrich von Kleist's Poetics of Passivity* (Rochester, New York: Camden House, 2009) observes that this passage plays out a "poetics of passivity" where "stress is placed upon the victim, the suffering individual, who—deprived of the ability to act and despite all efforts to the contrary—is reduced to the status of an object" (160).

[26] Mehigan, *After Kant*, 75.

The narrator seems to take on Josefa's perspective as she rejoices in the solidarity forged in "countless instances of fearlessness, of magnanimous contempt for danger, of self-denial and super-human self-sacrifice, of life unhesitatingly cast away as if it were the most trifling of possessions and could be recovered a moment later." Indeed, as the narrator continues:

> since there was no one who on that day had not experienced some touching kindness or had not himself performed some generous action, the sorrow in every heart was mingled with so much sweetness and delight that Josefa felt it would be hard to say whether the sum of general well-being had not increased on the one hand by as much as it had diminished on the other. (60)

"Hard to say," *indeed*! On a formal level, this eerily-calm, eye-of-the-storm interlude establishes a literary-archetypal contract with us, the readers, who, lulled into a false complacency, will potentially feel betrayed when Kleist sadistically forces us to watch the murderous frenzy that finally consumes Josefa and Jéronimo, along with the virtuous Don Fernando's infant son and sister-in-law. The narration's saccharine tone equivocates its own Leibnizian measure-for-measure balancing act as Kleist's third person narrator disingenuously accentuates the lack of accessible reality behind the happy appearance. This appearance will be reversed all too imminently by a primal horde that uncannily replicates the unmoved-mover violence of an earthquake.

The couple's fortunes reverse when, accompanied by Don Fernando's family, they foolishly travel to the Dominican Church in Santiago to offer joy-filled thanks to God for their miraculous salvation. The remainder of the story details the cataclysmic events that follow after the prior denounces Josefa and Jéronimo in his sermon, blaming their sins for the earthquake and commanding restitution for the unfulfilled sacrifice. Those assembled immediately coalesce into a Satanic mob with one aim: to wreak vengeance on the unpunished sinners in their midst. Lethal confusion ensues as the crowd bludgeons Don Fernando's sister-in-law, Doña Constanza, after mistaking her for Josefa, the "convent whore." Before the murderers attack Don Fernando, someone claiming to be Jéronimo's father helpfully identifies his own son to the mob who immediately beats him to death. The shoemaker, who previously worked for Josefa's family, levels her with a single blow before seeking her "bastard":

> Master Pedrillo struck [Josefa] dead with his club. Then, drenched with her blood, he shrieked: "Send her bastard to hell after her!" and pressed

> forward again, his lust for slaughter not yet sated. […] Master Pedrillo would not give up until he had seized one of the infants by its legs, dragged it from Don Fernando's grasp, and after whirling it round in the air above his head, dashed it against the edge of one of the pillars of the church. After this, silence fell and the whole crowd dispersed. When Don Fernando saw his little Juan lying at his feet with his brains oozing out, he raised his eyes to heaven in inexpressible anguish. (66-67)

The novella's blatant, structural parallel between the earthquake and the mob's malice align an exterior with an interior irruption of "first nature," thus insinuating an uncanny destiny: the innermost primal aggression that centuries of socialization should repress, if not forestall, explodes into a public arena with the relentlessness of an automatism.[27] Josefa and Jéronimo's Edenic reunion in the valley after surviving the earthquake cannot be taken as a harbinger of permanently reconsolidated solidarity; rather, this treacly scene borrows the plot tricks of fairy tales, ostensibly to ridicule Rousseau and perhaps also to beguile readers into taking down our guard. We might be all the more shocked, then, when preternatural bloodlust engulfs both Josefa and Jéronimo after they giddily disregard their memories of the prior injustices perpetrated against them and dare to rejoin a vindictively superstitious community.

2. "Visceral Reason" in Kleist's Precarious Modernity

"The Earthquake in Chili" simultaneously confirms and belies Jeffrey High's claim that Kleist was not prepared for the "self-aware superstition, half enlightened denial, and savage outrage" forecast by Kant and Schiller at the end of the eighteenth century.[28] The turbulence that sharpens Kleist's jagged political horizon foments a mood of crisis that proliferates wounded bodies throughout his novellas, plays, and anecdotes. Yet the

---

[27] As Andreas Gailus argues in *Passions of the Sign: Revolution and Language in Kant, Goethe, and Kleist* (Baltimore: The Johns Hopkins University Press, 2006), the "sovereignty of political, psychological, and linguistic orders" in Kleist and Goethe's foundational crisis texts is "shattered by the intrusion of a succession of uncanny undersides: of violence into the domain of law; of the body into speech; and of the extrasubjective—impersonal—into the subject" (Gailus 21).

[28] Jeffrey High, "Crisis, Denial, and Outrage: Kleist (Schiller, Kant) and the Path to the German Novella(s) of Modernity," in *Heinrich von Kleist and Modernity*, ed. Bernd Fischer and Tim Mehigan (Rochester, NY: Camden House, 2011), 193. High suggests that the age of Enlightenment did not fulfill its promise for Kleist's generation and he joins the generations of literary critics who have sought to trace the "denial of this promise" through Kleist's works and letters (Ibid., 187).

ripples of blood and torn open flesh that punctuate this oeuvre simultaneously betoken the fantasy of a peaceful existence that might be "live[d] within the bounds of the law in which obedience, discipline, and rules prevail."[29] This "contractualist" fantasy suffuses Kleist's critique of the Enlightenment presumption of "fidelity to the collective [that] underpin[s] the rule of law."[30]

Contractualist paradigms inevitably codify varying figurations, not just of "human nature," but also of a group psychology that envisions particular possibilities and limits for the individual-community-state matrix. Mehigan derives Kleist's pessimistic views about human nature and group behavior from an agonistic tension between Thomas Hobbes' on the one hand and Jean-Jacques Rousseau (with Kant) on the other who tend to occult the former's attention to the vexatious question of collective consent.[31] The Hobbesian position, as Mehigan characterizes it, prioritizes "powerful emotions, tied to the body" as the condition for collective agency, and the "commonwealth" as such. This position posits an intolerable "state of lawlessness where self-preservation is entirely the responsibility of individuals acting for themselves." Given that any agreement originating from the collective will be determined, for Hobbes, by sentiment rather than reason, only the sovereign can enforce communal commitment to the rule of law and thereby counteract a perilous "state of nature."[32]

---

[29] Galili Shahar, "Fragments and Wounded Bodies: Kafka after Kleist," *The German Quarterly* vol. 80, no. 4 (Fall 2007), 453.

[30] Mehigan, *After Kant,* 68. This trajectory evinces itself in narratives that "are replete with references to tacit or overt contracts, which are subjected to rigorous evaluation in the course of the works in which they appear" (ibid., 71).

[31] Ibid., 72.

[32]Ibid., 71. A testament to the historiographical and theological irony that pervades Kleist's works, no less a religious authority than Luther himself is brought in to denounce Kohlhaas's violence. A reasonable man in fiction at least, Luther's sympathy is aroused by the horse-dealer's account of callous authorities who do not merely fail to uphold the retroactive force of legal protections, but also answer requests for legal action with duplicity and repressive force. Yet even Luther is stalled in his efforts to fulfill his pledge to Kohlhaas as the former must surmount a lack of coordination between judicial authorities in Brandenburg and Saxony. At the frayed seams of the Empire in Luther's time, a pledge of justice is vouchsafed, not through the highest state and religious authorities, but through a soothsayer's magic, her *deus-ex-machina* power to hold everyone accountable to a preordained fate and thereby make a mockery of Kant's ideal of unshackled reason conquering superstition. Insofar as the novella's poetic reflexivity "denaturalizes historical reason" (Gailus, *Passions*, 136), this prophecy trope emerges as a vehicle of effective

In contrast, the position that Mehigan attributes to Rousseau and Kant domesticates the dangers that affectivity poses to reason's sovereignty by replacing sentiment with "a kind of second nature," which stems from the acceptance of a social contract as the foundation of civil society.[33] In Rousseau's world view, this position naturalizes reason's agency, since, as Mehigan observes, "it purportedly generates principles of agreement, such as the contract, of its own accord" as an extension of "intuitions about being that ordinary experience of the world makes available."[34] In a similar vein, Kant's "categorical" ideal of "mature" reason "legislates what it is to be a human being," and the efficacy (or appeal) of this regulative ideal removes the need for an active choice between a state of nature and civil society.[35]

---

causality in a world where everything solid (or constative) has melted into air. *Michael Kohlhaas*'s gypsy soothsayer, who ineffably resembles Frau Kohlhaas's mother, is a distinctive but by no means unique example of Kleist's employment of supernatural elements. Kleist's plots occasionally fulfill a longing for a supernatural justice that overturns the malicious intentions of those who trample a fundamental letting-live. In "The Beggarwoman of Locarno," a housekeeper takes in a sick old woman, but on returning from a hunt, the Marchese heartlessly commands the gravely ailing beggar to retreat behind the stove, where she passes away. When the accursed man subsequently witnesses the nightly signs of the beggarwoman's ghost retracing the weary path of her final fatal steps, his terror spurs him to immolate himself with his castle. The Marchese has belied the aristocrat-paternalist's *noblesse oblige* to protect the weak and vulnerable members of his community, yet it is a ghost rather than an act of reason or state that punishes this crime against survival. Likewise, in "Saint Cecilia" and "The Duel," Kleist paralyzes his would-be destroyers of the peace with uncanny deformities of mind and body, thereby allowing the innocent or slandered to triumph for a change; nevertheless, the stories' suspense depends on our understanding that perfidy would have certainly prevailed over survival through public acquiescence if the Saint Cecilia or twisted fate had not intervened. Along with the soothsaying gypsy from *Michael Kohlhaas*, these supernatural interventions topple the Enlightenment dream of a mature reason that intercedes on behalf of justice as birds of a feather flocking together. Supernatural forces in Kleist's *Novellen* retroactively confirm the continuing relevance of sloughed off puerile superstitions that define first nature over and against a second-naturalized civility, which repeatedly proves incapable of guaranteeing social responsibility or lawful behavior.

[33] Mehigan, *After Kant*, 71.

[34] Ibid.

[35] Ibid., 71-72. Mehigan asks us to recall that Kant's 1784 Enlightenment essay stipulated "private reason," or obedience, as an essential condition for maintaining the "consensual community" (ibid., 68). What Kant's "mature" perspective disavows, of course, is that affectivity and experience are inseparable; this is to suggest that the affective residues of experience might crucially condition

A passively preconscious inclination to abide by an unspoken truce not to attack those in our midst is the presupposed fulcrum of rational behavior—the Enlightenment's antidote to Hobbes' "war of all against all,' the specter of a demonic multitude, pitched on the brink of genocide, revolt, or both at once. Yet the ironically melodramatic tone of the narration that induces readers to *inspect* Little Juan's oozing brains in the penultimate scene of "The Earthquake in Chili" reproaches our complacent commitment to a second-natural civility that undergirds my survival in connection with yours as we share everyday social space. For while the civil-minded predictably condemn non-state violence as "irrational," in the pre-dawn hours of Kant's enlightenment, Kleist unfurls a "war of all against all" among churlishly temperamental and easily corrupted priests and monks who tussle with superstition and sometimes overtake a puerile state apparatus before it has had a chance to mature into a reliable threat. Paternalistic authorities fail over and over again to redress injustice; they will more likely foreclose rather than fulfill the countervailing "rational" agenda to ensure communal survival.

In exaggerating its confirmation of Hobbes over and against Rousseau and Kant, Kleist's literary barbarism makes mince meat out of the contractualist paradigm that expropriates sentiment in tautologically installing the "natural" appeal of reason. When Kleist's characters strive to behave in keeping with an a-pathetic regulative ideal as the ground of civil cooperation, they find themselves unequally pitted against Hobbesian subjects who give free rein to those very passions that "mature reason" brackets out.[36] Smashed skulls, lanced breasts, and raped nobility conjure the seductive promise that limns Hobbes' notion of a people's contract with a sovereign that permits him everything if only he will protect them from the dangers of "first nature." In short, Kleistean violence attests to an *inescapably volatile affective economy*, which preempts a social contract

---

"intuitively-based" agreement, which implies that sentiment operates preconsciously at the heart of reason itself.

[36] At the fulcrum of Hume's arguments against Leibniz's doctrine of sufficient reason, as Mehigan parses them, is the claim that, "[w]hile we can *imagine* how an effect arises from a cause, our experience of things does not reveal an actual cause to us." The overall implication is that "the rational interrogation of our experience does not elicit the shape of reality, no matter how regular the conjunction we find in it. It is custom and habit that give shape to our experience, not reason" (*After Kant*, 42). In allowing a Hobbesian "state of nature" to prevail, Kleist, as Mehigan insightfully demonstrates, inadvertently identifies with Hume's skepticism before Kant's: civic morality is a rickety byproduct of customs that merely simulate emotional bonds with others, yet there is no abiding affective infrastructure that dependably supports it.

that enlists emotional control while ensnaring Kleist's rationalistic protagonists in nasty, brutish, and foreshortened fates.

Carol Jacobs has argued that *Michael Kohlhaas* is structured around a pledge that "has been turned somewhat inside out."[37] This eviscerated pledge manifests itself for Jacobs in the vacillating vitality of the gleaming black horses that Kohlhaas entrusts with the Junker Wenzel von Tronka as insurance for a promise to return and pay the latter's arbitrary and legally groundless toll for passing through his land. The Junker scourges Kohlhaas's naïve trust in his fellow man's spirit of cooperation by mistreating the horses and lethally brutalizing their caretaker who faithfully sacrifices his life in the service of his master while protecting the latter's property.

Yet Wenzel von Tronka's truculence is not sufficient cause to drive the horse-dealer to cast off his noble ideals all at once in a furious reversion to brutality. Kohlhaas's peaceful attempts to seek justice for the rogue Junker's treachery set into motion a chain of events that expose a still more pernicious unreliability on the part of inconsistent or nepotistic governance structures that exacerbate rather than redress injustice. Kohlhaas's disillusion with the merits of positive law implodes after the Brandenburg Elector's bodyguard lances Frau Kohlhaas with deadly force as she seeks to intercede on her husband's behalf. A peaceful attempt to activate the state's commitment to lawfulness has brought about his wife's death and thereby undermined his family's survival.

The narration ratchets up the melodramatic impact[38] of the widower's situation in recounting how the answer to the deceased wife's petition belatedly comes back to him after the Pastor had "just delivered a moving

---

[37] Carol Jacobs, *Uncontainable Romanticism: Shelley, Brontë, Kleist* (Baltimore: The Johns Hopkins University Press, 1989), 153.

[38] Gailus comments perceptively on the use of melodramatic performatives depicting Kohlhaas's transformation from honest man to brigand, or "the perverse inversion of Kant's impersonal personality" (Gailus, *Passions*, 122). To Gailus's analysis, I would add that the third-person narration seems to be mocking Kohlhaas as he "[draws] up an edict in which, 'by virtue of the authority inborn in him', he ordered Junker Wenzel von Tronka, within three days of sight of the document, to bring back to Kohlhaasenbrück the two horses he had taken from him and worked to death on his fields, and to fatten them in person in Kohlhaas's stables" (Kleist 137-138). The arbitrariness of the "three days" that Kohlhaas allots to the Junker to respond to the edict exposes its whimsical futility: the horse-dealer's "edict" pathetically imitates a rhetoric of governance that wields force without signification. Kohlhaas's officious performatives thus refract the appalling inefficacy of a disordered legal redress system that can be countered, it would seem, only through a reversion to natural law.

address from beside [Lisbeth's] bier: it commanded him to fetch the horses from Tronka Castle and, upon pain of imprisonment, to make no further submissions on this matter" (137). In Kleist's monstrously disordered universe, legal authorities merely add insult to injury in responding to entreaties for justice with threats. It might come as no surprise, then, that an enraged Kohlhaas "immediately set[s] about the work of his vengeance," (137), for what course is left to Kleist's unfortunate horse-dealer, that one-time "paragon of civil virtues" (113), but a "blatant *withdrawal* from all communal obligation"?[39] The extremity of Kohlhaas's about-face attests to his gut-convulsing sense of betrayal as the state's arbitrary and unwarranted aggression against lawful cooperation transvalues Kohlhaas's "irrationally" insurrectional violence into his last recourse for self-determination.

Silke Weineck has observed that it is not merely law, but law as an avatar of the "symbolic father" (God, King, or Sovereign) that is chasing its own loose ends in Kleist's novellas and dramas.[40] In a letter

---

[39] Gailus, *Passions*, 119. Kohlhaas hereby plays the role of a proto-liberal subject outraged as he encounters the "ubiquity of the political" in Carl Schmitt's sense of a "post-liberal" state sovereignty not counteracted by "society" or by an attendant ethics of sociability (ibid., 127). If "this extraordinary man could have been considered a paragon of civil virtues" before his thirtieth birthday, then it is tragically ironic that "his sense of justice made him a robber and a murderer" (Kleist 114), or so Gailus contends (ibid., 110), as Kohlhaas ego-maniacally seeks exact compensation that goes beyond the law. In Gailus's interpretation, Kohlhaas's morally narcissistic anarchism "inaugurate[s] a state of exception, and the text that chronicles his exploits is an exploration of the problems posed by this state: the status of sovereignty, the relation between violence and law, and the place of the individual in the body politic" (ibid., 114). Citing Kant's *Contest of the Faculties*, Gailus additionally interprets Kohlhaas's "embrace of violence […] as an elaboration of a strain of excess that belongs to the dynamic of moral agency and, more specifically, to a moral enthusiasm unmoored from the regulatory framework of both reason and institution"—in short, as a model of revolutionary subjectivity (120).

[40] Silke Weineck, "Kleist and the Resurrection of the Father," *Eighteenth-Century Studies* 37, no. 1 (2003), 70. Weineck demonstrates how "[t]he distinction between biological, cultural, and symbolic fatherhood is at the center of three myths that are of central importance both to Kleist and to the Western construction of paternity in general: the story of God, Joseph, and Jesus (along with its prefiguration in Abraham's near-sacrifice of Isaac), the story of Laius, Polybus, and Oedipus, and the story of Zeus, Amphitryon, and Heracles." She adds that, "[i]n their numerous readings and retellings, these master narratives have shaped and continue to shape our thinking of fatherhood, positively and negatively, and their protean adaptability enables them to manifest fatherhood's *long*, that is mythical, history," by which

strategically addressed to his fiancée, Kleist instructs her about a woman's obligations towards her husband, whose happiness is her sole object, in contrast with the man's split obligations to his family and fatherland. In effect, this division of labor implies that he "cannot work for his wife *with all his strength,* whereas woman works for her husband *with her entire soul.*"[41] With absurd frankness, Kleist confesses his belief that the husband "'receives the entire sum of his domestic, that is to say *all* of his happiness' from [his wife]."[42] The implication, as Weineck proposes, is that a man's "happiness not only depends on the distinction between public and private, it is also entirely dependent on woman's recognition of him *as* private individual."[43]

If women might engender happiness in a patriarchal framework where biological fatherhood is never certain, it is because they are expected to foster the "private" emotional existence of their husbands who cannot expect personal affirmation from the state, the fatherland, or the public realm which more typically impede and thus deplete personal satisfaction.[44] Once again, this notion of the private cannot be separated from a regulative ideal of reason that expropriates emotion. The injury to Kohlhaas rendered by an erratic law is therefore manifold, since it includes his forfeiture of an entire affective economy—his wife as a source of recognition, solace, and ontological sustenance. No wonder, then, that his bereavement incites a once-shining beacon of honesty to erupt against the façade of paternalistic state authority—to burn down his ruthless antagonist's castle, and then to mobilize his pillaging militia to raze a sleeping Wittenberg in a ferocious pursuit of vengeance.

In "The Foundling," Kleist scrutinizes filial disloyalty as an adopted son repays his father's beneficence with seemingly boundless treachery. The merchant Piachi takes in the little boy Nicolo after the orphan's plague infects and kills the trader's biological son, Paolo, who accompanied his father on a business trip. Despite the presumably enlightening benefits of a good education, the "unnatural" son not only spurns his father's attempts to inculcate him with a sense of sexual propriety but opportunistically seeks to seduce the older man's virtuous

---

she means "patterns that both transform and are subject to what we think of more narrowly as the historical, the more rapid processes of institutional, political, and economic change" (ibid., 71).

[41] Ibid., 76, citing Kleist's letter to Wilhelmine von Zenge from May 1800.

[42] Ibid. See also *Sämtliche Werke*, 578.

[43] Ibid.

[44] Ibid.

yet psychologically fragile young wife, Elvire.[45] Piachi confronts Nicolo with this misdeed; however, the legal heir produces a decree, forged with the help of venal Carmelite monks, guaranteeing his absolute right over the father's property, and then kicks the old man out of his own estate. Overwhelmed by the depth of this dishonor and by his grief after burying the "unhappy Elvire," who has succumbed to a "burning fever," the homeless Piachi crushes his adopted son Nicolo's skull against the wall ["*drückte ihm das Gehirn an der Wand ein*"] and is discovered, with the one-time ward's head between his knees, in the process of ramming the injunction into the other's mouth (285; *Sämtliche Werke* 219).

Andreas Gailus overturns the obvious reading of this act that isomorphically identifies the head with reason, when he insists that Nicolo's skull "[embodies] reason's devitalization, the locus of ossified and deadened thought" rather than its vital inverse.[46] In the adopted son's maleficence, the father has glimpsed the void that lies behind the promise encoded in paternal solicitude that *kin* should repay *in kind.* "The Foundling" insinuates that "kindred" as such do not exist: Nicolo has *shuddered* the rationalist's faith in the underlying decency of his fellow man, a tacit contract to share a commitment to mutual survival.[47] Piachi's brutality vents his clammy revulsion upon confronting reified reason and empty legal expression, respectively, in his son's opportunism and the law's corruptibility. In shoving the decree down a dead Nicolo's throat, Piachi targets the duplicity that immobilizes justice and expression, leaving silent rage in its wake.[48]

---

[45] Nicolo pursues this seduction by dressing up as the Genoese knight, Colino (anagrammatically aligned with *Nicolo*), who perished slowly over the course of three years from wounds he sustained while rescuing the thirteen-year-old Elvire from a fire. Because the melancholic young woman retains an obsessive and ritualized reverence for Colino, Nicolo's trickery causes her to swoon into a high fever.

[46] Andreas Gailus, "Breaking Skulls: Kleist, Hegel, and the Force of Assertion," in *Heinrich von Kleist and Modernity*, ed. Bernd Fischer and Tim Mehigan (Rochester, NY: Camden House, 2011), 252.

[47] Mehigan argues that Piachi's collapsing world "is attributable, less to malevolent qualities in the foundling Nicolo's character than to Piachi's dogged allegiance to rational ideals." For, as Mehigan proposes, only his "belief in a rationally ordered universe" could prompt him to adopt the orphan in place of his deceased child (*After Kant,* 44).

[48] Piachi's post-rationalist revenge lust is not sated by the treacherous Nicolo's physical death. Even as the law requires confession before execution, our morally-unhinged patriarch refuses to receive the "blessed gift of salvation" in order to pursue Nicolo in hell: "On one side stood a priest who in a voice like the last trump

One of Hobbes' original contributions to contractual theory, according to Weineck, is his declaration in the *Leviathan* to the effect that the Commonwealth has been "'erected by the fathers, not by the mothers of families,'" even though (and perhaps because) biological fatherhood "'cannot be known.'" He thus deprives fatherhood of its "metaphysical anchor" at the same time that he deploys its metaphoric force to rewrite monarchic rule as contractual sovereignty.[49] Despite his own professed interest in a gendered division of affective labor, Kleist appears to deride the sentimentality that subsequently infuses this constellation[50] in "The Marquise of O—." The sexual violence suffered by Kleist's titular character is multifarious: The Russian Count, who initially represents himself as her savior after she falls into the clutches of a marauding army, eventually confesses that he lost control of himself at the sight of the beautiful and defenseless Marquise while she purportedly lay unconscious. Before this confession redeems the Marquise, her Commandant father refuses to believe her protestations of innocence and, in an outburst of severe temper, withdraws his affection and expels Kleist's mysteriously pregnant heroine from her family home.

The Commandant's implacable anger appears all the more egregious after the Russian Count owns up to his malfeasance, and Kleist's narrator treats us to an unexpectedly disturbing reconciliation scene between father and daughter. The Marquise is described as lying silently in the Commandant's lap "with her head thrown back and her eyes tightly shut" as her teary-eyed father "[presses] long, hot, and ardent kisses on to her mouth [*lange, heiße und lechzende Küsse*], just like a lover!" Meanwhile,

---

described to him all the terrors of hell into which his soul was about to be plunged; opposite stood another, holding in his hand the Body of Christ, the sacred means of redemption, and spoke to him of the glorious abodes of eternal peace. 'Will you accept the blessed gift of salvation?' they both asked him. 'Will you receive the sacrament?' 'No,' replied Piachi. 'Why not?' 'I do not want to be saved, I want to go down into the deepest pit of hell, I want to find Nicolo again—for he will not be in heaven—and continue my vengeance on him which I could not finish here to my full satisfaction'" (286). Kleist's agonistic poetics besets his arrested protagonist on each side with hell fire-threatening and heaven-beckoning priests. This absurdly exaggerated opposition underscores the righteousness of Piachi's new-found nihilism.

[49] Weineck, "Resurrection," 73 citing Hobbes's *Leviathan*, 102-103.

[50] Weineck notes that John Locke's *Treatises on Government* seem to mock Sir Robert Filmer's smooth analogy between paternal authority and state sovereignty; nevertheless, as Weineck points out, Filmer's sentimentalization of the family "continued to haunt private practice and political rhetoric," finding tangible expression in Rousseau (ibid., 75).

the ineffectual mother voyeuristically watches, through a keyhole and then from behind her husband's chair, "transported with delight" (107 translation modified/*Sämtliche Werke* 142). Weineck foregrounds the uncanny lewdness of the Commandant's "busy" fingers as he arranges his daughter's mouth, so as to kiss it all the more passionately with "inexpressible pleasure" [*mit Fingern und Lippen in unsäglicher Lust über den Mund seiner Tochter beschäftigt war*].[51] The reader might recall Don Fernando's "inexpressible anguish" as he raises his eyes heavenward at the sight of "his little Juan lying at his feet with his brains oozing out" or Toni's "inexpressible look," which I discuss below, as she reproaches her executioner/betrothed for his faithlessness. In those moments, the adjective *indescribable* [*unbeschreiblich*] conspicuously gestures toward the sublime pathos that a tragic reversal of fortune ineluctably precipitates (as if to deride the very logic of tragedy, which Kleistean viscerality overshadows). Here, the adjective *unsäglicher* [inexpressible] sardonically indicates the unspeakable pornography of the father-daughter bond. The incestuous quality of their communion retroactively stipulates the price of paternal forgiveness: it is paid in the obscene currency of masochistic enjoyment (or its performance) as the exceedingly passive Marquise ecstatically luxuriates in this mouth-stroking kissing business with her enraptured mother looking on.

The stakes are "visceral" in this story because the Marquise risks social death and bastardizes her own son if she does not accept an atrocious bargain: she purchases familial harmony and reaffirms her membership in the sex-gender system by consenting to marry her rapist, not once but twice—the first time, by coercion, to restore familial order, and the second to officiate her "genuine" acceptance of her role as the birthing machine of a "whole row of little Russians." The reader cannot experience the novella's "happy end" compromise as anything other than farcical after the Marchise's trust in male guardians has been interpenetrated by hypocritical contracts that, in quick succession, couple protection with rape or incest.[52] In the end, the story's glib punch line heightens the derisory effect of Kleist's fairy-tale tone as the wife satisfies her husband's curiosity about her violent change of heart following his confession: "Throwing her arms around [the Count's] neck, [the Marquise] answer[s] that she would not

---

[51] Weineck, "Resurrection," 77; *Sämtliche Werke* 142. Weineck notes that the daughter "is so passive that her very mouth needs to be arranged for the kiss—*erlegte ihr den Mund zurecht*, a formulation that invokes and conceals *Recht*, the word for both right and the law, fitting since this is a scene of repossession" (ibid., 77).

[52] Weineck, "Resurrection," 78.

have seen a devil in him then if she had not seen an angel in him at their first meeting" (113). In other words, the other is not what he claims to be—a "moral of the story" supplied in the paranoid syntax of visceral reasoning.

In "Betrothal in Santo Domingo," it only requires a momentary lapse of judgment for Gustav von der Ried to lose faith in the mestizo Toni by failing to recognize her performance of treachery as a life-saving strategy. Playing out the excruciating logic of Kleistean betrayal, Gustav not only shoots his lover point blank in the middle of her chest, he also kicks the dying "whore" (his word) before Herr Strömli compels the wretched man to realize his hideous error. She is beyond rescue, the narrator clarifies, as "she was completely penetrated/run through [*ganz durchbohrt*] by the bullet" (*Sämtliche Werke* 198).

Kleist opens up an agonizing space within the final climactic scene when the "noble girl" reaches out her hand to her betrothed, and, with an "inexpressible look" [*unbeschreiblichen Blick*], unfurls a last, heart-breaking conditional past-perfect reproach before "relinquishing her soul": "'Oh,' cried Toni, and these were her last words: 'you should not have mistrusted me!'" ["*'Ach,' rief Toni, und dies waren ihre letzen Wörter: 'du hättest mir nicht mißtrauen sollen!*'" (*Sämtliche Werke* 198)]. To identify with Toni's "inexpressible" look, a description that begs the question of its own performativity, is to judge Gustav's hot-headed execution of his lover with a body-and-soul-penetrating bullet as more appalling than his brain-splattering suicide. Once again, Kleist stages a scene that underscores the flimsiness of any intimate bond that might dependably vouchsafe survival.

Of course, it was not his fiancée who betrayed him, but rather, as Volker Kaiser claims, Gustav's own perversely obsessive investment in hermeneutical certainty,[53] though Kleist's more seasoned readers might just as easily expect the former. After failing to read the fidelity behind Toni's performance of betrayal, Gustav turns his rage on the vehicles of

---

[53] Volker Kaiser, "Epistemological Breakdown and Passionate Eruptions: Kleist's 'Die Verlobung in St. Domingo," *Studies in Romanticism* 42, no. 3 (2003). If, as Kaiser suggests, a racist narrator beguiles the reader into counter-intuitively investing in Gustav's faulty hermeneutical strategies and white-entitled value system, then "the monstrous suicide at the end of the story assumes an eminently critical significance, shocking the reader into a reconsideration of his/her own interpretative desires and anxieties" (ibid., 345). However, if the narrator's naturalized antipathy against the insurrectional Congo Hoango and his "rabble" [*Kerle*] (263; *Sämtliche Werke* 194-195) alienates a contemporary liberal gaze that is more sympathetic to anti-colonial struggle, then we will more likely identify with the self-consciously tactical Toni who has, in any case, shown herself to be the better reader all along.

communication and reason themselves, putting the gun in his mouth before pulling the trigger. The result is a completely shattered skull, which, "because he had placed the pistol in his mouth, clung in part to the surrounding walls [*des Ärmsten Schädel war ganz zerschmettert, und hing, da er sich das Pistol in den Mund gesetzt hatte, zum Theil an den Wänden umher*] (*Sämtliche Werke* 199). If "Betrothal" is haunted by the specter of the guillotine and the French Revolution, as Kaiser contends, then Gustav's catastrophic impulsivity confronts Kleist's readers with the visceral stakes of any vow traumatically forged in the state-of-nature midst of revolutionary Terror.[54]

Gustav's brain-splintering shot connects this scene to Master Pedrillo's infant-smashing malevolence in "The Earthquake in Chili," Piachi's skull-crushing vengeance against Nicolo in "The Foundling", as well as Michael Kohlhaas's "dashing out" of the Junker Hans von Tronka's brains "against the stones" (139). No Kleistean protagonist, no matter how noble or gracious, eludes the spray of innards when civility or its appearance collapses. Kleist's readers might nevertheless ask why brains splatter so regularly in Kleist's novellas, spurring us to shudder (or even laugh) as we witness an implied author's post-Kantian compulsion to eviscerate the mind as the presumed seat of rationality itself.

The prominence of visceral egress in Kleist's fiction recalls Arjun Appadurai's critical delineation of the "primordialist thesis," as an outgrowth of developmental-anthropological lineages of modernization theories.[55] While stressing his own commitment to investigating the interplay between affect and imagination in explosively changeable social interactions, Appadurai rejects the tendency of this thesis to collapse two avatars of "irrationality": violence, ethnocide, and terror on the one hand and resistance to modernization (comprising the ascendancy of positive over natural law, technological organization, and capitalist growth) on the other. As Appadurai notes, this conflation articulates ontogenetic and phylogenetic figurations of human development stemming from Western

---

[54] Gailus also makes a case for reading the French Revolution in German thought and letters, and the work of Kant, Goethe, and Kleist in particular, "as the historical manifestation of a new form of subjectivity whose divided and unstable nature reverberates within the foundations of symbolic life." Gailus's textual exemplars thus serve as "heteroclite" counter-testaments against the French Revolution insofar as they anxiously fulfill the presentiment that "to speak and act is to open oneself to an impersonal energy that threatens the integrity of language and subjectivity" (*Passions*, xiv).

[55] Arjun Appadurai, *Modernity at Large* (Minneapolis: University of Minnesota Press, 1996).

psychological analogies between the individual's instinctual latencies and a prehistorically rooted collective conscience that cannot be easily transformed but can be readily ignited "by new historical and political contingencies."[56]

Appadurai emphasizes the imagination's role in the sociocultural construction of emotion in order to distance himself from the presumption that "ethnic animosities" reside "in every national closet," but "mature" democracies regulate these "raw" affects while "less evolved" societies fail to hold them at bay.[57] Yet Appadurai also concedes that this emphasis does not explain "the brute contingency, the raw violence, the electric blood lust, the instinct to degradation" that fuel "rape, torture, cannibalism, and the brutal use of blood, feces, and body parts." When these *viscera* "enter the scenario of ethnic cleansing, we are faced with the limits, not just of social science but of language itself."[58]

Appadurai's speculations about these "viscera" spotlight the *intimacy* of neighbor-against-neighbor fights to the death. Such close-range ferocity derives from a "profound sense of betrayal" that arises when there is a "perceived violation of the sense of knowing who the Other was and of rage about who they really turn out to be."[59] Appadurai suggests that "[t]his sense of treachery, of betrayal, and thus of violated trust, rage, and hatred has everything to do with a world in which large-scale identities forcibly enter the local imagination and become dominant voice-overs in the traffic of ordinary life"; thus, "[w]hen these identities are convincingly portrayed as primary (indeed as primordial) loyalties by politicians, religious leaders, and the media, then," as Appadurai observes, "ordinary people self-fulfillingly seem to act as if only this kind of identity mattered and as if they were surrounded by a world of pretenders."[60] The alleged divergence between appearance and reality crystallizes when politicians, the media, and religious figures induce ordinary people to invest in local identifications and loyalties as "primordial" bulwarks against global insecurity.

As his quintessential figure for what I have been calling "visceral reason," Kleist's brain ejection scenes might be interpreted, after Appadurai, as a gory symptom of the paranoid compulsion to turn identity inside out—to *eviscerate* the lurid reality underneath the sociable façade. Gailus reads the "counter-linguistic aggression" evinced in such visceral imagery

---

[56] Ibid., 140-141.
[57] Ibid., 141.
[58] Ibid., 154.
[59] Ibid.
[60] Ibid., 154-155, 155.

as "the extreme manifestation of Kleist's energetic conception of language," which rebels against "language's tendency toward communicative decay, its hardening into repetition, cliché, and automaticity."[61] With Gailus, I am arguing that Kleist's apparent desire to "visceralize" language, to restore its full-blooded affectivity and injurious agency, opens the reader to a more trenchantly embodied concern.

In the interests of finessing an anachronism that my reading overtly risks, I should stress that Appadurai's *Modernity at Large* amplifies problems which unfold "as states lose their monopoly," and various groups resort to "the logic of the nation to capture some or all of the state, or some or all of their entitlements from the state" (157). Yet if we read Kleist's novellas as "perverse rewritings of Kant's Enlightenment project," as Gailus suggests (Gailus 27), then they do not arrive too early in the German-speaking, nation-building trajectory to reflect anxiety about political modernization. In Kleist's fiction, the very proto-state civil and legal entities that should buttress social harmony tend, fecklessly or belligerently, to ravage it. Two centuries before *globalization* became a flicker in Appadurai's eye, Kleist already fleshed out the gruesome volatility of a failed state in the making. Goaded by the furious specter of a Hobbesian society that erupts in the absence of a legibly consistent law, what is so devastating about Kleist's fiction is its coyly sadistic demonstration that the paranoid's worst assessment is the only dependable truth: the biosocial truce is flimsy at best, and no altruistic or hopeful gesture should restore our faith in it. His traumatic parables rattle thoughtless trust in the habits and conventions that simulate survival-committed civility, viscerally confronting us with an otherwise disavowed vulnerability.

---

[61] Gailus, "Skulls," 247. According to Gailus in *Passions of the Sign*, an investment in communication and sociability exposes Kleist's rationalistic characters to the havoc wreaked by collective and even revolutionary energies that destroy or block the force of speech. The sense of betrayal that results from a preemption of reasoned communication ineluctably spawns extreme, even foundational violence as the only effective "speech act" available when words fail (11). Gailus proposes the concept of the *energetic sign* to correspond to "the dynamic manifestation of a structural infirmity in the foundations of meaning" (xiv). This structural default is tied to the premise that "true speech is eventful in that it produces changes outside itself to the extent that it opens itself up to its *internal* outside, the extraverbal force of passion" (11). The energetic sign is, thus, "constitutively heterogeneous, divided between sense and force, the semantic and the countersemantic" (xiv).

CHAPTER FIVE

APPARENTLY UNRELATED: AFFECTIVE RESONANCE, CONCATENATION AND TRAUMATIC CIRCUITRY IN THE TERRAIN OF THE EVERYDAY

ANNA GIBBS

> I stumbled out of bed; I got ready for the struggle
> I smoked a cigarette; I tightened up my gut
> I said 'this can't be me, must be my double'
> And I can't forget, I can't forget, I can't forget
> But I don't remember what
>
> —Leonard Cohen

> From universalism [composition] takes up the task of building a common world; from relativism, the certainty that this common world has to be built from utterly heterogeneous parts that will never make a whole, but at best a fragile, revisable, and diverse composite material.
>
> —Bruno Latour, "An Attempt at a 'Compositionist Manifesto'"

When I was asked to produce a chapter for this volume I didn't want to write a purely theoretical paper about trauma. I felt too implicated in what I wanted to say to be able to distance myself in academic discourse. I didn't want to write fiction, either, since I did still want to formulate some concepts for thinking about what trauma might mean in the everyday, and about a structure of experience that might be to some extent generalizable, even though its contents would be specific. So what follows is neither theory, nor fiction, and yet also both: an impure mixture, a fragment from a larger piece of work that wants to address the affective resonance between images, stories and experience. This resonance, I contend, brings things that are thematically or otherwise unrelated into a relation organized solely by affect, and in doing so, gives rise to what I would describe as a kind of complex circuitry between things in which the effects of events concatenate to produce the everyday as a terrain of trauma. This is not the "trauma culture" decried by Lauren Berlant and others.[1] Nor is this terrain smooth and continuous. Rather, it is rocky, requiring negotiation, but also affording texture in the experience of passage through it.

Mark Selzer has described the present as a mediatized public culture mesmerized by the repetitive spectacle of traumatized ("torn and open") bodies, and the endless exposure—through confession and therapeutic discourse—of the psychic pain of trauma.[2] And we do now live in a more or less continuous state of mediatized emergency and traumatic aftermath, desensitized by the onslaught of images—many would argue—to the affect we ought to feel. Alternatively, we might be overwhelmed by exposure to this image stream and so be subject to a traumatic numbing that marks what has been called the "death of experience." Where Selzer, writing at the end of the era of broadcast media, emphasizes spectacle, I want instead to focus on processes of circulation, translation, accumulation and, especially, concatenation: concepts more adequate to the qualities of everyday life, which is, after all, composed of repetition into which time introduces both difference and the form of the cycle. Selzer and others seem to ignore the fact that so many people watching televised trauma have a firsthand relation to trauma of their own. Viewers might be refugees or migrants (given the radical uprooting migration can entail) watching the wars, arrests and disappearances, the earthquakes, or disasters of whatever kind, happening in their homelands, to their families, to people they know or to whom they feel a particular empathy. Or viewers might witness trauma in their own Australian backyard, to people with whom many of us do have some connection, however tenuous. I think here, for example, of places like Villawood Detention Centre in Sydney, where asylum-seekers are held for indeterminate periods of mandatory detention, or Pinjarra, a small town in Perth, the site of a massacre of indigenous people by white settlers (now described as the "Battle of Pinjarra," and where aboriginal people have been refused permission to place a memorial[3]). Viewers might be survivors of child sexual assault or domestic violence watching news of violent crime such as rape or murder. For such viewers the mediatized public culture Selzer critiques is something other than spectacle.

---

[1] Lauren Berlant, "Affect in the End Times" *Qui Parle: Critical Humanities and Social Sciences* 20, no. 2 (Spring/Summer 2012).

[2] Mark Selzer, *Serial killers: Death and Life in America's Wound Culture* (New York: Routledge, 1998).

[3] On this topic, see Robyn Ferrell, "Pinjarra 1970," in *The Real Desire*, ed. Briar Hill (Victoria: Indra Publishing, 2004).

I am equally unhappy, then, with the too simple concept of "vicarious trauma" and with too rigid distinctions between first and second hand or real and mediated experience. At the other end of the spectrum, the tendency to extend the definition of trauma to all distressing experience is also troubling. Trauma involves a shattering of self, that complex structure both relatively stable and yet of necessity open to ongoing transformation. This is a structure composed of the characteristics of continuity (an ongoing sense of itself in time), color (familiar patterns of feeling), cohesiveness (a sense of itself as distinct from others, though able to temporarily merge with others to a greater or lesser degree at certain moments—in love, in infancy, for example) and agency (a sense of purpose and relative confidence in our own capacity to act) which enables us to operate in a social world. With this in mind, clinical practice reveals that traumatic shattering on a small scale can be caused by something apparently minor, like a communicative disjunction between therapist and patient, created when a patient feels that they are not understood. We might describe this as traumatic stress, rather than trauma per se, which implies that the shattering is not total, but that there is a tendency toward the fragmentation of the self when subject to particular stimulus or stressors ongoing in time. Trauma *tout court* would seem to mean, rather, a shattering without repair, in which an abyss of vertiginous terror and perplexity threatens to open at any minute. Perhaps there is no cure for trauma in this sense. But maybe there can be amelioration of effects, by the same means that is used clinically for the repair of disjunctions and the strengthening of the structure of the self. This involves the progressive working through of "transsubjective translation"[4] in which the putting into words is both a reconnecting of referential layers and a reconnection with the other, on the condition that the other is capable both of listening and hearing, of affectively resonating with distress at a lower, (but not too much lower), level of intensity so as to modulate the experience of distress for the person experiencing it.[5]

First conceptualized by Silvan Tomkins, the term "affective resonance" refers to the positive feedback loops created by affect, and in particular to the tendency of someone witnessing the display of affect in another person

---

[4] Wilma Bucci, *Psychoanalysis and Cognitive Science* (New York and London: Guildford Press, 1997).

[5] Anna Gibbs, "Writing and Danger: The Intercorporeality of Affect," in *Creative Writing: Theory Beyond Practice*, eds. Nigel Krauth and Tess Brady (Teneriffe: Post Pressed, 2006).

to resonate with and experience the same affect in response.[6] Affective resonance does not produce "understanding" in the embracing sense of comprehension, but is a form of sympathy, (or mimetic communication), that senses a basic formal gestalt of feeling. To be effective therapeutically, this mimetic apprehension must also be tempered by a kind of empathy that knows its own limits, that understands the trauma in terms as close as possible to those of the subject experiencing it, and not merely in its own terms ("what I would feel like if I were in that position"). Of course, it is never completely possible to understand someone purely on their own terms, and this is what we mean when we say on the one hand, that we "can only imagine" the pain of others, and on the other that trauma is "unimaginable."

I have written elsewhere in other terms about the imbrication of images with the real, about the way so-called direct experience is always in some way mediatized, and the way in which images can become direct experience.[7] Here I want to try to do it differently, in part involving something like what Laleen Jayamanne has called "mimetic criticism,"[8] in order to attempt to open up questions about the process of what I will call "concatenation," and by which I mean a process of associational intensification, performed in part by the work of what Tomkins terms "affect scripting." [9] In this context, he introduces the concept of

---

[6] Silvan Tomkins, *Affect, Imagery, Consciousness*, 4 vols. (New York: Springer, 1962-92).

[7] Anna Gibbs "Horrified: Embodied Vision, Media Affect And The Images," in *Interrogating the War on Terror*, ed. Deborah Staines (London: Cambridge Scholars Publishing, 2007).

[8] Laleen Jayamanne, *Towards the Cinema and it's Double* (Bloomington: Indiana University Press, 2001).

[9] Silvan Tomkins and Donald Mosher, in "Scripting the macho man: Hypermasculine socialization and enculturation" *Journal of Sex Research* , 20, no. 1 (1988), write, "The function of scripts is to manage affect: they are sets of 'rules for the interpretation, prediction, production, control and evaluation of a set of scenes.'" Scenes—much as in the theatre—are events organizing people, props, affects and action in place and time. They render a particular affect salient and invest it with meaning. Script theory is complex, but essentially it posits that the meaning of behavior can be accounted for by identifying the scripts which drive it and the affect states these scripts attempt to manage. The growing importance of any particular affect and the proliferation of its potential sites of activation (which give rise to scripts) comprise a process Tomkins calls "magnification" (as opposed to amplification, in which an affect is intensified in the degree of its arousal). Magnification is the "experience of a new affect during a narrative review" of a family of scenes which are linked by affect. Such a review in turn increases the significance of the affect in question, and this will give rise to scripts designed to

"magnification," which names the process by which affects become meaningful by being discriminated and meaningfully linked to the particular contexts in which they are experienced: this forms part of the work of memory. Here I propose that traumatic experience dispenses with this form of secondary processing, and that instead, repeated experiences of affective resonance (whether "firsthand" or "mediated") produce a concatenation in which affect resonates with like affect, so as to link otherwise unrelated scenes without producing articulable meaning. Here we might say that something is simply undergone rather than fully experienced.

If one of the results of trauma for the first generation is the impossibility of finding "the words to say it," in the title of Marie Cardinal's exemplary novel about familial abuse, the problem of the unspeakable, of a horror so great that words are inadequate to it, and poetry an affront to it, the problem for the generations afterwards is how to translate what has *not* happened, at least not directly to them, but what is nevertheless transmitted as affect and an empty place where representation ought to be.[10] I want to suggest, without going so far as to make a metaphor out of this very particular experience, that *something* of this problem has become pervasive in mediatized cultures, where images communicate faster than we can make sense of them. I want, in this "enactive" writing, to try to diagram both the effects of this ambiguity of the image, and the processes of formation of traumatic short-circuiting through affective resonance between very different, apparently unrelated, events, times, and places, and the traumatic concatenation of experience this produces. Chantal Akerman's film *D'Est* (1993) is an important source for describing the workings of affective resonance, but the film itself also works as a *mise-en-abyme*[11] for the production of concatenation produced by this resonance.

---

maximize, minimize, counteract or neutralize particular affects. Scripts dealing with negative affect will produce analogues (i.e. once you are alert to negative affect you will see the potential for it everywhere, finding similarities in apparently different and increasingly remote scenes). Scripts dealing with positive affect, by contrast, aim to maximize it, will produce variants: e.g. "'one develops a talent by using it in many different ways or settings or a friendship grows through the sharing and rehearsal of diverse experiences' (Carlson, 1981)", in Gibbs, "Horrified."

[10] Marie Cardinal, *Les Mots Pour Le Dire* (Paris: Grasset, 1975).

[11] Lucien Dällenbach, *Le récit spéculaire. Essai sur la mise en abyme* (Paris: Seuil, 1977).

*

One night a man telephones my mother: I want to come and see you, he says, I am your uncle Jack. I don't have an uncle, my mother says, but of course it turned out she did, only my grandmother never spoke of him, her shamed silence digging a hole down which his existence disappeared.

I never knew my paternal grandfather. He fought in the First World War, my father tells me when I stumble on the one photograph we have of him. He was never the same afterwards, becoming silent and withdrawn.

I remember the utter, speechless horror of one afternoon as an undergraduate when a French lecturer screened Alain Resnais' *Night and Fog* (1955) on a rainy day in Adelaide. I had known next to nothing at all of the Second World War until then.

A friend has not been able to bear to listen to what her mother wants to tell her about her life in a concentration camp. Her mother makes a tape, and my friend drives around in her car, listening to her mother's voice and the story that is too intense to be born in the intimacy of the face to face. She can't stop weeping.

A Bosnian student tells me about the moment when she, aged five, and her slightly older brother, home alone, heard bombs begin falling nearby. It's war, he told her. It's started, and now we have to go.

A 12 year old my colleagues and I interview in Penrith as part of the "Power of the Image" project says he doesn't want to go into the city any more. When he's there, he says, he keeps looking up, expecting to see planes flying into buildings.

A friend who thought she was white tells me of going to work in an aboriginal community where they tell her they recognize her: they know who she is. They knew more about my family than I did, she says.

As we walk home form school together one day, my best friend tells me a secret she insists I not share with ANYONE: she is going to kill herself.

Another friend tells me over a glass of wine that she now thinks what she calls "convict shame" and its alcoholic aftermath has been transmitted through generation after generation of her mother's family.

I discover one day after the class where a French lecturer (the same one who screened Resnais' film) played Barbara singing "*Une petite cantate que nous jouions autrefois...*" (a song about a dead child), that this woman's husband and son had drowned in a boating accident.

I can't get the image of the boy in the detention center lying wasted and listless on his stepmother's lap out of my mind after the ABC *Four Corners* program.

Of course these resonances are not identical, nor even equivalent in any way. I list them more or less at random as they occur to me. They exemplify instances, fragments of horror, big or small, thrown out into the everyday like bits of shrapnel to lodge in the bodies of those who hear the stories, see the images or are suddenly pierced by the pain of others. There is so much shrapnel flying around. Some of it inevitably strikes us where we are vulnerable and might never be dislodged. But how much shrapnel can a body bear? What happens when shards begin circulating in a body that has absorbed them?

*

It's a balmy Paris evening in the summer of 2003, where I've arrived after months of traumatic stress at work, my closest colleague and I having —by the skin of our teeth—survived another major restructure, the second in three years, complete with all the dog-eat-dog and disregard for the niceties of the corridor that seem inevitably to accompany situations in which survival is uncertain and will likely be at the cost of others. My colleagues have behaved in ways I never anticipated (though perhaps I should have, having experienced the shock of betrayal of collegiality, and even friendship, on the previous occasion). Never mind the big picture issues about the future of the university these changes and the managerial ethos driving them portend; the devil in the details has left me fraught and exhausted. All I want now is to be a stranger in a strange city. I'm longing to lose myself in streets I once knew well, but haven't visited in years. Despite the recent misfortune back home, on this night I'm excited. I'm in Paris and on my way to a screening of a film by the Belgian francophone director, Chantal Akerman,[12] probably my favorite director. I had watched her films, transfixed, first in the freezing National Film Theatre cinema in Melbourne (*News From Home* (1977), *Les Rendez-vous d'Anna* (1978), and later, *Toute une nuit* (1982)), while people from the rows in front left in an intermittent stream throughout every one of these slow-moving films, with their long takes on almost empty spaces, deserted railway platforms at night, claustrophobic and impersonal hotel rooms, rare cuts and pans, anonymous comings and goings, minimal dialogue, voices on answering machines speaking to empty rooms: "Anna, where are you?"; and total lack of the familiar shot-reverse shot structure that Hollywood made second nature.

[12] Screening at Cinema MK2 Hautefeuille, 20 June 2003.

I couldn't understand this impulse to flee the scene. I couldn't have moved. For me, Akerman's films—especially the earlier ones—were riveting: deeply affecting, and profoundly melancholic, as if they took place to the rhythm of sobbing. This rhythm, I think now, was a kind of amodal communication in which the distress it mimetically induced resonated affectively with things in my own experience that may or may not have been thematically related to situations conjured by the films themselves. There is something in rhythm that strikes bodies at the presubjective level, entraining them and attuning them to the rhythms of a different experience, felt before it is understood. I would have said then that these films were about loss (but loss of what?), about the way communication fails, and how words separate us as often as they join us.

I didn't know, then, what I was to realize that summer evening in 2003: that Akerman was the daughter of a Holocaust survivor, Nelly Akerman, whose own mother was murdered in Auschwitz. I only know now, since reading Griselda Pollock's writing on Akerman, the story of how Nelly had been given her mother's diary in 1945, had inscribed it, and then put it away, to be found years later first by Chantal, then by her sister, each of whom in turn inscribed it.[13] In 1984 Akerman said her mother gave her the diary "instead of talking." Then in 2004 Akerman asked her mother to translate it aloud from the Polish as she filmed, and her mother began to weep as she realized what she was reading from this diary, that she had again forgotten. It is in the course of filming that Nelly caresses Chantal's face, and it is this gesture, the detail of this gesture, that resonates with Pollock, whose own daughter has recently left home and who she misses to the point of paralysis around writing.

My own response to Akerman's films in the early 80s was visceral—but if I had had to try to articulate something of it, I would have put it in the feminist terms in which her films were then received, as a way of resisting the putatively masculinist aesthetics of the spectacle in order to allow room for other registers of experience—like the stifling frustration of Jeanne Dielmann (the eponymous character of one film), and ours, as we watch her do the dishes in real time, and eventually murder a client. Marleen Gorris' *A Question of Silence*, in which a group of women, complete strangers to each other until that moment, murder a male boutique owner, would have been a more relevant point of comparison than Jean-Luc Godard's work or the films of the avant-garde.

---

[13] Griselda Pollock, "The Long Journey: Maternal Trauma, Tears and Kisses in a Work by Chantal Akerman" *Studies in the Maternal* 2, no. 1 (2010), www.mamsie.bbk.ac.uk.

Made in 1993, the film I am going to see is not new, but it is new to me—Akerman's work no longer seems to come to Australia—and what's more, Akerman will be at the screening to answer questions afterwards. The film is *D'Est* (from, or, of the East, that is, eastern Europe). The opening onto an image of a highway at night is abrupt, just as the ending will be. The film simply comes to a stop, almost arbitrarily. In between, the strict limitation of point of view is underscored by a certain lack of constructedness: although not completely synchronous, sound from one scene rarely carries over into another; and when it does one suddenly realizes with a shock that it is the footsteps of the crew one hears crunching in the snow.

Shot in 1991, only two years after the fall of the Berlin Wall and the break up of the Soviet Union, the film opens on the journey eastward through Europe from Berlin by car with long takes of landscapes filmed from the window interspersed with long slow takes on those "no places" of being on the road: a café on an otherwise empty stretch of road lined with fields; the occasional car passing at high speed. We see a car pass a single tree at an intersection on a rough rural road, and a little while later a horse-drawn cart labors through from another direction. Later still, another intersection: a motorbike crosses at full throttle, and a little while after, another horse and cart. The hint of transition is clear, but only gradually does the film approach the observable life of the cities, and as movement slows to the recurrent rhythms of everyday life, to the quotidian to and fro, a creeping stasis makes itself felt.

This is like no other travel film I have ever seen. What kind of journey is this? Where are we being taken?

These people don't behave the way they might in other places, where youths would surely clown in front of the camera, where people might openly show anger at being intruded upon, or might outright refuse the camera's gaze. In scenes shot in public places one observes people's initial, barely perceptible, surprise on discovering they are being filmed, and their realization that the camera will not stop to capture them but will simply pass on by, going about its own business. There are seemingly endless scenes of public queues: you could not say the camera is welcomed, but it is sometimes acknowledged, tolerated.

In the attitudes of people and the postures of their bodies we see what Akerman, later that night, would call "passivity," but which seemed to me at the time to be, rather, *impassivity*—a more complex state of resistance which refuses to manifest itself openly as resistance or hostility—a kind of *passive aggression*. As well as what Akerman no doubt intended by "passivity": a sheer stubborn ongoing "putting up with," as people had put up with so much else over the decades since the end of the war, and evidently continue to do so now, occasional riots and grass roots activist movements not withstanding. Both passivity and impassivity speak to history, to the social and political repression of the Soviet regime, to the food shortages and poverty then and since. Hostility had to be covert. There are few words exchanged. The danger of speaking in public apparently continues to be felt as a kind of after-effect or body habit, even after the actual danger has passed.

Endless waiting. Empty tedium in stark, empty rooms. The lack of the kind of busy familial interaction one sees in waiting rooms in Australia: the contained resignation of those who have been waiting too long. The object of waiting evaporates. The habit of waiting hardens into posture. A sweeping 360-degree pan around the grand old atrium of a railway station shows more queuing—for tickets and telephones—while others wait for trains or passengers in this cavernous space filled with a different kind of cold from the snow outside.

In another scene, a group of teenagers rock enthusiastically to an Elvis song, as if it were the latest hit. But even in the face of this animation the old technology gives the feeling of life in a time capsule, makes for a sense of "still life," as the film's domestic tableaux ("*nature mortes,*" and they don't call it that for nothing) strongly suggests. In these scenes people are filmed at home, doing what they normally do, making those small, routine gestures that compose the everyday—sitting, staring, drinking tea, putting on lipstick as the rest of the family moves around the same room, attending to a crying baby, watching… A woman listens to old records and prepares simple food. A child watches TV and aimlessly fiddles with a toy car while his mother plays the piano in the corner of the room. There is no privacy; only a feeling of claustrophobia, of proximity without the real contact of community. An old couple filmed through an open window play cards in their underwear. A man writes, while his wife hovers restlessly by.

A woman, formally dressed in a 1940s frock, sits, stares at the camera, waiting—for someone, or something. Or perhaps no longer even waiting, but simply, in spite of everything, enduring. Going on being, the only way she can, in a kind of hardening into existence as a meringue, drying out into its beautiful but brittle sculpted form, so that when you bite into it, it crumbles to nothing in your mouth.

Yes, this is about the fall of the wall, but there is something else going on here too, in this view of the other side of the divide, the time *after*, in which nevertheless little has changed. This is not just time after the collapse of communism: it is still the time after the end of the war. Images of women in headscarves and clothing that might date from the 1940s. So too the outdated technology seen in homes (phonographs, old radios). People carrying suitcases, or waiting in queues at train stations inevitably conjure the images of displacement so familiar to us from both archival footage and fictional reconstruction of the Second World War. (These were the cultural memories awakened by the images of refugees during the conflict in Bosnia in the 1990s). Suddenly, I know where the film has taken us. I know where we are. We are in a camp. A camp that has turned all the different countries of eastern Europe through which we have passed into "the East," all their languages into reticence, and all their seasons—even spring and summer—into an icy cold. A "glacial" age[14] in which things are immobilized, preserved in a living death.

Akerman has insisted on the subjectivity of responses to the film, on the personal nature of what is invoked by way of memory or association. And yet what is conjured up is not entirely subjective, but participates in a kind of "image repertoire," to borrow one of Barthes' terms,[15] so that one trauma is conjured up from the images of another. The silver birches so characteristic of eastern European landscapes are familiar to Australian viewers from documentary footage of the Second World War, seeing them again, here in his film reminds me of how spooked I felt travelling through southern Germany, near the Black Forest, with a gaggle of psychoanalysts from a clinical conference, without really knowing why I felt shadowed by something that made me anxious until we went to the remains of the psychoanalyst Georg Groddeck's summer house which had been destroyed, we were told, when the forest was set alight to flush out the fleeing Nazis.

This time no one leaves.

But, when the screening ends and Akerman is introduced to take questions, hostility bursts out. Someone comments on the way the film supposedly "silences" its subjects, does "violence" to them in not allowing them the opportunity to speak "for themselves."

The assumption here seemed to be that the spoken word would give greater access to truth than the corporeal language of movement, gesture, expression. Besides, it is said, though I can find no reference to it, that Akerman once remarked that "interviews in film only make television." And what would they have said, anyway, that we can't already apprehend ourselves from their faces and gestures, which seemed to me to speak so eloquently in their silent impassivity and their habitual guardedness. The shame of intellectuals (illegally) selling packets of spaghetti and other

[14] Akerman, "A propos d'est', in the pamphlet *De l'autre coté, Sud, D'Est, trois films de Chantal Akerman*, (Paris: Chloé Lorenzi, nd).
[15] Roland Barthes, *The Rustle of Language*, trans. Richard Howard (Berkeley: University of California Press, 1989).

foodstuffs in improvised street markets is palpable and exquisitely painful, even (or especially?) to me, who has daily witnessed the destruction of the university, the transformation of students into customers and the disintegration of teachers into frustrated functionaries.

And as if Akerman's entire oeuvre hasn't been, in some way, about the inadequacy of language, the affect-laden but emptied of content repetitions and clichés of *News From Home*, or, in a different way, the recycled jokes and anecdotes of *Histoires d'Amérique*.[16] Dialogue in all these films is spare, sparse and intermittent. In *Les Rendez-vous d'Anna* (1978) especially, speech almost never reaches its destination, seemingly unable to perform the phatic work of binding me to you, of making *us*. Shifters seem only to mark absence, even when someone says "I am here" because of the ambiguity of context of the shifter "here": here in the empty room, where the phone rings and the machine picks up, or here elsewhere, from where the voice is speaking? Conversations are one-sided, or else they are what the French call *dialogues de sourds,* where people speak past each other and there is no possibility of metalinguistic clarification. And yet understanding doesn't completely fail: it just can't be put into words—as if people speak a language they know but cannot translate, an analogue for traumatic knowing without knowing what it is we know, or even that we know.

Akerman's is a gaze not uninvolved. It is drawn by what attracts it, but not caught up in events, situations, people. Semi-detached. Her camera acts as a conductor to an audience whose responses are not programmed for us by the momentum of narrative or by the presentation of "characters," documentary or otherwise, nor conditioned by the conventions of the roots movie Akerman ironically references in voice over, since we are given no indication of what might be personal in the film's material. There is a certain openness allowed us here: an expectation even that our (in)attention will be selective, both dreaming and reflective.[17]

---

[16] See Akerman, quoted in Janet Bergstrom, *Endless Night: Cinema and Psychoanalysis, Parallel Histories* (Berkeley: University of California Press, 1999), 276: "Because they [people of her parents' generation] did not transmit their histories, I searched for a false memory, a kind of imaginary, reconstructed memory […] The jokes were told because life was unbearable. It was a way of denying what happened through mockery, keeping it at a distance by making fun of it. When history becomes unbearable, you stage your own misery and laugh at it."

[17] This is the kind of floating attention solicited by choreographer Pina Bausch, in her dance performances (about which Akerman has made several films), in which occasionally a fragment of narrative might seem to manifest itself, but incomplete, truncated, an arc only partially described.

Part of the experience of watching *D'Est* is the experience of your own assumptions revising themselves, the awareness of your own feelings as they shade subtly into something else, some other feeling. Your relation to what you are watching shifting, reconfiguring. It is like seeing in action the work of exemplarity undone by detail, as each new detail offered in the image qualifies other details, shifting the whole to be inferred from all these details sideways. Here, one detail cannot stand for the whole; cannot represent it. Details form a sequence that adds up to no totality, nor finds any order in narrative. This is, rather, an open-ended account(ing) in which one more detail could transform the whole picture. It is this proliferation of details without exemplarity that allows particular moments of the film to resonate affectively with different people, some of whom may have no other contact with the trauma of the Holocaust or that of the partition of Germany than the associational link with a single detail that resonates with their own traumatic scenes.

What resonated for me most at the time of writing was the scene in which intellectuals were shown as completely *déclassés*, depressed, and silent. I remembered watching Akerman's film during a trip to a city that was full of memories of my own postgraduate work, of a time when ideas mattered, when a shopkeeper might know the name of your supervisor (and not simply as a celebrity). That 2003 trip was an all-too short escape from what I had been experiencing as an extremely hostile work environment in the wake of a major restructure. Now, in 2012, at another moment of crisis in the institution, and more iatrogenic restructuring, these memories are entwined with others involving discussions about the film with a colleague who spent time in Berlin before the fall of the Wall, and since. She tells me that her impression is that in East Germany everyone worked and everyone had a sense of belonging and purpose. It was only after reunification that people became unemployed and dislocated and lost any sense of their own value. It doesn't quite fit with our idea of the social disease of the Stasi and repression, but everyone I have spoken to talks about very strong family life and very close communal relationships in the former East, she tells me. I wonder, she continues, if they see "impassiveness" as a public position very far from the daily experience of living in the east?[18]

A few months after this discussion we find ourselves in Berlin together, trying to set up a project that forms part of our plan for how to survive ever-worsening conditions at work and to be able to do the research and writing that is so important to each of us. We go together to the Mauer

[18]Anne Rutherford, private conversation.

museum and thrill at the ingenuity of various means of escape from the East: tunnels, home-made submarines, home-made flying machines, balloons, shopping bags containing babies, secret spaces built into cars… Afterwards we laugh maniacally, and neither of us actually articulates what is so clearly in the air between us: an intensely felt resonance between these forms of ingenuity and our own project of escape.

Then, to show me the other side of the German Democratic Republic (GDR), the side she apprehends through her friends that lived there, my friend takes me to a "nostalgia" restaurant where East German food is served in an unrenovated setting. I'm keen to see this, though the last thing I (who have fallen prey to the decadent worship of chefs) want to do is eat there. It turns out to be closed. I'm not sure whether I'm sorry or relieved.

Since that moment, nostalgia has come to form another point of resonance between my imaginings about the GDR (formed on the basis of Akerman's images, and haunted, in turn, by her familial experience of the Holocaust) and, in a completely different register, my experience of the contemporary university. Academics who resist some of the neoliberal "reforms" in universities are constantly accused of nostalgia for a past that—almost by definition—never existed. The institutionalized misogyny of sexual harassment, the routine sexual exploitation of female students by male academics, and the rule of the God Professors are all cited as evidence that the past was never perfect.

If I was to admit to nostalgia, I would say that it was for a single aspect of the brief period in the very early 1980s when the feminist forms of resistance to such things made for intense and sustaining forms of collegiality, and for a great deal of intellectual pleasure. I remember three of us being so annoyed by the way the men at meetings droned on to each other and ignored us, that my two women colleagues and I decided to knit our way through the meetings, knowing how irritated our male colleagues would be by this. It turned out to be more incendiary than we could have predicted—partly because I, who was no expert knitter and used needles the size of broomsticks and two balls of wool at once, found my production growing at such a rate that I had to carry the work around with me in a giant green garbage bag. We soon had their attention, and we used it. Those two female colleagues taught me how to teach, and they also taught me, as we collaborated on panels for conferences, that intellectual excitement could be knitted together with the sensual pleasures of eating, drinking and dressing.

Now, just sometimes, I am tempted to say that I preferred the days when campuses were places of sexual desire, no matter that it so often (though not always) played out in asymmetrical ways between men as teachers and women as students, to the dispirited desireless deserts that pedagogical relations have become today. And I especially preferred them to a time when state of the art policy against discrimination and sexual harassment simply serves as window-dressing, or a kind of decorative wrought-iron curtain distracting attention from the new neoliberal forms of discrimination, bullying and harassment (there are also policies dealing with the latter two) that are becoming so familiar.

Eventually, as women became less of a minority, at least in the Humanities (and is this simply coincidental?), decision-making committees were progressively turned into consultative committees whose recommendations were more often than not ignored so that participation came to feel increasingly futile. This situation, and the bigger picture within which it is embedded, has formed the background mood of distress and disaffection that increasingly characterizes university life for many.[19] It is the local effect of all this that has shaped my own experience, producing alternating anger, distress and fear, contrasted with rare

[19] In the 1970s, however, a crack opened by feminism allowed women to move into the university in greater numbers, bringing with them, often (though admittedly not always), a commitment to greater democracy and to transparency in the decision-making processes of the institution. In Australia, this moment, which coincided with the Whitlam reforms that made tertiary education free, was quickly overtaken by the Dawkins reforms of the 1980s, which abolished the two tier tertiary system to facilitate wider access to universities. This last reform, however, produced all manner of unintended consequences, inaugurating an endless process of institutional merger and restructure which most affected newer and less well-resourced universities, but did not leave the more established, wealthier universities untouched either. The Howard decade saw a progressive defunding of the universities combined with a ramping up of rhetoric against academics (classed, along with various other groups, as latte-drinking or chardonnay-sipping elites). It also saw dramatic changes to the working lives of academics, with increasing amounts of time given to administration despite shrinking staff-student ratios, and it placed the onus on academics to fund their own research by means of Australian Research Council Discovery grants (with a success rate of about 18% in the Humanities) or partnerships with industry. Most recently, the uncapping of university places and rise of MOOCS ("massive online open courses") has intensified a process in which research and teaching have come uncoupled (research, it seems, is henceforth to be carried out at some universities, anyway, by a privileged few in dedicated centers or on research-only appointments); administrative staff have come to outnumber academic staff (again, more in some institutions than others); face to face teaching is in rapid decline and education has become ever more commodified and instrumentalized. Moreover, restructuring and cost-cutting has produced a series of waves of so-called "voluntary redundancies" in Australian universities over the last 5 years.

experiences of joy in moments of agency and collegiality. Most depressing, though, is the abject state of resignation and learned helplessness into which so many academics have fallen. Like frogs tossed into a pot of lukewarm water which is then put on the burner and slowly heated, so the frogs don't realize what is happening to them and don't try to escape, they have been unable to protest effectively against change, have become passive and quietist, hostages to a culture of fear.[20] When I think about this, it is the impassive, resigned faces of *D'Est* that come to mind, even though in actuality the faces of my colleagues hardly ever show that expression. In reality, in fact, they hardly ever show: the corridors are empty most of the time, and the doors to empty offices are firmly closed. People go in, do what they have to do, and leave. When I go there I feel the way I felt watching *D'Est*. There is the something of the glacial feeling of the camp in this institutional emptiness. It took the writing of this paper to recognize that feeling, though my body had already made the connection. The spaces of the institution are stark and desolate, even though the walls are hung with artworks. Of course, they are artworks made by the redundant staff of the "too expensive" and now defunct art school.

Many colleagues don't recognize the signatures on the works in the corridors; they don't recognize the artist in the work. No one wants to hear the history: that's all in the past. The affective withdrawal of so many colleagues means they are also blind and deaf to present distress. They have erected an unbreachable "empathic wall" between themselves and it, and this only increases the sense the rest of us have of going unheard and unrecognized, a sense so pervasive in traumatic states.[21] The university of the present could be described as a zone in which loss of communal and institutional memory has produced traumatic amnesia—traumatic, at least, for those who have been marginalized as institutions attempt to change the culture of the university by changing the personnel. Where there is memory now, it is corporate. It is memory as "RAM, not ROM,"[22] obliterated when the system goes down, and sometimes by design.

*

[20] Perhaps this fear is not unrealistic, given the penchant of universities everywhere for sacking those who criticize their management.

[21] Donald Nathanson, *Shame and Pride: Affect, Sex and the Birth of the Self* (New York and London: WW Norton, 1992).

[22] Brett Neilson "Data, Zone, Territory," position paper, *Data, Memory, Territory* 1 (http//digitalmediaresearch.org, 2012), 16.

The idea of a traumatic circuitry begs the question of how to break such circuits. This question becomes particularly acute in relation to the university, a large part of whose *raison d'être* is, after all, the formal transmission of culture, and therefore of cultural memory. Karyn Ball suggests that we risk passing on incapacitating melancholy identifications to students—and, I would add, independently of what is ostensibly taught.[23] Of course it's hard not to do this when we recognize how few jobs there are, and how the conditions of academic work are changing almost beyond recognition, especially in the newer, less wealthy institutions than, say Cambridge in the UK, or the Ivy Leagues of the US. Shoshana Felman once wrote powerfully about the way the pedagogical face to face positioned the teacher as analysand, and the student body as analyst, who diagnose the teacher's own implication in what is being taught.[24] On the one hand, this is precisely the problem Ball identifies, on the other, it is too much to expect of our students that they perform the repair work of the analyst for us, rather than for themselves, as Felman envisages they do. Ball suggests that the rise of the affect paradigm in the Humanities is tied to the melancholy of an "unfulfilled longing for public respect," and that affect "stands in for an auratic sense of a presence-in-knowledge that has diminished with the rationalization of academic labor."[25] That resonates with me, especially when I remember the juncture at which I simultaneously decided to do clinical training as a psychodynamic psychotherapist in an affect-oriented modality (in part in the light of the demand of the university to do empirical rather than scholarly research), and discovered the work of Tomkins via Eve Sedgwick and Adam Frank's edited collection of his writings.[26] In Australia I think the Howard decade also impelled a new consideration of the non-rational in politics—certainly the rise of Pauline Hanson in 1999 made that urgent for me.[27] Ball's critique notwithstanding, affect theory, it seems to me, can help us out of potential capture by melancholic identification, and the silencing culture of fear in so many universities, where criticizing management seems increasingly to lead to charges of serious misconduct and ultimately to dismissal.

---

[23] Karyn Ball "The Longing for the Material," *Differences: A Journal of Feminist Cultural Studies* 17, no. 1 (2006).

[24] Shoshana Felman, "Psychoanalysis and Education: Teaching Terminable and Interminable," *Yale French Studies*, 63 (1982).

[25] Ball, "Longing," 78.

[26] Eve Kosofsky Sedgwick and Adam Frank, *Shame and Its Sisters: A Silvan Tomkins Reader* (Durham: Duke University Press, 1995).

[27] Anna Gibbs, "Pauline Hanson and the Epidemiology of Affect," *The Australian Humanities Review,* http://www.lib.latrobe.edu.au/AHR/gibbs.htm 2001.

If this writing is an attempt to articulate the process by which traumatic experience is concatenated in the temporality of the everyday, it is in the hope that understanding this particular non-rational process will help ameliorate it by enabling the undoing of melancholic identification to open the way for other more challenging but ultimately more life-affirming identifications, and to a regained sense of agency. In so doing, it attempts to take up what Ned Rossiter identifies as the "challenge for biopolitical labor," which "will be to assert the autonomy of the common from emergent apparatuses of capture," as he writes in the *Edu-Factory* journal.[28] By "the common" he means a creative force arising out of biopolitical labor, rather than a pre-existing resource (like "the commons"). "The common" is a form of surplus value which capital seeks to expropriate by its "apparatuses of capture" (of which melancholic identification and being silenced by the culture of fear are examples) or "regimes of measure," which melancholy and silence prevent us adequately resisting. Rossiter writes that "the affirmation of the common is offered as a condition of possibility for collaborative constitution, for the sharing of affects of love, solidarity or wrath, and for the translation of such affects and experiences across the 'irreducible idiomaticity' of ethico-political practices."[29] Essential to such affirmation is the capacity to jam the circuitry of traumatic stress and put a stop to the process of concatenation, and recovering the linkages forced by affective resonance across diverse scenes might be one way to do this. More important though, might be the generation of countervailing affects that tend to produce a sense of agency rather than melancholic paralysis or the freeze or flight response to fear.

At my own institution, the establishment (by a group of unknown individuals) of UWS Dissenter, a blog site which facilitates anonymous (but moderated) commentary on the effects of the corporatization of the university on the everyday lives of those who teach and study there has made a small but palpable difference to the capacity of staff to resist the latest round of cuts and the particular vision of the university these are intended to bring about. Satirical pieces produce the joy of recognition among readers, give rise to laughter and provide a powerful antidote to melancholy. For the writer they must surely revive the "sense of presence-in-knowledge" gone missing elsewhere. They may on occasion run the risk of the "foreshortened critique." This is a process in which the larger processes and contradictions which inflate administration and capital

---

[28] Ned Rossiter, "The Informational University, the Uneven Distribution of Expertise and the Racialization of Labour," *Edu-Factory Journal* 0 (January 2010), 71. http://www.edu-factory.org/wp/wp-content/uploads/2011/08/Rossiter.pdf
[29] Ibid., 64.

investment and deflate teaching resources are obscured by the belief in the personal culpability of the individuals in place, identified by one contributor, but the laughter to which they give rise is a circuit-breaker which creates a sense of communion and feelings of agency rather than incapacitated isolation. In itself this blog will not produce change, but it does help create the condition of possibility for meaningful resistance to traumatic concatenation and beyond that, to the particular local "Organizational Changes" which would further instantiate the neoliberal university.

CHAPTER SIX

TORTUROUS AFFECT: WRITING AND THE PROBLEM OF PAIN

MICHAEL RICHARDSON

1.

"It would be totally senseless to try and describe here the pain that was inflicted on me," writes Jean Améry of his torture by the Nazis.

> Was it 'like a red-hot iron in my shoulders,' and was another 'like a dull wooden stake that had been driven into the back of my head'? One comparison would only stand for the other, and in the end we would be hoaxed by turn on the hopeless merry-go-round of figurative speech. The pain was what it was. Beyond that there is nothing to say.[1]

Here Améry points to a double injury: representation fails, even as his pain is shown to be something he alone can experience. Or as he puts it, such feelings of pain "mark the limit of the capacity of language to communicate."[2] What Améry seems to arrive at is a kind of futility: the pain was what it was, and what it was is indescribable. This is not, of course, futility of spirit or lack of courage, but a futility inherent to the relation between language and pain. Figural language cannot do justice to his experience of torture; there remains an irreducible gap between what his body knows and what words can express. Perhaps Améry simply finds himself at the vanishing point of representation, where the signs of language cannot do justice to that for which they stand.

The incommunicability or unsharability of the pain of torture at which Améry arrives is not a side effect, argues Elaine Scarry, but constitutive of its harmfulness.

---

[1] Jean Améry, *At the Mind's Limits: Contemplations by a Survivor on Auschwitz and Its Realities*, trans. Sidney Rosenfeld and Stella P. Rosenfeld (Bloomington, IN: Indiana University Press, 1980), 33.

[2] Ibid.

> Physical pain does not simply resist language but actively destroys it, bringing about an immediate reversion to a state anterior to language, to the sounds and cries a human being makes before language is learned.[3]

This is why pain is such a radical demarcation of self and other. "To have pain is to have *certainty*; to hear about pain is to have *doubt*."[4] It is what it is, at once known and unknowable. In Scarry's famous formulation, pain makes and unmakes the world.

Not only does Améry's pain refuse description, his torture performs that very destruction of language to which he succumbs. Torture proves how absolutely real and singular his pain is. It makes him witness to the inexpressibility of his own pain. Or as Scarry puts it, "torture also mimes (objectifies in the external environment) this language-destroying capacity in its interrogation, the purpose of which is not to elicit needed information but to visibly deconstruct the prisoner's voice."[5] There is an inescapable logic to Scarry's forceful and eloquent analysis of the pain of torture. Torture not only sharpens the distinction between self and other, it violently reasserts the unbridgeable difference between subject and object. In rendering the subject object, torture reinstates the absolute nature of each position: one can only be subject or object, signifier or signified. To try to speak or write the pain of torture is thus to rage against an incommensurable gap between language and experience.

Yet perhaps the problem is not simply that representation reaches its limits, but that its conceptual inadequacies as a theoretical frame for expression are radically and irrevocably exposed. Perhaps the problem resides in ontology, in distinguishing so resolutely between self and other, subject and object. Perhaps thinking *between-ness* instead of *separateness* will reveal something both of this incommensurability and of the capacity for art in general, and fiction in particular, to both say something other than "it was what it was" and avoid the hopeless figurative comparisons that so concerned Améry.

This essay, then, is an act of speculative thinking and a response to the notion that language must fall short before the pain of torture. It is not a denial of Améry's contention about the limits of language, but rather an attempt to think this problem into fiction. Améry, after all, is in the midst of his own testimony when he says that it would be "totally senseless to try and describe here the pain that was inflicted on [him]." My concern is to

---

[3] Elaine Scarry, *The Body in Pain: The Making and Unmaking of the World* (New York: Oxford University Press, 1985), 4.

[4] Ibid., 13.

[5] Ibid., 19-20.

consider how creative practice might approach this problem in writing, and in doing so to think pain differently to the structure established by Scarry. My intention in this respect is not to supplant testimony, but rather to consider how fiction might approach writing torture. I should be clear, then, that I—unlike Améry—am not a torture survivor. While this essay seeks to explore the writing of torture from "within" the act, it does so from within the writing of fictive, literary testimony of the kind considered by Shoshana Felman and Dori Laub in their book *Testimony*.[6]

2.

That torture should feature so prominently in the American response to 9/11 is hardly surprising.[7] Torture, as Darius Rejali so persuasively shows, was and is pervasive in democracies, whether in the form of confessions beaten out of criminals by police or in the name of national security, as is the case in the war on terror.[8] What is startling is not so much its American resurgence (the Algerians, Irish, and many others will attest to the extreme actions that purportedly democratic governments will take given certain circumstances), but that its necessity has been so openly debated and—by virtue of that necessity—all too readily legitimized by significant numbers of thinkers and policymakers.[9] No doubt such positions are spurred on by

---

[6] Shoshana Felman and Dori Laub, *Testimony: Crises of Witnessing in Literature, Psychoanalysis, and History* (New York: Routledge, 1992), 108. For further discussion of the ethics of writing torture, and the relationship between literary and eyewitness testimony, see Michael Richardson, "Who speaks? Torture and the ethics of voice " *TEXT* 16, no. 1 (2012).

[7] My intention is not to show how so-called "enhanced interrogation" techniques constitute torture. In my view, it is clear from the extensive literature on the subject that many of these techniques are torture when used separately and that together they unquestionably constitute torture on the part of the United States. The fact that defenders of such techniques by and large resort to arguments about the efficacy of torture demonstrates the extent to which the various euphemisms employed by the US military and intelligence services are little more than legal sophistry.

[8] Darius M. Rejali, *Torture and Democracy* (Princeton: Princeton University Press, 2007).

[9] Alan M. Dershowitz, *Why Terrorism Works* (Connecticut: Yale University Press, 2002); Mirko Bagaric and Julie Clarke, *Torture: When the Unthinkable is Morally Permissible* (Albany, NY: State University of New York Press, 2007); as well as various arguments and supporters noted in Michael Plaxton, "Justifying Absolute Prohibitions on Torture as if Consequences Mattered," in *Warrior's Dishonour: Barbarity, Morality and Torture in Modern Warfare*, ed. George Kassimeris (Hampshire, UK: Ashgate, 2006).

fear (and even perverse forms of patriotic love and grief), yet they also indicate a profound willingness to elide the "world-destroying" pain of torture.[10] Paradoxically, it is as if the sheer unknowability of such pain, its capacity to erase language, were enough to excise pain itself from certain discourses of torture's legitimacy.

In the aftermath of 9/11 this problem of pain was to be found right at the heart of the American state. As the now-notorious Bybee Memo to then White House Counsel Alberto R. Gonzales states:

> torture is not the mere infliction of pain or suffering on another, but is instead a step well removed. The victim must experience intense pain or suffering of the kind that is equivalent to the pain that would be associated with serious physical injury so severe that death, organ failure, or permanent damage resulting in a loss of significant body function will likely result.[11]

Leaving aside the obvious moral repugnancy of such a definition (let alone the pages of pedantic consideration that precede it), the incommunicability of pain actually enables the legitimation, however spurious, of torture. Phrases such as "of the kind that is equivalent" and "would be associated" defer knowing into likeness—they are so indeterminate as to be almost meaningless. Yet where Améry and Scarry find tragic the failure of language to account for awful experience, Bybee and his masters see an opportunity for the justification of violence. In this, the authorization of American torture performs the distinction between the subject of torture (who becomes object), and the torturer, whose agency is vastly and willfully expanded by exerting power over another.

Many would argue that resistance must occur first and foremost in the purely political arena. President Obama has, as of 2012, made some headway in that regard, such as banning most aspects of "enhanced interrogation." But there is, it seems to me, a crucial role for cultural and philosophical response. If Jack Bauer of the television drama *24* can help sanitize and legitimize torture,[12] then it is possible for other cultural responses to express something of the awful price of torture in the war on terror. Film, perhaps because the cinematic image, diagetic sound and

---

[10] Scarry, *Pain,* 29.

[11] Cited in David Cole, *Torture Memos: Rationalizing the Unthinkable* (Oxford: Oneworld, 2009), 56.

[12] Jinee Lokaneeta, "A rose by another name: legal definitions, sanitized terms, and imagery of torture in *24*," *Law, Culture and the Humanities* 6, no. 2 (2010); Elspeth Van Veeren, "Interrogating 24: making sense of US counterterrorism in the global war on terrorism," *New Political Science* 31, no. 3 (2009).

musical scores allow modes of expression other than language, has more readily confronted torture.[13] My interest here, however, is not to consider what film can do, nor to ask—as interesting as the question is—what social, political or psychological factors might be at work in the paucity of fiction on American torture and the war on terror. Rather, I want to examine why it is that literature finds torture, its intimate violence and traumatic remnants, so difficult to write—and consider how that writing might be reconceived to better bring torture and its pain into the ambit of fiction.

3.

Améry: "Pain, we said, is the most extreme intensification imaginable of our bodily being. But maybe it is even more, that is: death."[14] This proximity to death is what makes the pain of torture so devastating and totalizing, yet also contains its political risk. For the state that has no regard for the death of its victims—and there have been many such regimes—this is of far less concern than it is to the state that writes legal memoranda designed to define torture out of existence. For the United States, the survival of its detainees—even those Defense Secretary Rumsfeld called "the worst of the worst"—was (and is) crucial.[15] Perhaps this is why the tortures of the United States rarely work only through pain.

Consider the detainee at Guantánamo Bay, Bagram, Abu Ghraib or one of the CIA black sites scattered around the globe. Waterboarding works on and through fear: in the first instance a fear of death and then a fear of the event itself, a fear of fearing death. The muscles contract, spasm. The victim chokes, heaves up water. The body shrinks away yet is bound in place. The torturer fears too. Fear of what the other might know fuels the desire to break the victim, and yet the torture fears failing, falling short, never knowing. The detainee, stripped naked, feels shame and humiliation. Not only is the naked body exposed to the gaze of others, it is helpless

---

[13] Classic films such as *Death and the Maiden* (1994) and *The Battle of Algiers* (1966) have torture as a central theme. In recent years, Hollywood films such as *Syriana* (2005) and *Rendition* (2007) have also critiqued torture. In addition, there are numerous documentaries about American detention and torture, including *The Road to Guantanamo* (2006), *Taxi to the Dark Side* (2007), and *Standard Operating Procedure* (2008).

[14] Améry, *Mind's Limits*, 33.

[15] For Rumsfeld's quote see Scott Horton, "The Worst of the Worst?," *Harper's Magazine*, October 2, 2009, accessed 24 September 2012, http://harpers.org/blog/2009/10/the-worst-of-the-worst/.

before that gaze. The victim tries to turn away, to hide the shame, but cannot. There is no place to turn in a tiny cell, interrogation booth or wire cage. The attempt to turn away creates a further exposure. Or, worse still, the detainee may be shackled naked in place, overcome by the desire to hide and yet utterly unable to do so. And if the guard or interrogator is female and the detainee a Muslim male, an added depth is present in the shame. Stress positions involve shame, and even more so disgust. Forced to stand for hours, the detainee defecates and urinates on themselves, feels these excretions on their skin and cannot pull away. Disgust, too, in the moment of confession—the self-disgust of the detainee who has betrayed friends, or lied to end the torture. Torturer and jailers look on, lips curling at the abject victim, humanity stripped slowly away. Then there is the impression in the detainee's face from an open hand slap, just hard enough to hurt, not hard enough to signal anything other than contempt. Pain is here too. Bursting lungs that fill with water. Feet and ankles swelling while the back aches, jabs shooting through muscle. Sting in the cheek where the hand has struck. But it is shame, fear, disgust and contempt that amplify pain, resonate with one another, bring the body in all its fullness and knowledge of the world into the ambit of torture.

Pain is never pain alone. No small part of the horror of torture is that when the pain recedes, when its extreme intensification of bodily being is no longer total, more awaits. That *more*—shame, fear, disgust, contempt—is not simply more within the body. It is a *more than body* that holds the possibility of conceiving both torture and pain in a way that is, I want to suggest, less resistant to expression.

4.

A body encounters itself, encounters other bodies, encounters the world. Such encounters are *events*. "Nothing is prefigured in the event," writes Brian Massumi. "It is the collapse of structured distinction into intensity, rules into paradox."[16] For Massumi, the event is a way of thinking existence.

> Every event is singular. It has an arc that carries it through its phases to a culmination all its own: a dynamic unity no other event can have in just

[16] Brian Massumi, *Parables for the Virtual: Movement, Affect, Sensation*, (Durham: Duke University Press, 2002), 27.

> this way. The unity of the occasion is the just-this-way in which the phases of the arced unfolding hold together as belonging to the same event.[17]

Or, to put this differently, every event creates the new, even when it repeats or destroys. Indeed, in repetition there is always the prior occurrence(s), and the very fact of each following instance being thus related to the prior one(s) gives it new distinctiveness.[18] Newness, in this reading, is not so much amoral as outside any order of morality. It simply is, although not *is*, not *being*—newness becomes.

Conceiving of the encounter of bodies as event means seeing bodies differently; not as fixed and bounded entities, but as both actually existing and always potentially something else. "The body is as immediately virtual as it is actual. The virtual, the pressing crowd of incipiencies and tendencies, is a realm of *potential.*"[19] To say that nothing is prefigured is not to say that what bodies might become is without constraint. This is why Massumi writes of tendencies that press and crowd the body. Tendencies are what the future makes of the past, more than the body.

What does *more than the body* mean?

Affect, then, is the relational stuff of encounter, its forces and capacities. It is precisely that which is always in formation, not yet concrete; potential, always exceeding the body's actual. It is the substance of relationality, that which connects body to body, body to itself, world to body. Affect is both of and more than the body. "Actually existing, structured things live in and through that which escapes them," writes Brian Massumi. "Their autonomy is the autonomy of affect."[20] Thus the capacity or power of a body is its ability to affect and be affected.[21] This is the conception Deleuze follows (including in his work with Guattari). Affect, understood in the Deleuzian sense, is concerned primarily with potential and the capacity for becoming, for bodies to change in encounter. For Deleuze and Guattari, affect operates with particular force in art; indeed, affect (rather than concept) is central to how art thinks.[22]

---

[17] Brian Massumi, *Semblance and Event: Activist Philosophy and the Occurrent Arts* (Cambridge, Mass: The MIT Press, 2011), 3.

[18] Deleuze discusses the relationship between repetition and singularity in detail throughout *Difference and Repetition*, trans. Paul Patton (London: Continuum, 2004). Massumi's philosophy draws heavily on Deleuze's work, both alone and with Guattari.

[19] Massumi, *Parables*, 30, emphasis in original.

[20] Ibid., 35.

[21] Ibid., 15.

[22] Gilles Deleuze and Felix Guattari, *What Is Philosophy?*, trans. Hugh Tomlinson and Graham Burchell (New York: Columbia University Press, 1994).

If Deleuze and Guattari, and Massumi following them, offer one perspective on affect, a substantively different conception is that of Silvan Tomkins. For Silvan Tomkins, affects are discrete, specific and biological.[23] He identifies nine affects—shame-humiliation, distress-anguish, fear-terror, enjoyment-joy, interest-excitement, contempt-disgust, surprise-startle, anger-rage, dissmell[24]— which are not quite the emotions with which they share names but involuntary, pre-cognitive and visceral experiences felt on and in the body. Crucially, however, Tomkins' affects are always in response to the body—one's own, or that of another. They are concerned with the experience of *this body here* in relation to both other bodies and the world. What Tomkins describes would be sensation within the Deleuzian approach, and thus there is no easy fit between the two conceptions. Nor do I wish to propose one. My interest is, rather, in what might productively be done with their resonance. Roughly speaking, if what Deleuze does is enable an understanding of bodies within the world as intimately connected and connectable, Tomkins reveals something of the specific nature of those connections in lived experience. Both approaches show that when thinking affect, "a body is as much outside itself as in itself—webbed in relations—until ultimately such firm distinctions cease to matter."[25]

As much as affect is relationality, it is also intensity; never uniform or static, the forcefulness of affect varies. Some bodies have more capacity to affect, others to be affected. Yet affect is not a synonym for communicability: a relation can negate, limit, cut off. A relation of negation is as possible as one of unification, and equally binding. Nor is affect without constraint. Potential is always tied to the actual, and thus context matters. Tortured and torturer affect and are affected differently. Affect's between-ness and beside-ness, its more-than, is experienced differently by different bodies. One person places the black cloth over the face of another, the body whose eyes widen white, pulse racing. One body is disgusted at seeing the other naked; one is shamed by being stripped bare. "With heart and soul they went about their business," writes Améry

[23] Silvan S. Tomkins, *Affect, Imagery, Consciousness, Vol 1, The Positive Affects*, (New York: Springer, 1962) and *Affect, Imagery, Consciousness, Vol. 2, The Negative Affects* (New York; London: Springer; Tavistock, 1963).

[24] Tomkins sees affects as operating along spectrums of intensity, hence the pairings of terms. Dissmell, a later addition to his affect theory, is similar to what might commonly be called revulsion.

[25] Melissa Gregg and Gregory J. Seigworth, "An Inventory of Shimmers" in *The Affect Theory Reader*, ed. Melissa Gregg and Gregory J. Seigworth (Durham, NC: Duke University Press, 2010), 3.

of his torturers, "and the name of it was power, dominion over spirit and flesh, orgy of unchecked self-expansion."[26] Or in Scarry's words:

> It is the intense pain that destroys a person's self and world, a destruction experienced spatially as either the contraction of the universe down to the immediate vicinity of the body or as the body swelling to fill the entire universe.[27]

Certain bodies expanding, unchecked, to fill the world into which another is thrown. Others contracting. Affect spilling over, potential for the destruction of the world felt—bodily felt—on the skin of the tortured. Think of the tortures of the war on terror—waterboarding, stress positions, sleep deprivation, sensory assault. Think of Tomkins' affects, their taking hold of the body before the brain knows. In each instance the impact of affect is amplified by the restraint of the body's desired response. What might have been a brief expression is prolonged indefinitely. The only possibility is that affects remain, staying on and in the body. There is no turning away, no shrinking back, no recoil that can return the victim to any kind of affective equilibrium.

"Affect *is* the whole world: from the precise angle of its differential emergence."[28] Bodies in event, beyond the limits of the skin and the fixities of language.

5.

What happened to the subject and object? They are absent, but not quite gone; not defined out of existence, but shifted in their ontological status. "*There is no subject separate from the event.*"[29] Neither cognitive nor discursive, Massumi's activist philosophy resituates subjectivity. The subject is what finds itself in the middle of the event, experiencing its occurrence. Objects take new form too, which is to say that object-ness is neither inherent to any entity nor granted by the subject. "Subject and object are given *operative* definitions by pragmatism [...] Subject and object are grasped directly as variations—not only of themselves but of each other."[30] This resituating is both more drastic and subtler than it might appear at first glance. "Thought and thing, subject and object, are

---

[26] Améry, *Mind's Limits,* 36.
[27] Scarry, *Pain,* 35.
[28] Massumi, *Parables*, 43.
[29] Massumi, *Semblance,* 8.
[30] Massumi, *Semblance*, 31.

not separate entities or substances. They are irreducibly temporal *modes of relation to experience itself.*"[31]

Now something of the significance of affect becomes clear. Affect can be understood not only as a conception of relation and intensity but constitutive, at least in part, of an ontology—what Massumi terms an ontogenetics—that shifts the locus of being from subject and object to experience itself. Relation and intensity, aesthetic and political, virtual and actual—in each, dichotomy is displaced by differential. Enter spectrums of relation rather than unbridgeable division. Emergence of relation, rather than distinction.

Such a move matters, since, as Massumi notes, "the subject-object dichotomy itself has far-reaching consequences. It extends itself into a division between ways of knowing, and from there into a hierarchy between modes of practice."[32] This hierarchy is no esoteric concern. Teresa Brennan, whose critique of psychoanalysis and conception of the transmission of affect shares certain affinities with Silvan Tomkins, argues that:

> whether one insists on the subjective or the objective, whether one believes that the object can be known in itself or for itself, one tacitly assumes the foundational associations between mind, form, activity, will, and the subject, on the one hand, and, on the other, body, matter, passivity, lack of agency, and the object.[33]

Brennan resists such foundational distinctions and recognizes that the subject/object dichotomy is a "lived thing" with significant costs.[34] One such cost might well be how we understand the body in pain.

6.

"Whoever is overcome by pain through torture experiences his body as never before," writes Améry. "In self-negation, his flesh becomes a total reality."[35] Does this mean pain is utterly contained within the body that experiences it? Is the gulf between the pain you feel and I witness, or that I

---

[31] Ibid., 34.
[32] Ibid., 11.
[33] Teresa Brennan, *The Transmission of Affect* (Ithaca: Cornell University Press, 2004), 19.
[34] Ibid., 23.
[35] Améry, *Mind's Limits*, 33.

feel and you witness, too vast ever to know? Is it pure sensation, without affect, or is there an affective dimension to pain?

Simply because the pain of torture is so frequently preceded, followed and penetrated by other affects does not mean it is itself affective. Tomkins conceives of pain as part of an intermediate system between affects and drives, which relates to learning how to manage and respond to affect.[36] Affect can be "about pain" but, implicitly, "pain per se" is distinct from affect.[37] Brennan's approach is similar: affects are crucial in forming judgments about "how to avoid pain and increase pleasure."[38] Comfortable with the singularity of the experience of pain—"Pain is a response of the sympathetic nervous system, and, after all, each body has its own"[39]—she suspects that pain and affect are of a closer order than Tomkins suggests. "It is well known that anxiety 'increases' pain, which leads me to wonder if pain and anxiety are not in some way of the same genus, both composed of the same nerve-racking stuff."[40] If there is some constitutive similarity between anxiety and pain then perhaps some aspect of pain is sharable, *more than* its sensual experience.

Distinctions between sensation and affect can be tricky to navigate, particularly when emotion is added to the terrain. Within the heterogeneous field of affect theory conceptual differences can at times be simply definitional, but at others the nuances of distinction can be revealing. Massumi means something quite precise when he refers to both sensation and emotion—distinct, in each case, from affect. "Sensation is the mode in which potential is present in the perceiving body," as well as its "direct registering."[41] There is an affinity here to that unordered, involuntary aspect of Tomkins' visceral affect. Its aliveness in the skin, its racing through the nervous system, always in that instant before knowing, is nothing if not "sheerness of experience" at the "extremity of perception."[42] For Massumi, an "emotion is a subjective content, the sociolinguistic fixing of the quality of an experience which is from that point onward defined as personal."[43] In other words, emotion is what results from bodily learning, from the playing and replaying of experience, affect complicated

[36] Eve Kosofsky Sedgwick and Adam Frank, *Shame and Its Sisters: A Silvan Tomkins Reader* (Durham: Duke University Press, 1995), 47, 53-4.
[37] Ibid., 52.
[38] Brennan, *Transmission,* 106.
[39] Ibid., 167.
[40] Ibid.
[41] Massumi, *Parables*, 75; 97.
[42] Ibid., 98.
[43] Ibid., 28.

by cognition. Tomkins and Massumi/Deleuze present different taxonomies but both grapple with how to reconceive experience. Massumi's thinking, for all its abstraction, is not un-embodied—it is simply not concerned with the biological specificity that preoccupies Tomkins.

What, then, of pain? Perhaps thinking pain as an aspect of an event, operating across multiple orders of experience—affect, sensation, emotion—offers a way forward. Sara Ahmed notes that pain is usually designated as sensation. But,

> pain is not simply the feeling that corresponds to bodily damage. Whilst pain might seem self-evident—we all know our own pain, it burns through us—the experience and indeed recognition of pain *as pain* involves complex forms of association between sensations and other kinds of 'feeling states'.[44]

For Ahmed, pain is "bound up with how we inhabit the world, how we live in relationship to the surfaces, bodies and objects that make up our dwelling space. Our question becomes not so much what *is* pain, but what *does* pain do."[45] The pain of drowning and the painful explosion in the lungs of a waterboarded detainee are not the same thing. It is what the pain *does* that is its affective quality. If I begin to drown, my relation to my own body might be refigured. Water as weapon, lungs as enemy. Or body revealed in totality, pain awakening self to specificities of form, not dividing but completing. Either way, self-relation: the body in the event of pain cast into sudden relation with its changing experience of being, becoming newly self. Not so in torture. Waterboarding, repeated encounter with virtual death, engenders different relations. A detainee's body is affected by the possibility of its death, awoken to its own frailness, to pain of a similar sensation—choking, heaving, bursting lungs—and yet in an utterly different way to simply drowning. Marched from a cell, strapped in place, a black cloth on his mouth, a hand that tips a canister barely seen against the glare of overhead lights. A voice that questions. This is contingent pain, pain at the hands of another.

What is at stake here is not the unmaking of the world from the position of the subject, but something else. Recall the re-situation of both subject and object from the primacy in which Scarry places them to modes of relation to experience, as "takes" on the event. One body tortures another and "it is through the flow of sensations and feelings that *become*

---

[44] Sara Ahmed, *The Cultural Politics of Emotion* (New York: Routledge, 2004), 23.
[45] Ibid., 27.

conscious as pain and pleasure that different surfaces are established."[46] Transformation of bodies—becoming-tortured, becoming-torturer. More than this, "the experience of pain does not cut off the body in the present, but attaches this body to the world of other bodies, an attachment that is contingent on elements that are absent in the lived experience of pain."[47] What is absent? Precisely between-ness, Massumi's virtual inextricable from the actual. Absent, too, is the potential that it might be my body (some body, your body, even the torturer's body) in pain soon enough. Pain that is not pure affect but affective nonetheless. "The affectivity of pain is crucial to the forming of the body as both a material and lived entity."[48] And it is also vital to some line of flight between the pain of torture and its expression.

7.

It is now necessary to consider what I have so far deliberately excluded from these consideration of events and affects and torture: time. Not only does time matter in the occurrence of these things, it is inescapable in their aftermath.

"It was over for a while. It still is not over."[49] Améry's beautifully simple statement of profound insight. Time figures here in all its folding mutability, over for an indeterminate while, still not over. Temporal aporia, slippery and uncertain. Torture that lives in the traumatized body. "Whoever was tortured, stays tortured," writes Améry. "Torture is ineradicably burned into him, even when no clinically objective traces can be detected."[50] This lasting quality of torture, its presence within the body outside the clinical, its incorporeal yet bodily traces, demands consideration.

This is trauma, described in its classic psychoanalytic terms, in which, as Patricia Clough notes, "trauma makes the past and the future meet without there being a present."[51] Trauma is an event that ruptures the present and later returns, unwanted and unavoidable. It is experience out of time, re-experienced. This shattering of time is critical. Cathy Caruth recognizes that "trauma is not locatable in the simple violent or original event in an individual's past, but rather in the way that its very

---

[46] Ibid., 24.
[47] Ibid., 28.
[48] Ibid., 24.
[49] Améry, *Mind's Limits*, 36.
[50] Ibid., 34.
[51] Patricia Ticiento Clough, "Introduction," in *The Affective Turn: Theorizing the Social*, ed. Patricia Ticiento Clough (Durham: Duke University Press, 2007), 13.

unassimilated nature—the way it was precisely *not known* in the first instance—returns to haunt the survivor later on."[52] This *return* of trauma has important implications for thinking the pain of torture: it is not only the event itself that assaults language, but the traumatic after.

Some resonance with the processual ontology Massumi presents is immediately evident. Events do not occur in an instant, but over time. "Process—event, change, production of novelty, becoming—all imply duration. They are time concepts. Past, present, future are always co-implicating."[53] Trauma, then, might be thought of as an interruption in the arc of an event, the sudden overload of a circuit, an unexpected charge that transforms one becoming into another. The violence of torture leaves its mark in the relations of actual and virtual, of potential, that are always co-constitutive of the body in time. "The body doesn't just absorb pulses or discrete stimulations; it infolds *contexts*, it infolds volitions and cognitions that are nothing if not situated."[54] Dominick LaCapra articulates something similar, despite the grounding of his work in psychoanalysis and deconstructionism. For LaCapra, the undecidability within trauma threatens to "disarticulate relations, confuse self and other, and collapse all distinctions, including that between present and past," through "compulsive repetition of traumatic scenes—scenes in which the past returns and the future is blocked or fantastically caught up in a melancholic feedback loop."[55]

Whether read through pragmatic philosophy, deconstruction, or psychoanalysis, something happens in trauma to infold time. To not simply stutter the relation between time-of-the-body and time-of-the-world but radically disrupt it, to fracture experience and have those fragments cling to bodies, recurring. Negative affects penetrate and take up residence within the traumatized body; "there is something in trauma that permits such affects a permanent entry," says Brennan.[56] As Anna Gibbs writes, "when we see an action performed, the same neural networks that would be involved if we were to perform it ourselves are activated."[57] When

---

[52] Cathy Caruth, *Unclaimed Experience: Trauma, Narrative, and History* (Baltimore: Johns Hopkins University Press, 1996), 4.
[53] Massumi, *Semblance*, 24.
[54] —. *Parables*, 30.
[55] Dominick LaCapra, *Writing History, Writing Trauma* (Baltimore: The Johns Hopkins University Press, 2001), 21.
[56] Brennan, *Transmission*, 48.
[57] Anna Gibbs, "After Affect: Sympathy, Synchrony and Mimetic Communication," in *The Affect Theory Reader*, ed. Melissa Gregg and Gregory J. Seigworth (Durham, NC: Duke University Press, 2010), 196.

negative affects occur at radical intensities their encounter with the body wreaks lasting violence. Such trauma "does not fade […] with time or distance […] it is as if the psyche has incorporated the very structure of abuse in some malformation, which keeps the trauma current by repeating it in the imagination."[58]

Layers and secretions, stratas of the body. Affect sticks to skin, fires neurons, constrains and generates potential, hardens on and in bodies. It is the shared substance of the experience of the traumatic event, the force of its relation between past and future, virtual and actual, understood not as binaries but as poles of experience between which the body fluctuates. Trauma, then, depends on affect in time, pain in time—both its affective and qualitative dimensions. "Pain is not simply an effect of a history of harm; it is the *bodily life of that history*."[59]

Crucially, the event from which trauma springs ruptures the aware experience of the event ending. "The experience of trauma […] would thus seem to consist, not in the forgetting of a reality that can hence never be fully known, but in an inherent latency within the experience itself."[60] This is the shock, the lack of immediate recognition *that this is happening* that begins the traumatic event. This delay works with the destruction of language to submerge the event and its meaning. For meaning to emerge, time is necessary, although whether this will be three days, weeks or years is always unknown. The event occurs, is experienced, and at once deferred. Even as the bare facts emerge, its meaning or the lived experience may remain obscured. This does not mean that its effects are not felt or manifested symptomatically—rather that those symptoms (sleeplessness, flashbacks, fits of anger or grief or paranoia) bear little or no relation to known, meaningful memory. Time allows the sediment of affect to bring out the remnants of the trauma of torture on and in the body. In a very real sense, the event of torture never ends. "The past is living rather than dead; the past lives in the very wounds that remain open in the present."[61]

---

[58] Brennan, *Transmission*, 47-8. Some aspects of this account of affect and trauma draws on previous work of mine. For more, see Michael Richardson, "Writing Trauma: Affected in the Act," *New Writing: The International Journal for the Practice and Theory of Creative Writing*, 10 (2013, forthcoming).`

[59] Ahmed, *Cultural Politics*, 34.

[60] Caruth, *Unclaimed Experience*, 17. To avoid overlaying yet more theoretical terminology, I have excised from this quotation Caruth's reference to the Freudian concept of *latency*. Psychoanalysis, as this essay obliquely shows, provides important contributions to understanding trauma, which are not altogether incongruous with the ideas discussed herein.

[61] Ahmed, *Cultural Politics*, 33.

Perhaps "the *trace* of past actions, *including a trace of their contexts*," is "conserved in the brain and in the flesh, but out of mind and body understood as qualifiable interiorities, active and passive respectively, direct spirit and dumb matter."[62]

When trauma emerges it does so violently, not just on the body but in and on language. Just as the traumatic event is a schism within narrative and a denial of language, so too its return. There is a tension here between the return of the event and the capacity of language to express it, since trauma is exactly that which refuses language in its occurrence. What, then, to make of its return?

In Arthur Koestler's novel *Arrival and Departure*, Peter, a survivor of torture by an unnamed totalitarian regime, wakes from a dream in which he is a "prisoner of empty time" to a "queer, numb feeling in the bend of the knee, round the burn scar"[63] left by his torturers. The leg ceases to respond or have any feeling; Peter is paralyzed. He falls into a fevered sleep in which he explores in dreams and hallucinations the "forgotten islands of his past,"[64] namely his detention and torture. This trauma returns only in fragmentary moments, pieces of the past that refuse to be memory—the past known as the past—and repeatedly surface to take hold of his body. In the narrative that Koestler presents, it is not simply that the present collapses into the past, but that temporality infolds. This fits with LaCapra's description of how "tenses implode" such that "[a]ny duality of time (past and present or future) is experientially collapsed or productive only of aporias and double binds."[65] Peter cannot speak the event that repeatedly takes hold of his body, yet there is no distinction in language between the past event and its present occurrence. "The first three strokes seemed to split his body into two; he had never imagined that flesh could experience such mortal pain and yet survive to feel it, and feel it repeated once more, and again."[66] As Caruth puts it, trauma "is always the story of a wound that cries out, that addresses us in the attempt to tell us of a reality or truth that is not otherwise available."[67]

It is as if something were occurring just beyond the limits of language, an event whose shape is recognizable but which cannot fully enter into words. Representation as an expressive practice, the attempt of language to

---

[62] Massumi, *Parables*, 30, emphasis in original.
[63] Arthur Koestler, *Arrival and Departure* (Harmondsworth, UK: Penguin, 1969), 62; 63.
[64] Ibid., 71.
[65] LaCapra, *Writing*, 21.
[66] Koestler, *Arrival,* 108.
[67] Caruth, *Unclaimed Experience,* 4.

stand in for the event, appears inadequate. It is as if Massumi were writing of such limits of language, a crying out against time destructively infolded, when he says, "Language cannot reach this directly future-feeling limit of thought. But in imagination it can approach it. When it does, words resonate with virtual thought-events lying on the linguistic horizon."[68]

Simply recognizing "the legacy of incomprehensibility at the heart of the catastrophic experience"[69] offers no escape from what Améry calls the "nothing more to say" of torture, the "it was what it was" with which this essay began. Scarry's recognition that language is destroyed in the act of torture does not mean that language returns to the event in its aftermath. The event remains, language erased by pain. But this reading of torture against the grain of the subject/object divide, of articulating its trauma in relation to affect, calls forth something new. What emerges is necessarily incomplete because the totality of the trauma remains unknowable. Yet, I want to suggest, this incompleteness marks out certain silences that speak through their very presence as absence. Such silences are not always negative: they can attest to a refusal to be defined, contained or controlled by torture. In this sense, silence can empower. But it can equally mark out precisely what is terrible in torture: the destruction of voice and a refiguring of the very constitution of the body. "Literature," Caruth famously writes, "is interested in the complex relations between knowing and not knowing."[70] What I have sought to arrive at is something of the substance of those complex relations, and in doing so reach a point at which what literature can do may be (re)imagined.

8.

One of the very few literary novels to address torture and the war on terror is *Orpheus Lost* by Janette Turner Hospital, an Australian-born author who has lived most of her adult life in Canada and the United States.[71] As the title suggests, the novel recasts the Orpheus myth in a post-9/11 context. Terror attacks are occurring in Boston, where Leela is a mathematician at Harvard and her boyfriend Mishka, an Australian of Hungarian extraction, studies music. While much of the novel involves flashbacks to Mishka's childhood in the Daintree Rainforest in north-

---

[68] Massumi, *Semblance*, 122.
[69] Caruth, *Unclaimed Experience*, 4.
[70] Ibid., 3.
[71] Janette Turner Hospital, *Orpheus Lost* (New York: W. W. Norton, 2007). For the remainder of this section, I refer to page numbers in parentheses following quotes.

eastern Australia and Leela's in the American South, the main action centers around Mishka's possible involvement in a subway bombing, his detention and torture, and Leela's search to find him. The novel is laden with weighty themes: Mishka's troubled and ambiguous identity as the son of a refugee mother and a not-as-dead-as-he-thought jihadist father; responsibility for the actions of parents, embodied not just by Mishka but also by Leela and Cobb, the latter her childhood friend turned Special Forces officer and torturer; cultures of fear in contemporary America; the guilty until proven innocent paradigm of national security; questions of guilt and redemption.

Torture first enters the text as a kind of haunting potential, yet strangely lacking in affective impact. Cobb Slaughter, on the hunt for the men behind a bombing on the Boston subway, pulls Leela, the novel's central character, into a secret security center for questioning, to which she responds with all the emotive force of someone taking a telephone survey. No fear, no anxiety, almost no *affect* of which to speak—despite being snatched and hooded, kept alone for hours. She blows kisses, gives a viewing window the finger "in a manner more flirtatious than obscene," and is in "a perfect state of repose" (51). When Cobb enters the room, she is "startled" by his ski mask but otherwise "relaxed" (58). This can be read as a dissociative state, reflected in her failure to "recognize any of the houses" in the neighborhood street to which she is returned (84). Dissociation certainly prefigures the way the text later recounts Mishka's torture, but this also produces an oddly disembodied quality to the writing of torture.

Elaine Scarry notes that pain readily encounters an "as if…" structure of similarity and likeness in language,[72] and this occurs immediately in Mishka's torture in *Orpheus Lost*: "Mostly he was not conscious of breathing but he was conscious of something that felt *like hot skewers in his shoulders*. His wrists were tied together, crosswise, and held in a carpenter's vice. Someone was tightening the vice" (245, emphasis mine). The sensation of pain is immediately deferred, and what follows is bare, direct description. This is characteristic of testimonial accounts of political violence, as I have discussed elsewhere.[73] Tellingly, however, Hospital emphasizes cognition and consciousness, rather than the bodily presence of pain. Still, there is promise here and the next line—"The pain came and went" (245)—and those that follow carry within them something of the

[72] Scarry, *Pain*, 15.

[73] Michael Richardson, "Writing Torture's Remnants," in *Speaking the Unspeakable*, ed. Jeanne Clark and Catherine Collins (Oxford: ID Press, 2013).

erasing force of pain, its collapse of past moments into the present, the body's hunger for release.

But then the body in pain vanishes. "The pain was like a crowded city street," writes Hospital (245), and the simile shifts into metaphor and takes hold of the text. There is a long description of a noisy city street, imagined cars and faces, from which pain resurfaces in the most fleeting of ways: "He could identify one strand of the pain. He became conscious of a savage chafing where the hood was tied" (246). Then his imagined streetscape provides a way out: "the car can drive us away and we can leave your body behind" (246). Here the metaphors perform a dissociation, displacing the pain of torture from experience. Suddenly Mishka is disembodied, in a hallucinatory world, no longer part of torture: "He joined his mother at the window and they stared at the effigy wearing the costume of his body. It was swinging by its wrists from a hook. Its feet did not quite touch the floor. Apart from the hood, it was naked. The light changed, the car moved, and Mishka left his effigy behind" (246-7). He hears screams and wonders if they are his own or from the next cell. Then he is literally returned to a pre-traumatic past into which the present intrudes only briefly via the questions of his torturer, and sparse and sparing glimpses of "burning shoulders" and the "tightening vice" (247). The torturer, too, is replaced by "the voice of a hostile schoolteacher and Mishka was being caned again and again," which again defers the violent present to the remembered past (250). Torturer becomes schoolteacher, an almost impossible diminution.

When Mishka returns to the present he has become something other than himself. At one point he identifies as Prometheus (252), then as Orpheus (253). His torturer, too, becomes a mythical figure. "[Mishka] tried to explain that he had not descended into the dark world of Cerberus to steal secrets" (253). His pain becomes the pain of mythic fantasy. "Cerberus growled and continued to tear at Mishka's flesh. Mishka's wings—he was suspended in flight, his wings caught in a tree perhaps, or in a net—were dislocated along the muscle where his feathered limbs were attached to his back" (253). In Hospital's construction, torture is over-signifying rather than destroying of signification—represented here by the aestheticization of that over-signification into mythic figures. He gives names to stop the pain, names of friends and mentors, then returns to nightmares. This section—his last direct presence in the text beyond his spoken-of absence—ends with an almost heavenly vision in which his music has tamed Cerberus and he wrestles with a "radiant being," after which "the music of the spheres was all around him and he felt no pain at all" (257). The aestheticization of displaced pain completed, Mishka disappears from the novel. His torture, then, performs a becoming-object, from which art—here represented by mythic figures that become music—affords some form of escape.

It is tempting to say that the ungraspability of pain has infected the text itself, driven away the entire instance of its occurrence. But this is not quite the case. Hospital does not so much recount the unmaking of the world as its blotting out, a slide into dissociation represented by a series of metaphors—cities, mythic figures, music. In this sense, the text proposes a stylistic mode of representing the displacement of the pain of torture, but not the pain itself. To write the pain itself, and the traumatic aftermath of that pain, asks for a different approach. In Hospital's writing of torture, affect figures little. Fear, shame, disgust, contempt, and even anger slip away from the act of torture. Nor does the novel have anything to say about what comes after torture, its traumatic effects/affects. Mishka, the reader learns, does indeed live, but in the ninety-odd pages that follow his torture he exists only as a cipher through which redemption is sought, love and faith expressed, and maternal bonds renewed. Time does not infold, the event slips away into narrative past-ness, hardly punctuated by its present violence. The virtuality of potential is nowhere to be found; there is only the Orpheus fantasy and "no pain at all." "Trauma," writes LaCapra, "brings about a dissociation of affect and representation: one disconcertingly feels what one cannot represent; one numbingly represents what one cannot feel."[74] In Hospital's text, dissociation of affect and representation occurs within the act itself—performed as a displacement into art and aesthetics. What this paper has, to this point, sort to explore is the latter part of LaCapra's equation, the tension between feeling and representing, reconceived as constituted by affect and its traumatic remnants.

9.

Massumi describes seeing a mouse from the corner of your eye: you "*feel* the arc of its movement" even though "you don't actually 'see' the vector of the mouse's movement, or your own."[75] A semblance of movement occurring. "*Semblance* is another way of saying 'the experience of a virtual reality.' Which is to say: 'the experience of the reality of the virtual.'"[76] Thinking the fictive writing of torture and its trauma as seeking their *semblance* is very different to trying to *represent* them. Nor is

---

[74] LaCapra, *Writing*, 42.
[75] Massumi, *Semblance*, 17.
[76] Ibid., 15-6.

semblance at all the same as resemblance. "Resemblance comes before the event, and takes precedence over it [...] With the precedence of resemblance comes the dominance of *interpretation*."[77] *Orpheus Lost* can be read as resemblance, since its mythic metaphor predetermines the meaning of Mishka's torture and in doing so closes off all realms of expression that are not symbolic, not contained in figural language, not dependent on the deconstructive undoing of fixed meanings. I want to suggest that *semblance* offers an alternative approach to writing torture, one concerned less with displacement and more with its traumatic aftermath.

"When a semblance is 'seen,' it is virtually seen," writes Massumi. "How else could the virtual actually appear—if not *as* virtual?"[78] This might seem conceptually impossible, but what Massumi points to is the capacity for art to impart some experience of the not-yet, the could-have-been, the more-than-occurred—"the virtual as a coincident dimension of every event's occurrence."[79] If the subject/object dichotomy resists betweenness, semblance embraces it by concerning itself with the relational and differential rather than the distinctive and disjunctive. Direct connection is not necessary, as Massumi shows in discussing the emergence of perspective painting alongside courtly sovereignty; perspective's dominant vanishing point a semblance of power that descends from the figure of the king. Royal authority and perspective painting are not the same. Rather than *connection,* something else joins them: "a *relation of nonrelation*."[80] Turning to torture, perhaps the problem is thinking that language *can* represent pain, when perhaps what it could strive for is something of the relation of nonrelation—the affective substance of its ungraspability. "Semblances of a certain artistic kind make gestures of revealing a content that lies beneath their surface. They reveal that depth in the very gesture of veiling it."[81] Sketches of aporia, glimpsed vectors of flight across caesura. Not so much accepting the unspeakable as expressing the affective experience of its unspeakability.

If torturous affects—the shame, fear, disgust, contempt, and pain (in its affective dimensions) experienced by detainees at Guantánamo, Abu

[77] Ibid., 177.
[78] Ibid., 18, emphasis in original.
[79] Ibid.. In *Semblance and Event*, Massumi considers what he calls "occurrent arts," which in his examples are primarily dance, painting and what might best be termed "art events." However, as he notes, "All arts are occurrent arts" (ibid, 82), such that his theorizing is as applicable to literature as to dance, if more difficultly realized in the former.
[80] Ibid., 61, emphasis in original.
[81] Ibid., 176.

Ghraib, and elsewhere—are the relations of violent encounter, the in-between-ness and forceful dynamism of event, then their expression might call forth precisely this *more than*. This could be the case even with a diminishment or paucity of language—I am suggesting a *more than* of relationality, not quantity. "A semblance is a *form of inclusion* of what exceeds the artifact's actuality."[82] Writing torture, its affects and its pain, could mean writing fiction that is *primarily* affective, rather than symbolic, figural or concerned with linguistic play. It means writing that gestures beyond the page, beyond language even. There is no space, here, for totalizing metaphors in which the event itself falls away and only the symbols remain. "A semblance isn't just like a force. Its "likeness" *is* a force, an abstract force of life."[83] What can generate semblance is likeness and metaphor liberated from sheer symbolism, allowed semantic incompleteness precisely so that what is relational, what is virtual, can actually occur in the act of reading. Such writing might ask that trauma not be totalized. That if death ends the traumatized body, torturous affect has already spilled over, exceeded limits.

Remember Améry's disrupted and de-structured temporality—"It was over for a while. It still is not over."[84] Semblance offers a kind of response. "A semblance is always an expression of time" and "a lived expression of the eternal matter-of-fact that is time's passing."[85] Or its failure to pass, its ruptured fragments clinging to bodies, traumatic remnants of violence transforming the tortured body. The virtual actually seen, not the totality of trauma but the suddenly recognized trajectory of its infolding of time and affect. It seems to me that if writing is to achieve this semblance, the act of torture cannot be the endpoint of narrative. Neither tortured nor torturing body should slip free. Fiction that writes torture, its pain and trauma, might seek semblance of time's passing, its infolding and rupturing, its sedimenting of affect, and the continuing of event into an always affected after. This after, even more than the event of torture itself, offers the capacity for written expression precisely because it allows time itself to work on traumatized bodies.

10.

A return to the beginning. "The pain was what it was," writes Améry. But the pain also *is what it is* and everything that passes in the time

[82] Ibid., 58.
[83] Ibid., 56.
[84] Améry, *Mind's Limits*, 36.
[85] Massumi, *Semblance*, 24.

between *was* and *is*. If the pain of torture is to be written, it might cease to be a thing on its own, alone and distinct, and be both known and unknown in relation to the affects that work with it, on it and through it to shape, define and silence bodies. Pain must be understood as relational and contingent as well as individual. As Sara Ahmed writes, "The impossibility of feeling the pain of others does not mean that the pain is simply theirs, or that their pain has nothing to do with me."[86] Or that it has nothing to do with affect, relation, the potential of expression. To assign the pain of torture to permanent unspeakability risks—however unintentionally—repeating the original violence. This is not to suggest that all silence does so, only that silence contains a kind of ambiguity. Indeed, more than ambiguity, silence can be loaded with complexity—particularly when that silence is unspeakable, a site of collision between bodies, and with power. Such unspeakability is hardly empty, hardly still—it has shape and content, relations of nonrelation. That it operates against language means that it can be expressed obliquely, in the effects of sedimented affect, in the changing of bodies in the passing of time. In semblance.

"An art practice can be aesthetically political, inventive of new life potentials, of new potential forms of life, and have no political content."[87] Writing the tortures of the war on terror into fiction is to engage political content, but it must do more than this. Writing torture needs not only to write *against* the kind of thinking manifest in the Bybee Memo but to grasp the potential of writing to be more than representation. This means approaching the problem of pain from the angle of its emergence into relation, into contingency. It means expressing the folding, rupturing and fragmenting of time, not simply to replace it in narrative but to chart its affective force on bodies and worlds. It means being willing to see the unmaking of the world from the corner of your eye, a semblance of an event beyond the vast dichotomy of subject and object. It means writing—messy, incomplete, gestural—the terrible *more than* that is constitutive of torturous affect.

[86] Ahmed, *Cultural Politics*, 30.
[87] Massumi, *Semblance*, 54.

PART III:

MEDIATIZED

CHAPTER SEVEN

GOJIRA'S BONES: THE MONSTER AS A VESSEL OF AFFECTIVE ENERGY

AARON KERNER

> One gets the feeling, particularly in the Japanese films but not only there, that a mass trauma exists over the use of nuclear weapons and the possibility of future nuclear wars. Most of the science fiction films bear witness to this trauma, and, in a way, attempt to exorcise it.
>
> —Susan Sontag, "The Imagination of the Disaster"

Context

Gojira (ゴジラ), or Godzilla as it is known outside Japan, is a complex matrix of highly fluid historical and socio-cultural concerns.[1] The Gojira franchise is the longest running film series in cinematic history. The Japanese name is a compound word, coming from the Japanese phonetic equivalent of "gorilla," (ゴリラ) and the word for "whale" (kujira—鯨). While the latter evokes enormity, the former refers to *King Kong*—a film that had made the rounds in Japanese theaters some time prior to the development of the first Gojira film, released in 1954 and directed by Ishiro Honda. In fact Toho—the studio that produced the film—experimented with stop-motion animation, emulating Merian Cooper and Ernest Schoedsack's 1933 film *King Kong*, but quickly determined that the process of stop-motion was too cumbersome and too expensive. Abandoning stop-motion led to the innovation of "suitmation," placing a man in a rubber suit. (Of course the original Gojira film also follows close

---

[1] I would like to express my gratitude to Kyosuke Yamagishi who helped with the research on this project and was an invaluable interlocutor—we had a number of fruitful conversations that helped to shape my thinking on the subject.

on the heels of Eugène Lourié's 1953 film *The Beast from 20,000 Fathoms.*)

Toho was exceptionally well-positioned for this production because during the war the studio had produced documentaries and dramatized accounts of the war using miniature sets. For instance, Kajiro Yamamoto's 1942 film *Hawaii mare oki kaisen* (*The War at Sea from Hawaii to Malay*), produced by Toho, included a reenactment of the attack on Pearl Harbor using miniatures. Eiji Tsuburaya developed many of the special effects, most notably the miniature sets used in Yamamoto's film (among many other films), and would later employ his trade in the Gojira series. Notably too, Honda worked his way through the ranks as an assistant director for Yamamoto.

It is too easy to dismiss the Gojira series as tawdry camp, and contrary to conventional thinking there is far more to the monster series than cheap B-movie thrills. It serves as an over-determined site of complex and even contradictory sentiments. The longevity of the Gojira enterprise speaks to the traumatic experiences that it negotiates—*repetition* of course being one of the signatures of the traumatic. In a published chapter entitled, "Gojira vs. Godzilla,"[2] I explored the significance of the monster in relation to hibakusha—the Japanese term for atomic bomb survivors. Hibakusha are treated as lepers and while viewed with sympathy they are also feared—perceived as agents of some terrible communicable disease, in a word they are "abject." Stemming from her extensive psychoanalytic research (and practice) Julia Kristeva develops this conception of the abject: those "things"—and they really aren't "things"—for which there is no category; it is a non-object, a signifier without a signified, those "things" that are felt, the sensational experience, and have little recourse to a signifying system.

One of the central observations of "Gojira vs. Godzilla" is that despite the monster's evolution over the past half-century its skin remains the same—curiously rough, and not particularly reptilian. This is of supreme importance because the monster's skin resembles the keloid scars of (some) hibakusha. The significance of suitmation comes into focus here too, because the monster has far more to do with the victims of the catastrophic atomic attacks, than the bomb and its destruction of infrastructure. Gojira *has to be* a man in a rubber suit precisely because it's about the traumatic experience the Japanese people endured. While the innovation of suitmation might have been the product of production

[2] Aaron Kerner, "Gojira vs. Godzilla: Catastrophic Allegories," in *Ritual and Event: Interdisciplinary Perspectives*, ed. Mark Franko (New York: Routledge, 2007), 109-124.

necessity, the final result was a figure that deeply resonated with the Japanese audience.

The monster is frequently attributed as "foreign"; the monster almost invariably emerges from the ocean, coming from "outside" Japan. Likewise, most Gojira films end with the monster returning to the sea: an expulsion of what is impure, what is abject. The monster then materializes as a visible manifestation of social anxiety in the face of the stranger within the national-self. Placing hibakusha in contrast to the Japanese imagined sense of (national) self, throws identity into crisis: hibakusha are in-between, recognizably Japanese but also categorically different too. Not one or the other, but simultaneously inhabiting both paradigms—a liminal non-category.[3] It is precisely in this unnamable position, this indefinable space, the domain of the non-object that affect resides; beyond the proper registers of communicative values lies feeling (I will discuss this at greater length later).

Gojira then functions as a provisional vessel where affect is coaxed into communicative form. Foreignness is in itself neutral; it has no inherent value.[4] The drive energy that fuels hatred, fear, racism comes from within the angst-ridden-subject, and is projected onto the foreigner. And what prompts the foreign body to serve as an abject referent is that it brings the subject to the place where meaning collapses, to the dissolution of stable subject-object relations, in short, death (i.e., dissolution of boundaries). Hibakusha are routinely cast as outsiders, while some are visibly marked as "other" with the characteristic keloid scarring from the atomic blast, some are not. Gojira's skin renders the indicators of otherness in its visible form, lending form to what is a non-object—that is to say the anxiety prompted by a referent that threatens the stability of subject-object relations. Keloid scarring (or its manifestation in Gojira's skin) is symptomatic of defilement, of impurity. Kristeva reminds us that "filth is not a quality in itself, but it applies only to what relates to a

---

[3] See Julia Kristeva, *Strangers to Ourselves*, trans. Leon S. Roudiez (New York: Columbia University Press, 1991), 187.

[4] I don't wish to make light of the existential realities of being "foreign," what I am seeking to address here are the ontological motivations for xenophobia, racism, and rigid nationalistic posturing which is erroneously predicated on a sense of a "pure self." Platforms that rest on hate of an-other, "like political commitment," as Kristeva advises, "to the extent that it settles the subject within a socially justified illusion—is a security blanket" (*Powers of Horror: an Essay on Abjection*, trans. Leon S. Roudiez (New York: Columbia University Press, 1982), 136-137). Of course the experience of the foreigner is far from "neutral," the point remains that there is nothing inherent to the position of foreigner—fascination (e.g., attributing the other as exotic), or revulsion/hatred are values assigned from another site.

boundary,"[5] and more specifically the violation of it, and like the leper, hibakusha and their scars are not inherently abject, but are visual referents of a porous body, a body between, mutating, or mutilated (i.e., contaminated, changed, changing, malformed, disfigured). This is just one way in which the monster functions as an affective vessel. What I intend to do in this paper, then, is trace some of the other ways in which the monster functions as an affective vessel, most particularly with respect to the national(ist) trauma.

Akira Ifukube: Scoring the Voices of the Dead

Akira Ifukube, who composed the hallmark scores for the Gojira films, and is responsible for developing the monster's distinctive roar, recounts that the monster, "was like the souls of the Japanese soldiers who died in the Pacific Ocean during the war."[6] Like his filmmaking compatriots, Ifukube also applied his trade to the wartime effort, writing marches for the military, and the militaristic elements in his work for the Gojira films is distinctly evident.[7] And indeed Ifukube's music goes a long way in conveying the nationalist sensibility, though his work perhaps at the same time reveals the instability of the nationalist project, which like all nationalisms is premised on an imagined "pure" community. While Ifukube's work owes a clear debt to militaristic motifs (as found in Western music), his work is also "strongly influenced by the folkloric music of the ethnic minorities from northern Japan such as the Ainus and Nivkhi."[8] The trademark compositions, including the monster's theme song *Allegro Marciale*, inflected with Western and aboriginal elements, then, already places the national(ist) project on tenuous ground.

Allegro Marciale bears the clear hallmarks of a military march, playing to jingoistic sentiments, but other pieces strive to elicit more solemn affect. *Prayer for Peace* is a funerary-like piece, sung by schoolgirls, and while overwrought nonetheless tugs at the heartstrings. The piece is featured in the wake of Gojira's raid, with the throngs of the wounded filling up the

---

[5] Ibid., 69.

[6] Akira Ifukube cited in Yoshikuni Igarashi, *Bodies of Memory: Narrative of War in Postwar Japanese Culture, 1945-1970* (Princeton: Princeton University Press, 2000), 114; 116.

[7] Samara Lea Allsop, "Gojira/Godzilla," in *The Cinema of Japan and Korea*, ed. Justin Bowyer (New York: Wallflower Press, 2004), 66.

[8] Inuhiko Yomota, "The Menace from the South Seas: Honda Ishiro's *Godzilla* (1954)," trans. Sachiko Shikoda, in *Japanese Cinema: Texts and Contexts*, eds. Alastair Phillips and Julian Stringer (London: Routledge, 2007), 103.

halls of an overwhelmed hospital. It also comes in the latter moments of the film—a requiem for Dr. Serizawa, Gojira, or both. In the first film Serizawa designs a device—the Oxygen Destroyer—that is powerful enough to kill Gojira, but is apprehensive about using it. After languishing over the ethics of using his device (and the knowledge associated with its creation) Serizawa finally agrees to use the Oxygen Destroyer on the condition that he deploys it himself. After triggering the device under water Serizawa cuts his airline to the surface and dies along with the monster. Serizawa's sacrifice finds certain affinities with the suicide missions of kamikaze pilots—the last desperate bid to save Japan, but significantly in this case the desperate act proves successful. The shots in the hospital call to mind the aftermath of the firebombing raids, or the atomic attacks; in one instance during the original 1954 film a doctor inspects a little girl with a Geiger counter and shakes his head suggesting a poor prognosis. The imagery and score appears to be drawn from Hideo Sekikawa's 1953 film *Hiroshima*—a "realistic" representation of the atomic bombing.[9] *Prayer for Peace* and its emotional affect evoke the souls of the dead, and its presence in the latter moments of the film, when Serizawa and his compatriot Ogata descend into Tokyo Bay to deploy the oxygen destroyer:

> It looks like the mythical descent to 'another world.' The scene has no dialogue and its audio track comprises bubbling sound effects and solemn music. The music subtly associates Godzilla's atrocity on land with his being victim of human aggression to marine ecology. This double aspect is crucial to the story and the music functions as a hinge to connect one with the other.[10]

Indeed, and perhaps more than the visual register—the characters' descent into what is about to become a mass grave (the oxygen destroyer will not only kill Gojira, but it will destroy all life in Tokyo Bay)—the angelic call of the voices harmonizes with the souls of the dead. Gojira then straddles these contradictory poles, perpetrator and victim, a vessel capable of containing a complex matrix of ambivalent feelings. Fittingly, Ifukube recycled the melody of *Prayer for Peace* for Kon Ichikawa's 1956 film *Biruma no tategoto* (*The Burmese Harp*)—which features a former soldier, who becomes a Buddhist monk, returning to the site of a battle to pray for

---

[9] Shuhei Hosokawa, "Atomic Overtones and Primitive Undertones: Akira Ifukube's Sound Design for Godzilla," in *Off the Planet: Music, Sound and Science Fiction Cinema*, ed. Philip Hayward (London: John Libbey, 2004), 56.
[10] Ibid., 56.

the souls of the dead.[11] The immaterial voices of the dead—emanating from the non-diegetic space—negotiate a traumatized national(ist) self, and Gojira is the provisional materialization of the return of the repressed, an uncanny specter.

Gojira as National(ist) Specter

The Gojira film series is deeply indebted to Japan's incredibly rich pantheon of supernatural figures that populate its folklore. The tradition of Japanese ghost stories is known as kaidan (怪談), and although Gojira manifests in material form, unlike a ghost, the monster shares certain affinities with the specter. In fact, the generic term of Gojira films, kaiju eiga (怪獣映画) mysterious monster movies, shares a common root. These monster movies are also referred to as daikaiju (大怪獣), meaning giant monsters. The prefix of the two previously mentioned terms, kaiju (怪獣) and kaidan (怪談), as well as daikaiju, use the same kanji character (kai—怪) for mysterious, strange, or haunting. And in all cases evoke an "other worldliness" that we might call the "uncanny." And it is possible to think of Gojira as something like a ghost that haunts, and returns to Japanese cities over and over again to wreak cataclysmic destruction. Though it is important to keep in mind that, as Noriko Reider urges, "kaidan need not evoke fear in the minds of an audience," but that "frequently there is a revenge motif with an element of horror."[12] And in many of the Gojira narratives the monster manifests as a form of retribution for disturbing the natural order of things (e.g., pollution, irresponsible use of nuclear energy), or, and this is particularly true of the films from the 1990s and early 2000s, some form of divine punishment for offending ancestors.

In its association with the netherworld—ghosts, and other supernatural figures—the monster is closely linked with the Japanese conception of kami in the Shinto tradition—nature spirits, or nature gods. Like the Judaic tradition where nothing is outside of God, incorporating even what the Christian tradition would characterize as evil (and therefore separate from God), the division between "good" and "evil" with respect to kami is sometimes difficult to differentiate. Throughout the series Gojira vacillates between these moral polarities, but unbound by human mores the monster shares more in common with the will of the natural world. In keeping with its affiliation with kami, Gojira emerges from the natural world, and is

[11] Ibid., 60, note 22.

[12] Noriko T. Reider, "The Appeal of 'Kaidan' Tales of the Strange," *Asian Folklore Studies* 59, no. 2 (2000): 266.

closely associated with the element of water—namely the Pacific. In addition, in a number of the films when the monster first appears it emerges from the ocean depths during a typhoon or some other natural cataclysm such as volcanic eruptions.

The figure of the demon (oni) also furnishes some of the characteristics associated with Gojira—the monster—and the narrative motifs found in the series. In fact the original film includes a short scene with the people of Odo Island watching an age-old ceremony intended to placate the monster that they call "Gojira." The performers in the ceremony wear Tengu masks—a monstrous creature with an elongated phallic-like nose. There are in fact historical precedents for mobilizing supernatural figures like oni for ideological purposes. As part of the war effort, for instance, other races, and more specifically the enemies of the Japanese Empire, were rendered as demons. Reider notes that:

> the oni as enemy during wartime in Japan was quickly and artificially created by Japanese leaders and enthusiastic nationalists. Far from an image that evolved over time, this use of oni was a ploy that exploited fearful associations [with the demon] and thus advanced the Japanese wartime ultra-nationalist agenda.[13]

Rendering the referent as monstrous positions it as a convenient, malleable vessel with effectively boundless potential to house cultural anxiety. Although in the wake of the Second World War the political legitimacy of the nationalist regime—and its associated visual culture—effectively collapsed, the strategy of mobilizing the supernatural figure nevertheless changed to meet contemporary needs. As I have stated already though, over the course of half a century, the Gojira series has evolved to reflect an ever-increasing nationalist sensibility to negotiate the trauma of the Second World War, the sacrifice of Japanese soldiers, and nostalgic mourning for its once mighty military prowess.

Nationalist Motifs in the Gojira Series

> There is a vast amount of wishful thinking in science fiction films, some of it touching, some of it depressing. Again and again, one detects the hunger for a 'good war,' which poses no moral problems, admits of no moral qualifications. The imagery of science fiction films will satisfy the most

---

[13] Noriko T. Reider, *Japanese Demon Lore: Oni from Ancient Times to the Present* (Logan, Utah: Utah State University Press, 2010), 110.

> bellicose addict of war films, for a lot of the satisfactions of war films pass, untransformed, into science fiction films.[14]

The original 1954 film seeded the earth for nationalistic sentiments to take root in the film series. No one in Japan went unscathed by the trauma of war and the humiliation of occupation, and many involved in the Gojira franchise (e.g., Honda, Ifukube, Tsuburaya) either worked in the film industry that propagated nationalistic and militaristic rhetoric, served in tours of duty, or even both. The destruction that the original monster visits upon Tokyo resembles the firebombing campaign that leveled entire districts in the capital city; and Honda admits as much that the destruction of the city in the 1954 film was modeled with the aftermath of American bombing campaigns in mind. In fact, the specific districts that Gojira levels corresponds to historical events and the American strategic pattern of destruction, and what is particularly striking is what *remains intact* (though always out of frame) in the original Gojira film: namely, the Imperial Palace.[15] This oblique approach to the Emperor's residence—if not to the Emperor himself—figures as a haunting specter of the countless Japanese soldiers that died abroad leaving their souls restless.[16] Yasukuni—Japan's national shrine for its war-dead—was intended to enshrine the souls of the dead, a site for both private and public memory, where the souls of the dead are worshipped/commemorated and revered as kami. Finding certain affinities with Yasukuni, Gojira also functions as a vessel that accommodates the souls of the dead.

---

[14] Susan Sontag, "The Imagination of Disaster," *Against Interpretation, and Other Essays* (New York: Picador; Farrar, Straus and Giroux, 2001), 219.

[15] Inuhiko Yomota notes: "For those possessing even the slightest knowledge of Tokyo's spatial layout it must be noticeable that there is one important monument, the Imperial Palace, that is never depicted or referred to—despite the fact that geographical logic decrees that Godzilla would have certainly walked past it on this route [i.e., during its rampage]. The question therefore remains: why did this monster, having travelled all the way from the South Seas to Japan, return into the sea at the very point where it should have reached the Imperial Palace?" Yomota, "Menace," 107. Masahide Tabata also discusses the significance of what does and doesn't get demolished in the Gojira series, noting that no Buddhist temple or Shinto shrine is ever destroyed by Gojira, and of all the historical sites—the castles in Osaka and Nagoya—that get crushed these are concrete replicas. It is only Gidora—the alien outsider—that ever attacks a sacred site, specifically the Asama shrine.

[16] See Norio Akasaka's, "Gojira wa naze koukyo wo fumenainoka?" ("What Makes Godzilla Hesitate to Stomp about the Imperial Palace?"), in *Bessatsu-Takarajima: Kaijugaku nyumon* (Tokyo: JICC-shuppankyoku, 1992), referenced in Yomota, "Menace," 107.

The worship of ancestors, paying due deference to the spirits of the dead, proper treatment of remains, all deeply rooted elements of the Japanese religious/cultural experience, materializes as motifs found in later Gojira films as well. In a number of the films the monster is explicitly or implicitly related to Japanese war-dead, and in fact the Japanese Self Defense Force (SDF) plays an increasingly significant role in these later films. While the first film clearly draws from Toho's archive of wartime documentary and dramatized accounts of military exercises (e.g., a demonstration of naval vessels launching depth charges), the SDF does not lend material support to the production of the Gojira films until the late 1980s. It is interesting to also note that the Japanese military was reconstituted as the SDF in July of 1954, the same year that the first Gojira film was released. Many films from the Heisei series (1984-1995), and the Millennium series (1999-) feature a thinly-veiled special unit of the SDF known as G-Force. This unit is specifically charged with defending Japan against monsters, namely, Gojira. In these films the G-Force is frequently associated with the United Nations and even cooperates with the American military. This reflects Japan's very real ambition to be recognized as a major political (and even a military) force in the community of nations, and Japan has made it no secret that it seeks a permanent seat on the UN Security Council.

The Gojira narratives generally couch the SDF well within constitutionally prescribed bounds, charged with defending the homeland —and casting SDF or G-Force leaders as measured agents of the state, in no way belligerent or overly zealous in their application of personnel or military force. Kazuki Omori's 1989 film *Gojira tai Biorante* (*Godzilla vs. Biollante*) was the first film to gain direct support from the SDF, shooting many of the scenes at the SDF Fuji training grounds, and includes footage of live ammunition exercises (under the provision that no soldiers actually appear in the film). Reportedly, following Omori's 1989 film, the SDF then began to pitch possible scenarios for future film projects.[17]

Masaaki Tezuka's films *Gojira tai Mekagojira* (*Godzilla Against MechaGodzilla*, 2002) followed by *Gojira tai Mosura tai Mekagojira: Tokyo S.O.S.* (*Godzilla: Tokyo S.O.S.*, 2003) explicitly correspond from one film to the next. Tezuka's films negotiate the national(ist) trauma by evoking the restless souls of the dead. In the first of these films, when Gojira emerges from the sea, a team of scientists (a reference to Serizawa) is assembled to create a weapons system, generally referred to as Kiryu

[17] Sabine Frühstück and Eyal Ben-Ari, "'Now We Show It All!' Normalization and the Management of Violence in Japan's Armed Forces," *The Journal of Japanese Studies* 28, no. 1 (Winter 2002): 22.

(meaning—mechanized dragon), to defend Japan. We learn that the bones from the 1954 Gojira have been stored in a secret facility and the team use Gojira's bones as the basic armature for the bio-robot. Kiryu is later dubbed Mekagojira because the spirit of the original Gojira manifests in the bio-robot, causing it to malfunction. Mekagojira does in the end force Gojira to retreat into the sea, and the SDF/G-Force claim this as a victory. The film is laced with militaristic and nationalistic content, including kamikaze and ideologically loaded imagery. One of the SDF commanders proclaims in the latter moments of the film, "We couldn't kill it. But we did expel Gojira." Perhaps one of the most explicit manifestations of expelling the "foreign other," while all at the same time confronting the disavowal of repressed traumatic memories; if Gojira embodies the souls of the dead, then here is an outward manifestation of a negation of the traumatic memory, cast back into the oblivion of the Pacific. (And here—though deeply intertwined with nationalistic sentiments—the evocation of past traumatic events enacts a type of mourning that acknowledges it, a subject I'll address later.) The imagery of expulsion is immediately followed with the swelling of heroic non-diegetic music. The jingoistic score carries across a series of other shots until we are finally brought to the immobile body of Mekagojira—spent after battling Gojira—its pilot (a woman) emerging from inside the bio-robot to see *the rising sun* over the Pacific and Gojira wading back out to sea. In this victory the SDF—and notably the female pilot of Mekagojira—reaffirms (or even births) the Japanese national body by expelling the monstrous outsider, and re-mapping the borders of a clean and proper national body.

The succeeding film *Tokyo S.O.S.* begins with Mosura (Mothra) threatening to wage war on humanity—and more specifically the Japanese—if they do not properly dispose of Gojira's bones used in Mekagojira. As with Masaaki Tezuka's previous film, *Tokyo S.O.S.* is also loaded with nationalistic imagery and narrative motifs. Gojira returns to Japan because of its continued violation of the natural order and running afoul of the taboo against handling bodily remains, using the 1954 Gojira's bones as an armature for the bio-robot Mekagojira. It is important to note here that the Japanese cremate their dead in the Buddhist tradition. And when the body is reduced to ash family members gather around the cremated remains and in pairs pick out bones that are then interned in a vessel, which in 49 days will be finally laid to rest in the family's plot. Only through this ritual of cremation and final burial will the soul of the dead pass into the Western Paradise to rest in peace. Providing final sanctuary, then, is what is at stake in *Tokyo S.O.S.*—and beyond that, if Gojira's body and bones embody the spirit of deceased ancestors (especially the soldiers from the Second World War), the cultural stakes are all that much higher.

The twin fairies associated with Mosura act as liaisons between the monster and humans. In the original 1961 film *Mosura* the Linguist Shinichi Chujo encounters the fairies, and was instrumental in determining how to appease the monster. In *Tokyo S.O.S.* the fairies make an appeal to Chujo once again (Hiroshi Koizumi plays Chujo in the original 1961 film and Tezuka's 2003 film). The fairies explain to Chujo that they have a problem, and plead with him: "It's Godzilla's bones. You must send them back to sea. Human beings made a weapon using the bones from Godzilla. That was a mistake." In a stroke of narrative convenience Chujo's nephew, Yoshito Chujo, happens to be a member of the SDF/G-Force ground crew working on the Mekagojira program; Yoshito interrupts, insisting that it's the only defense that Japan has against Gojira. The fairies implore, "No human being may touch the souls of the dead. We came to tell you that Godzilla's bones must return to the sea, and remain there." The fairies rebuff Yoshito's insistence that they need to keep Mekagojira for protection, promising that if Gojira should return: "then Mothra will be there to protect you." The fairies continue to beg that they help to lay Gojira's bones to rest, "If they're not, then Mothra will declare war on the human race. Naturally, we don't want war to happen. And neither does Mothra." In relatively explicit terms we see the national(ist) narrative motif materializing.

Like Tezuka's 2002 film *Gojira tai Mekagojira* the sun features prominently in the narrative. When Mosura arrives to defend Japan against Gojira, its initial encounter with the monster exhibits Mosura with the blazing sun behind it. The closing shot, similar to Tezuka's previous film, also ends with the rising sun. Between Mosura and Mekagojira, Gojira is defeated. The twin Mosura larva spins a cocoon around the gravely injured Gojira. The film concludes with the bones within Mekagojira seizing command of the bio-robot. Clamping onto the immobilized Gojira, the pair launch from the ruins of the Diet—trampled during the battle between the monsters—and set a course for the Pacific. Mekagojira plunges the pair into the Japan Trench, finally laying the bodies of both monsters to rest in the ocean depths. Mosura as an agent of the natural world—which in the Japanese worldview is inseparable from kami—ensures that balance is restored.

Locating Affect

What I have discussed thus far pertains largely to narrative content, and the nationalistic motifs that are woven into the Gojira films. Affect, though, does not reside in content, but rather in form. Moreover while many film theorists relate affect to synesthesia, or the haptic experience—where it is posited that the visual and aural cinematic landscape wields the capacity to elicit a sensuous experience such as touch or smell—an enterprise I view with suspicion (because they tend to function only as analogies—"it's as if …", or hyperbolic descriptions[18]), what I rather wish to call attention to are those experiences that are quite inexplicable: when the body suddenly goes flush with goose bumps, hair stands on end, tears are brought on by an encounter with the beautiful, physiological responses such as averting one's eyes, a knee-jerk gasp, a lurching backwards or jumping out of one's seat. These visceral experiences are most commonly elicited through style and form.

Undeniably the content of what is presented in many of the Gojira films is crass adolescent entertainment (though they didn't necessarily start out this way), laced with overwrought moralizing. The generally inane content, nevertheless, hosts the aesthetic embellishments that fuel its affective charge. There are specific tropes that wield the potential to elicit an aesthetic experience, and I use "aesthetic" here in the Kantian sense. The aesthetic experience, as Kant deems it, becomes more self-evident when we consider the antonym "anesthetic"—that which is supposed to "dull the senses"—"aesthetics," then, in contrast, is an experience that "stimulates the senses." In his *Critique of Judgment* Kant refuses to outline the qualities of the aesthetic referent, because the aesthetic experience is subjective and completely divorced from the referent (and utility), what he posits as "disinterested." Kristeva, on the other hand, equipped with an arsenal of theoretical models capable of apprehending the "discourse of feelings," offers a cadre of tropes that potentially harbor affective force: rhythm and harmony, extra-communicative utterances, lektons (a signifier without a signified), the playful interventions in syntax, and those "things" that fall outside the objectal economy (e.g., the abject, the semiotic, drives).

The "things" that typically elicit an affective response are those referents that, as Kristeva posits in *Powers of Horror*, upset "identity, system, order. What does not respect borders, positions, rules. The in-

[18] I'm thinking here of scholars like Laura Marks who talks about "the skin of film"; see *The Skin of the Film: Intercultural Cinema, Embodiment, and the Senses* (Durham: Duke University Press, 2000); and *Touch: Sensuous Theory and Multisensory Media* (Minneapolis: University of Minnesota Press, 2002).

between, the ambiguous, the composite."[19] There is an inherent paradox built into the critique of affect, because once the innately visceral experience is subject to critical engagement (i.e., a process that occurs within the Symbolic register) then it ceases to exist. The Symbolic being that plane where meaning resides: discourse, narrative, communicative systems. One of the consistent themes that run through Kristeva's research, from its earliest moments in the 1970s through to the present, is an effort to critically engage with the "discourse" of affect. And, of course, this is what prompts Kristeva's intervention in the Structuralist paradigm and its application of linguistics that "established itself as the science of an object ('language,' 'speech' or 'discourse')." But Kristeva's interest lies outside the objectal economy, those "things" that have no communicative value (properly speaking) and have "non-utilitarian use, the areas of transgression and pleasure."[20] And the difficulty comes particularly in assimilating what is inherently outside discourse. Once the referent that elicits the affective experience is rendered—if only tenuously—within the object economy, it is linked with what is ostensibly a "thing" and at that very instant we lose hold of it.[21] This is not to suggest that affect is hopelessly beyond our capacity to critically engage with it, but rather we have to know where to find it to begin with—and from this perspective it is not located in content as such, but in form, those elements of the cinematic arts that have no communicative value.

Takao Okawara's 1995 film *Gojira tai Desutoroia* (*Godzilla vs. Destroyer*) closes with a deeply affecting scene depicting the death of the monster and offers an example of affect in form. Toho intended to kill the monster to clear the way for the American film *Godzilla* (directed by Roland Emmerich, 1998). The opening title sequence for the 1995 film begins with an animated depiction of the Oxygen Destroyer deployed by Dr. Serizawa in the 1954 film. We eventually learn that the monster that emerges to challenge Gojira, dubbed Destroyer, evolved from the Oxygen Destroyer. The monster initially begins as a collection of microorganisms, but quickly grows and evolves into crustacean-like creatures (clearly deriving from the alien in the *Alien* series), before finally merging into a single lumbering monster. The life form is initially detected in an under-

---

[19] Kristeva, *Powers*, 4. Pertaining to "things" Kristeva observes: "A 'something' that I do not recognize as a thing. A weight of meaninglessness, about which there is nothing insignificant, and which crushes me. On the edge of non-existence and hallucination, of a reality that, if I acknowledge it, annihilates me" (2).

[20] Julia Kristeva, "The System and the Speaking Subject," in *The Kristeva Reader*, ed. Toril Moi (Oxford: Blackwell, 1995), 26.

[21] Ibid., 30.

the-bay tunnel, where there is a sudden and sharp rise in temperature; the site, as it turns out, is where the original 1954 Gojira died. Although the 1995 film remains relatively subtle in its nationalist rhetoric, and in this case Gojira does not necessarily embody Japan's war-dead (though it could), Destroyer, on the other hand, is born from the site of the original Gojira, where it's bones came to rest and Serizawa sacrificed himself—and thus places the narrative as a whole in a continuum of films that are more explicitly nationalist.

Where the historical narrative in the immediate postwar era necessitated a recalibration of the Emperor's role—from divine ruler to victim of a belligerent military regime—the figure of Serizawa refuses to yield to the new order. Gojira films, and specifically the original 1954 film, invite spectators to revisit the destruction of their nation, and a national narrative, as Yoshikuni Igarashi observes:

> The [1954] film brings the audience back to the scene of destruction, a space shared with the war dead. The audience is then provided with a final closure to memories of destruction by a Japanese character. Dr. Serizawa's invention and final intervention destroy the monster. However, through his act of bringing about a final resolution, Dr. Serizawa remains forever at the scene of destruction, joined by the souls of the dead at the bottom of the sea. Previously, the film has established that Dr. Serizawa had been injured in the war and has been determined to stay aloof from postwar society; his final act completes his reunion with the community of the war dead. The young scientist's self-sacrifice is an act that stubbornly refuses absorption into the historical narrative.[22]

Okawara effectively resurrects Serizawa's character in Kenichi Yamane, the adopted grandson of the paleontologist, Dr. Yamane, from the 1954 film. The young Yamane—a self-trained Gojira expert—is recruited to determine the best way to neutralize the monster. A conventional attack is deemed too dangerous, potentially prompting the monster to go into meltdown, and Yamane determines that a "chemical attack" is the only option, and insists that the Oxygen Destroyer be deployed once again to dispatch Gojira. But more importantly, Yamane pulls the veil off the postwar historical narrative and seeks answers (to Japan's problems) ostensibly in what has been designated as taboo—the knowledge and power associated with Serizawa, a war veteran, a character that refused to assimilate to the new world order.

While this provides some of the narrative contextualization of the film, the true affective force of the film materializes in its cinematic

[22] Igarashi, *Bodies of Memory*, 118.

embellishments: the use of lighting, movement of form, editing, composition, and audio-design. In addition to Gojira, another monster of the same species appears, a smaller, apparently younger monster christened as Junior. Before Gojira arrives in Tokyo, Junior—akin to the Japanese spirit in the final days of the war—attempts to challenge Destroyer despite being hopelessly outmatched. And indeed Destroyer makes short shrift of Junior. When Gojira approaches Junior's incapacitated body, the monster bellows a lament-filled roar. Barely perceptible, a bubbling, or churning, references the instability of the monster's body, that is ready to burst at the seams. Using dramatic backlighting Okawara creates a powerfully affecting scene, outlining the shape of the mourning monster, transforming the monster from a solid form into a ghostly figure. The lighting here (and it is used later for a similar effect), by placing the monster in near silhouette, offers a "material" referent of a body in transition, a body slipping between life and death. The steam that rises from the monster's body also confers the monster's tenuous grip on life, the vessel that can no longer contain itself, that leaks.

Ifukube's music accompanies the scene charging it with emotive force (but let's admit it—the music is overwrought and saccharine). When Gojira finally reaches Junior the monster appears to bow down to "breathe life" into it, but we are then presented with a somewhat shocking shot—a point-of-view shot taken from Gojira's perspective as Junior closes his eyes (perhaps the youngster dies?). The passing of Gojira's "life-force"—visualized as a ghostly orange gas—has an audio accompaniment that is equally ghostly. Although the audio element associated with Gojira's "life-force" is motivated by the actions represented in the scene, it nevertheless straddles the diegetic/non-diegetic register; the character of this audio element suggests a thin drawn-out scream, *like* the souls of the dead screaming out from the nether regions.

The editing—specifically the POV shot—invites the spectator to participate in the communion with the monsters that straddle the threshold between life and death. When Junior closes its eyes the string instruments swell and an oboe enters the musical arrangement and wails a sorrowful cry on Gojira's behalf. The following shots include close-ups of Gojira's head and medium close-ups outlining the monster's figure with light as steam continues to emit from its body; bolts of light literally explode from its skin as the integrity of Gojira's body becomes increasingly compromised. The relatively low tonal range of the wind instrument—at once melodic and reedy (which to my untrained musical ear sounds slightly dissonant)—along with all the other aesthetic embellishments accompanying the scene intends to elicit an emotive response in the spectator. The meditative quality of these aesthetic embellishments is interrupted, though, when Destroyer once again attacks Gojira.

As Gojira tips ever closer to meltdown, its dorsal spines begin to melt, and its body uncontrollably emits pulses of light, its body temperature so hot—approaching 1200 degrees centigrade—that the air around the monster spontaneously combusts. The monster unleashes, with unprecedented force, volleys of its radioactive breath against Destroyer, causing Destroyer's flesh to explode open. After Gojira finally vanquishes Destroyer, Gojira truly begins the process of nuclear meltdown; Okawara slows the image ever so slightly, as the monster utters a death rattle—a low grumbling or gurgling—suggesting the break down of boundaries within the body, the membranes of organs and flesh disintegrating. Its body continues to emit pulses of light, and cast plumes of steam against the black background of the night sky. The monster's body writhes in a sort of death dance, as it is showered in a rain of particles (nuclear fallout?) that sparkle in the light. When the monster finally reaches 1200 degrees centigrade the image is slowed even further and is accompanied by the strum of a harp and a cacophony of multiple piano-keys slamming down all at once (an audio reference to the original 1954 film, which used a similar technique—for instance, when Serizawa demonstrates the destructive power of the Oxygen Destroyer for his fiancé).[23] The forlorn trumpeting of an oboe enters the non-diegetic track once again as the monster writhes in agony. The SDF/G-Force attempt to mitigate the damage caused by a meltdown and fire "freezer lasers"—the impact of the blasts explode in clouds of white smoke, but the diegetic sound of weapons fire is eclipsed by the non-diegetic score which now includes the hailing of angelic voices—a solemn beckoning that shepherds the monster between the world of the living and the dead. The figure of the monster—in slow motion—contorts in a cloud of steam and smoke as the swelling of string instruments amplify the aesthetic charge of the lament-filled scene. Gojira's flesh begins to melt away, exposing raw bone—its death rattle more distinctly signifying the disintegration of bodily boundaries, the bubbling of a hemorrhaging body. The monster utters one last death bellow—as its life force, embodied in a brilliant orange spewing of light—escapes the bounds of flesh; the monster, having thrown off this mortal coil, is life without body, life without form. The angelic voices answer

---

[23] Multiple piano-keys coming down simultaneously had a specific function in Ifukube's view of scoring: "To represent the volume and weight of the monster, it [the score] features brass instruments and emphasises the bass sound (trombones, tubas). A piano tone cluster [i.e., multiple keys played at once] amplifies the shock effect." Hosokawa, "Atomic Overtones," 55; also see 60 note 21.

Gojira's death call and herald the monster's unbound spirit—as life without a container, it dissolves into nothingness, and the faint outline of Gojira's bones crumble, a frame ripped apart without a body to hold it together. Unbound by flesh the monster dissolves into light, a white-hot mass, but as the camera pulls away the light becomes more defuse, less intense, and the hail of angelic voices recedes and gives way to a low (non?)diegetic rumble.

At the SDF/G-Force command center Yamane monitors radioactivity levels and notices a sudden drop in the level of radioactivity; echoing the previous shot pulling away from the site of catastrophic destruction, the camera now moves towards a black void filled with smoke—a non-space, a spatial field divorced from referents in the objective narrative diegesis. As we move increasingly forward, the figure of Gojira (or is it Junior?) vaguely emerges in silhouette—bathed in a sea of smoke—enveloped in the diegetic sound of a wind-swept landscape. Backlit, the figure of Gojira (or Junior) is seen bellowing its echoing roar, though we hear nothing but the low timbre of a rumbling wind. The silhouette of the monster cuts shadows through the smoke. Though still veiled behind a layer of smoke, the monster finally, in the last seconds of the film, belts out its distinctive cry—though as heard in a chamber, or filtered through an unseen membrane; the qualities of the image and audio-design suggests that what is exhibited is coming from another dimension, another world, beyond the world of the living, the echoing voice of a ghost.

The aesthetic embellishments charge the narrative content with affective potency, and this enhances the nationalistic motifs. It is possible, for instance, to imagine here that Gojira, and now Junior, assume the burden not only of radiation (hence the drop in radioactive readings) such as experienced by hibakusha, but also a troubled history that to one degree or another disavows its war-dead. The malleability of the monster allows it to straddle multiple positions at once. In this case Gojira and Junior are perhaps closer to Dr. Serizawa who sacrificed himself so that Japan can live on. Yomota describes Serizawa's sacrifice as set against a backdrop of relative prosperity for post-war Japan, and concludes that, "he is thus portrayed as an enigmatic critic of society,"[24] a conclusion that is equally applicable to our monsters. The aesthetic treatment of the narrative content charges the film with affective potency.

One of the key elements that elicit an affective response in Okawara's 1995 film is the exhibition of bodies in transition. The affective power, though, comes in Okawara's capacity to "represent" those liminal

[24] Yomota, "Menace," 106.

moments/spaces. And more than this, the "representation" of these bodies in-between is located not necessarily in the content (the narrative—Gojira is dying), or in visible forms (the monster's body itself), but in style and other non-communicative elements: the harmonics and nasal-quality of the oboe, the gurgling (of a hemorrhaging body), the audio elements associated with the monster (signifying the "screams of the souls of the dead"), the character of singing voices (the harmonics of the angelic voices that narrate nothing, simply singing "ahhh"), the straddling of non-diegetic/diegetic registers (the ambiguity of audio elements), the ambiguity of spatial relations (in the final seconds of the film), the editing that destabilizes viewing positions, the writhing body in slow motion (at once not part of the "realist" narrative diegesis, but still clearly with a foot in it), the play between light and shadow, etc. And just to focus on the qualities of the oboe's sound for a moment, there is perhaps more than any other instrument, a certain haptic character—the sound intimately bound with the body of the oboist: the embouchure and the very breath resonates through the spittle-soaked double reed. The vibrations of the body and organic qualities of the reed lend—not representation as such, because the sound of the oboe does not have "meaning"—but rather offers the "resonance" of living flesh that throws a provisional netting around a body in-between, a body straddling life and death, lending a "voice" to the restless souls trussed to the figure of Gojira. The aesthetic embellishments amplify the force of the narrative content, but owe its affect to, as Kristeva might say, a "semiotization of the Symbolic." In fact narrative content might very well impede, or distract from the non-communicative "discourses" that are the thoroughfare to the cinema of sensation. The tracing of the monster's boundaries—the aural and visual referents that "signify" a lining—and finally the dissolution of bounds illustrates yet another example of how the monster serves as an affective vessel.

And to make a confession: I find the closing moments of Okawara's film utterly sublime. My body goes flush with goose-bumps, I am brought nearly to tears, it is not the content of the narrative that achieves this affective experience, rather it is the proliferation of cinematic and aesthetic embellishments. And by-and-large the tropes that invite the affective experience are those that negotiate the presence of a referent in-between, in transition, without definable form, liminal. Shuhei Hosokawa describes the closing of the original 1954 film in similar terms:

> When the oxygen destroyer starts operating, the music changes key. When he is awakened and doomed to *decomposition*, the piano plays Spanish-like tonic chords in fortissimo (E major- F major) to dramatize the monster's final agonies [i.e., slipping between life and death]. Its last chord (E major)

> is a strong expression, dedicated to the sublime death of the *transcendental creature*. Such a sublime moment is unusual and hard to find elsewhere in the monster film genre. What follows it is a mournful choir. Again, the music is used twice to aurally illustrate *the double face—the violence and vulnerability*—of Godzilla.[25]

Without saying as much, though nevertheless clearly registered, Hosokawa also identifies the key tropes that elicit affect—those aural elements that evoke decomposition, the transcendental character of the monster, the double face, etc. In other words, referents associated with the fragility of borders, linings, categories that potentially collapse in on themselves.

And finally, the confrontation with the abject referent—delivering the spectator to the place where meaning collapses—wields the potential for catharsis. The malleability of the monster, its status as a provisional object, and the poetic narrative form (as an allegory) in which it is placed, does not directly confront the national(ist) trauma, but approaches it obliquely. There is no effort whatsoever to formulate a coherent narrative, or an attempt to fabricate "meaning" for the countless lost in the Pacific conflict, or the traumatic experience of a systemized firebombing campaign followed by two nuclear bombs. Rather the veiled Gojira narratives offer, at best, a fragmentary narrative, and this strikes me as productive. The traumatic might elicit from us a desire to know, or if not to know then to construct a narrative of coherence, to wrap it up in a tidy box (with a bow on top) and summarily cast it back to oblivion. "The over-valuation of wholeness and coherence goes hand-in-hand with a disavowal of partiality and fragmentation," Bill Nichols observes. "When we over-value, we fetishize."[26] The Gojira narrative does not impose closure on the traumatic narrative, it's not fetishistic, but rather as a malleable vessel makes allowances for a narrative that can only ever be partial and fragmentary. Drawing heavily from Eric Santer's work, Nichols notes that, "Recounting traumatic events must either engage in the work of mourning or resort to what he [Santer] calls narrative fetishism. Mourning begins with the acknowledgment of trauma and its destabilizing effect on the psyche; narrative fetishism begins with the disavowal of trauma."[27] In its role as a provisional vessel lending a voice to the souls of the dead, its visible

---

[25] Hosokawa, "Atomic Overtones," 56. Emphasis added.

[26] Bill Nichols, "The Terrorist Event," in *Ritual and Event*, ed. Mark Franko (New York: Routledge, 2007), 98.

[27] Ibid., 99. See Eric Santer, "History beyond the pleasure principle: some thoughts on the representation of trauma," in *Probing the Limits of Representation Nazism and the Final Solution*, ed. Saul Friedlander (Cambridge: Harvard University Press, 1992), 143-154.

marks of uncanny otherness, Gojira's body becomes the site/sight of mourning. And this again perhaps speaks to the longevity of the Gojira series as part of the on-going process of mourning.

Conclusion: "the stupider the better ..."

The confusion between emotion and sensation is endlessly propagated in contemporary film/media studies. Where emotion pertains to the object economy—narrative investment, and definable experiences (e.g., sadness over a character's death)—sensation, on the other hand, pertains to the economy of non-objects, the ineffable experiences that elicit peculiar physiological responses in the spectator, and it is here that affect is located. The conflation of emotion and sensation potentially sends us off on a "wild goose chase," diverting our critical attention to narrative content, when in fact a more productive enterprise might involve an appraisal of cinematic embellishments—style, form, non-communicative elements. The privileging of narrative content over form, at least in part, stems from the inception of our discipline; of course many film studies programs emerged from, or are still attached to, Literature departments. This is not to say, though, that it is necessary to "throw the baby out with the bath water," it would be a mistake to disregard narrative content, but rather than locating the affective charge as only woven into narrative fabric, one must marshal nuanced tools that precisely locate the ruptures in "meaning"—allowing us to identify those referents that offer provisional form to the non-object.

The national(ist) trauma plays out in the Gojira narrative, and the monster plays host to the affective charge associated with that trauma. These films—despite their campy aesthetic—exploit aesthetic strategies that elicit an affective response in the viewer. And in fact this might seem counterintuitive, but "the stupider it is, the better," Kristeva argues:

> for the filmic image does not need to be intelligent: what counts is that the specular presents the drive—aggression—through its directed signified (the object or situation represented) and encodes it through its plastic rhythm (the network of lektonic elements: sounds, tone, colors, space, figures), which can come back to us from the other without response and which consequently has remained uncaptured, unsymbolized, unconsumed.[28]

[28] Julia Kristeva, *Intimate Revolt: The Powers and Limits of Psychoanalysis*, trans. Jeanine Herman (New York: Columbia University, 2002), 77.

As Okawara's 1995 film, *Gojira tai Desutoroia*, demonstrates, the narrative content, the "meaning of the text," might very well be "inane," but it hosts referents that bear the potential to elicit affect. So "the stupider it is, the better," precisely because it frees the filmmaker and the scholar from the shackles of the imperative to "communicate," where the filmmaker makes "meaning" the scholar is traditionally commissioned to "unearth (deeper?) meaning." Instead filmmakers and scholars are afforded the luxury of concentrating on aesthetic embellishments (e.g., sound, light)—the place where affective energy ferments.

In his book, *Francis Bacon: The Logic of Sensation*, Gilles Deleuze arrives at a similar conclusion. Repeatedly Deleuze attempts to isolate in Bacon's painting the Figure—the embodiment of sensation—without "the danger of reintroducing a 'story' or falling back into narrative painting."[29] Deleuze, from a different theoretical framework, outlines many of the same tropes that Kristeva does—the undifferentiated body, the boundaries between self and meat, and these Figures (not figures, or the figurative—which pertains to concepts, narrative) materialize in color, rhythm and other elements that exceed figuration. The Figure, capital "F," in Deleuze directly accesses the nervous system, whereas figuration is channeled through cognitive faculties. Deleuze posits that "the Figure is the body without organs," which he characterizes not as a body that "lacks organs," but rather that "it simply lacks the organism," in other words, it is not governed by a socializing system.[30] The Figure manifests in the "zone of indiscernibility", where the territory between animal and human is effaced, between the socialized body and flesh/meat, between the living and dead, and finally in its relation in the state of "becoming." And it is precisely in these liminal non-categories, non-objects, that Kristeva locates affect: in artistic practices that negotiate "fragile border[s] (borderline cases) where identities (subject/object, etc.) do not exist or only barely so—double, fuzzy, heterogeneous, animal, metamorphosed, altered, abject."[31] And these "things" manifest in *form* precisely because they *do not* pertain to meaning as such, but to affect. The use of light, slow-motion, and non-diegetic/diegetic audio design in these films, by means of cinematic form, trade heavily in affect, serving a cathartic function for the traumatic (nationalistic) wound that still festers. The politics here are problematic to be sure, but the films nevertheless negotiates the open wound of a national(ist) trauma.

---

[29] Gilles Deleuze, *Francis Bacon: The Logic of Sensation*, trans. Daniel W. Smith (Minneapolis: University of Minnesota Press, 2004), 55.
[30] Ibid., 40; 41.
[31] Kristeva, *Powers*, 207.

CHAPTER EIGHT

THE MEDIATIZATION OF TRAUMA AND THE TRAUMA OF MEDIATIZATION: BENJAMIN, TULLOCH, AND THE STRUGGLE TO SPEAK

BEN O'LOUGHLIN

Introduction

Mediatization refers to the manner in which a social event, process or practice becomes considered by those participating in it as a media phenomenon, and any media organisations involved are aware of themselves as integral to that phenomenon.[1] Religion, sport, conflict, party politics—even history itself—have internalised today's media logics to the extent that we must say they are constituted through media. But what of a traumatic experience that defies representation, intelligibility and media logics? Is the silence, working-through, and emergence of trauma subject to the same digitization, acceleration and visualisation as the rest of mediatized 21st century life? Who is subjected to trauma, and witness to it, appears less determined; a global media ecology and archive creates indefinite listeners, new attention economies for trauma events, and allows the non-traumatised to re-tweet, mash-up and generally play with the eventual accounts of the traumatised. Trauma's widespread presence in contemporary society means it becomes enmeshed in mediatized practices. Have new rituals emerged to allow for the management of affect around trauma?

At the same time, has mediatization itself, as a social fact and inescapable condition, actually contributed to trauma? The ubiquity and centrality of mediatization to contemporary society masks the inescapable

[1] Thanks to Nathan Widder and Andrew J. Morley for discussions about this chapter, and to Meera Atkinson and Michael Richardson for commenting with great care and insight.

fact that many people are unprepared or unwilling for their lives to become public. As more of life becomes visible, recordable and searchable thanks to the diffusion of digital media, so the chances of details of one's life "going public" increase. Being caught up in an accident or becoming indirectly connected to a news story entails a permanent risk of being thrust into the media spotlight on the media's terms.

With this double-play of media and trauma in mind, this chapter explores the ways in which trauma becomes publicly present in a mediatized environment but also examines the trauma of finding oneself mediatized. These explorations are possible because a number of individuals have willingly shared their experience of the drama and trauma of mediatization. This chapter looks in particular at the shock of survivors of the 7/7 London bombings in 2005 as they found themselves becoming public property. Some experienced an inability in the immediate aftermath to articulate resistance against monolithic media representations. However, some individuals harnessed new media technologies to manage their trauma, for instance to form groups with other terrorist attack survivors. The analysis that follows also responds to Shoshana Felman's essay, "Benjamin's Silence," reprinted in this volume. Walter Benjamin was another individual who dealt with the mediatization of trauma and the trauma mediatization itself brings. His attempts to make public the trauma of the outbreak of world war and the suicide of his friends opens further space to think about how trauma is communicated from generation to generation. For instance, Benjamin was concerned that all that younger generations would know of the world wars would be images, since survivors would be stunned into silence and incapable of rendering their narratives and moral evaluations of their experiences to their children. This chapter focuses at length on the case of John Tulloch, a 7/7 survivor who opposed the war on terror and the 2003 Iraq War of the time. Benjamin too was opposed to wars unfolding but struggled with different modalities to get his opposition across to wider publics. The contrast of their periods of mediatization helps illuminate the continuities of structural power and individuals' uneven authority and capacity to communicate.

Trauma, defined by Cathy Caruth, refers to:

> a response, sometimes delayed, to an overwhelming event or events, which takes the form of repeated, intrusive hallucinations, dreams, thoughts or behaviors stemming from this event, along with numbing that may have

> begun during or after the experience, and possibly also increased arousal to (and avoidance of) stimuli recalling the event.[2]

Mediatization should be incommensurable with trauma. Mediatization involves the transformation of social practices and institutions into public, expressive, performing practices. Trauma leads to "numbing" and possibly avoidance, as Caruth states—the opposite of public expression. Furthermore, the victim of trauma may not recall the experience or event at the time. In some cases it may be repressed, emerging months and years later, perhaps in the process of giving testimony to a listener. Memory can return as fragments or aspects, or as an incongruent episode or sense of incongruence; there is not necessarily a narrative to relay. Trauma appears unsuited to news media presentation events as "stories" with cause and effect, with a past, present and likely future. While a traumatic event might have the drama, emotion and cast of characters that fulfill the news values of a good story, the slipperiness and variability of traumatic experience and memory create difficulties and risks for both journalist and traumatized interviewee in any attempt to report what happened and what the interviewee remembers.

This chapter is about the struggle to speak and bring to a new audience a traumatic experience. Such efforts are in many ways doomed. As Lyotard has written in the context of the Holocaust, there is an obligation to write about it and yet it is impossible, for innumerable reasons.[3] We should not invoke such horror; we are incapable of fully narrating such horror; if I narrate it, the horror will not hold the significance it had; and what if my narration is used as a tool by others, beyond my intention—is there an unavoidable risk I may betray the victims? Striving for certainty and a clear narrative will fail, and the resulting voice will be indirect and, when speaking for the suffering of others, lack authority. Yet, still, we must wrestle with it. Benjamin tries to relay the trauma of the simultaneous suicide of a friend and the outbreak of World War I. Tulloch tries to relay the trauma of being bombed in the 7/7 terrorist attacks in London in 2005 and the trauma of being thrust into the media spotlight as a supporter of Tony Blair. Indeed, journalists quickly labeled the image of Tulloch an "icon" of the 7/7 attacks.[4] He had to face the possibility his

---

[2] Cathy Caruth, *Trauma: Explorations in Memory* (Baltimore: Johns Hopkins University Press, 1995), 4.

[3] Jean-Francois Lyotard, *Heidegger and "the jews,"* trans. A. Michel and M.S. Roberts. (Minneapolis and London: University of Minnesota Press, 1990).

[4] John Tulloch and R.Warwick Blood, *Icons of War and Terror: Media Images in an Age of International Risk* (New York and Abingdon: Routledge, 2012).

face would be an image forever displayed when the attacks were remembered. Both Benjamin and Tulloch failed in the short term but eventually found a way to relate their experience of trauma.

Mediatization and Control

Mediatization is central to a long historical transformation in which institutions and practices take on a "media form."[5] All communication is *mediated*, if only by language and symbols. Mediated politics, for example, would refer to all politics. In contrast, *mediatization* describes "the meta process by which everyday practices and social relations are historically shaped by mediating technologies and media organizations."[6] The study of mediatization addresses the manner in which a social event, process or practice becomes considered by those participating in it as a media phenomenon, and any media organisations involved are aware of themselves as integral to that phenomenon. Another way to understand this is in terms of "media logics": certain mediums, and the production and consumption practices that emerge around them, privilege particular ways of behaving. Television prioritizes a visually compelling and verbally fluent mode of action which political leaders and organisations soon learnt to adapt to in the late 20th century to the degree that politics was *done differently* thereafter.[7]

A classic example pointed out by Baudrillard is the May '68 protests. Students could follow their actions in mass media. They began to identify with the subjects they saw presented on screen, at the expense of seeing through their immediate experience on the streets. This "mass mediatization" of the protests involved the "imposition" of news media

---

[5] Stig Hjarvard, "The Mediatization of Society: A Theory of the Media as Agents of Social and Cultural Change," *Nordicom Review*, 29, no. 2 (2008).

[6] Sonia Livingstone, "Foreword: Coming to Terms with 'Mediatization'," in *Mediatization: Concept, Changes, Consequences*, ed. Knut Lundby (New York: Peter Lang 2009), x.

[7] David L. Altheide and Robert P. Snow, *Media Logic* (London: Sage, 1979). For its application see Andrew Hoskins and Ben O'Loughlin, *War and Media: The Emergence of Diffuse War* (Cambridge: Polity, 2010), 103; Gianpetro Mazzoleni, "Mediatization of Politics," in *The International Encyclopedia of Communication*, ed. Wolfgang Donsbach (Malden, MA: Blackwell, 2008); Andrew Chadwick, *The Hybrid Media System: Power and Politics* (Oxford: Oxford University Press, forthcoming).

temporalities, news values and news' narrative frameworks.[8] The protests stopped following their own logics, and played out according to the news story template. The result was the protest movement's defeat. Hence, mediatization has concrete effects. The effects of mediatization have been documented in various fields of social life, including children's play,[9] religion,[10] war,[11] terrorism,[12] memory,[13] and electoral politics.[14]

The Internet has its own affordances that enable and constrain human action. Today, across a range of fields of social life, mediatization might be expected to become more intensive. More of life is digitized as media content. It is recorded, archived, retrieved, and transformed or remediated. Digital media create a potentially destabilizing dynamic here, a "contingent openness,"[15] since digital content can emerge to force the reconsideration of some event or phenomenon. The emergence of the chaotic phone video of Saddam Hussein's execution, photos from Abu Ghraib, or Wikileaks; all resulted in the unsettling of established meanings inside and outside the

---

[8] Jean Baudrillard, *For a Critique of the Political Economy of Signs* (St. Louis: Telos, 1981), 164-184. Cf. William Merrin, *Baudrillard and the Media: A Critical Introduction* (Cambridge: Polity, 2005).

[9] Stig Hjarvard, "From Bricks to Bytes: The Mediatization of a Global Toy Industry," in *European Culture and the Media*, eds. I. Bondebjerg and P. Golding (Bristol: Intellect Books, 2004); and Stine Liv Johansen, "The Mediatization of Children's Play," project at the University of Copenhagen, (no date), http://mediatization.ku.dk/publications/children/ (accessed September 29, 2012).

[10] Stig Hjarvard, "The Mediatization of Religion: A Theory of the Media as Agents of Religious Change," *Northern Lights* 6, no. 1 (2008).

[11] Simon Cottle, *Mediatized Conflict: Developments in Media and Conflict Studies*, (Maidenhead: Open University Press, 2006).

[12] Akil Awan, et al. *Radicalisation and Media: Terrorism and Connectivity in the New Media Ecology* (London: Routledge, 2011).

[13] Andrew Hoskins, "The Mediatization of Memory," in *Save As . . . Digital Memories*, eds. J. Garde-Hansen, et al. (Palgrave Macmillan, Basingstoke, 2009), and Andrew Hoskins, *The Mediatization of Memory: Media and the End of Collective Memory* (Cambridge, MA: MIT Press, forthcoming).

[14] Lawrence Ampofo, Nick Anstead, and Ben O'Loughlin, "Trust, Confidence and Credability: Citizen Responses on Twitter to Opinion Polls During the 2010 UK General Election," *Information, Communication & Society* 14, no. 6 (2011); Gianpetro Mazzoleni and W. Schulz, "'Mediatization of Politics': A Challenge for Democracy?" *Political Communication* 16, no. 3 (1999); and Jesper Strömbäck and Daniela V. Dimitrova, "Mediatization and Media Interventionism: A Comparative Analysis of Sweden and the United States," *International Journal of Press/Politics* 16, no. 1 (2011).

[15] John Urry, "The Complexity Turn," *Theory, Culture & Society* 22, no. 5 (2005), 3.

US about its foreign policy. For this reason, since the emergence of the Internet, and especially Web 2.0 and what Manuel Castells calls "mass self-communication,"[16] the last decade has seen great concern among power-holders about the "chaos" and "flux" of information. What Andrew Hoskins and I have called this "second phase of mediatization"[17] is one that has particularly problematized concepts and practices of control and cause-effect relationships in global affairs.

In his concept of mediatization, Baudrillard identifies even more fundamental effects. Mediatization is more than a matter of shaping institutions and behavior; it is epistemological and phenomenological. The way in which media institutions cut and edit live occurrences and stock footage into "events," "stories" and other semiotic structures comes to "define our experience and knowledge."[18] For instance, in the late 20th century "history" became what television had covered.[19] Events without accessible footage received less significance; "Vietnam" as storyline, event and catastrophe eclipsed the Korean War. Political leaders learnt to work with this. By the 2003 Iraq War, the US staged a series of televisual moments such as the felling of Saddam Hussein's statue and the "mission accomplished" celebration on an aircraft carrier. This recognition of television's role in defining audiences' understanding of history shows how leaders instrumentalise mediatization to establish the truth or reality of events. Given this instrumentalization, it is a short leap to ask whether the mediatized event even happened at all or was just a simulation, a non-event, as Baudrillard famously suggested of the first Gulf War.

The relation of trauma and affect to mediatization is important because it throws ordinary people into public presence in quite unexpected ways. Trauma is not something that necessarily involves media professionals who have been trained in how to speak fluently to camera. It entails people coping with the demands and expectations of performing for media. This is why it is useful to look both at how trauma becomes mediatized but also whether being mediatized is itself traumatic. The sheer relentlessness and ubiquity of mediatization would appear to represent a structural power that ordinary people would have little chance to influence. For example, Madianou has shown how losing control of one's media exposure can lead to shame, and that unwanted media representations of oneself can impact

[16] Manuel Castells, *Communication Power* (Oxford: Oxford University Press, 2009).
[17] Hoskins and O'Loughlin, *War and Media.*
[18] Merrin, *Baudrillard*, 65.
[19] Andrew Hoskins, *Televising War: From Vietnam to Iraq* (London: Continuum, 2004).

one's sense of self.[20] In 2003 Madianou interviewed "Laura," 25, who had become carnival queen for her London borough when she was 16, a year-long position that involved charity work and appearing in a parade. Laura became pregnant, the local newspaper published an article that upset her, and she withdrew as carnival queen. The article referred to the working class area she lived in and associated her with binge drinking among young women—an implied explanation of how she became pregnant. Whether or not Laura felt any shame at becoming pregnant, she imagined how a presumed audience would interpret the story. As Madianou writes, "Watching oneself on the media is bound to be an emotional experience involving pride, affirmation, confidence, but also possibly, rejection, shame and anger." [21] Laura felt unable to respond other than by withdrawing from her public role. She did not complain to the newspaper—the shame was "debilitating."[22] Laura was left "wordless" both publicly and in the interview with Madianou, in which she was reluctant to talk about the event. Laura's case demonstrated the structural power and indifference of mainstream news and how many ordinary people lack the agency to exert any control over their public appearance.

John Tulloch's case lies at the very limit of this. Journalists and editors using his photo assumed he was just another survivor. As it happened, he was a Research Professor of Sociology and Communications at Brunel University in London and formerly Head of the School for Journalism, Media and Cultural Studies at Cardiff University. He would have expected himself to know the mechanics of news reporting and what was happening around him. However, having just narrowly survived a major terrorist attack, physically debilitated and traumatized, he was not in a position to exert his full agency immediately.[23] Like Laura, Tulloch had to cope with the shock of being represented in ways he did not expect or welcome.

Despite the difficult cases of Laura and Tulloch and the pessimism of Baudrillard, mediatized trauma is not always hurtful or disempowering to those involved. It is through mediatized practices that survivors of 7/7 are able not only to represent their actual, immediate experiences, but also to create new, positive social ties. It is not that mediatization or the "simulacra" Baudrillard writes of are necessarily at the expense of actual social relations. Participatory media can be productive for ordinary people; in this case, as they try to deal with trauma. For instance, Tulloch

[20] Mirca Madianou, "News as a looking-glass: Shame and the symbolic power of mediation," *International Journal of Cultural Studies* 15, no. 1 (2011).
[21] Ibid., 7.
[22] Ibid., 9.
[23] John Tulloch, *One Day in July: Experiencing 7/7* (London: Little, Brown, 2006).

eventually contested the mediatized representation of himself and thus laid bare the process by which the truth or even the "history" of an event gets written by mainstream media. He used his expert knowledge of mediatization to inject critique and reflexivity into the process. He was permitted backroom access to news production after the event and used interviews to contest the categorizations journalists used, for instance reducing individuals to either attacker or victim. He was able to manage the trauma of his own mediatization, of seeing himself on the front cover of the best selling newspaper in the country expressing a political view he diametrically opposed. It was not a determined process. The rest of this chapter draws out some of the intricacies of these relationships.

The Mediatization of Trauma

Walter Benjamin's theory of war and silence is helpful for thinking about the representation and even mediatization of trauma today. In the opening chapter to this volume, Shoshana Felman describes Benjamin's long silence following the German invasion of Belgium at the outbreak of World War I on 4 August 1914 and the death of his friend, poet Fritz Heinle, four days later. Heinle committed suicide with his girlfriend Rika Seligson and left a note for Benjamin to come and find them, dead. Benjamin did not address either trauma directly, but through a lecture on Hölderlin and his autobiographical "A Berlin Chronicle" he implied a link between the outbreak of war and his friend's death as symbolizing both the extinguishing of life and the resistance and hope in youth. These reflections stand alongside two scholarly essays. In "The Storyteller" (1936), Benjamin argued that the trauma of World War I left participants unable to communicate their experience.[24] A number of conditions contributed to this outcome: capitalism, the diffusion of dull bourgeois values, the decline of craftsmanship, and the pervasiveness of mass media. All of these factors exist today at even further extremes, with critical scholars continuing to question the increasing penetration of everyday life by capitalism, a risk-averse bourgeois culture, the decline of craftsmanship, and the pervasiveness of mass media.[25] However, the primary cause for

---

[24] Walter Benjamin, *Illuminations*, trans. Harry Zohn (New York: Schocken, 1969), 83.

[25] Capitalism, see Luc Boltanski and Eve Chiapello, *The New Spirit of Capitalism* trans. Gregory Elliot (London: Verso, 2005); bourgeois culture, see Frank Furedi *Therapy Culture: Cultivating Vulnerability in an Uncertain Age* (London: Routledge, 2004); craftsmanship, see Richard Sennett *The Craftsman* (New Haven,

this subjective en masse silence, for Benjamin, was the experience of the First World War, a "collective, massive trauma."[26] Body and mind were exposed to destructive forces and violence beyond intelligibility and that people could not readily communicate. Individuals could not share their experiences; "Their trauma must remain a private matter that cannot be symbolized collectively."[27]

Several of Benjamin's assumptions no longer hold. The distinction of public/private and individual/collective underpinning his account are problematic in today's media environment. When the BBC, ABC or CNN position themselves as much as platforms for audience commentary as channels of one-to-many broadcasting, the dualism of mass media versus personalized communication has clearly blurred.[28] Castells uses the term "mass self-communication" because the global dispersion of social media means people everywhere can engage in the same media practices of self-publishing and content sharing as well as old-fashioned consumption of professionally-produced content. John Thompson argues that the distinction between public and private remains important morally but is becoming less easy to demonstrate empirically.[29] These trends manifest themselves on Benjamin's terrain of the trauma of war. Since the early 2000s there has been a proliferation of public communication by soldiers, for instance the phenomenon of war—or milblogs. There has been increasing public recognition of private trauma, with Post-Traumatic Stress Disorder (PTSD) more widely recognized and less stigmatized. A digital media ecology has also resulted in the occasional leaking of private military information that describes the trauma being suffered by soldiers. For instance, in October 2010 Wikileaks published information from the US Army War Logs about suicides, mental breakdowns and violence between US soldiers.[30] Finally, an endless series of wars, conflicts and catastrophes feeds a media ecology characterized by the 24/7 presence of traumatic events, a surround of suffering whose social and long term effects have yet

---

CT: Yale University Press, 2008); mass media, see Sherry Turkle, *Alone Together* (New York: Basic Books, 2011).

[26] Felman, "Benjamin's Silence," 206 / 27.

[27] Ibid., 207 / 28.

[28] Cf. Livingstone, "Foreword."

[29] John Thompson, "Shifting Boundaries of Public and Private Life," *Theory, Culture & Society* 28, no. 4 (2011).

[30] Spiegel *The WikiLeaks Iraq Logs: A Protocol of Barbarity*. Spiegel Online International, October 25, 2010. http://www.spiegel.de/international/world/the-wikileaks-iraq-logs-a-protocol-of-barbarity-a-724026-7.html (accessed September 26, 2012).

to be understood and documented. It is no coincidence that in recent years literature on media "witnessing" has flourished.[31] We can ask whether these images and self-reporting practices offer accurate accounts of the experience of war given that it is difficult if not impossible for trauma to be adequately represented.[32] Nevertheless, there is no doubt that there has been an increasing mediatization of trauma and the likelihood of witnessing mediatized trauma.

Given these changes, we must also re-assess one implication Benjamin drew from his theory of war and silence: that the loss of personal and collective narration implies the loss of moral thinking. Here, Benjamin refers to the figure of the dying man on his deathbed, who draws authority from directly facing death and is thus able to speak. At such a moment an individual can evaluate his or her own life and ethical conduct. If survivors of the world wars could not narrate even on their deathbeds, then moral evaluation evaporates. Storytelling is evaluative, and if individuals cannot tell stories they have no framework to evaluate.

To the extent that these propositions were valid, they are again problematic today. Narrative too has been mediatized, that is, disciplined by the logics of media forms and institutions. To return to personal narratives of war and its traumas, there is greater reflexivity about how these should be represented in public. When individuals record with their own mobile devices, they exhibit media literacy about what constitutes desirable footage ("what shoots well"[33]), they make presumptions about likely audiences and their tastes, and possible critiques or misunderstandings. They consider the criteria by which amateur footage may be picked up by mainstream media organisations and used in professional broadcasts. Narrative is also formed and concretized through the pre-construction of stories. The majority of news stories in mainstream media follow "templates" in which breaking news events are fitted into the

---

[31] John Ellis, *Documentary: Witness and Self-Revelation* (London : Routledge, 2011) Paul Frosh and Amit Pinchevski, eds. *Media Witnessing: Testimony in the Age of Mass Communication* (Basingstoke: Palgrave Macmillan, 2009); Frances Guerin and Roger Hallas, eds. *The Image and the Witness: Trauma, Memory and Visual Culture* (London: Wallflower Press, 2007); John Durham Peters "Witnessing," *Media, Culture & Society* 23, no. 6 (2001); and Leshu Torchin, *Creating the Witness: Documenting Genocide on Film, Video, and the Internet* (Minneapolis: University of Minnesota Press, 2012).

[32] Lytord, *Heidegger*; Guerin and Hallas, *Image and Witness*.

[33] Ben Mor, "Public Diplomacy in Grand Strategy," *Foreign Policy Analysis* 2, no. 2 (2006).

narrative of a previous event audiences are expected to be familiar with.[34] These conventions mean that morality and righteousness can be invoked and assumed to be intelligible by an event's reporters, participants and audiences. The construction of a new event as "scandal" or "bombing" or "new accord" invokes the problems, dilemmas, heroes and villains of previous iterations of that event type.

Such conventions are most evident when breached. On 5 September 2012 three members of a British family holidaying in Annecy, France were murdered, as well as a passing French cyclist. One four-year-old girl survived the attack by lying under the legs of her dead mother for eight hours, until discovered by police. Two days later, *The Guardian* published an opinion article asking whether it would be possible for the four-year-old daughter to return to a "normal" life, and what that might mean.[35] The article byline ran, "Is forgetting or rationalizing such trauma the best path to a normal life?" It was published in *The Guardian*'s online "Comment is Free Section", in which readers are invited to leave comments and discuss the article topic on the pages below the line area. The comments indicate how uncomfortable readers were being put in a position to comment on this traumatic event. Only 15 comments were posted before *The Guardian* closed the comment function. The first comment from username Definitelynotashark was, "Im really not sure what type of comments you are expecting on here?" While a few users then commented on trauma itself, others argued that *The Guardian* had overstepped a boundary by publishing this article or making it a topic for debate. It is "too soon," *The Guardian* was being "sensationalist," the newspaper was "rushing in." The comment about sensationalism illustrated a degree of media reflexivity in analyzing the editorial decision to publish, the content of the article, the likely knowledge of the story held by other readers, and the intention or "angle" *Guardian* editors were taking. That comment received by far the most recommends. That readers agreed a line had been overstepped, and the newspaper cut off comments, shows normative conventions operating and that moral evaluation had not disappeared even when the individual's trauma had not been narrated.

Does war still create silence in a mediatized society by reducing unfolding events to a single history? This is an important question

---

[34] Jenny Kitzinger, "Media Templates: Key Events and the (Re)construction of Meaning," *Media, Culture & Society* 22, no. 1 (2000).

[35] Anouchka Grose, "In Annecy, a child witnesses murder. It can't be sewn into 'normal'," *The Guardian*, September 7, 2012, http://www.guardian.co.uk/commentisfree/2012/sep/07/annecy-child-witnessed-murder?INTCMP=SRCH (accessed September 26, 2012).

politically. In the context of world war, Benjamin attacked history as a field and discourse on two grounds. On the one hand history at the time lacked the conceptual resources or frames of reference to make sense of the world wars. Historians were reduced to amazement, but this only exposed the poverty of historians' grasp of political change. He wrote, "This amazement is not the beginning of knowledge—unless it is knowledge that the view of history which gives rise to it is untenable."[36] This amazement at shocking events remains present in political statements about war and security today. The 9/11 Commission Report is notable for describing the 11 September 2011 attacks on New York and Washington DC as "unprecedented" and "resistant to any analysis."[37] Such thinking absolves any authority of blame and steers directly away from systematic judgment about the complexities that led to the attacks. Similarly, Wikileaks' release of US diplomatic cables created amazement among US political elites. The *New York Times* Editor Bill Keller defended the release of the information, saying on television that "it's history in real time."[38] However, an unnamed official briefed the *Washington Post*, saying US diplomats were "in shock" and that Hillary Clinton found that "As the nation's diplomat-in-chief, this is really unpleasant, and difficult and uncomfortable."[39] The Italian Foreign Minister, Franco Frattini, called the leaks the "September 11th of world diplomacy."[40] Confusion was evident in the response of US policy elites. On Fox News, one former Defense Intelligence Agency officer proposed military action against Assange: "I would look at this very much as a military issue. With potentially military action against him and his organization."[41] Hence, political and media discourse gravitates quickly to a singular narrative in

[36] Benjamin, *Illuminations*, 257.
[37] Cited in Tulloch and Blood, *Icons*, 173.
[38] Scott Neuman, "Clinton: WikiLeaks 'Tear At Fabric' Of Government," *NPR*, November 29, 2010, 2012 http://www.npr.org/2010/11/29/131668950/white-house-aims-to-limit-wikileaks-damage (accessed September 26),
[39] Mary Beth Sheridan, "Hillary Clinton: WikiLeaks release an 'attack on international community'," *Washington Post*, November 29, 2010, http://www.washingtonpost.com/wp-dyn/content/article/2010/11/29/AR2010112903231.html (accessed September 26, 2012).
[40] Spiegel. *Outrage and Apologies: Washington Fights to Rebuild Battered Reputation*. Spiegel Online International, December 6, 2010. http://www.spiegel.de/international/world/outrage-and-apologies-washington-fights-to-rebuild-battered-reputation-a-733088.html (accessed September 26, 2011).
[41] Declan McCullagh, "Congressman wants WikiLeaks listed as terrorist group," *CNET*, November 28, 2010, http://news.cnet.com/8301-13578_3-20023941-38.html (accessed September 26, 2012).

order to minimize or negate shock. In this case, the story became one of "what to do about Wikileaks" rather than "what do the cables reveal about US foreign policy."

For Benjamin, the losers and the powerless have no say in history; they do not get to write history books. "The continuum of history is that of the oppressors," Benjamin writes.[42] Benjamin's "Theses" essay invokes Paul Klee's painting of an angel facing backwards, being blown into the future, witnessing a pile of debris piling up at its own feet. Benjamin interprets this as a parable. The debris stands for ideas of universal history and progress, the ideas of Kant and Hegel, an "ideological sham" that distracted us from the victims of history and the violence of today.[43] There is no telos or line into the future because if humanity is facing backwards we cannot see what is coming or any signposts showing direction or progress. However, that accumulation of debris offers hope: an imperative for a messianic moment of seeing history's wreckage and realizing a new direction. That new direction might not bring progress, but it could bring redemption.[44]

More recent thinking on time and politics has led attention to a question that follows from Benjamin's analysis. If there is no clear line into the future, and there are multiple histories, not just the winner's, then how can politics incorporate representations of multiple histories and multiple trajectories that exist simultaneously? For instance, Kimberley Hutchings argues that such heterotemporality can be found both empirically and conceptually in international affairs. Western humanitarian interventions are viewed by some groups as missions of progress towards a universal liberal order and by others as a continuation of global power asymmetries. For Hutchings this indicates "a mutual contamination of 'nows' […] which do not derive their significance from one meta-narrative about how they all fit together."[45]

Can mediatized news cope with heterotemporality and thus be able to offer public representation to different histories of trauma? It remains the case that news media cannot proceed on this basis. News works through recursivity, the assumption that audiences are familiar with the past of a story and that each story has a linear narrative that audiences can catch up with, drop back in to. Hetero-recursivity would be a fundamental challenge

---

[42] Felman, "Benjamin's Silence," 210 / 32.

[43] David Hoy, *The Time of Our Lives: A Critical History of Temporality* (Cambridge, MA: The MIT Press, 2009), 154.

[44] Felman, "Benjamin's Silence."

[45] Kimberly Hutchings, *Time and World Politics: Thinking the Present*, (Manchester: Manchester University Press, 2008), 166.

to the way news works. Furthermore, on any given story, mainstream news organisations "index" their reporting to those with the power to determine its outcome.[46] This makes sense because journalists seek to keep their audiences informed about the likely course of events. However, those with the power to determine outcomes are usually governments and large corporations. After the 7/7 bombings, a dominant narrative did form through statements of political leaders and the reporting of mainstream media. The narrative emphasized the inevitability of attacks on London, the motives of the attackers, practical responses and the need for moving on.[47] Indeed, it was already in place before the bombings: in May 2003 the BBC broadcast a prime time simulation, "London under attack," to prepare citizens—and any policymakers, journalists and emergency response workers watching—for how a real crisis might unfold, and that featured many of the same "experts" who appeared in the reporting of the actual terrorist incidents in 2005.[48] Hoskins writes of "gravitational memorial forces"[49] that kick in to fix meaning immediately or even before an event unfolds, forces including mainstream television and later public inquests and other institutional processes.

As mainstream media and political practices gravitate towards a dominant (or "mainstream") narrative today, so too did the historian in Benjamin's day, he argued. It was for this reason that Benjamin proposed the historian's task *should be* "to give voice to the dead and to the vanquished and to resuscitate the unrecorded, silenced, hidden story of the oppressed."[50] But today, in some situations the dead, the vanquished and the oppressed have made their own recordings and published them. Mediatization enables pluralized content and innovative media practices, albeit with no promise of "mainstream" or mass audiences. One instance

[46] Daniel C. Hallin, *The "Uncensored War"* (Berkeley: University of California Press, 1986); W. Lance Bennett, "Toward a theory of press-state relations," *Journal of Communication* 40, no. 2 (1991); Lance Bennett and Sonia Livinstone, "A semi-independent press: Government control and journalistic autonomy in the political construction of news," *Political Communication*, 20 (2003); W. Lance Bennett, RG Lawrence, and Steven Livingston, "None dare call it torture: indexing and the limits of press independence in the Abu Ghraib scandal," *Journal of Communication* 56, no. 4 (2006).

[47] Nuria Lorenzo-Dus and Annie Bryan, "Dynamics of memory: Commemorating the 2005 London bombings in British television news," *Memory Studies* 4, no. 3 (2011), 285-6.

[48] Awan, et al. *Radicalisation*, 66-83.

[49] Andrew Hoskins, "7/7 and Connective Memory: Interactional Trajectories of Remembering in Post-Scarcity Culture," *Memory Studies* 4, no. 3 (2011).

[50] Felman, "Benjamin's Silence," 214 / 35.

after the 7/7 bombings was the "living memorial" created through the website of the Miriam Hyman Memorial Trust, set up by Miriam's sister Esther after Miriam was killed in the attacks.[51] The memorial functioned as an interactive space through which interested parties could learn about Miriam Hyman's life and about how the trust was using funds to sponsor medical treatment for people with optical disease. It was a site designed for people to visit, consume content, share stories, and find and begin new interactions with other people. This mediatized space shows how new relationships and digital content can together be set in-motion, supplementing mainstream media narratives and conventions.[52]

Many of the tendencies Benjamin identifies concerning the silencing of trauma and gravitational pull towards a singular historical narrative appear to operate in a mediatized news environment. However, there have been some important changes to the relation of mass to personal and public to private that begin to unravel, or at least work alongside these gravitational forces. In the next section, I explore the tension between the structures of power that sustain these forces and individual agency, and, in a different way, examine the struggle to control the communication of one's trauma. What happens when individuals are thrust into the public eye? What resources and opportunities are there in a mediatized environment to control their public representation?

The Trauma of Mediatization

As discussed earlier, for Benjamin world war ushered in a silence of narration that resulted in a generalized crisis of narrative in Germany. The consequence of this was diminished morality, since it is through stories that people can evaluate events and conduct. In "Theses on the Philosophy of History" (1940) Benjamin argued that 19th century historicism and the Nazi regime in Germany each reduced history to a single, linear narrative. In the process, they silenced the powerless, the oppressed and, in most cases, the dead. As Shoshana Felman notes, it is through these indirect reflections on war, trauma and silence that Benjamin finds a way to express his own trauma while remaining seemingly silent about it. And with his eventual suicide in 1940, during his attempt to escape Nazi-occupied France while carrying a manuscript, Felman argues Benjamin became a symbol himself, "a proverb", what today we might call an icon.

---

[51] Matthew J. Allen, and Steve D. Brown, "Embodiment and living memorials: The affective labour of remembering the 2005 London bombings," *Memory Studies* 4, no. 3 (2011).
[52] Hoskins, "7/7."

Subsequent generations have heard of his trauma, and the trauma of those lives he described, because, by echoing the suicide of Heinle, Benjamin enacted a repetition of the utmost severity and this, for Felman, increased his authority as a narrator.

What becomes clear in Felman's account is Benjamin's continued failure to find an overt way to articulate these traumas. He used a variety of media forms and practices, but it was perhaps suicide that proved the most successful mode of communication. Critics did not realize that his post-1914 silence, as later narrated in "A Berlin Chronicle," was a way of expressing the critical position taken in his essays "The Storyteller" and "Theses on the Philosophy of History"; instead, his silence was "at once dismissed and trivialized", Felman writes. She also thinks the Hölderlin lecture "failed to translate the impact of the event" of Heinle's death and war's outbreak. The lecture was "roundabout," she argues. This makes sense if trauma is understood as the inability to address or articulate an event directly, as suggested earlier. Finally, "A Berlin Chronicle" is addressed to Stefan, Benjamin's son who was then a child. It is an attempt to convey his traumatic experiences to the next generation, to create a chain of memory of those traumas. He was concerned that the inability of war veterans and survivors to narrate their experiences would create a gap between the next generation and his. Carrying a manuscript presumed to be the "Theses" essay, Benjamin was arrested at the French/Spanish border and feared he would be handed over to the Gestapo. It was at that point that Benjamin killed himself.

In a radically different media ecology, John Tulloch has been through several attempts to relay his traumatic experience and his political critique. On 5 July 2005 Tulloch was sitting a meter from one of the four suicide bombers on a London underground train. He was photographed an hour later with bandages on his head held together by another survivor's silk tie, hair thick with dust, and his face covered in dried blood. The next morning, this photo was on the front page of *The Sun* newspaper.[53] On 8 November *The Sun* printed the photo again, with the headline, "Terror Laws: Tell Tony He's Right." Using what was effectively a cartoon speech bubble, *The Sun* presented Tulloch as supporting the war on terror legislation of Tony Blair and his Labour Government. On 10 November, Tulloch told *The Guardian* newspaper:

> This is using my image to push through draconian and utterly unnecessary terrorism legislation. Its incredibly ironic that *The Sun*'s rhetoric is as the voice of the people yet they don't actually ask the people involved, the

[53] Online at publication at: http://news.bbc.co.uk/2/hi/uk_news/5118048.stm

> victims, what they think. If you want to use my image, the words coming out of my mouth would be, 'Not in my name, Tony'. I haven't read anything or seen anything in the past few months to convince me these laws are necessary.[54]

Years later, in a scholarly monograph *Icons of War and Terror*, Tulloch reflects that the ordeal gave him the opportunity to reflect on how media create iconic images in the first place. He experienced "close-up, and somewhat powerlessly, the construction, circulation and manipulation of [my] image in the world's media."[55] Among other iconic images of trauma such as Kim Phuc, the girl running from napalm in Vietnam, or the "falling man" images from the 11 September 2001 attacks on New York's twin towers. Unlike those, however, Tulloch was an icon who was able to bring agency to his trauma.

Tulluch used media interviews to try to convey the multiple identities of those involved. He felt neither he nor the suicide bomber next to him, Mohammad Siddique Khan, could or should be understood as only "survivor" and "attacker." For example, in an ITN national news broadcast on 7 July 2006 Tulloch writes that he "secured conceptual, voice-over and editing control of [my] item on the identities of Mohammad Siddique Khan."[56]

Nevertheless, Tulloch's relationship to media was complex because trauma is so difficult to narrate. His therapist tried several ways to get Tulloch to recover "trapped" memories of the bombing, but Tulloch himself writes (in the third person):

> Tulloch was only too aware that what 'trapped' him most (consciously, at least) in these therapy recall sessions was the realization that his memories of 7/7 had been constructed in part via his process of talking about the event to the media. By the time he reached the final session with his PTSD [Post Traumatic Stress Disorder] therapist, he was so aware of this imagistic media narrative obstructing his therapy that he was ever more urgently searching for 'new images' of the 7/7 event.[57]

Not only did Tulloch scan media for different images of the event, he searched the Internet to find more information about the science of trauma

---

[54] Ros Coward, "'They have given me somebody else's voice—Blair's voice'," *The Guardian*, November 10, 2005, http://www.guardian.co.uk/politics/2005/nov/10/media.media (accessed September 29, 2012).
[55] Tulloch and Blood, *Icons*, 7.
[56] Ibid., 177.
[57] Ibid., 179.

and therapy. He had previously written on different modalities of risk and was aware of disjunctures between expert and lay discourses of risk. This knowledge, and his ability to survey news and the Internet to find more information about his own case and others, enabled him to explore and construct his own subject position vis-a-vis the event, journalists and therapists. Hence, as well as satisfying his emerging interest in how icons emerge, Tulloch was able to use the mediatized ecology of 21st century Britain to gain empowerment in his own situation.

Even then, Tulloch has been unable to arrive at the kind of stable narrative that might please mainstream media. In 2012 the UK government threatened to withdraw Tulloch's right to stay in the UK, following his adoption of Australian citizenship in the 1980s. In the BBC's reporting, the suitcases re-emerged into the public eye:

> Prof Tulloch was one of hundreds injured in the 7/7 blasts in 2005 when four suicide bombers attacked central London, killing 52 people.
>
> He became a symbol of the country's resilience after his picture was published in the media after the 7/7 attacks. He was also visited by Prince Charles in hospital.
>
> Shards of shrapnel were embedded in his face and he has suffered symptoms of post-traumatic stress disorder.
>
> He told the inquest into the 7/7 deaths that he was partially shielded from the blast by the luggage at his feet.
>
> Prof Tulloch says the uncertainty over remaining in the UK is worse for him than 7/7 because had been 'lucky' on that day [sic]. He had survived then managed to go on a 'journey' which saw him write two books related to his experiences.[58]

In an interview with Hoskins (2011), Tulloch describes the surprise of learning a year after the 7/7 bombings that the suitcases that covered and perhaps saved his legs when a bomb exploded in his train carriage turned out to have stopped somebody trying to cover the body of a victim and afford them more dignity. Tulloch had celebrated those cases, but now the cases "were the guilty party, the bad guys, not the good guys that had saved my legs." In being asked to move between, Tulloch was placed back there (the event) with his original understanding of what happened, placed now (in the inquest) to learn of what actually happened, and back there

[58] Caroline Evans, "Prof John Tulloch, 7/7 London bomb survivor, fights to stay in UK," *BBC News Wales*, September 2, 2012, http://www.bbc.co.uk/news/uk-wales-19455691 (accessed September 29, 2012).

again (the event) with a new understanding of the role of his suitcases.[59] This new meaning of the cases has not been woven into the public narrative of John Tulloch. In the BBC's 2012 report, the fact that the suitcases were now "the bad guys" was omitted.

Conclusion

William Connolly says that it is in the traumatic or uncanny event that the ambiguity of morality becomes strikingly clear.[60] What might have seemed black and white, right or wrong, legal or illegal, suddenly loses its straightforwardness. Indeed this is partly what makes trauma such an unsettling experience; the ground is shifting under us. In a mediatized environment in which trauma becomes increasingly enmeshed in media practices and representations, it remains the case that mainstream media operates in a way that channels audiences to forget the ambiguities of morality. News media in particular seeks a clean, clear narrative. For the person who has experienced trauma, part of what is uncanny is the realization that this is impossible. The media are being dishonest in their aims but the individual has little recourse.

Tulloch was caught in the middle of this dilemma. Not only did he see the rapid imposition of a clean, clear narrative that did not fit his understanding of the political ambiguities and contradictions in play, but that clean, clear narrative was attributed to him without his consent. His professional background gave him the agentic capacities to seek control of his presentation, gain information on his medical situation, and carve out a particular subject position for himself.[61]

The form of mediatization that has brought participatory digital platforms and increased media literacy and reflexivity affords individuals new ways to deal with traumatic experiences. From the websites created by 7/7 survivors to readers' critical comments on *The Guardian* website about its treatment of a trauma event, it is clear that the breakdown of distinctions between mass and personal communication, and between public and private, creates new opportunities for ordinary citizens to mediatize trauma on their own terms.

---

[59] Ben O'Loughlin, "Commentary: The Phenomenology of the Event: Remembering the 2005 London Bombings," *Memory Studies*, 4:3 (2011).

[60] William Connolly, *The Augustian Imperative: A Reflection on the Politics of Morality* (London: Sage, 1993), 131-138.

[61] Diana Coole, "Rethinking Agency: A Phenomenological Approach to Embodiment and Agentic Capacities," *Political Studies* 53, no. 1 (2005).

How would news media address trauma in a way that satisfies the critiques of Benjamin and Tulloch? Trauma and mainstream news media appear inherently mismatched, and yet the drama of trauma is irresistible to news media. Trauma offers no simple narrative, no certain truth, and these are the very axioms of a news "story." Thinking forward, however, could we be bold enough to imagine a journalism that might cover trauma by reporting that very uncertainty and that represents how people cope with certainty's absence, and the strategies they use to come to terms with their experience? At the very least, in a mediatized age in which so much detail of events is searchable and accessible, audience members may feel curious enough to investigate the event themselves, to do "homework," to source alternative accounts to those offered up by the mainstream media.[62]

A second agenda for further research concerns the ways in which mediatization affects those not expecting to appear in news media, such as Laura and Tulloch. Does the "contingent openness"[63] of mediatization and the ever-present threat of becoming public create trauma beyond the individual cases explored here? Karin Jürs-Munby asks "whether traumatization may not also reside in the very form of global mediatization itself."[64] It might reasonably be asked whether ubiquitous footage on daily news of traumatic death and injury creates conditions for a secondary trauma among audiences-cum-witnesses. As Hoskins and I have pointed out, there have been no systematic studies of the effects of a global media ecology of violence and trauma on audiences.[65] What forms of anxiety, compassion or apathy are produced through routine engagement with such news? Despite much speculation we simply do not know, and it will take much methodological imagination to even begin to address this.

Digital media enables unprecedented voice *and* unprecedented risks to the private- or self-image. There may be less of a struggle to speak in the first place, but more of a struggle to retain control of one's words and images. We need to examine theoretically and empirically how these tensions play out and whether, in some cases and for some people, the prospect of navigating these tensions shuts down communication altogether. It is not unthinkable that mediatization and silence can live together and with political effects, meaning the old questions about structural power and the agency of creativity are as important as ever.

---

[62] Karin Jürs-Munby, "'Did You mean Post-Traumatic Theatre?': The Vicissitudes of Traumatic Memory in Contemporary Postdramatic Performance," *Performance Paradigm* 5, no. 2 (2009), 20.
[63] Urry, "Complexity," 3.
[64] Jürs-Munby, "Vicissitudes," 24.
[65] Hoskins and O'Loughlin, *War and Media*, 37-39

CHAPTER NINE

WHERE THE BUFFALO NO LONGER ROAM: AFFECT AND ALLEGORY IN *THE LAST HUNT* AND *THE LAST BUFFALO HUNT*

JONATHAN L. KNAPP

Lee Anne Schmitt's and Lee Lynch's *The Last Buffalo Hunt* (2011) is part of a growing body of experimental documentaries that deconstruct the history and iconography of the North American West.[1] The American bison, or buffalo, is one of the frontier's most enduring symbols.[2] The near extinction of the species is deeply intertwined with government policies toward American Indians as well as the rise of ranching and the railroad, making the buffalo a particularly appropriate emblem of the West's complex history.[3] This essay will explore the dark side of westward expansion by comparing *The Last Buffalo Hunt* to Richard Brooks' 1956 Western *The Last Hunt*.[4] Though these films come from very different eras and generic traditions, each projects legacies of racism and environmental catastrophe onto the body of the buffalo.

Both films revolve around buffalo hunting—with *The Last Hunt* detailing the twilight years of the frontier, when buffalo had nearly

---

This essay would not have come about without the guidance and encouragement of Aaron Kerner.

[1] *The Last Buffalo Hunt,* directed by Lee Anne Schmitt and Lee Lynch (2011, from the artist), DVD. Other key examples include the work of James Benning, as well as Lucien Castaing-Taylor and Ilisa Barbash's *Sweetgrass* (2009).

[2] Patricia Nelson Limerick, *The Legacy of Conquest: The Unbroken Past of the American West* (New York: Norton, 1987), 314-316.

[3] Richard Slotkin, *The Fatal Environment: The Myth of the Frontier in the Age of Industrialization, 1800-1890* (Middletown, CT: Wesleyan University Press, 1985), 408, 427.

[4] *The Last Hunt*, directed by Richard Brooks (1956; Burbank, CA: Warner Archive Collection, 2012), DVD.

disappeared from the landscape. Though a fictional narrative, Brooks' film incorporates real footage of the government's annual hunt of the buffalo herd in Custer State Park in South Dakota. This contemporaneous footage serves as an allegory for the systematic slaughter of buffalo that took place during the late 19th century, and for the violent acts committed against American Indians and their land. *The Last Buffalo Hunt* shows how this traumatic history lingers in the present: a vast landscape that was once vibrant and diverse has given way to one of isolated herds and impoverished reservations, while images of buffalo and American Indians have been subsumed within commercial culture—used to signify rural casinos and convenience stores that flank lonely desert freeways. Much of *The Last Buffalo Hunt* focuses on safari-like chartered hunts that take place in Utah's remote Henry Mountains, which culminate in long, excruciating scenes of death. Drawing from the work of Jeffrey Skoller,[5] I will use Walter Benjamin's theory of the allegory and Gilles Deleuze's concept of the time-image to analyze how these films use real footage of buffalo slaughters, the bloody scenes of death and mutilation serving two functions: to elicit affect and to allegorize the traumatic history of violence—against animals, humans, and the land itself—that haunts the Western landscape.

Allegory and *The Last Hunt*

When Richard Brooks adapted Milton Lott's novel *The Last Hunt* for the screen, he had been working in Hollywood for over a decade, initially as a screenwriter, and then as a writer-director, a role he took on with the film *Crisis* (1950). The film Brooks made just prior to *The Last Hunt*, *The Blackboard Jungle* (1955), generated controversy for its social commentary, for showcasing rock & roll, and for fears that it might contribute to juvenile delinquency.[6] Thus, Brooks had a reputation as a provocateur, a label *The Last Hunt* only reinforces. With the film, Brooks intended to force American audiences to confront their nation's legacy of buffalo hunting, which nearly drove the species to extinction. According to Stewart Granger, one of the film's stars, Brooks seemed to take a perverse pleasure in capturing the gore of the buffalo hunts.[7] Because of this focus on brutality, censors demanded cuts to the film, and audiences protested its

---

[5] See Jeffrey Skoller, *Shadows, Specters, Shards: Making History in Avant-Garde Film* (Minneapolis: University of Minnesota Press, 2005).
[6] Douglass K. Daniel, *Tough as Nails: The Life and Films of Richard Brooks* (Madison: University of Wisconsin Press, 2011), 92-94.
[7] Ibid., 97.

violence.[8] The relevance of the buffalo to American Indian culture—and the allegorical parallels that could be drawn between the plight of the buffalo and that of American Indians—was not lost on Brooks, nor was the power of the bloody imagery. The degree to which contemporary audiences consciously understood Brooks' correlation between buffalo hunting and the treatment of American Indians is unclear, but the connection was made explicit by reviewers of the day.[9] What is clear is that audiences who protested the film were troubled by the gruesome footage. The film succeeds because it fuses its allegorical elements with footage that gives the audience an affective charge.

To understand how the film connects its buffalo hunting footage to historical buffalo hunting and to violence against American Indians, it is necessary to establish Walter Benjamin's theories of history and allegory. Benjamin conceives history as a continuum, as an endlessly unfolding catastrophe in which the past, present, and future have a complex, dynamic relationship. The past haunts the present like a ghost, and its traces are embedded in the objects that surround us. The way that one can capture these "ghostly signals," and come to see and understand how the past is embedded in the present, is through a process that Benjamin calls "profane illumination."[10] Avery F. Gordon describes this as a type of "conjuring,"[11] as remnants of the past are animated in such a way that their presence and their complexity become apparent. One, therefore, comes to view the present moment as being in communion with what has already occurred. Richard J. Lane has summed up how the past and present are in dialogue, how a single space or a single object "not only holds historical traces and contains explosive forces, but encompasses parallel existences."[12]

One of the ways that art can illuminate these past histories is through allegory, which Benjamin discusses in *The Origin of German Tragic*

---

[8] Ibid., 98.

[9] See Bosley Crowther, "Screen: Out Where the Buffalo Roam: 'The Last Hunt' Has Premiere at State," *New York Times*, March 1, 1956, 37. Also B.G. Marple, "*The Last Hunt*," *Films in Review* 7, no. 3 (1956): 131-132.

[10] Walter Benjamin, "Surrealism: The Last Snapshot of the European Intelligensia," in *Reflections: Essays, Aphorisms, Autobiographical Writings*, trans. Edmund Jephcott, ed. Peter Demetz, (New York: Harcourt Brace Jovanovich, 1978), 179-183.

[11] Avery Gordon, *Ghostly Matters: Haunting and the Sociological Imagination* (Minneapolis: University of Minnesota Press, 1997), 205.

[12] Richard Lane, *Reading Walter Benjamin: Writing Through the Catastrophe* (New York: Manchester University Press, 2005), 68.

Drama.[13] Craig Owens explains Benjamin's notion of allegory as a sort of doubling, a layering similar to the parallel existences that Lane identifies. "In allegorical structure, then, one text is *read through* another, however fragmentary, intermittent, or chaotic their relationship may be; the paradigm for the allegorical work is thus the palimpsest."[14] When an image is used within allegory, Owens argues, it becomes a hieroglyph, which he means in the sense elaborated by Roland Barthes: "[it is] a radical condensation of narrative into a single, emblematic instant […] in which the past, present, and future, that is, the *historical* meaning, of the depicted action might be read."[15]

In its use of 20th century footage of real buffalo deaths, *The Last Hunt* condenses the past and present in a single instant that illuminates the historical meaning of buffalo hunting. This footage of death is an allegory for the devastation that took place across the American West in the 19th century, when buffalo were hunted en masse and nearly removed from the landscape altogether. Historians have shown that the U.S. government sanctioned this activity because many American Indians depended on the buffalo for their livelihood, as a source of food, clothing, and tools.[16] Thus, *The Last Hunt*'s buffalo hunting also allegorizes the government's genocidal policies toward American Indians, in which men, women, and children were systematically isolated, starved, and killed. The goal was to erase the presence of American Indians from the landscape, as happened with the buffalo. *The Last Hunt* and *The Last Buffalo Hunt* show how this goal simultaneously succeeded and failed. Buffalo and American Indians now live in far fewer numbers and in far more contained and isolated environments, but their histories loom over the West's barren landscapes and endure, in mutated form, within the imagery of popular and corporate culture. The traumatic violence that scars the Western landscape also persists in the minds of American audiences as ghostly traces, and *The Last Hunt* and *The Last Buffalo Hunt* conjure these traces through their bloody scenes of death.

After opening title cards that explain the origin of the buffalo hunting footage ("the required annual thinning of the largest buffalo herd in America") and historical context about the extent of the buffalo decimation, Brooks' *The Last Hunt* cuts to a series of shots of buffalo

[13] Walter Benjamin, *The Origin of German Tragic Drama*, trans. John Osborne (New York: Verso, 1998).
[14] Craig Owens, "The Allegorical Impulse: Toward a Theory of Postmodernism," *October* 12 (Spring 1980), 69.
[15] Ibid., 74-76.
[16] Slotkin, *Fatal Environment*.

thundering across the plains. The stampede riles the stock of cattle rancher Sandy McKenzie (Stewart Granger), who begins shooting the buffalo, which draws the attention of a nearby horseback rider, Charley Gilson (Robert Taylor). The two men decide to partner on a hunting venture that includes two buffalo skinners—one an old alcoholic white man named Woodfoot (Lloyd Nolan) and the other a "half-breed" Indian named Jimmy O'Brien (Russ Tamblyn)—plus two American Indians they pick up along the way: a young, unnamed woman (Debra Paget) and the male toddler in her care. This opening scene jolts the audience with its goriness. A wounded buffalo abruptly leaps forward and, in a last gasp, prepares to charge the men, before Charley shoots it dead. Sandy walks over and bends down to the animal, its face smeared in blood. This is the first of a few scenes of real buffalo death, footage that affects the viewer with its pure, visceral power.

Animal Violence, Sensation, and Film

Jonathan Burt has discussed the fact that audiences, and censors, have historically responded more harshly to animal violence than human violence, regardless of whether the violence is real or simulated. This is a curious paradox, given that humans kill countless animals daily—for food, for fashion, or for "sport"—with little protest. According to Burt, these images of animal violence affect viewers so intensely because, "the animal film image […] is more prone to collapse the boundary of representation and reality than other forms of imagery."[17] For Burt, there are two impulses behind this difficulty in reading animal imagery: "metaphorical parallels that seek to collapse human and animal at some level and which highlight a shared experience of suffering […and the] second [which] detaches human and animal suffering as separate issues, but also bases itself on a refusal to read the image purely as an image."[18] In other words, humans become conscious of their own fragility and mortality through images of animals in pain and in death. Humans see traces of themselves, their bodies, in the animals. This imagery unsettles viewers in ways that images of human suffering do not, for these human images can more easily be grasped as simulation. Humans are easily understood as actors—"unreal" in a sense, while animals are always animals; they are real. This connection to the real gives viewers feelings of discomfort; in other words: *affect*.

[17] Jonathan Burt, *Animals in Film* (London: Reaktion Books, 2002), 140-141.
[18] Ibid., 162-163.

The Last Hunt and *The Last Buffalo Hunt* conflate human (American Indian) and animal (buffalo) suffering through allegory or, put in Burt's terms, by collapsing these distinct streams of suffering into one. The suffering of American Indians can be read through the images of mutilated buffalo flesh. Historical trauma erupts from the audience's disgust at unflinching scenes of brutality, and disgust gives way to anger and guilt: the indiscriminate slaughter of buffalo is shameful and its connection to the organized genocide of American Indians is criminal. For this convergence of physical disgust and historical shame to occur, the viewer must see the death of a buffalo and know that it is footage of an actual, *real* death, not just a simulation.

This begs the question of whether one can justify the death of an animal for the service of allegory, be it in a narrative film (*The Last Hunt*) or in a documentary (*The Last Buffalo Hunt*). We must see these animal deaths for what they are: brutal and traumatic. Animals die needlessly and endure tremendous pain. Both *The Last Hunt* and *The Last Buffalo Hunt* force audiences to witness suffering. Importantly, animals were not killed *because* of these films. In *The Last Hunt*, the U.S. government granted Brooks permission to shoot the "required annual thinning" of the buffalo herd at Custer State Park, a distinct event that would have occurred whether or not cameras were present.[19] In *The Last Buffalo Hunt*, filmmakers Schmitt and Lynch did not charter the hunts; rather, they documented expeditions that were scheduled independently and separately. Their work on the film is similar to that of embedded war journalists. Both films invite audiences to question the ethics of the hunting that they depict.

As Akira Lippit has argued, and Burt has summarized, the animal on film cannot die because it is beyond language and is constantly reanimated by the filmic image.[20] Through the reanimation of the filmic image—and the affective charge that it gives the audience—*The Last Hunt* and *The Last Buffalo Hunt* create meaning from what is essentially senseless slaughter. One might say that the reanimated animal haunts through its simultaneous absence and presence. Vivian Sobchack has examined the death of the animal on film in a different light, but one that also leads

---

[19] Douglass K. Daniel writes: "Overpopulation demanded a regular thinning, several dozen in all, and Richard [Brooks]'s cameras caught the exact moments in which the bullets slammed into the animals. At least the meat did not go to waste: it was either sold or given to the Sioux reservation." Daniel, *Tough As Nails*, 97.

[20] Akira M. Lippit, "Arche texts: Lascaux, Eros, and the Anamorphic Subject," *Discourse* 24, no. 2 (Spring 2002); Jonathan Burt, "Morbidity and Vitalism: Derrida, Bergson, Deleuze, and Animal Film Imagery," *Configurations* 14, no. 1-2 (Winter-Spring 2006).

viewers to have a bodily, affective response. In her influential essay "The Charge of the Real," Sobchack articulates how the inclusion of footage of a real rabbit death in Jean Renoir's fiction film *The Rules of the Game* (1939) ruptures the film's fictional world:

> the rabbit's death [...] transformed fictional into documentary space, symbolic into indexical representation, [her] affective investments in the irreal and fictional into a documentary consciousness charged with a sense of the world, existence, bodily mortification and mortality, and all the rest of the real that is in excess of fiction.[21]

Sobchack's project is in part designed to examine cinema less as "a *phenomenal object* than as a *phenomenological experience*."[22] The experience of watching a real rabbit die jolted Sobchack's body and took her mind out of the narrative of the film, which led her to contemplate the broader context in which this particular rabbit lost its life. This might shed light on *The Last Hunt*, as some audiences protested the real footage of death. The buffalo deaths rupture the narrative; they bring the history of real death into the unreal world of the film and, in doing so, encourage contemplation of the tragic historical legacy of buffalo hunting and its role in the genocide of American Indians.

Sensation and senses beyond sight and sound are a recurring theme in the content of *The Last Hunt*, with the dialogue frequently discussing the messiness of buffalo hunting. Woodfoot talks about skinning so many buffalo that his "clothes [were] stiff from buffalo grease." References to the smell of buffalo hide are littered throughout the film, as hunters are repeatedly said to "smell like a stinkin' buffalo." Significantly, American Indians are also associated with smell. When Sandy hires Jimmy, "the half-breed," as a second skinner, the racist Charley snarls that Jimmy "smells like the same Injun to me." Other characters refer to Jimmy as a "stinkin' Indian." Scholars such as Laura Marks and Martine Beugnet have argued that certain films elicit sensation through a synesthetic process, in which the film stimulates the audience's eyes and ears, the organs of sight and sound, to elicit different sensations, or affect, in other parts of the body.[23] *The Last Hunt* does not actually provide viewers with an affective

---

[21] Vivian Sobchack, "The Charge of the Real: Embodied Knowledge and Cinematic Consciousness," in *Carnal Thoughts* (Berkeley: University of California Press, 2004), 269, emphasis in original.
[22] Ibid., 260.
[23] Laura Marks, *The Skin of the Film: Intercultural Cinema, Embodiment, and the Senses* (Durham, NC: Duke University Press, 2000); Martine Beugnet, *Cinema and*

olfactory response, (indeed it is debatable whether this is even possible), but Brooks repeatedly foregrounds smell, specifically unpleasant smell, within the film's content. This invites viewers to think about the stench of decay, which complements, and enhances, their affective response to the images of buffalo death. Because the film aligns its American Indian characters with the buffalo through smell—at least in the imagination of its white characters—stench fuses the film's allegorical and affective elements.

The Last Hunt also foregrounds decay in other ways. Though the monomaniacal Charley refuses to admit it, the buffalo are disappearing. The great herds that once roamed the plains have dissipated to only include scattered herds in the Dakota Territory or, as Sandy says, "just bones, millions of bones. The stink of it. The shame of it." In this line, the film links physical disgust with moral disgust, or shame, a connection that becomes more explicit in the use of time-images. The scenes of Sandy and Charley hunting in *The Last Hunt* are shockingly blunt, with one buffalo after another dropping, lifeless. After Charley kills an entire herd of buffalo, the film cuts to a ground-level shot of carcasses. Blood smears the face of the buffalo on the left of the frame. Sitting in the middle of the carnage, Charley smiles wildly and breathes heavily, almost orgasmically. The camera remains focused on this image, giving the viewer an uncomfortable choice: look at the bloodied face of the dead buffalo and the exhilarated face of Charley, or look away. The lingering of the camera calls to mind Deleuze's concept of the time-image—an image that disarms the viewer through its prolonged duration, eliciting unpleasant affect—an idea that will be particularly relevant to the discussion of Schmitt's and Lynch's *The Last Buffalo Hunt*.

Shortly after this scene, Sandy suppresses his growing disgust with hunting and slaughters an entire herd. When a white buffalo suddenly appears from behind a veil of smoke, Sandy pauses to marvel at the extremely rare beast. Unimpressed with Sandy's reluctance, Charley brutally destroys the animal. The camera, at a closer range than the film's other kills, shows the white buffalo being shot in the head, the impact of the bullet sending a puff—of smoke or perhaps decimated flesh and skull—into the frame. Jimmy and Sandy explain that the white buffalo are revered by American Indians as "Big Medicine," the basis of their religion. In this instant, Charley attacks not only an animal but American Indian culture itself. The film's final shot shows the white buffalo hide splayed on a tree to rot, a sacrificial offering to the sun as part of the religion "Big

---

Sensation: French Film and the Art of Transgression (Carbondale, IL: Southern Illinois University Press, 2007).

Medicine." The specter of death thus darkens the American landscape: that of the buffalo and, through the religion that the animal skin signifies, that of the American Indian.

The Last Buffalo Hunt and the Time-image

The Last Buffalo Hunt—like Lee Anne Schmitt's previous film, *California Company Town*—draws from the essay film tradition, prominently featuring voiceover narration from the director herself. *The Last Buffalo Hunt*, which lists Lee Lynch as a co-director, incorporates other formal strategies as well. Whereas *California Company Town* combined narration with stationary 16mm color shots of the landscape, *The Last Buffalo Hunt* intersperses this aesthetic with video footage documenting guided buffalo hunts that take place in Utah's remote Henry Mountains. The filmmakers alternate between on-camera interviews with hunters and vérité-style footage of their expeditions.

Like *The Last Hunt*, *The Last Buffalo Hunt* opens with an image of running buffalo. Here, however, the animals are in an enclosed area and chased by cars. The film cuts to a shot of the herd from within a moving vehicle, an allegorical image that evokes both the past that Brooks' *The Last Hunt* recreates and the present, in which the few remaining animals are highly regulated by humans and their technologies. After a sequence of contemplative shots of the landscape—of corporate signage along empty roads and peaceful, empty grasslands—the film cuts to its title card and 16mm footage of a tent camp. The grainy 16mm color image lends the scenes a feeling of the past, of a way-of-life lost, that contrasts with the feel of the video footage that immediately follows it. The film cuts to the inhabitants of the camp, a buffalo hunting party led by Terry Albrecht. During the film's first hunt, Albrecht and his client stalk to the edge of a ridge, and the latter man fires at a small herd below, instantly dropping a large buffalo. The camera jolts backward from the shot, as if mirroring the audience's affective shock. The camera, now stabilized, focuses on the slain buffalo, its tail twitching involuntarily. The scene then cuts to the aftermath: the sound of saw against flesh and bone, as the skinners slice guts from meat, hide from skeleton, giving the audience an affective shudder. This scene only hints at the gore that lies ahead: a particularly slow death, and the meticulous gutting of a buffalo carcass.

Jeffrey Skoller has shown how certain avant-garde films access history by employing time-images, which break from the more conventional movement-images, the hallmark of action-oriented classical Hollywood cinema. The epitome of the time-image, a Deleuzian concept, is the long take, an extended shot that draws attention to its temporal nature. The static 16mm shots of landscape that have been characteristic of Schmitt's cinema are a good example. For Skoller, the time-image can achieve something similar to Benjamin's allegory, for "[t]ime-images can evoke temporalities that are not necessarily actualized in the image itself [...] they 'make perceptible ...[more complicated relationships of time] which cannot be seen in the represented object and do not allow themselves to be reduced to the present.'"[24] In other words, time-images can, like allegories, encompass parallel existences in a single instant. At the same time, Skoller explains, the body and sensation are essential aspects of the time-image: "It is not only the result of what is represented that opens the image beyond itself; it is also the bodily and affective experience of real-time duration. Such direct images of time access virtual temporalities through memory, desire, and bodily sensation."[25] Thus, time-images can be used to not only re-animate history but also to elicit affect, for they can cause viewers to *feel* physical sensations, to be aware of affect in their own bodies. Skoller's words here resemble Sobchack's description of the real death of the rabbit rupturing the narrative space of *The Rules of the Game*. In both cases, the viewer becomes aware of the image's indexical quality and of the broader context—historical, circumstantial, and personal—that informs the image's form and content. This is achieved through affect, by making the viewer aware of the length of the shot, aware of his or her status as a viewer, and, in some instances, physically uncomfortable.

Both *The Last Hunt* and *The Last Buffalo Hunt* affect viewers by stimulating feelings of disgust and grief. In the case of Schmitt's and Lee's *The Last Buffalo Hunt* in particular, these feelings of disgust are achieved through time-images, in which the camera lingers on long, excruciating scenes of death. In refusing to cut away from these scenes of suffering, the film forces the viewer to witness the intense pain of the animal and feel profound discomfort at this suffering. Through the time-image's evocation of parallel existences, as well as the film's other allegorical elements, this anguish takes on historical and political dimensions. Many of the film's non-hunting scenes are time-images that show icons of the buffalo and the American Indian scattered throughout the landscape, which underlines their allegorical connection. In watching the footage of buffalo death, the viewer *feels* the suffering of the animal and reacts to it viscerally—with shudders of physical disgust, flashes of rage and agony, and waves of grief. Some viewers might feel sick, while others might turn away. Regardless,

[24] Skoller, *Shadows*, xx, citing Gilles Deleuze, *Cinema 2: The Time-Image*, trans. Hugh Tomlinson and Barbara Habberjam (New York: Zone, 1992), xii.
[25] Ibid.

the viewer *feels*. And, through the use of allegory, the viewer experiences the history of the mass buffalo hunts of the late 19th century and the human atrocity that accompanied it: the genocide of American Indians.

The Last Buffalo Hunt's most brutal death recalls the beginning of Brooks' *The Last Hunt*, when the injured buffalo desperately attempts a final charge at Sandy. Though bleeding from multiple bullet wounds, the buffalo in *The Last Buffalo Hunt*'s final hunting scene repeatedly struggles back to his feet. The camera shows one bullet after another smacking the buffalo's head and neck, but the animal somehow clings to life and begins hemorrhaging blood, as thick red strands gush from his nostrils and mouth. "I still see it breathing," the distraught hunter exclaims, while strained breaths punctuate the stream of blood like faint waves. Finally, a bullet knocks the animal sideways. The legs continue to convulse, causing the audibly upset hunter, who remains outside of the frame during these death throes, to doubt whether the animal has died. A slap to the buffalo's eye causes not so much as a twitch, which leads the hunting party to declare the animal dead. The ordeal has evidently been excruciating for the hunter, who had earlier told the filmmakers stories of previous hunts in which she failed to instantly kill her prey.

By focusing so unflinchingly on the prolonged suffering that led to the buffalo's death, *The Last Buffalo Hunt* exposes the hunter's naivety and hypocrisy. Hunting is a gruesome business, and the extended shot that depicts the culmination of this particular hunt, a time-image, forces the audience to recognize this fact. Although this hunter claims to dislike animal suffering, she seems unwilling to accept that her actions guarantee it. The spectacle of such intense suffering wrought by her own hands induces guilt, even if it is unconscious. She explains the joys of hunting but admits that she does not like "roughing it" (she also likes to go to the mall each day). In other words, she wants to kill animals without getting her hands, or her conscience, dirty. *The Last Buffalo Hunt* proves this is an impossible task and a questionable desire. Hunting involves futile suffering and death, and a refusal to admit this is shameful. *The Last Hunt* and *The Last Buffalo Hunt* bring this shame to bear through their affective shock. The audience is called upon, as witness, to experience the shame denied by the hunters of the present and the past. The films stop short of completely demonizing hunting or hunters, but they do not sidestep the violence that inevitably results from hunting; they force audiences to encounter the historical shame for the traumas of buffalo hunting and genocide. Perhaps this heightened shame and guilt helps to explain the frequently adverse reactions to these films: the audience protests against

The Last Hunt and reviews of Schmitt's and Lynch's film criticizing its goriness.[26]

The Color of Meat and Hunting by Disguise

In his book-length examination of the paintings of Francis Bacon, Deleuze locates art's ability to capture sensation—or, put differently, to elicit affect—in the depiction of color, which, for Bacon, finds its greatest material in meat. "Bacon's painting," Deleuze writes,

> Constitutes […] a *zone of indiscernibility or undecidability* between man and animal […] The body is revealed only […] when the flesh ceases to cover the bones […] This pictorial tension between flesh and bone is […] achieved […] by *meat*, through the splendor of its colors.[27]

It is color, Deleuze argues, that enables a painting to transcend the world of the visual, and become more tactile, as if one can feel its textures through the sensation of seeing: "color, and the relations between colors […] form[s] this haptic world and haptic sense."[28] This concept of meat can help to illuminate a scene at the end of *The Last Buffalo Hunt*, but first a discussion of the zone between man and animal is in order. *The Last Hunt* and *The Last Buffalo Hunt* generally keep distinctions between man and animal intact, although the climax of *The Last Hunt* blurs these boundaries, as Charley freezes to death while wrapped in buffalo hide, the hardened skin of the animal meshing with his own, echoing both a taxidermy model and, ironically, the very American Indians that he so passionately despises.

Garry Marvin has argued that there is an element of blurring inherent in the type of hunting he identifies as "hunting by *disguise*," as opposed to "hunting by *disturbance*."[29] In hunting by disguise, which the hunters in both *The Last Hunt* and *The Last Buffalo Hunt* practice,

---

[26] See, for example, Dennis Harvey, "*The Last Buffalo Hunt*; a Meandering Jumble That's Unpleasantly Vivid when Portraying Hunting Tourism in Modern-day Utah," *Daily Variety*, May 2, 2011,
http://www.variety.com/review/VE1117945133/ (accessed August 8, 2012).

[27] Gilles Deleuze, *Francis Bacon: The Logic of Sensation*, trans. Daniel W. Smith (Minneapolis: University of Minnesota Press, 2004), 20, emphasis in original.

[28] Ibid., 111.

[29] Garry Marvin, "Wild Killing," in *Killing Animals*, ed. The Animal Studies Group, (Urbana, IL: University of Illinois Press, 2006), 22, emphasis in original.

> the distinction between human and the animal becomes blurred; the hunter attempts to become animal; the physical, behavioral, and emotional distance is closed. Here the human slips, unobtrusively, rather than openly intruding, into the countryside.[30]

In *The Last Hunt*, both Charley and Sandy become increasingly disturbed, even altered, by their hunting. Though Sandy recognizes this, Charley is completely unaware of his transformation, of his becoming animal; he remains stubbornly blind to the disappearance of the buffalo and to his escalating obsession. Charley becomes, as the skinner Woodfoot describes, "spooked" by the buffalo, "hearin' and seein' 'em when there weren't nary a one." Charley's behavior is increasingly irrational and erratic, ultimately destroying him; in his death, he goes the way of the buffalo.

The hunters in *The Last Buffalo Hunt* stalk their prey (like Charley and Sandy) by remaining undetected within the landscape.[31] For Charley from *The Last Hunt*, killing is the "natural state of things" and "the only proof you're alive." The hunters in Schmitt's and Lynch's film express their belief that hunting is a way to reconnect with and experience nature, "what you don't see everyday," a sort of wilderness untouched by man, which is ironic given that buffalo hunting was one of the historical practices that contributed to the destruction of the vast wilderness of the West. This irony is central to Schmitt's and Lynch's *The Last Buffalo Hunt*, which finds buffalo hunting and the frontier way of life—as epitomized by the figure of the cowboy—simultaneously absent and present. On the one hand, cowboys and buffalo hunters seem to be part of a dying lifestyle (Albrecht claims that he is going to retire from guided hunts and bemoans the lack of interest by younger people), but the traces of these histories remain visible within the traumatised American landscape.

Both buffalo and American Indians continue to physically exist, even if their numbers are far lower than they were prior to European contact and if the area that they inhabit is significantly smaller and more regulated. They

---

[30] Ibid.

[31] How respectfully Schmitt's and Lynch's film treats its hunters is open to debate. Upon my first viewing of the film, at the San Francisco International Film Festival, with an audience that was unafraid to verbalize displeasure with the hunting footage and with some of the hunting party's dialogue (which, sadly, fulfills stereotypes that liberal urban Americans have about conservatives and hunters), I felt that Schmitt and Lynch looked down upon their human subjects. Subsequent viewings have taken place at home, alone, with a DVD provided by Schmitt. I now feel that the filmmakers have a more nuanced, objective view of the hunters, particularly Albrecht, while not shying away from the inherently destructive nature of hunting. I feel they are respectful, but critical.

have become integral parts of American visual culture—with the icons of cowboys, buffalo, and Indians all being widely appropriated through corporate imagery, signifying gas stations and casinos throughout the vast West. These icons, insofar as they are intended to spur reflection, are designed to evoke and reinforce nostalgic feelings about the frontier. They are shorthand for what is perceived as the rugged individualism of the American spirit. But, through Schmitt's and Lynch's camera, they hover over the American landscape, haunting reminders of a bloody, shameful history.

This history is revivified through the buffalo slaughters that both *The Last Hunt* and *The Last Buffalo Hunt* depict. Having already witnessed scenes of buffalo being shot down, Schmitt and Lynch show in graphic detail the "cleaning" of a buffalo carcass. They do so through a time-image, with a camera that remains focused on the scene, as men eviscerate a dead buffalo that hangs from the back of a truck. The men do not simply skin the buffalo, but instead hollow it out, meticulously separating slabs of meat from the bloody innards. The blood and guts of the dead animal rush onto the earth, which calls to mind the flesh and meat that Deleuze found so moving in the work of Francis Bacon. For Deleuze, it was in this rendering of meat's physicality that Bacon captured sensation, where his work elicited affect. At the center of the frame in the shots of buffalo gutting, vibrant swaths of red ripple with the men's slicing motions, which separate skin, muscle, tissue, and bone. In one shot, what appears to be the animal's massive stomach bulges outward from its splayed body, protruding from the carcass, looking almost womb-like. Heat from the recently slaughtered animal meets the crisp air outside, and steam rises from the mangled pile of organs that gathers on the frozen grass. This bloody heap of buffalo guts is deeply unsettling, as it reminds the viewer of his or her own physical, animal nature. At the same time, it is difficult to differentiate between organs; stomach, intestines, and other sinewy matter intertwine in a shapeless pile, in what Deleuze would call a "*flow* of broken tones."[32] In light of the buffalo's near-extinction and its relation to the plight of American Indians, this gory scene feels uncanny, like the return of a repressed history that continues to scar the American landscape.

The theorist Winfried Menninghaus has linked the concept of formlessness to disgust through the work of philosopher Aurel Kolnai. For Kolnai, as Menninghaus points out, the morally disgusting has an analogy in the "'haptic softness' and [...] the 'swampy flourishing of a [...] mass

[32] Deleuze, *Francis Bacon*, 117, emphasis in original.

grown formless and uniformly pulpy.'"[33] This shapeless mass of buffalo on one level affects the viewer by being physically disgusting. But the swampy, formless guts connect to moral disgust in the way that Schmitt and Lynch situate the slaughter of buffalo within the larger context of the settlement, exploitation, and destruction of the American West. This is in a way what the film—and what Brooks' *The Last Hunt*—achieves: the physical disgust, the shame and anguish, the overwhelming affect, that viewers feel at the prolonged scenes of death, suffering, and mutilation leads to moral disgust, which the films' allegorical elements reinforce. Affect connects to historical trauma. The films achieve this multi-layered disgust in a way that fuses two of Deleuze's ideas: the time-image and the rendering of meat, of a zone of indiscernibility that blurs the boundaries between animal (buffalo) and human (the American Indian and the viewer).

In an essay on contemporary visual art that incorporates dead animal bodies as formal elements, Steve Baker employs Elaine Scarry's work to explore how people struggle to interpret the "visual intensity" of the wounded body, both human and animal.[34] As Scarry argues, the body—and particularly the wounded one—eludes easy comprehension. Baker sees in this "conceptual instability" something akin to Deleuze and Felix Guattari's concept of becoming-animal: "To become animal is […] to find a world of pure intensities where all forms come undone."[35] The buffalo guts get their affective power not from any narrative elements, but rather from formal ones: from the broken tones of the flesh, which create a zone of indiscernibility through which life becomes death. The body of the buffalo has become formless, and the image is pure intensity; it elicits affect. The viewer is not simply conscious of death; he or she on some level feels it through the ripples of flesh and the spurts of blood. Through this feeling, this *affect*, boundaries are blurred and the viewer becomes animal. He or she becomes conscious of mortality: of his or her own, of the American Indian, of the buffalo.

---

[33] Winfred Menninghaus, *Disgust: Theory and History of a Strong Sensation*, trans. Howard Eiland and Joel Golb (New York: State University of New York Press, 2003), 20.

[34] Steve Baker, "'You Kill Things to Look at Them': Animal Death in Contemporary Art," in *Killing Animals*, ed. The Animal Studies Group (Urbana, IL: University of Illinois Press, 2006), 81-84.

[35] Ibid., 84 citing Gilles Deleuze and Félix Guattari, *Kafka: Toward a Minor Literature*, trans. Dana Polan (Minneapolis: University of Minnesota Press, 1986), 13.

Taxidermy: A Conclusion

Shortly before the gutting scene, *The Last Buffalo Hunt* contains a brief sequence of taxidermists at work. One of the men labors over a buffalo's eye, explaining that "the whole key in any taxidermy is making your animals look alive, like they are out in the wild [...] like they're looking at you." Steve Baker has articulated a mode of looking that pertains to the killing of animals "in which the troubling or even accusatory power of the animal's gaze is engaged."[36] Here, "the killed animal's own glazed gaze [turns] back to meet and to confront that of the sometimes too complacent human viewer."[37] This accusatory mode is the one that *The Last Buffalo Hunt* accesses, which is made startlingly clear in the film's final shot. A handheld camera lingers on several animatronic busts that move back and forth robotically. A taxidermic moose and a wax-like American Indian chief occupy the left of the image, while a longhorn cow flanks the right edge. People wander in and out of the frame, occasionally obscuring the busts. At the center of the image are a taxidermic buffalo and a ghoulish cowboy (a ghost?) that jerks spastically. The prolonged nature of this time-image affects the viewer, eliciting feelings of confusion and anger. This accusatory gaze implicates the viewer in that which the film has repeatedly evoked through its scenes of animal suffering. *The Last Buffalo Hunt*—just like *The Last Hunt* some fifty years earlier—assaults the viewer with traumatic death, generating feelings of disgust both physical and moral. These scenes spur reflection on what came before—both within the film and, more broadly, within culture. What came before? Buffalo were slaughtered mercilessly. American Indians were persecuted and killed. A once plentiful land was extinguished. The traces of this history are evident in the carcasses that litter the landscape and in the statues that advertise casinos. And these traces are evident in the eyes of the mummified buffalo and the ghoulish cowboy—and in the anguished bodies of the animals that succumb to the hunters' bullets. Forever re-animated by the filmic image, they stare back at us and challenge us: do not dare to forget.

---

[36] Ibid.

[37] Ibid., 85.

PART IV:

EMBODIED

CHAPTER TEN

RADICAL REALISM AND OTHER POSSIBILITIES IN CONTEMPORARY INTERCULTURAL INDIGENOUS AUSTRALIAN CINEMA

JENNIFER L. BIDDLE

Jacob Nash, *Bloodlines*, 2007, single channel film, 5 min, 46 sec

Pauline Whyman, *Back Seat*, 2007, single channel film, 5 min, 46 sec

Warwick Thornton, *Nana*, 2007, single channel film, 5 min, 46 sec

Adrian Wills, *Jackie Jackie*, 2007, single channel film, 5 min, 46 sec[1]

These four films by Indigenous Aboriginal Australian Directors were produced in 2007, and exhibited as part of the international exhibition *Un_imaginable*[2] in 2008, at the Ivan Dougherty Gallery, COFA, UNSW, in Sydney. This essay is about how these films operate, formally and

---

[1] All films courtesy and copyright Australian Film Commission, Special Broadcasting Corporation, New South Wales Film and Television Office and Scarlet Pictures Pty Ltd, Sydney

[2] *Un_imaginable*, curated by Felicity Fenner, July 10-17 August, Ivan Dougherty Gallery, COFA, UNSW, 2008. The international exhibition *Un_imaginable*, curated by Peter Wiebel, July 3—August 24, 2008, ZKM Museum of Contemporary Art, Karlsruhe. See the associated publication Dennis Del Favero, Ursula Frohne, Peter Weibel, eds., *Un_imaginable*, (ZKM/Centre for Art and Media; iCinema/University of New South Wales; University of Pittsburgh, Karlsruhe; Sydney; Pittsburgh, 2008). I would like to thank the Ivan Dougherty Gallery and, specifically, Curator, Felicity Fenner, for permission to update for inclusion here an original essay I wrote for the Sydney *Un_imaginable*, an in-house exhibition catalogue published by Ivan-Dougherty Gallery (2008).

aesthetically, to evoke traumatic affect as they contend, in radically differing ways, with the violence of colonial occupation in the present.

2008 was a landmark year in Aboriginal history. It is not arbitrary that these four films were made in the lead up to it. Their release, in 2007, preceded the formal, public "Apology" of the (then) Prime Minister of Australia Kevin Rudd, to the Aboriginal people of Australia, issued in 2008. Under considerable pressure from Aboriginal and other political lobbyists, Rudd finally undertook to conduct the nationally-telecast, highly media-orchestrated Parliamentary "Apology," including wide screen viewings in major national parks and squares (notably, Aboriginally-significant public places) as well as inviting Aboriginal luminaries to attend Parliament on the day as formal, dignitary, representative witnesses. Rudd's "Apology" was not really addressed to the entirety of the Aboriginal population, nor was it a generic apology for colonial occupation. Rather, it was specifically addressed to those Aboriginal people, and their families, who are now referred to as *The Stolen Generation*. This term acknowledges the injustice done to the thousands of Aboriginal children forcibly removed from their families and either adopted out to non-Aboriginal families and/or placed on missions to be raised. This practice of forced removal was carried out un-officially from the inception of British colonial occupation of Australia but continued under various State legislations and national policy sanctions, until as recently as 1969 (in New South Wales).[3]

In his "Apology," Rudd did not revoke but in fact, subtly endorsed, new national government policy that had taken shape in 2007, called variously, *The NT* [Northern Territory] *Emergency Response, The Intervention*, or now, in new 10-year-future policy form passed in 2012 (with bipartisan support), *Stronger Futures*. These policies have seen remote-based Aboriginal communities and people subjected to what are recognized by Amnesty International and the United Nations to be human rights violations, including draconian and discriminatory changes to welfare policy and payments, quarantining of traditional lands and rights to housing, dismantling of Aboriginally-determined local community governments, and the cessation of bilingual and bicultural schooling programs in favor of English-only accelerated literacy and numeracy[4].

This is the broad historical context in which the production of these films took shape.

[3] See the award winning Indigenous documentary Darlene Johnson, *Stolen Generations*, (Tapestry International Cinema, 2000), for further details.

[4] For further discussion see Jennifer Biddle "Art under Intervention: the radical ordinary of June Walkutjukurr Richards" *Art Monthly* 227 (March 2010): 35-39.

*

These four experimental films may be short (5 minutes each), but they pack no small punch. We do not so much "view" these films as we are "hit by" them.[5] The works shock, stun; they hurt, humiliate; they tantalize, delight and tickle. Their effectiveness/affectiveness resides in their very troubling of the supposed distinction between the drama taking place on the screen and the experience incited in viewer response. Disbelief, incredulity, the absurd—the anguish of breeched identity, the violence of words, the burden of representation itself— in these films, the so-called unimaginable becomes palpable, proximate, inescapable. No longer do distinctive Aboriginal life worlds remain othered, over there or elsewhere, but are brought into sharp and pointed relief within the realm of our experience through the cinematic.

Laura Marks has defined intercultural cinema as "characterized by experimental styles that attempt to represent the experience of living between two or more cultural regimes of knowledge, or living as minority in the still majority white, Euro-American West."[6] Intercultural films record "the unrecordable memories of the senses"[7]—experience and perception that differ from those of White Euro-American societies, particularly where optical visuality has predominated. It turns to the senses because other resources—history, records, representation in any form—may simply not exist. The violent disjunctions in space and time which characterize the contemporary diasporic condition of exile, immigration, and displacement, in her terms, require an appeal to memory and other non-visual forms of knowledge, both collective and individual, in order to engender otherwise unknown, unrepresented, even disavowed versions of history, experience, event. Marks figures intercultural cinema as the "scent that rises from the funeral garlands,"[8] a figure at once resilient but tethered to a past that has yet to cease its hauntings. And it is the past that burns yet in contemporary Australia, as these four pithy intercultural vignettes suggest.

---

[5] I borrow this phrase from Michael Taussig, *Mimesis and Alterity: A particular history of the senses* (London and New York: Routledge, 1993), who, in another context altogether, discusses the illuminations affective imagery has to literally "hit" its mark.

[6] Laura Marks, *The Skin of the Film: Intercultural Cinema, Embodiment and the Senses* (Durham: Duke University Press, 2001), 1.

[7] Ibid., 5.

[8] Ibid.

Bloodlines is less a depiction than a deployment of uncertainty. Reminiscent of Tracy Moffatt's *Night Cries* (1989), the film is driven by anxiety. It evokes in the viewer what it purports to depict: fear and anticipation, inaction and inhibition, hope thwarted in advance. Trauma is made our own. Delay, deferral and disassociation become our only response because the film in no way resolves the dilemma it instigates. The real time of watching is almost unbearable. What we see in the film is less than even a day in the life of a young Aboriginal man, but these few minutes of screen time manage to evoke a lifetime of not knowing at once intensified and condensed in micro visibilities of sweat, flesh, face. The human cost of a past that can have no reconciliation, the obscenity of an Apology offered in the early days of *The Intervention*, the helpless lack of clues that Stolen victims and institutions like Link Up[9] have (not) to go on—in an instant, all of this. The legacy of the Stolen Generation as it lives on, literally and affectively, today.

From the opening haunting scenes of a telephone line that travels nowhere, a hanging and headless cord turned black snake to the high stark modernism of the interior of the young man's apartment, where the opulence of technology, the matte exterior of Apple, Bang and Olufsen, white couch, abstract art, space itself, become prime signifiers of the vacuity that "White" success, assimilation, ultimately affords. Alienation screams with sounds as much as vision. The crack of ice cubes shattering, taps turned on and off, water splashed hands to face, to no avail. The young man's bare feet pace the wooden floors in time with mounting anxiety. The few "family" photographs on his shelves are blurry, barely discernable, serving to heighten the existential fact of his brutal aloneness. A single lone piano note repeated turns into his heart beat amplified, and in turn, becomes our own blood coursing in sheer symptomatic corporeography. He tries to write "it" out, but words begin and are halted, frustrated, again and again, the mute realities of silenced survivors.

The last sequence of the film, the first and only time we hear voice, speech, at all, operates backward by providing only in retrospect, and only provisionally, a rationale for what we have been made to bear witness to. He dials, hangs up, dials again, finally succeeds to blurt his introduction, identify his existence, to who we can only surmise, is his Aboriginal birth mother. The film ends exactly there. Neither he, nor we as the audience,

---

[9] *Link Up* is an Aboriginal-run, community-based national organization established in 1980 (originally on a volunteer basis, incorporated since 1995) to assist "Stolen Generation" survivors of enforced removal to "link up" again with their Aboriginal families and communities.

are let “off the hook” but are left hanging, desperately, on the line and at the end of the line (bloodline, lifeline, lifetime).

In terms of narrative, *Back Seat* by comparison, is more conventional: the story of a young Aboriginal girl’s visit to her (Aboriginal) mother and siblings with her (White) step-mother and father. But there is nothing simple in this story, nor is anywhere safe. “Go on dear, why don’t you go in first” the White step-mother says, bright blue eye shadow, white button earrings. This is thick ethnography, circa late 1960s, no less evident in the “mother’s” home, where glass ashtrays, gold trophies, as well as requisite white tulle curtains are pulled closed to entertain privately, no less bourgeois, no less proper, than her White counterparts. The Hermannsberg-esque boomerangs adorning the lounge room wall could almost be anywhere; a signifier not of Aboriginal difference but of a similitude that renders forced policies of removal, or the need for fostering, a travesty. It is what happens between the subjects present—the infinitesimal attention to detail of what is manifest in only a few seconds of close up—that allows unconscious histories of affect and nuances of feeling to flood our experience.

The smallest of gestures is here the greatest source of politics. Multiple points of identification are offered, yes, but it is the absenting of the daughter’s experience that becomes the subject matter of this film. Her disassociation is made ours. Ventriloquist doll struck dumb between two masters at odds, unable to mouth the polite discourse between the two mothers (this is maternal territory, a battle field, no less). Tea is offered, politely and not so politely declined (the White mother “slaps” the White father’s hand as he reaches for a biscuit). Our protagonist is unable to speak, or rather to scream, the sole question banished—the question, as audience, we equally cannot ask: why, why, why? Why was I taken away? What’s wrong with my family? What’s wrong with me? Why can’t I stay here? In whose world, according to what logic, can this happen?

The camera stills to a single shot of the daughter in sharp, still, frontal focus, where sounds drown and diffuse, everything stills, dissolves, focus is lost altogether. The next sequence finds her having fled the scene, back to the car. The subsequent slap of her hand on the car lock (repetitious slapping, four times each door), fast, too loud, the screeching of the windows rolling shut too slow yet to close out, to escape from, what cannot be borne. The back seat the only refuge for the Aboriginal disposed, the dispossessed, the homeless, in occupied territory. It is her (not-stolen, Aboriginal) sister who saves her, who can normalize what is revealed to be a mad, incomprehensible, adult world. Her siblings stand in this film as her mirror equivalents evoking, in their over-enthusiastic embrace of her, far more yet of the unspeakable injustice of the Stolen legacy.

The hands of the two separated sisters reach to touch across a glass dividing, palm to palm matched perfect, before the "outside" sister, also, must, inevitably, turn her back on the situation. *Back Seat* finishes with the "backseat" daughter being driven away with her two White parents, rubbing sensuously time and again, a Polaroid snapshot of her happy (stolen) family, where she sat, at the front alongside her mother, for only this brief "stolen" moment. Analogous to the instigatory effects of the film itself, saturated by longing and loss, this so called family is graspable only by a making visible of what cannot otherwise (and even then, can it ever?) be seen.

Nana is also told from the child's point of view. Technically, *Nana* is a docu-fiction. Not a real story as such, but social realism, or what Mark Nash might call an "experiment with the truth."[10] There is a marked turn towards experimental documentary forms in intercultural cinema, as these four films indicate, in a move to redress colonial histories and dominant representations by creating collective authorizations, legitimate memory and counter-histories for the first time—what needs to be remembered, what must not be forgotten.

The doco-fictive form is signatory across Warwick Thornton's now award-winning film career (his feature *Samson and Delilah* won the *Camera D'or* at the 2009 Cannes Film Festival and was nominated for Best Foreign Film at the 2009 Academy Awards). Classic documentary turned upside down, the child's voice in *Nana* is utilized as the expert voice-over, speaking directly to us throughout the film as if reading a script in word perfect English, a subtle thumbs up to the supposed need for current *Intervention* government driven accelerated literacy programs in remote communities perhaps? The film is set in an Aboriginal Desert "remote" context. The child's "Nana" (grandmother) by contrast, the real "star" of the film, speaks, sings, and later yells, but only in a Central Desert Indigenous language, Warlpiri.

This is the third world linguistic zone of the contemporary real, where languages vie, shift, and aren't necessarily shared or spoken by the same generations of person. But this reality is not disturbing to the child—no two worlds of bilingualism, no bifurcated experience, no alienation is here proffered. This in fact is a poignant story of family, safety and security. "Wurra" Nana breathes out, after tender care with nit removal and hair brushing replete with head scarf to frame the contented face of her

---

[10] Mark Nash, "Experiments with the Truth: The Documentary Turn" *Anglistica* 11, no. 1-2 (2007): 33-40.

granddaughter on her knee; "wurra" which in Warlpiri means "wait, stay, be here" (my translation, the film does not translate Nana's Warlpiri, nor does it identify that *Nanna* is speaking Warlpiri).

Nana is depicted as a Super Hero in her granddaughter's eyes, with all the exaggerated abilities of comic book realism and grandeur both—boiling so many sausages at once in order to feed elders in the community, to almost be witch-like in her stirring of a cauldron of a lethal looking stew in the opening scene as she, at the same time, (mock) performs ceremonial song and dance. Later, we will see her hunt Herculean prolifically and fast, shot-gun accurate replete, slapping carcasses of goanna, kangaroo, lizard in piles on the hood bonnet of her Toyota, triumphant. She paints possibly "faux" classic acrylic *Jukurrpa* (Dreaming) art for sale to unsuspecting naive Whitefellas, as she winks at her granddaughter complicit, and thus, to us. And finally, *Nana* wards-off grog runners, as a member of the now famous community-led initiative "Night Patrol,"[11] where elder members of Warlpiri communities patrol Yuendumu and Lajamanu to ensure that they remain, at community decision, "dry" and free from alcohol and drunks both.

Here, the child's perspective—writ large literally—becomes the source of the absurd, where exaggerations of the everyday and un-natural naturalness become ludicrous in extreme. The laughter that erupts may evoke the realm of childhood innocence, but this absurdity is an embittered criticism, subversive and cathartic, dislodging repression and affording relief to what cannot be said. Might it suggest that the reverence for tradition, art, for ceremony, for so called "high" Aboriginal culture privileged by both the ethnographic and tourist gaze is too great? A gesture towards the killing-off the living that this reverence entails? The perversity of picking peaches in order to preserve them? Cauterized culture that cannot live, breathe, self-determine, laugh at itself, at us? Does this not show us that speaking English doesn't mean a loss of language, culture? That old people aren't left starving in camps like dogs (and indeed, that old people are, like those Ancestors they always emulate, cheeky, licentious characters, the slap on *Nana's* bottom by that old man in camp, a slap in the face literally of those who might think otherwise)?

The child's perspective is cleverly, strategically, mapped onto that of "our" own, where, as John von Sturmer has figured it, Aborigines are always represented in terms of excess. As he puts it, they "fight too much,

[11] See Warlpiri Media Association *Night Patrol (Munga Wardingki Partu)*. Co-production with CAAMA (1997).

fuck too much and drink too much."[12] Here, the abject and the innocent coalesce: do "they" really cook that many sausages at once? Do Warlpiri really use the bonnet of their cars (pace *Bush Mechanics*)[13] to transport hunted meat? The dots on those paintings, are they really too big, ludicrous, or might this be new "Emily"?[14] The irreverence is somber and sobering (too), laced with the fact that any and all images of Aborigines can never be dislodged from a violent history of colonial representation which is not yet past, as the mocking terms of both the film, and the mirth it engenders, attest.

Jackie Jackie is a story of gleeful, girly, redemption. Its art is not so much an excavation of the past as it is fantastical fabulation, blending hyper real estrangements to offer new affective resonances and resources to what, in fact, ought to be by now an all too trite parable of modern racism. The very terrain of this film seems intentionally un-original, in harkening back to familiar terrain and devices in order to harness the already known of memory, mood, gesture, and fashion to new effect. This film excels in the Derridian adage that it is only through repetition that the new can emerge. Equally, it harkens to the repetitious nature of trauma itself as delayed and continuous return.

Jackie Jackie is a modern mall melodrama, set in what can only be called the contemporary present-past of the 1970s. Shades of Baz Lurhman and Andy Warhol both, helmet-headed White blondes predominate the fantasy, domestic and deeply feminine world of shopping and consumerism, whose dazzling and facile façade hides the no uncertain truth of the racist agenda that is really at stake. The white shop owner/manager cannot pronounce the name of the protagonist, "Jinaali", despite the fact that she is wearing a name-tag with her name spelt properly on it (as she points out to him). His incapacity to simply call her by her proper name incites a greater history of what Gayatri Spivak has called "catachresis"[15]—the colonial violence done to the colonized by

[12] John von Sturmer, "Aborigines, Representation, Necrophilia" *Art and Text* 32 (1989): 127-139.

[13] *Bush Mechanics* (Dir. David Batty) A film Australia National Interest Program in association with Warlpiri Media Association Inc (2001).

[14] "Emily" refers to perhaps the most famous of Western Desert Aboriginal art painters, Emily Kame Kngwarre, who transformed the movement with her radical innovation of using a traditional acrylic painting aesthetic and style. See Jennifer Biddle, *Breasts, Bodies, Canvas: Central Desert Art as Experience* (Sydney: UNSW Press, 2007) for further discussion.

[15] See Gayatri Spivak, "Can the Subaltern Speak?" in *Marxism and the Interpretation of Culture*, eds. Cary Nelson and Lawrence Grossberg (Chicago: University of Illinois Press, 1988), 271-313.

names (identities, histories) not being able to be pronounced, written, said; and the obscene re-naming in colonial languages and terms (identities, histories) that has taken shape. The shop manager calls Jinaali "Jamimah, Gin-a-loo, Jedda."[16]

In order to rally support against his relentless slurs, the heroine Jinaali mail orders, no less, from late night sit-com television advertising, a "Jacki Jacki" doll. "Jacki Jacki" is itself a racist "no name", a generic name for Aboriginal stock men, specifically from an Australian history of frontier occupation. This "Jacki Jacki" is a phantasmagorical Aboriginal action figure in pint-sized, boxed form, able to be ordered, bought, in order to defend Aboriginal people today, whose greater purpose it is to fight off racists with his super-sized powers. In the final scene of the film, however, back at the Grocery Store Jinaali is seen having to re-box her purchased "Jacki Jacki" as his anti-racist brutalism is found by her to be both annoying and uncouth; too black and white, too simply a reversal and over-empowering ultimately of her own authority to defend herself, to speak for herself.

Jinaali names herself both "Jinaali" and an "(Ab)original" in a public performative to the manager, the shoppers, and to us. A performance that outdoes both her white male boss's racism and "Jacki Jacki" action figure's equally categorical anti-racism. In so doing, "race" becomes ludicrous. "Whiteness" is shown to be what it is: performative, banal, obvious, repetitive and ultimately boring, in the sense that it is simply uncool and un-savvy to not get where the "the human race" is "at". In this case, the "human race" is lining up for service at Jinaali's cash register—comprised of (in visually normative signifier terms): "Aboriginal," "Gay," "Muslim," "Goth" and "Punk" people. In a better performance of "Blackness" (not a loin clothed, spear toting, "Jacki Jacki" doll version) the very genuine heroine of the film, Jinaali, simply outshines the other cashiers. Her check-out line is now the place to be checked "in". The White shoppers, now equally gleeful, surge forward convinced to join her

[16] "Jedda" is a name made famous by the cinematic figure of "Jedda", in fact, a fictive female Aboriginal character in the Charles Chauvel film of the same name, *Jedda*, Charles Chauvel Productions, Columbia Pictures and British Lion (1955). The character of "Jedda" was played by Ngarla (Rosalie) Kunoth. The complex relationship between Kunoth's own biography and the making of the film (its real historical effects as it were, on her life) are explored by Warwick Thornton in an earlier short documentary *Rosalie's Journey*, CAAMA Productions (2003). The shop manager's use of the name "Jedda" for Jinaali evokes a greater suspicion yet of colonial representation and pointedly locates the history of cinema itself as no less suspicious, as it is potently important in very real terms today.

"human" queue, and her cheeky direct wink at the camera in the final dissolving moments flirtatiously invites us all.

Theatricality is not outside or separate from the real world of politics, race, economy; the theatricality of affect resides precisely in the artful act of the everyday.

CHAPTER ELEVEN

TRAUMA STIMULATED ART, OR THE EMBODIMENT OF AFFECT IN LEBANON: AN ALLEGORY

RICARDO MBARKHO

The process of doing art in Lebanon is closely linked to politics; it has its root in the traumatic Lebanese civil war that took place from 1975 to 1990. The heightened political environment in Beirut influences affective circulations and expressions within communities, and as Kaelen Wilson-Goldie notes, the divisions in the political landscape often generate divisions in the art scene.[1] In other words, for the Lebanese people, affect is inherently political. It is also economic, as politically biased funding fuels the fires of this politicized affect, revealing certain values and prejudices. Since trauma in Lebanon is most manifestly a result of war, death looms ever-present and is often a major focus of art practice. Artists face an ethical problem since they might be seen to exploit people's misery in mining this political and traumatic history for their art productions. The risk here is that death becomes the point to which all the aesthetic discourses lead: dying for country, for the cause, for religion, for politics, for ideology, and so on. This is evident in a number of artworks, as well as in observable behavioral ideology, and in various social, individual, or national conflicts. Traumatic and violent death becomes a justified aspect of life. This has led some artists to refuse the political and nationalistic glorification of death and to promote life instead. In this way, Lebanese artists attempt to use art to overcome trauma and to affirm life in the face of traumatic affect.

---

[1] Kaelen Wilson-Goldie, "An art scene divided," *The National*, 2008, www.thenational.ae (no longer available online) (accessed July 2, 2008).

This attempt to overcome trauma in art often involves the construction of narratives, of artworks that tell stories. However, if this storytelling is subject to political interference it is reduced to advertising a certain political ideology. Art can only operate as an overcoming of trauma when it is working on a different platform than that of political propaganda. Politically funded artists fail to truly question and incite people to think. They are no longer engaging with the affective residue of trauma in such a way as to invite productive potential. Instead, they become puppetry for a post-war ideology that robs the artist of autonomy and integrity, and manipulates stories and affect for political purpose. In doing so, art is denied its crucial function of opposing or questioning the alteration of ethical values that politics seek to change. Thus some trauma stimulated art practitioners in Lebanon fail to avoid the trap of fascism in their attempts to address, and express, traumatic affect. In this sense, art in Lebanon has no way out but to deal with its own absurdity. Thus, the story begins.

On Sunday 13th of April 1975, the Lebanese civil war erupted. Clashes between Palestinians and Lebanese Christian Militias led to mass killings on both sides. The heat of the war didn't cool off until years later. During the harsh and gloomy winter of 1976 Charbel turned two. His family, Lebanese Maronite Christians, hid in the safe house of a building not far from the frontlines in Ain el Remmaneh, the Lebanese Stalingrad. Charbel was cold there, and his father, Joseph, went up to his apartment on the 2nd floor to bring him an extra blanket. Joseph grabbed the white cotton blanket from the bedroom that faced the street, and as he headed toward the door, a Palestinian missile dropped near the building. Dozens of shards of metal spread from the missile; many shards entered Joseph, who happened to be standing in the way. The blanket's white turned to red. Charbel, the two-year old, became a man, a traumatized man. In the same year, Dimitri, another Lebanese Greek Orthodox Christian set out to visit his sister in West Beirut, which was partly occupied by the Palestinians. He travelled from East Beirut where the Phalangists, the Christian militia, drew the defense line. Phalangist snipers stood on top of every building and on every corner. Dimitri was carrying clothes for his girl, Caroline, when a sniper's shot killed him. Caroline the little girl became a woman, a traumatised woman. Joseph and Dimitri had never met each other, and growing up, Charbel and Caroline blamed the deaths of their fathers on the Palestinians in the case of the former and the Phalangists in the case of the latter. Not only did they blame the deaths of their fathers on the Palestinians and Phalangists, but also the deaths of those who died fighting to serve their causes. Traumatic memory consumed them both, setting them on the path of channeling their grief into their work: they both became active in the field of art.

Growing up in a sphere where everyone is socially well-connected, Caroline evolved within the so-called Pro-Palestinian left-wing circles, where she eventually found her way to art curating. Working hard to build up a name in the art scene, Caroline could be seen every day, at the famous Rawda café, known as the left-wingers' meeting place. Caroline fraternized with others involved in art and politics who were committed to helping each other achieve their respective goals. Friends with similar political views were likely candidates in volunteering time for art at the beginning of Beirut's vibrant art scene in 1994; the time of the genesis of the now prosperous art organization initiated and headed up by Caroline. This lively postwar art wave, perhaps destined to happen, shook Lebanon and reverberated around the world. It shook the country because for the first time ever, Lebanon built a globally recognized identity for its local art scene, one that reflected Lebanese issues. And it reverberated around the world because through the Lebanese art scene the West had a window onto the Islam majority in the Middle-East, as well as the Christian minorities in the region, which gave the West an opportunity to explore and understand a region closely linked to terrorism and eventually implicit in the devastating events of 9/11.

While Caroline both discovered and nurtured this bourgeoning scene, Charbel struggled to find his creative and political place. He wondered if he'd become a right-wing Phalangist; his parents had always told him not to become affiliated with any militia, for, according to them, militias end up annihilating one another. When he was 10 years old, his neighbor, Roy, a Phalangist was killed, felled by one of the other militia groups, or worse by another Phalangist, which seemed only to prove his parents' point. Charbel's loyalty to mainstream ideology as inherited by the right-wing would be questioned years later when in 1999 he initiated a discussion forum on the Internet about Lebanese-related concerns, a project undertaken while he was an art student.[2] These conversations, relating not only to religion, politics, identity, but also to gay and lesbian issues, and a mixture of other Lebanese relevant topics of the day, created a problem for Charbel when they were brought to the attention of the Lebanese Sureté Générale, who were known to be dominated by the Syrian regime after the civil war. Tracked and observed, his file was sent to all borders of the

[2] In keeping with the use of aliases in this article, the reference for this website is withheld, since its disclosure would identify individuals. It is my intention to offer the characters of this chapter as representative of not only a specific artist, but a number of artists working in Lebanon today.

country. But for Charbel, this desire to engage the other and to understand the conflicting points of view of political parties was motivated by his questioning of his naïve understanding of the Lebanese civil war, so he pressed on. He needed to uncover the thoughts of the other. For him, communicating opened up new possibilities to discover the other, and more specifically, to ascertain the trauma of the other. Charbel had begun his project with the intention of confirming the guilt of his father's killers, and to hold them to account, but the online forum took another direction, one that challenged Charbel's perceptions. Day after day, Charbel was learning that these alien others and their parties also had their ideologies, their motives and causes, and that it was the clash of these conflictive points of view that had materialized into war. Art critics linked Charbel's forum project to communicational and relational art aesthetics. Charbel himself considered that this project was an attempt to address and overcome trauma by utilizing an online textual setting, a discussion forum, as a place where affect is not facially expressed. In this way he hoped to uncover the others' true intentions and thoughts, reasoning that the absence of the facial expression, the absence of visible affect, for instance, might reveal the participants' actual thoughts and opinions in a way that was less charged and dangerous, and therefore more accurate. The speaking body, and facial expression, would be removed, replaced by the avatar and the assurance of physical safety, with the speaker's real identity hidden at all times.

It so happened that Caroline was running another online forum about Lebanese issues at the same time as Charbel. Though it may seem to be coincidence, it is perhaps more likely that there is an organic postwar, post-traumatic attitude or reaction informed by the need to know the other and to communicate online—in other words at a safe distance—to avoid the potential of physical harm. Despite this joint impulse, the cases of Charbel and Caroline illustrate a critical division in Beirut's art scene. Caroline's art projects are now funded by international organizations, as part of the pro-Palestinian left wing oriented art, while Charbel has struggled to find support and backing. Without the luxury of having a curator with the means of international funds taking care of him, Charbel has become the curator of his art circle, though it is a role he neither sought nor wanted. The press has subsequently positioned Charbel and Caroline as the principal figures in the divided Beirut art scene for the past two decades.

In 1996, Charbel had travelled to France and the USA to continue his art studies. It was not until he was back in Lebanon in 2002 that the balance tipped. During the war, Charbel was young. As he read the legacy of war on people's faces, it became clear to him that the misery had to stop, and that it was essential to affirm ideals that do not promote dying for one's country. Charbel's anti-romantic view of war and loss formed in contrast to the many artworks that, post-war, paved the way for the Lebanese people to attempt to cope with trauma by justifying dying for the country. For Charbel, such artworks are a catastrophe, since they justify Lebanese people dying in war. They teach people how to welcome death as an old friend, and how to do the duty of dying for an imagined and deeply problematic ideal.

Accepting death for the sake of a nation is not a concept that existed naturally; it is the result of traumatically shifting values and acceptance of these new values. It's a kind of forced behavior cultivated in conditions of war and violence. When contact with death becomes a habit, trauma becomes a habit too, and habits engender justifications, justifications that support the continuation of the habit. And so, the choice to fight and to traumatize is transmuted into the belief that there is no choice but to accept war, death and trauma. This amounts to an attempt to justify trauma by neutralizing it: trauma stops being recognized as trauma and begins masquerading as national pride. Further, affects, such as sadness, anger and fear, that surround trauma become nullified and normalized in this masquerade. This is best illustrated with the rituals of religious fundamentalists. Before sacrificing themselves to destroy enemy sites, they write love letters to their daughters describing how they will never forget their beauty and hair, how they will always carry their smile and laughter in their hearts. In this act the fundamentalists present themselves a dilemma: their duty for their religion vs. their love for their daughters. But both are to be questioned; is it only their duty that leads them to sacrifice their life or is it revenge? Is their love for their daughters real or a posturing to win the favor of their God and the forgiveness of people? For Charbel, such incidents provoked disgust.

It is unsurprising that performance art in Lebanon excelled during this period. In post-war Lebanon, performance was an effective strategy that offered to protect the performer from the naked insecurity and difficulty of expressing traumatic affect around the Lebanese civil war as a mere subject and citizen. With more and more artists performing, life in Lebanon became something of a performance of affects; affectivity became increasingly visible but it was presented devoid of genuine inner emotion, strangely dis-embodied as it were. Affect became a mask used to disarm the viewer who, at any time, might emerge as a potential enemy, a threat to physical safety and the body that housed authentic traumatic affect. This fakery amounts to the refusal of representation, the limits of what can be risked in art in Beirut. Performance art questioned not only war, but also performance acts themselves, producing a society of performers and artistic questioning, in which the act of performance and the realities of war merged. After the events of 9/11 suddenly brought the Middle East to the notice of the international art scene, Lebanon became one of the most mediatized regions of the world. International curators, artists, writers, media, critics, art dealers, and gallery owners flooded to Beirut to explore the city and study its religions, economy, politics, culture, history and creative industries. This global attention has become one of the principal preoccupations of Lebanon. In this renewed Lebanese context, people come to Lebanon to observe and mingle with both sides: Caroline's and Charbel's. The new challenge for Lebanese artists is the potential for their work to be co-opted, and not to become, in short, propaganda art. The onus is on them to question, to investigate, to query, to explore, rather than give in to mainstream or gendered demands. The international art community has largely endorsed those artists who seek to understand the conditions surrounding stereotyped concepts of the Middle East, the rise of terrorism, sectarianism, the oppression of women, and Arabism. The danger is that Lebanese artists and organizations unwittingly endorse and feed foreign motives and the projections of the west around the region's symbols and icons.

Whether it was an investigation of local concerns, or an exploration via the point of view of global and international clichés, Lebanese artists started generating narratives in relation to traumatic events, resulting in a plethora of works more narrative-oriented rather than experience-oriented, a move addressed in Anthony Downey's discussion of narrative-oriented works in Lebanon today.[3] Charbel created works that transposed narrative texts into images— he used visual codes to give an alternative reading and interpretation to selected texts, while Caroline defended "docufictional"[4] artworks. Despite their differing approaches, they were both iterating the same themes: war, crime, violence and loss—one as artist and the other as curator. This theme is alive and well today in the ongoing postwar art scene of Beirut, where all alike struggle with the affective aftermath of trauma and the failures of human culture.

---

[3] Anothony Downer, "In the Event of Fire: Precarious Images, the Aesthetics of Conflict, and the Future of an Anachronism," *Ibraaz*, July 13 2012, http://www.ibraaz.org/essays/30 (accessed October 4, 2012).

[4] An example of docufictional techniques can be seen at the blog *Beirut Art Critics*, in a post by Maya Hage, "Akram Zaatari: clin d'oeil," 24 May 2011, http://artsbeirut.wordpress.com/2011/05/24/akram-zaatari-clin-doeil/ (accessed October 4, 2012).

In this real and imaginary domain, art is investigating the intermediate space between two fields: trauma and affect. Consequently, one can say that if art in Lebanon has a distinct form, it is largely an affective form created in response to trauma. In this process, an economic engine that involves political alliances, ethical choices and aesthetic considerations influences art production. If the questions posed by artists and art works problematize conventions, then they may prove useful, but if they threaten the human rights charter, they become dangerous. In traumatic societies this danger often involves discourses that defend a so-called constructive self-negation. This is why for art to negotiate trauma it sometimes needs to mutate into other kinds of art that can exist in a traumatized society without compromise.

The current Lebanese art scene is a reflection of Charbel's and Caroline's evolution over the years; they both entered the international art scene from two different perspectives, from two different doors—one that opened out from the Lebanese "left," and one that opened out from the Lebanese "right." Both Charbel and Caroline have engaged with narrative oriented art, stimulated by similar traumatic histories, in an effort to undo trauma by experimenting, manipulating and embodying the residual traumatic affect of those histories into their different modes of art. It is an ongoing quest of Lebanese art and artists to process the affective fallout of still being a profoundly and communally traumatized country.

CHAPTER TWELVE

CHANNELING THE SPECTER AND TRANSLATING PHANTOMS: HAUNTOLOGY AND THE SPOOKED TEXT

MEERA ATKINSON

Introduction

You are reading—a poem, a novel, a memoir. You may not identify directly with what you are reading (the story, the character, the event). And yet. And yet you experience affect—anger, anxiety, sadness. You are in the past in the present intensely and imaginatively, not vicariously. You are in the spirit world of the writer, with the writer. The spirits are in dialogue and you are part of the dialogue, listening, contributing with your thoughts and responses. You meet the ghosts and phantoms of the text with your own hauntedness, a hauntedness that cannot only be your own. This is the power and potential of the radically spooked text: the experimental art of trans-traumatic narrative. This is its gift in guiding us to undead losses, its mode of helping us understand so that we may, in the words of Jacques Derrida, "learn to live."[1]

Creative writing based on traumatic familial history and theoretical readings of it are traditionally divided practices that appear in distinct and different contexts. This chapter primarily uses examples from my poetic prose novel, *Luna Alaska*, as well as Derrida's theory of hauntology and Nicolas Abraham and Maria Torok's concept of the phantom, to explore the affective operations of trans-traumatic practice, aiming to show that some writing exceeds the "about" of trauma to embody its subjective and cultural processes, thereby becoming literature of traumatic heritage.

"Traumatic writing" (otherwise known as post-traumatic writing) is a term used in trauma theory to describe writing, often historical, which

[1] Jacques Derrida, *Specters of Marx*, trans. Peggy Kamuf (New York: Routledge, 1994), xvii.

represents usually catastrophic or apocalyptic traumatic experience, such as the Holocaust.[2] In literary theory, traumatic writing has been positioned as an attempt to liberate the unconscious and speak the unspeakable and the literally unthinkable. Some have hailed the singular capacity of poetry to say the unsayable, but the claim is perhaps better made that poetry (as well as other art such as visual art and music) expressed the *otherwise* unsayable.[3] The great German poet Rilke affirmed the intimacy between the poetic word and affective silence when he wrote, "Words gently end at the edge / of the Unsayable" in *Sonnets to Orpheus*.[4] I once attended a master class[5] with eminent American poet Michael Palmer in which he spoke of the likeness between poetry and dance in their ability to express the otherwise inexpressible through rhythm, meter and gesture (made physically or viscerally in language). Palmer spoke too of the poetic reach to say the unsayable and poetry's attempt to articulate the potential, and prior-to-language, of experience. If we think of that potential and prior-to-language unsayableness as the existential unsayable, I asked him, what of the poetics of the traumatic unsayable, which is not potential nor prior to, but past, present, and widely considered to resist language? In answer, Palmer mentioned psychotic poetry and its incantorary, magical and "outside the psyche" quality, before admitting that he hadn't given the matter of the traumatic unsayable much thought.

I take up that question by way of a form of writing I call the poetics of trans-trauma—trans-trauma being my abbreviation for the familial transgenerational transmission of trauma and its relations with cultural and collective trauma. I discuss the work this kind of writing does and the means by which it might be accomplished, seeking to show that such literature is writing in which movement between the past and the present takes place within a current of heightened affect capable of generating a textual embodiment of trauma spanning generations. To that end I employ a definition of psychic trauma that does not simply indicate repression or

---

[2] Dominick LaCapra, "Trauma, Absence, Loss." *Critical Inquiry* 25, no.4 (1999), 696-727, and *Writing History, Writing Trauma* (Baltimore: Johns Hopkins University Press, 2001).

[3] Cathy Caruth, "Unclaimed Experience: Trauma and the Possibility of History," Yale French Studies 79: 181-192 (1991) and *Unclaimed Experience: Trauma, Narrative, and History* (Baltimore: Johns Hopkins University Press 1996).

Shshana Felman and Dori Laub, *Testimony: Crisis of Witnessing in Literature, Psychoanalysis and History* (New York: Routledge, 1992).

[4] Rainer Maria Rilke, *Sonnets to Orpheus,* trans. Stephen Cohn (New York: Routledge, 2002).

[5] Hosted by the Writing and Society Research Centre at University of Western Sydney, May 26, 2010.

the failure to process an event of the past, but rather an understanding that trauma is the past operative in the present, which may, in part, be brought to light through the act of writing. As Cathy Caruth states, "Trauma is not locatable in a single violent or original event in an individual's past but rather in the way that its very unassimilated nature—the way it was precisely *not known* in the first instance—returns to haunt the survivor later on."[6] Here Caruth hints at that which is at the heart of both Derrida's and Abraham and Torok's hauntologies, sharing, as they do, the quality of being *not locatable in a single violent or original event in an individual's past*. They share too an evocation of the *unassimilated nature* of trauma, the way it is *not known in the first instance*, and its tendency to *haunt*. For such reasons these theories prove useful in identifying the ways in which this past in the present operates textually and the means by which it might be written. Commenting on these oft-cited words of Caruth, Jill Bennett adds "Traumatic memory is, in this regard, resolutely an issue of the present."[7] Bennett's point that trauma is *resolutely an issue of the present* is also crucial to my conception of a poetics of trans-trauma, though as will become clear, Derrida's hauntology even questions the notion of a static present.

This essay is not a textual analysis as such, nor is it interested in reading literature for "hidden" traumas. I am concerned with a grander venture. Dori Laub has suggested that massive psychic trauma is "a record that has yet to be made."[8] My interest lies in addressing the question of how and why a writer chronicles a record yet to be made, and how such a chronicle of transgenerational trauma might be made in a manner that illuminates the cultural conditions and collective trauma associated with it. To my mind, the enquiry is not so much whether or not a given text contains specters, but to what degree they are present and through what strategies; whether or not they are consciously acknowledged and articulated, and in what manner. I view the poetics of trans-trauma as a particularly haunted literature that actively engages with the specter, either in its amorphous ghostly form or its more pointedly named or indicated phantom/s. In order to write this kind of text a writer must defy the conventions that would negate and avoid such hauntings; it must surpass writings that deny the existence of ghosts. This is perhaps why haunted textuality is more likely in creative writing than in formulaic, journalistic or academic writing. Derrida speaks of the hostility toward ghosts when he

---

[6] Caruth, *Unclaimed Experience: Trauma, Narrative, and History*, 4.
[7] Jill Bennett, *Empathic Vision: Affect, Trauma, and Contemporary Art* (Stanford, Calif: Stanford University Press, 2005), 40.
[8] Felman and Laub, *Testimony*, 57.

says, "There has never been a scholar who really, and as scholar, deals with ghosts. A traditional scholar does not believe in ghosts—nor in all that could be called the virtual space of spectrality."[9]

I maintain that part of the efficacy of this super-spooked practice of writing is that though it is unable to fully articulate trauma in language, it nevertheless speaks of, and to, that which hovers between presence and absence, unnamable and unknowable in the usual sense. I turn now to an outline of the modes by which it does this, drawing on Derrida's notion of the "specter" and Abraham and Torok's "phantom."

Derrida's Specter vs. the Psychoanalytic Phantom

Colin Davis's essay, "Hauntology, Spectres and Phantoms," [10] contrasting Derrida's notion of the "specter" and Abraham and Torok's concept of the "phantom," offers a distinguishing framework for thinking about narrative in the writing of trauma, its capacity to embody the trauma of past generations and to illuminate the nature of traumatic memory in its tendency to surface as repetition. Hauntology, Davis assures us, is far from a hackneyed belief in the supernatural. Rather it is a philosophy of trauma and mourning. He summarizes it thus:

> [I]n literary critical circles, Derrida's rehabilitation of ghosts as a respectable subject of enquiry has proved to be extraordinarily fertile. Hauntology supplants its near-homonym ontology, replacing the priority of being and presence with the figure of the ghost as that which is neither present nor absent, neither dead nor alive. Attending to the ghost is an ethical injunction insofar as it occupies the place of the Levinasian Other: a wholly irrecuperable intrusion in our world, which is not comprehensible within our available intellectual frameworks, but whose otherness we are responsible for preserving [...] It has nothing to do with whether or not one believes in ghosts.[11]

Abraham and Torok only use the idiom "the phantom" for their concept, while Derrida employs the words "specter," "ghost," and occasionally "phantom," interchangeably. Davis describes Abraham and Torok's phantom as the site of transgenerational transmission and communication —the way in which the undisclosed traumas of one generation influence

[9] Derrida, *Specters of Marx*, 11.

[10] Colin Davis, "Hauntology, Spectres and Phantoms," *French Studies* 59, no. 3 (2005), 373-379.

[11] Ibid., 373.

and disturb the life of another.[12]. Abraham and Torok themselves position the phantom as an alternative, multi-generational, operation, an alternative to the individualist construction of Freudian thought, writing that:

> The concept of the phantom moves the focus of psychoanalytic inquiry beyond the individual being analyzed because it postulates that some people unwittingly inherit the secret psychic substance of the ancestors' lives. The 'phantom' represents a radical reorientation of Freudian and Post-Freudian theories of psychopathology, since here symptoms do not spring from the individual's own life experiences but from someone else's psychic conflicts, traumas, or secrets.[13]

Also crucial is Abraham and Torok's concept of "the secret," which is not just, or even, a secret in the usual sense, but an entombed event or experience bound to an internal silence which results in a subjective split that is inherently shameful and diminishing.

The phantom then is the manner in which the secret(s) of a previous generation embed in and haunt subsequent generations, with or without their awareness of the traumatic event or events. Abraham and Torok posit the phantom as the "presence of a dead ancestor in the living Ego, still intent on preventing its traumatic and usually shameful secrets from coming to light," and they seek to "return the ghost to the order of knowledge."[14] In contrast, Davis explains, Derrida:

> wants to avoid any such restoration and to encounter what is strange, unheard, *other*, about the ghost. For Derrida, the ghost's secret is not a puzzle to be solved; it is the structural openness or address directed towards the living by the voices of the past or the not yet formulated possibilities of the future.[15]

Derrida's hauntology resists an interpretive project. Rather, as Davis assures us, "Derrida's specter is a deconstructive figure hovering between life and death, presence and absence, and making established certainties vacillate. It does not belong to the order of knowledge."[16]

---

[12] Ibid., 376.
[13] Nicolas Abraham and Maria Torok, *The Shell and the Kernel: Renewals of Psychoanalysis*, ed. Nicholas Rand (Chicago: University of Chicago Press, 1994), 166.
[14] Davis, "Hauntology, Spectres and Phantoms," 374; 378.
[15] Ibid.
[16] Ibid., 376.

This Derridean notion of the ghost will, throughout this chapter, be applied to textual hauntings more diffuse, diluted, or hybrid than phantomological haunting, and the term specter will be employed as a reference to either, both, or to haunting in general. I want to retain something of the specificity of the concept of the phantom, while questioning the assumption that a return to the order of knowledge is necessary, or even achievable.

In the beginning (Biblical pun intended), trauma and affect were theorized by the early pioneers of psychoanalysis, such as Pierre Janet, Josef Breuer, Sigmund Freud, and Sándor Ferenczi. Abraham and Torok, Hungarian-French analysts and theorists, were credited with a renewal of psychoanalytic theory during the 1960s and 70s; they fused philosophy, psychology, linguistics, and literary theory to posit a unique view of trauma, with particular attention to transgenerational transmission, partly advancing and partly challenging the foundational psychoanalytic legacy. Freud, at the forefront of the bourgeoning new "science," had hypothesized trauma and affect in terms of "personal identity as beset by unconscious conflicts, desires, and fantasies,"[17] and as editor Nicholas T. Rand is quick to point out in his introduction to the collected essays of Abraham and Torok, *The Shell and the Kernel*, the critical difference between their approach and that of traditional psychoanalysis lies in the fact that: "In Abraham and Torok's view, attempting to analyze a person in the light of predetermined ideas (such as theories of repressed incestuous wishes or fear of the castrating father) runs the risk of condemning the person's genuine suffering to eternal silence."[18]

According to Davis, Derrida was somewhat influenced by Abraham and Torok, and he was instrumental in bringing about their publication.[19] Paradoxically, despite Derrida's effort to bring the writings of Abraham and Torok to a wider audience, it is, Davis suggests, largely because of Derrida that they have drifted into semi-obscurity. Davis writes:

> Despite the intellectual vigor of works by Rand, Rashkin and others, the direct impact of Abraham and Torok on literary studies has in fact been limited, perhaps because the endeavor to find undisclosed secrets is likely to succeed in only a small number of cases. By contrast, Derrida's *Spectres de Marx* has spawned a minor academic industry. His hauntology has

[17] Rand, "Introduction: Renewals of Psychoanalysis." In *The Shell and the Kernel*, by Nicolas Abraham and Maria Torok, ed. Nicholas Rand (Chicago: University of Chicago Press, 1994), 18.
[18] Ibid., 1.
[19] Davis, "Hauntology, Spectres and Phantoms," 373.

> virtually removed Abraham and Torok from the agenda of literary ghost studies; or, to be more precise, when Abraham and Torok are now discussed by deconstructive-minded critics, their work is most frequently given a distinctly Derridean inflection.[20]

As will become clear, I too distance myself from the investigative project of which Davis speaks and view Abraham and Torok's phantom with a "Derridean inflection" in terms of textual analysis, but I also want to reaffirm the value of the phantom, as conceived by Abraham and Torok, and its usefulness in thinking about the operations of traumatic affect in narrative. I will begin my exploration of their differences and contributions, via Davis, with a focus on what the two theories agree on—the critical involvement of grief in spectrality—in order to argue that the poetics of trans-trauma illustrates the mournful phenomenon of trauma by way of a kind of writing through tears.

Luna Alaska[21] is a synthesis of fiction and memoir. It is fuelled by affect and its words are the indelible marks of love: the love of and for my family, first love, and the love of a therapeutic relationship. It is, above all, a work of love and mourning. Indeed, the novel begins with the grieving of the protagonist:

> Crying on the bus one day, looking out the window at people on the street, it suddenly struck Luna as incredible that everyone wasn't crying. Watching them scurry, she was seized with the conviction that they should, each and every one of them, be crying in banks, in elevators, at the hairdressers, and while eating lunch. How would the world be if a spell were cast disabling all the mechanisms, the avoiding, refusing, masking, displacing, suppressing, sublimating and medicating? Wouldn't we be stopped in our tracks and transformed into a sinking mass of grief, melded out of the hardness of our forms by our pooling suffering? Wouldn't every heart crack open and pour out its secret hurts? Wouldn't humanity shiver with light as its armor dropped, leaving nothing but pulsing tenderness? Is there anyone you would not love?[22]

If I have done my work correctly—if I have *worked* at all—it stands as an account of spectrality, both in its phantomatic and ghostly guises. And by "work" I mean a creative act of the mourning so central in hauntology. Derrida states:

---

[20] Ibid., 376.
[21] Meera Atkinson, *Luna Alaska* (unpublished manuscript, December 27, 2013), Microsoft Word file.
[22] Ibid., 1.

> Mourning always follows a trauma. I have tried to show elsewhere that the work of mourning is not one kind of work among others. It is work itself, work in general, the trait by means of which one ought perhaps to reconsider the very concept of production—in what links it to trauma, to mourning, to the idealizing iterability of exappropriation, thus to the spectral spiritualization that is at work in any *tekhnë*.[23]

Mourning always follows a trauma, says Derrida, but since trauma is, as Caruth asserts, "*not known* in the first instance,"[24] and is therefore doomed to return to "haunt the survivor later on," mourning, recognized as such or not, hints Derrida, is the mark of such haunting. If, by tekhnë, Derrida means craft, art, labor itself, the inference is that traumatic compulsivity is an inherent aspect of work, and of writing. A pause to unpack his reference to *idealizing iterability* will help clarify the scope of his notion of hauntology. Stanely E. Fish explains that:

> when Derrida declares that 'the sign possesses the characteristic of being readable even if the moment of its production is irrevocably lost' ("SEC" 182),[25] we must understand that the moment of production is itself a moment of loss, in that its components—including sender, receiver, referents, and message—are never transparently present but must be interpreted or 'read' into being… To say that something is iterable is usually understood to mean that after an original use it can be used *again* (*iter*); but for Derrida, iterability is a *general* condition that applies to the original use, which is therefore not original in the sense of being known or experienced without reference to anything but itself.[26]

For Derrida, then, iterability implies both repetition and a lack of an original, fixed motive for the action of work. If repetition is, as Caruth points out, characteristic of trauma, and if we accept Derrida's positing of mourning as an open-ended operation with no categorical, identifiable beginning and no neat parameters *and* as the condition of production, it emerges that it is traumatic affect, most essentially grief, and, as I would add and will later show, shame, that informs the practice of the poetics of trans-trauma. Hence Derrida's vision of "*hantologie*" comes into being as

---

[23] Derrida, *Specters of Marx,* 97.
[24] Caruth, *Unclaimed Experience,* 4.
[25] Abbreviation for Jacques Derrida's "Signature Event Context," in *Margins of Philosophy,* trans. Alan Bass (Chicago: University of Chicago Press, 1984).
[26] Stanely E. Fish, "With the Compliments of the Author: Reflections on Austin and Derrida," *Critical Inquiry* 8, no. 4 (1982), 703.

"the structural openness or address directed towards the living by the voices of the past or the not yet formulated possibilities of the future."[27]

In *Specters of Marx* Derrida builds his notion of hauntology on the foundation of Marx and larger-than-life historical and political hauntings; it is explicit in the text that he views the nature of the specter, and hauntology itself, as an essentially traumatic phenomenon. It is our living, always, with loss, and with its timeless reverberations. He states:

> The logic of the key in which I hoped to orient this keynote address was one of a politico-logic of trauma and a topology of mourning. A mourning in fact and by right interminable, without possible normality, without reliable limit.[28]

Bringing this traumatic affect to consciousness is a central concern of the poetics of trans-trauma, as is its functioning as avatar of the "structural openness" and "address directed towards the living by the voices of the past." It is at this point that the critical difference between Derrida's hauntology and Abraham and Torok's phantom emerges, for though Abraham and Torok also confirm the mournful nature of spectrality, they do pursue, unlike Derrida, an endpoint, an outcome, a direct engagement which might be said to constitute "closure". Rand describes Abraham and Torok's view of haunting as the process by which: "unfelt mourning, unassimilated trauma, the unwitting psychical inheritance of someone else's secrets—drive a wedge between us and our society," before posing the question, "How can people be helped to initiate a process of introjection that has failed to occur spontaneously?"[29]

Let me return to Derrida for a moment before taking up this question of "introjection." On point one of his three-part description of the specter as "thing" Derrida says: "First of all mourning. We will be speaking of nothing else."[30] We will be speaking of nothing else in everything we speak about. Work, the work of mourning and the work of writing, "consists always in attempting to ontologize remains, to make them present, in the first place by *identifying* the bodily remains and by *localizing* the dead."[31] On point two he writes, rather poetically: "Next, one cannot speak of generations of skulls or spirits except on the condition of language—and the voice, in any case of that which *marks* the name or

---

[27] Davis, "Hauntology, Spectres and Phantoms," 378.
[28] Derrida, *Specters of Marx*, 97.
[29] Rand, "Introduction" in *The Shell and the Kernel*, 22.
[30] Derrida, *Specters of Marx*, 9.
[31] Ibid.

takes its place."[32] The condition of language is essential, but, if we are to *speak of generations of skulls or spirits* our idea of language may need to be expanded to include language (as a system of signs and symbols) outside of language proper, such as affect. On point three Derrida insists: "Finally, the thing *works*, whether it transforms or transforms itself, poses or decomposes itself: the spirit, the 'spirit of the spirit' is *work*."[33] I concern myself with this issue of work—the work of art, of writing, of therapy, of love, of *introjection*—and with what it is and does in the poetics of trans-trauma. And here we circle back to Abraham and Torok, who wait patiently, now themselves spectral, for me to ground this difficult Derrida into flesh and blood. What Derrida is talking of is, in my view, the same process that Abraham and Torok understand by the term introjection, although for Derrida the imperative is encounter, while for Abraham and Torok it has a more procedural interpretation. The term introjection itself has a long and problematic history, meaning many things to many theorists, so I take this opportunity to define my understanding and usage.

Introjection and the Paradox of the Poetics of Trans-trauma

In claiming that the poetics of trans-trauma surpasses the mere telling of a traumatic tale to facilitate the work of introjection, I use the term "introjection" in the Abraham and Torok sense of the word. Rejecting the negatively oriented Freudian use of introjection— akin to notions of incorporation and internalization—Abraham and Torok make clear the differentiation of these views with the simple assertion that, "Incorporation denotes a fantasy, introjection a process."[34] In "The Illness of Mourning and the Fantasy of the Exquisite Corpse," Torok further distinguishes their redefinition:

> Introjection does not tend toward compensation, but growth. By broadening and enriching the ego, introjection seeks to introduce into it the unconscious, nameless, or repressed libido. Thus, it is not at all a matter of 'introjecting' the object, as is all too commonly stated, but of introjecting the sum total of

[32] Ibid.
[33] Ibid.
[34] Abraham and Torok, *The Shell and the Kernel*, 125.

> the drives, and their vicissitudes as occasioned and mediated by the object.[35]

Abraham and Torok adopt a positive meaning that posits introjection as the driving force of psychic life: an intricate, life affirming and enriching endeavor by which trauma, and indeed all experience, is endured, adapted to, worked through and transformed through a process of openness, awareness and expression.[36] Elsewhere, Rand describes Abraham and Torok's interpretation of introjection, and the importance they ascribe to it, as "more than elements of therapy; it designates the driving force of psychic life in its entirety … Abraham and Torok's concept of introjection appears to be a synthetic enlargement of abreaction, binding, working out, working-through, and the work of mourning."[37].

Rand goes on to add that:

> A preliminary definition might be that it is a constant process of acquisition and assimilation, the active expansion of our potential to accommodate our own emerging desires and feelings as well as the events and influences of the external world.[38]

This question of introjection, of how people might "be helped to initiate a process of introjection that has failed to occur spontaneously,"[39] specifically through writing and reading, is one I will elaborate on further in order to disavow any affiliations with introjection as constructed as a mandate to be obeyed, a search and destroy mission, or as textual therapy. In relation to the poetics of trans-trauma, I employ introjection in terms of the gentler, Derridean inflected description of "psychic opening and expansion" put forth by Rand. It is here, in this understanding of introjection as it relates to spectrality, that I assert the significance of traumatic affect.

Trauma presents an enormous challenge to the work of introjection since it resists being known, spoken and written. Transgenerational trauma, in which a subject is called upon not only to address their own experience of trauma, but also that of preceding generations, makes introjection even more challenging and often downright elusive. To the degree that it is possible or achieved, the introjection of transgenerational trauma is

[35] Torok, "The Illness of Mourning and the Fantasy of the Exquisite Corpse" in *The Shell and the Kernel*, 113.
[36] Abraham and Torok, *Shell and the Kernel*, 1994.
[37] Rand, "Introduction" in *Shell and the Kernel*, 8.
[38] Ibid., 9.
[39] Ibid., 22.

accomplished by various means, though I am most concerned with how a writer goes about it in the act of writing. In this case, I suggest, transmitted affect appears as the incarnation of trauma, including transgenerational trauma, and that it is this traumatic affect that offers enhanced promise for introjection through an intimate exchange, communicated and mediated by the process of writing and reading. However—and this is key to my argument—a vital aspect of the unique introjectory capacity of the poetics of trans-trauma is its paradoxical refusal of the credence that trauma can ever be entirely reckoned with, or tidily or lineally "worked through." It is, therefore, this acceptance of the limitations of language in the face of trauma that gives rise to the strategies this poetic practice employs, which, when skillfully employed in creative combination, can conversely loosen those limitations.

Modes of Textual Specter: Ghostliness

In my view a text can be highly ghosted—without either dealing directly or specifically with traumatic content or history—by embodying the ghosts of distant generational traumas, or cultural traumas so collectively well tolerated as to have become accepted norm. Indeed, this kind of ghosting may be so fundamental to writing as to be its very foundation. Davis points to this in reference to Julian Wolfreys' *Victorian Hauntings: Spectrality, Gothic, the Uncanny and Literature*,[40] outlining his bold assertion that ghostliness is not just one theme among others, not merely an aspect of textuality, but rather, in the words of Wolfreys, "the ungrounded grounding of representation and a key to all forms of storytelling." Davis goes on to quote Wolfreys as stating that ghosts "exceed any narrative modality, genre or textual manifestation," and that "all forms of narrative are spectral to some extent."[41]

If we consider the transgenerational transmission of trauma as a social operation and force—that is, one that is both informed by the culture and history within which it takes place and one that in turn informs culture—Wolfreys's claim seems less far fetched. I would, however, contest that even if we accept ghostliness as the "ungrounded grounding of representation and a key to all forms of storytelling," and even if it does "exceed any narrative modality, genre or textual manifestation," it does not follow that all texts are equally spooked, or that the presence of ghosts

---

[40] Julian Wolfreys, *Victorian Hauntings: Spectrality, Gothic, the Uncanny and Literature* (New York: Palgrave, 2002).
[41] Davis, "Hauntology, Spectres and Phantoms," 378.

is as keenly encountered across all texts. When it comes to writing, it is the measure by which an experience, reality, or cultural condition resists communication in language that determines its propensity to ghostliness; hence ghostliness operates as an apparition of trauma.

Evident in elements such as mood, tone and ambiance, ghostliness is channeled by a writer affectively as that which does not quite make it into text but which the text nevertheless conjures up. Toni Morrison's novel *Beloved*,[42] is not only spooked with Sethe's murdered daughter, it is spooked with the entire American slave trade, the history and impact of which is simply too colossal, communal and prolonged to be written as a phantomological secret. A writer like Kathy Acker[43] may have been channeling ghostly traumas around patriarchy; misogyny and sexuality too socially entrenched, eroticized and romanticized to be revealed in any more exact and rational way in her violent and confronting books. Haruki Murakami's[44] surreal and atmospheric novels are ghosted with the specter of Japan's relationship to the West, the shared history of war and cultural produce. Texts such as these are more haunted by Derrida's "vacillating of established certainties" than by Abraham and Torok's explicitly coded traumas.

It stands to reason that a text can be both ghosted and phantomized. The ghostliness of *Luna Alaska* has to do with the specters of war and of the double move of both the patriarchal rejection and sexual objectification of women, palpable in Luna's mother's sex addiction, Luna's grandmother's troubled fusion of frigidity and flirty glamour, and in the youthful Luna's obsessive and insecure relationship with an ageing underground rock star. The ghosting of the legacy of war makes its way into the novel in a chapter that involves an exchange between Luna and her therapist, Marie Ducrot Louzon, in which Luna recounts a series of family stories passed down from her mother, Jean, and grandmother, Essie:

> Marie looked up from her furious note taking.
> - Do you know much about Essie's parents and her relationship with them, she asked.

[42] Toni Morrison, *Beloved* (New York: Plume, 1987).
[43] Kathy Acker, *Blood and Guts in High School: A Novel* (New York: Grove Press, 1994), *Don Quixote: A Novel* (New York: Grove Press, 1994), *My Mother: Demonology* (New York: Grove Press, 1994).
[44] Haruki Murakami, *South of the Border, West of the Sun* (New York: Vintage, 2000) and *Kafka on the Shore* (New York: Vintage, 2006).

- Essie talked about her mother, Iris, a lot, answered Luna. Iris had been a good student, above average, but she gave up her studies to work in a laundry and support the family—her mother and younger twin sisters—after her older brother died in the 1918 flu pandemic. Iris's father had been killed in the Boer War when Iris was only five. Essie once declared proudly that her grandfather had been an 'Imperial Bushman', but I never understood what that meant. Essie told me once, in hushed, humiliated tones, that Iris was only 17 when Essie was born, out of wedlock, to a boy who'd gone to war. She said the family thought she'd be a bastard forever, but he surprised everyone twice: first by returning and then by making an honest woman of Iris. Stan was never the same after the war though. From what Essie said Iris was miserable in the marriage. The shell shock made him hard to live with and I suppose Iris must have been frustrated, being smart and reduced to menial chores. I don't remember my great-grandmother, though she was still alive for the first six or seven years of my life. I don't think we had much to do with her, but I vaguely remember her as a caring woman, and Essie worshipped her.
- And Essie's father, Stan? Do you remember him? Marie asked.
- He died before I was born. Essie rarely talked about him, only to say that he'd been a solider in WWI and that he was 'never quite right' after that. Once she told me he got into very maudlin states and was often despondent. She said one day she found him crying in the bathroom with a razor to his neck and that he only dropped it because she started crying and begged him not to hurt himself. He died mysteriously when she was eighteen, just shy of his fortieth birthday. Essie said she had no idea what happened to him, that no one ever told her and the family never spoke of it. I got the feeling it might have been suicide.[45]

This is the only section in the novel in which war is mentioned in relation to the family, yet it ghosts the text and its characters throughout with modes of masculinity: violent, absent and broken, and gender and familial relations. Pat Barker's *Regeneration trilogy* (*Regeneration*, *The Eye in the Door* and *The Ghost Road*,[46] is an example of a more dedicated and detailed spooking of the cyclical effects of war and its spectrality. While not obviously "experimental," the trilogy embodies the poetics of trans-trauma by means of a subtle yet profound radicality, and though it is globally revered as among the finest works of literature about WWI and war trauma in English, less observed is the way Barker's profoundly layered epic testifies to the cyclical haunting of war—familial and nationalistic—by exposing the multi-generational familial transmission of trauma at the heart of war.

---

[45] Atkinson, *Luna Alaska*, 78.
[46] Pat Barker, *Regeneration Trilogy* (Ringwood, Vic: Penguin, 1999).

It is surely no accident, then, that I am discussing cultural conflict and war in relation to ghostliness, or that the gender and war ghosting in *Luna Alaska* is made most manifest in the context of the therapeutic relationship, with its ethical imperative of justice. Derrida insists that it is ethically necessary to speak of, to, and with the ghost, going so far as to state:

> No justice—let us not say no law and once again we are not speaking here of laws—seems possible or thinkable without the principle of some *responsibility* [emphasis in original], beyond all living present, within that which disjoins the living present, before the ghosts of those who are not yet born or who are already dead, be they victims of wars, political or other kinds of violence, nationalist, racist, colonialist, sexist, or other kinds of exterminations, victims of the oppressions of capitalist imperialism or any of the forms of totalitarianism.[47]

And here it is apt to remember that for Derrida the specter is not a matter of the past spooking the present, or the dead spooking the living as such. Rather, his conception of hauntology refers to that which cannot be located in time as we know it and that which acts as a kind of continuum of presents less solid than we like to imagine, describing it as: "A spectral moment, a moment that no longer belongs to time, if one understands by the word the linking of modalized presents (past present, actual present: 'now,' future present)."[48] Derrida maintains that the ghost should not be made to speak clearly and precisely but rather that it should be engaged with as an uncertainty. The ghost in the poetics of trans-trauma might be thought of as the affective traces of traumas so far past or so unspeakably pervasive as to be outside reference to an identifiable or singular phantom. In the phantomized poetics of trans-trauma, however, Derrida's poststructural hauntology and Abraham and Torok's psychoanalytic hauntology might be seen to feed off, of and into each other in suspenseful density, because as well as translating what is translatable of the phantom, the trans-trauma writer also necessarily channels the ghostly specter of what remains unknowable, unspeakable, and timeless. Such channeled affect may be less influential in a text than the phantom in a generative sense, and might rather amorphously spook the text in an energetic manner. In this way, I propose the poetics of trans-trauma as an affective witnessing of inter-generational ghost stories.

---

[47] Derrida, *Specters of Marx*, xix.
[48] Ibid., xx.

Modes of Textual Specter: The Phantom

The phantom is a different proposition to ghostly spooking since it marks the site of a particular psychic splitting, or network of splittings, and the attendant shame and weakening produced in the living subject that is host to it. Abraham states:

> To be sure, all the departed may return but some are destined to haunt: the dead who were shamed during their lifetime or those who took unspeakable secrets to the grave … the phantom is meant to objectify, even if under the guise of individual or collective hallucinations, the gap produced in us by the concealment of some part of a love object's life. The phantom is therefore also a metapsychological fact: what haunts are not the dead, but the gaps left within us by the secrets of others."[49]

As Davis sets out, the central disparity between Derridean and psychoanalytic spectrality is found in this concept of "the secret," which amounts to a traumatic gap. Davis points out that for Abraham and Torok the secrets of the lying phantom are unspeakable because of their roots in shame and prohibition. He states that for them it is not that the secret "cannot be spoken; on the contrary, they can and should be put into words so that the phantom and its noxious effects on the living can be exorcized," while for Derrida, "the ghost and its secrets are unspeakable in a quite different sense."[50]

For Derrida, Davis continues, "The secret is not unspeakable because it is taboo, but because it cannot not (yet) be articulated in the languages available to us."[51] To my mind, the introjectory value of the poetics of trans-trauma lies in precisely this tension between these two positions, in the manner in which a Derridean inflection on the phantom opens up the process of introjecting the phantom by freeing it from the demand for a definitive solution. My view of the phantomized text integrates aspects of both these spins on the secret and eschews others. In keeping with Abraham and Torok's model, I treat the phantom as an evasive and inherited site of shame and prohibition within subjectivity, one that indeed has "noxious effects on the living." I also concur that the phantom can, and must, to some degree, and in certain respects, be "put into words" in such a way as to disempower and shrink its hold. Davis emphasizes that for

---

[49] Abraham, "Notes on the Phantom: A Complement to Freud's Metapsychology," *The Shell and the Kernel*, 171.
[50] Davis, "Hauntology, Spectres and Phantoms," 378.
[51] Ibid.

Abraham and Torok the "phantom is a liar; its effects are designed to mislead the haunted subject and to ensure that its secret remains shrouded in mystery."[52]

Yet while the phantom does involve lying it is not just that the phantom lies and (mis)leads its host away from itself; the site of the phantom marks the formation of an entrenched traumatic lie in the sense that trauma shapes and changes subjectivity, especially that of children in relation to the familial other. The shame and mourning that accompany the phantom might be viewed as the affective tombstones of a traumatic lie. For these reasons I see the phantomized text as offering increased potential for the "working-through" and introjection of traumatic affect, and most particularly shame and grief, given they are the affects most central to hauntological operations.

On the other hand, I embrace Derrida's view of the hauntological secret as unspeakable "because it cannot not (yet) be articulated in the languages available to us" as integral to the understanding of trauma employed in my theorizing of the poetics of trans-trauma. I also hold to his vision of spectrality as the "structural openness or address directed towards the living by the voices of the past or the not yet formulated possibilities of the future,"[53] and heed his insistence that the specter is "a deconstructive figure hovering between life and death, presence and absence, and making established certainties vacillate" such that "[they do] not belong to the order of knowledge."[54] My perception of the phantom, then, is formed within the productive tension between these two views of haunting.

Accordingly, my novel plays with the Abraham and Torok idea that only the return of the secret to its original recipient can release the subject from the spell of a previous generation's trauma, in part exploring this potential, and in part repudiating it by declining a denouement that suggests the outing of a phantom/secret equals "case closed". A phantomological site and the revelation of a secret is, indeed, key in the novel's denouement, but this working through is not posited as an ultimate resolution of trauma, much less a cure. Rather, it merely initiates a conscious process of mourning and leaves the "structural openness or address directed towards the living by the voices of the past" well and truly open for business. In an attempt to pull off this tricky tight-rope walking maneuver, *Luna Alaska* constructs an ambitious metaphor in which a family secret, in the traditional sense of the word, stands in for a

---

[52] Ibid., 374.
[53] Ibid., 378.
[54] Ibid., 376.

phantomological secret in the Abraham and Torok sense of the word; that is, a family secret, revealed in the process of therapy, embodies the subjective splits within Luna in which the trauma of Luna Alaska's dead mother resides:

> - And then what does he do, asked Marie.
> - He follows her, answered Luna.
> - Where?
> - To her room. She's climbing the stairs and he climbs the stairs behind her and I climb the stairs behind him and . . .
> - And what?
> - I think she knows he's there, following, and the scent comes off her and he follows her like a dog and her strap falls down off her shoulder. She leaves it there, dangling around her arm. She lets the door of her room swing slow behind her and he goes in. The door doesn't close all the way and I peer in through the crack. I see him pressed hard against her, kissing her and ...
> - And what?
> - I remember the magazines.
>
> Luna's eyes opened at the same moment as she let out a terrible sound, between a groan and a whimper.
> - Oh God, I'm going to be sick. I'm going to be sick.
>
> She held her stomach with one hand and pressed the other against her mouth.
> - It's okay. It's okay. Use this, said Marie, extending the waste-paper basket.
>
> Luna took the basket and fell to the ground facing the corner, retching into the plastic bagged basket before a gust of vomit spewed forth. Marie stood behind her making strange movements with her hands, running them down Luna's spine without touching, then flicking them away.
> - Hand it back to them Luna, she said as she did so. Hand it back.
> - What, cried Luna, the taste of vomit on her lips, pressure in her chest. What?
> - The shame, said Marie. Hand it back to them. It's not yours. Hand it back. They're over there, on the other side of the room. Give it to them. Get it off you. Run your hands over your body and gather it up. Hand it back to them. You've carried it long enough.[55]

Unsurprisingly, such experimentation does exact a price. In not seeking to resolve the tension between these two claims on the secret, *Luna Alaska* toys with it. Needless to say this toying produces a sense of inevitable guilt. Mid-way through the first draft I wrote in my writing diary:

---

[55] Atkinson, *Luna Alaska*,170.

> Yesterday, writing about my grandparents who are not my grandparents but characters in my novel, part memory, part make-believe, I felt a queasy discomfort wondering what they would make of what I make these characters do. What would they themselves, my dead grandparents and my mother—cast in the novel as a four times married nymphomaniac—think of what I'm doing with their memory, of how I am distorting them, elaborating them, performing them?

It is by these guilt-inducing means that the poetics of trans-trauma makes possible a bearing witness to a familial phantomological haunting that is explicit in nature though not necessarily accurate in disclosure, one that is less the factual telling of a secreted story and more akin to a translation of it. As Walter Benjamin shows in his essay "The Task of the Translator,"[56] translation is not the straightforward transcribing from one source and language to another, but rather an art form in itself, an interpretive and creative act. If we consider traumatic experience as the source and the language of trauma as foreign—that is, outside of our language and unreadable in our own—then the work of the poetics of trans-trauma involves re-creating and re-casting its material into a narrative in the language of writing. During the writing of *Luna Alaska* a combination of sundry snippets of evidence of familial life and traumatic experience, and the affects associated with them, suggested the story that I, as a writer of transgenerational trauma, translated. So it is that by writing (through) familial trauma *affectively*, drawing on various sources—stories, rumor, official records, documents, remembered conversations, gossip, diaries, letters, photos and memory, including fragmented, distorted and unreliable memory—a writer, (in the case of *Luna Alaska*, me), channels the unassimilated trauma of familial ancestors and culture. Anything that constitutes the unassimilated nature of trauma, the very ways in which it has not been known and yet registers its attendance in individual and family life, becomes the phantomological source material of the secret the writer of trans-trauma translates. This is not to say that what actually happens in a traumatic event or family history is of no consequence in its specifics or impact; or that uncovering, speaking, writing, and reading those specifics is unimportant. Rather, it is a way of re-thinking the *truth* of traumatic experience and of considering how, in the poetics of trauma, it may be testified without reliance on *fact*.

First and second generation traumatic writing, like the poetry of Lily Brett and Alison Bechdel's graphic memoir, *Fun Home: A Family*

---

[56] Walter Benjamin, "The Task of the Translator," in *Illuminations*, trans. Harry Zohn ed. Hannah Arendt, (New York: Schocken, 1969).

Tragicomic,[57] tend to be phantom-rich, and as such they are examples of what I am referring to as a mode of translation. Brett's collection, *The Auschwitz Poems*[58] is utterly infused with the energy, memory and profound trauma of her survivor mother. Its deceptively simple poetics, appearing in lower case and unpunctuated, with titles like "Everything looked normal" and "I wear your face", packs relentless punches to the power base of the phantom. Her later collection, *After the War: Poems*,[59] charts the post-traumatic experience with a focus on second-generation acting-out and working through. Bechdel's hybrid memoir-comic uses a combination of mediums to embody the complex nature of trans-trauma narrative. With its repetition of frames about the death of her father, standing for all the unspeakable, refused losses and identifications that haunt the family and Bechdel herself, this innovative work creates a temporal texture that, in combination with other embodiments, addresses not only a familial heritage but also a cultural one. Bechdel not only translates the phantom of her father's sexual and emotional repression, she translates the historical and traumatic legacy around the oppression and persecution of homosexuals.

In this practice, the trauma of ancestors is not a matter of the past but, as Caruth[60] and Bennett[61] confirm, resolutely operative in the present of the living. In my novel, the generational trauma of Luna Alaska's family is manifest in her life: in her panic attacks and agoraphobia, in her inability to experience a full range of emotions, in her isolation, and in the seething anger and overwhelming sorrow the process of therapy allows her to access. And it is the generative power of affect that has fuelled its writing, that led the way, so to speak. Jill Bennett discusses the capacity of a deep and affective mode of thought, saying that for philosopher, Gilles Deleuze, and French poet and Holocaust survivor, Charlotte Delbo, "deep thought entails circumventing conventional thought and moving into darker regions; it is also motivated by an affective connection. But, most important, the affective encounter becomes the means by which *thought proceeds* and ultimately moves toward deeper truth."[62]

---

[57] Alison Bechdel, *Fun Home: A Family Tragicomic* (Boston: Houghton Mifflin, 2006).
[58] Lily Brett, *The Auschwitz Poems* (Brunswick, Vic: Scribe, 1986).
[59] Lily Brett, *After the War: Poems* (Carlton, Vic: Melbourne University Press, 1990).
[60] Caruth, *Unclaimed Experience*.
[61] Bennett, *Empathic Vision*.
[62] Ibid., 37, my emphasis.

It is in this way—affect and affective encounter leading thought—that the writer of trans-trauma can write about, or out of, familial or multi-generational trauma without knowledge of secrets and traumatic history, or with only patchy or distorted knowledge. It becomes possible then, to adhere to the specificity of Abraham and Torok's hypothesis of the phantom without approaching it as a problem to be solved, but rather, as dynamic source material for an exploration and translation independent of concrete personal or familial revelations (but which may nevertheless also contain them).

"The Personal Is Political" Redux

A fervent introjectory and creative motivation is needed in order to write through the inescapable shame of the secret—the ghostly or phantomatic traumatic gap. I myself had been, dare I say it, haunted by the specter of *Luna Alaska* for two decades before its completion in 2012, having scribbled the first tentative and embryonic passages way back in 1996. What kept me returning to it and redrafting until I eventually realized what the novel was about and what I was attempting to write was this keen pull of introjectory promise and the propensity for ghosts and phantoms to inhabit that mysterious inspiration called creativity. This promise and inspiration was, however, held in tension with a persistent sense of shame: why must I write this? Will it matter to anyone else? Am I being narcissistic and self-indulgent? In their introduction to *Scenes of Shame: Psychoanalysis, Shame, and Writing*, Joseph Adamson and Hilary Clark speak of shame in relation to writing, and of the "painful feeling of exposed vulnerability"[63] for the writer. Acknowledging the dangers of writing, Adamson and Clark go on to claim that, "writing, precisely because it allows one to hide and reveal oneself at the same time, also allows for an intimacy and trust to be established with another or others, perhaps, in a way that no other situation provides."[64]

Elsewhere Adamson and Clark identify "shame as the primary negative affect involved in 'empathic failure'."[65] It is the capacity of writing and literature to create a context of "dangerous exposure," along with its invitation to empathic connection that summons the hauntological spirits. In the poetics of trans-trauma a writer does this intentionally and mindfully,

[63] Joseph Adamson, and Hillary Clark, "Introduction: Shame, Affect, Writing," in *Scenes of Shame: Psychoanalysis, Shame, and Writing*, eds. Joseph Adamson and Hilary Clark (New York: State University of New York Press, 1999), 28.
[64] Ibid.
[65] Ibid., 20.

in much the same way the atmosphere of the séance is created to intensify sensitivity and receptivity to the voices of dead (whether the subsequent visitations and conversations are real, imagined or uncertain is not so much the question).

Rand says:

> Abraham and Torok explore the mental landscapes of submerged family secrets and traumatic tombs in which, for example, actual events are treated as if they had never occurred [...] What matters is the preservation of a shut-up or excluded reality. This is why the authors speak of *preservative* repression, or the topography of encrypted secrets, and contrast it with Freud's concept of *dynamic repression*. Preservative repression seals off access to part of one's own life in order to shelter from view the traumatic monument of an obliterated event.[66]

The writer of the poetics of trans-trauma must negotiate and pass through the shamefulness of the phantom, and successfully doing so in the act of writing can act as a kind of initiation and reclamation, if not a final resting place. However, the writing and reading of the phantom can, I think, assist both writer and reader to gain "access to part of one's life" that has exposed, through affective writing, "the traumatic monument of an obliterated event."

I am intimating here that the operations of the phantom in the poetics of trans-trauma means literary readers, critics and theorists need not be limited to a choice between an Abraham and Torok inspired detective-like interpretive zeal and a poststructuralist insistence on the "openness to what exceeds knowledge."[67] In its disruption of binaries that privilege logic and rationality over bodily knowing and relational intangibility, such writing constitutes a feminist practice that confronts temptations toward a binary view that would require obedient subscription to either position. While Davis stresses the importance of distinguishing between Abraham and Torok's *phantoms* and Derrida's *specters*, he also admits that theorists themselves are "not always consistent"[68] in their distinction between the terms. The usefulness in teasing out a distinction perhaps lies less in establishing conflict between them and more in collapsing the two approaches into a complimentary amalgamation, at least in relation to trans-traumatic texts. In other words, I want to entertain a Derridean inflected reading of the psychoanalytic phantom that subverts the impulse

[66] Rand, "Introduction" in *The Shell and the Kernel*, 18.
[67] Davis, "Hauntology, Spectres and Phantoms," 379.
[68] Ibid., 376.

toward interrogation in favor of a kind of experiential witnessing, one that can relax the need for outcomes and "closure," while still accomplishing the work of introjection. In this way the secrets of phantoms can be viewed less as fixed and necessarily knowable—the slipperiness of trauma, in terms of meaning, access and expression, being notorious in trauma theory—and more as fertile territory for literary testimony. As Derrida says, sounding rather Abraham and Torok phantom-like:

> the specter is a paradoxical incorporation, the becoming-body, a certain phenomenal and carnal form of the spirit. It becomes, rather some "thing" that remains difficult to name: neither soul nor body, and both one and the other. For it is flesh and the phenomenality that give to the spirit its spectral apparition, but which disappear right away in the apparition, in the very coming of the *revenant* or the return of the specter.[69]

In such literature, the process of introjection is not at odds with a *revenant* of the specter. I cast the poetics of trans-trauma as writing that draws from the depths, informed by a bodily knowledge that defies rationality, though it nevertheless involves a complex cognitive and emotional process of channeling and translation. In this way Derrida's "structural openness or address directed towards the living by the voices of the past"[70] becomes a portal for a "thinking through the body"[71] feminist practice of writing that deals with trauma as a "personal is political"[72] cultural operation.

So it is that ghosts come forth to whisper, inaudibly, into the spaces between words and grammar, and phantoms spill their secrets through the embodied affect of the writer, channeled and translated, dynamically entangled, and encountered through, and by, an affected reader.

You finish reading and put down the book—of poetry, fiction, memoir. You feel illuminated, clearer, altered, like you remembered something you have never quite known nor forgotten, like some part of you has been returned to you. You have, through the *medium* of literature, engaged with

---

[69] Derrida, *Specters of Marx*, 6.

[70] Davis, "Hauntology, Spectres and Phantoms," 379.

[71] Jane Gallop, *Thinking Through the Body, Gender and Culture* (New York: Columbia University Press,1988), 1.

[72] The term 'the personal is political' is commonly credited to Carol Hanisch, the author of 'The Personal is Political', in *Notes From the Second Year: Women's Liberation: Major Writings of Radical Feminists,* eds. Shulamith Firestone and Anne Koedt (New York: Radical Feminist Publications, 1970), but in an updated version of the essay that appears on her website, Hanisch states that it was not she, but editors Firestone and Koedt who came up with the title, http://www.carolhanisch.org/CHwritings/PIP.html (accessed December 27, 2012).

the ghosts and phantoms with whom you pass the days, and you have emerged from this dance with death incredibly alive.

Bibliography

"Abraham Bomba." Visual History Biographic Profiles, USC Shoah Foundation Institute. http://tc.usc.edu/vhiechoes/bios/Bomba.Abraham .pdf.

A Poet: Unconcealed Poetry (Puisi Tak Terkuburkan). Directed by Garin Nugroho, 1999.

A Silence Full of Things. Directed by Alejandra Canales, 2005 http://vimeo.com/3504830.

Abraham, Nicolas and Maria Torok. *The Shell and the Kernel: Renewals of Psychoanalysis*. Edited and translated by Nicholas Rand. Chicago: University of Chicago Press, 1994.

Acker, Kathy. *Blood and Guts in High School: A Novel.* New York: Grove Press, 1994a.

—. *Don Quixote: A Novel.* New York: Grove Press, 1994b.

—. *My Mother: Demonology.* New York: Grove Press, 1994c.

Adamson, Joseph, and Hillary Clark. "Introduction: Shame, Affect, Writing." In *Scenes of Shame: Psychoanalysis, Shame, and Writing*, edited by Joseph Adamson and Hilary Clark, 1-35. New York: State University of New York Press, 1999.

Adorno, Theodor W. *Ästetische Theorie*. Frankfurt am Main: Suhrkamp, 1970.

—. *Notes to Literature Volume One*. Translated by Shierry Weber Nicholsen. New York: Columbia University Press, 1991.

—. *Negative Dialectics.* Translated by E.B. Ashton. New York: Continuum, 1996.

—. *Aesthetic Theory*. Translated by Robert Hullot-Kentor. Minneapolis: University of Minnesota Press, 1997.

Agamben, Giorgio. "Kommerell, or On Gesture." In *Potentialities. Collected Essays in Philosophy,* edited and translated by Daniel Heller-Roazen 77-85. Stanford: Stanford University Press, 1999.

—. "Notes on Gesture." In *Infancy and History. On the Destruction of Experience*, translated by Liz Heron, 133-140. London: Verso, 2007.

Ahmed, Sara. *The Cultural Politics of Emotion*. New York: Routledge, 2004.

—. *The Promise of Happiness*. Durham: Duke University Press, 2010.

Akasaka, Norio. *Yanagita Kunio no yomikata: Mo hitotsu no minzokugaku wa kano ka*. Tokyo: Chikuma shinsho, 1994.

Allen, Matthew J. and Steve D. Brown. "Embodiment and Living Memorials: The Affective Labour of Remembering the 2005 London Bombings." *Memory Studies* 4, no. 3 (2011): 312-327.

Allsop, Samara Lea. "Gojira/Godzilla." In *The Cinema of Japan and Korea*, edited by Justin Bowyer, 63-70. New York: Wallflower Press, 2004.

Altheide, David L. and Robert P. Snow. *Media Logic*. London: Sage, 1979.

Améry, Jean. *At the Mind's Limits: Contemplations by a Survivor on Auschwitz and Its Realities*. Translated by Sidney Rosenfeld and Stella P. Rosenfeld. Bloomington, Indiana: Indiana University Press, 1980.

Ampofo, Lawrence, Nick Anstead, and Ben O'Loughlin. "Trust, Confidence and Credability: Citizen Responses on Twitter to Opinion Polls During the 2010 UK General Election." *Information, Communication & Society* 14, no. 6 (2011): 850-871.

Appadurai, Arjun. *Modernity at Large*. Minneapolis: University of Minnesota Press, 1996.

Arendt, Hanna. *On Revolution*. Harmondsworth: Penguin, 1990.

Atkinson, Meera. *Luna Alaska*. Sydney: Humanities and Communication Arts, University of Western Sydney.

Awan, Akil, Andrew Hoskins, and Ben O'Loughlin. *Radicalisation and Media: Terrorism and Connectivity in the New Media Ecology*. London: Routledge, 2011.

Baer, Ulrich. *Spectral Evidence: The Photography of Trauma*. Cambridge, MA: MIT Press, 2005.

Bagaric, Mirko, and Julie Clarke. *Torture: When the Unthinkable Is Morally Permissible*. Albany, NY: State University of New York Press, 2007.

Baker, Steve. "'You Kill Things to Look at Them': Animal Death in Contemporary Art." In *Killing Animals*, edited by The Animal Studies Group, 69-98. Urbana, IL: University of Illinois Press, 2006.

Ball, Karyn. "The Longing for the Material." *Differences: A Journal of Feminist Cultural Studies* 17, no. 1 (2006): 47-87.

Barker, Pat. *Regeneration Trilogy*. Ringwood, Vic: Penguin, 1999.

Barthes, Roland. *The Rustle of Language*. Translated by Richard Howard. Berkeley: University of California Press, 1989.

Bashu (*The Little Stranger*). Directed by Bahram Beyzai, 1986.

Bush Mechanics. Directed by Bahram Beyzai. A film Australia National Interest Program in association with Warlpiri Media Association Inc., 2001.

Baudrillard, Jean. *For a Critique of the Political Economy of Signs*. St. Louis: Telos, 1981.
Bechdel, Alison. *Fun Home: A Family Tragicomic*. Boston: Houghton Mifflin, 2006.
Benjamin, Walter. *Illuminations: Essays and Reflections*, translated by Harry Zohn, edited by Hannah Arendt, 253-264. New York: Schocken, 1968.
—. *Gesammelte Schriften*, edited by Hermann Schweppenhäuser and Rolf Tiedemann, 7 vols. in 14. Frankfurt am Main: Suhrkamp, 1972-89.
—. *The Origin of German Tragic Drama*, Translated by. John Osborne. London: NLB, 1977 and New York: Verso, 1998.
—. *Reflections: Essays, Aphorisms, Autobiographical Writings*, translated by Edmund Jephcott, edited by Peter Demetz, 177-192. New York: Harcourt Brace Jovanovich, 1978.
—. *Écrits français*, ed. Jean-Maurice Monnoyer. Paris: Gallimard, 1991.
—. *Selected Writings, 1913-1926*, translated by Rodney Livingstone, edited by Marcus Bullock and Michael W. Jennings, 6-17. Cambridge, MA: Harvard University Press, 1996.
Bennett, Jill. *Empathic Vision: Affect, Trauma, and Contemporary Art*. Stanford: Stanford University Press, 2005.
Bennett, W. Lance. "Toward a theory of press-state relations." *Journal of Communication* 40, no. 2 (1991): 103-125.
Bennett, W. Lance and Steven Livingston. "A Semi-independent Press: Government Control and Journalistic Autonomy in the Political Construction of News." *Political Communication* 20 (2003): 359-362.
Bennett W. Lance, R. G. Lawrence and Steven Livingston. "None Dare Call it Torture: Indexing and the Limits of Press Independence in the Abu Ghraib Scandal." *Journal of Communication* 56 (2006):467-485.
Berlant, Lauren. "Affect in the End Times." *Qui Parle: Critical Humanities and Social Sciences* 20, no. 2 (Spring/Summer 2012): 71-89.
Bernstein, J.M. *The Fate of Art: Aesthetic Alienation from Kant to Derrida and Adorno*. University Park, PA: The Pennsylvania State University Press, 1992.
Besterman, Theodore. *Voltaire*. Oxford: Blackwell, 1976.
Beugnet, Martine. *Cinema and Sensation: French Film and the Art of Transgression*. Carbondale: Southern Illinois University Press, 2007.
Biddle, Jennifer. *Breasts, Bodies, Canvas: Central Desert Art as Experience*. Sydney: UNSW Press, 2007.
—. "Art Under Intervention: The Radical Ordinary of June Walkutjukurr Richards." *Art Monthly* 227 (March 2010): 35-39.

Boltanski, Luc and Eve Chiapello. *The New Spirit of Capitalism*. Translated by Gregory Elliot. London: Verso, 2005.

Bradshaw, John. *Healing the Shame That Binds You*. Florida: Health Communications, Inc, 1988.

Brand, Alice. "Hot Cognition: Emotions and Writing Behavior." *Journal of Advanced Composition* 6 (1985-6): 11.

Branden, Joseph. "John Cage and the Architecture of Silence." *October* (1997): 80-104.

Breen, John ed., *Yasukuni, the War Dead, and the Struggle for Japan's Past*. New York: Columbia University Press, 2008.

Brennan, Teresa. *History After Lacan*. London: Routledge, 1993.

—. *The Transmission of Affect*. Ithaca: Cornell University Press, 2004.

Brett, Lily. *The Auschwitz Poems*. Brunswick, Vic: Scribe, 1986.

—. *After the War: Poems*. Carlton, Vic: Melbourne University Press, 1990.

Brodersen, Momme. *Walter Benjamin: A Biography*, translated by Maclolm R. Green and Ingrida Ligers, edited by Martina Dervis. London: Verso, 1996

Brothers, Peter H. "Japan's Nuclear Nightmare: How the Bomb Became a Beast Called *Godzilla*." *Cineaste* 36, no. 3 (Summer 2011): 36-40.

Bruno Latour. "An Attempt at a 'Compositionist Manifesto'." *New Literary History* 41 (2010): 471-490.

Bucci, Wilma. *Psychoanalysis and Cognitive Science*. New York and London: Guilford Press, 1997.

Burt, Jonathan. *Animals in Film*, London: Reaktion Books, 2002.

—. "Morbidity and Vitalism: Derrida, Bergson, Deleuze, and Animal Film Imagery." *Configurations* 14, no. 1-2 (Winter-Spring 2006): 157-179.

Callard, Felicity and Constantina Papoulias. "Affect and Embodiment." In *Memory: Histories, Theories, Debates*, edited by Susannah Radstone and Bill Schwarz, 246-262. New York: Fordham University Press, 2010.

Cardinal, Marie. *Les Mots Pour Le Dire*. Paris: Grasset, 1975.

Caruth, Cathy, "Unclaimed Experience: Trauma and the Possibility of History." *Yale French Studies* 79 (1991): 181-192.

—. ed. *Trauma: Explorations in Memory*. Baltimore: Johns Hopkins University Press, 1995.

—. *Unclaimed Experience: Trauma, Narrative, and History*. Baltimore: Johns Hopkins University Press, 1996.

Castells, Manuel. *Communication Power*. Oxford: Oxford University Press, 2009.

Caygill, Howard. *A Kant Dictionary*. Malden, MA: Blackwell Publishing, 1995.

Chadwick, Andrew. *The Hybrid Media System: Power and Politics*. Oxford: Oxford University Press, forthcoming.

Chelkowski, Peter. *Ritual and Drama in Iran*. New York: New York University Press, 1979.

Chevrie, Marc and Hervé Le Roux. "Site and Speech. An Interview with Clause Lanzmann about *Shoah*." In *Claude Lanzmann's Shoah. Key Essays*, edited by Stuart Liebman, 37-49. Oxford: Oxford University Press, 2007.

Clough, Patricia Ticiento, ed. *The Affective Turn: Theorizing the Social*. Durham: Duke University Press, 2007.

Cole, David. *Torture Memos: Rationalizing the Unthinkable*. Oxford: Oneworld, 2009.

Connolly, William. *The Augustian Imperative: A Reflection on the Politics of Morality*, London: Sage, 1993.

Coole, Diana. "Rethinking Agency: A Phenomenological Approach to Embodiment and Agentic Capacities." *Political Studies* 53, no. 1 (2005): 124-142.

Cottle, Simon. *Mediatized Conflict: Developments in Media and Conflict Studies*. Maidenhead: Open University Press, 2006.

Coward, Ros. "'They Have Given Me Somebody Else's Voice—Blair's Voice'." *The Guardian*, November 10, 2005, accessed September 29, 2012. http://www.guardian.co.uk/politics/2005/nov/10/media.media.

D'est. Directed by Chantal Akerman, 1993.

Dällenbach, Lucien. *Le récit spéculaire. Essai sur la mise en abyme*. Paris: Seuil, 1977.

Daniel, Douglass K. *Tough as Nails: The Life and Films of Richard Brooks*. Madison: University of Wisconsin Press, 2011.

Darwin, Charles. *The Expression of the Emotions in Man and Animals*. Edited by F. Darwin. London: John Murray, 1904.

Davis, Colin. "Hauntology, Spectres and Phantoms." *French Studies* 59, no. 3 (2005): 373-379.

de Man, Paul. *Allegories of Reading*. New Haven: Yale University Press, 1979.

—. *The Rhetoric of Romanticism*. New York: Columbia University Press, 1984.

Del Favero, Dennis, Ursula Frohne and Peter Weibel, eds. *Un_imaginable*. Sydney: iCinema/University of New South Wales, 2008.

Deleuze, Gilles. *Cinema 1: The Movement-Image*. Translated by H Tomlinson and B. Habberjam. Minneapolis: University of Minnesota Press, 1986.

—. *Spinoza: Practical Philosophy*. Translated by Robert Hurley. San Francisco: City Lights Books, 1988.

—. *Cinema 2: The Time-Image*. Translated by Hugh Tomlinson and Barbara Habberjam. New York: Zone, 1992.

—. "Ethology: Spinoza and Us." In *Incorporations*, edited by Jonathan Crary and Sanford Kwinter, 625-633. New York: Zone, 1992.

—. *Difference and Repetition*. Translated by Paul Patton. London: Continuum, 2004.

—. *Francis Bacon: The Logic of Sensation*. Translated by Daniel W. Smith. Minneapolis: University of Minnesota Press, 2004.

Deleuze, Gilles and Félix Guattari. *Kafka: Toward a Minor Literature*. Translated by Dana Polan. Minneapolis: University of Minnesota Press, 1986.

—. *A Thousand Plateaus: Capitalism and Schizophrenia*. Translated by Brian Massumi. Minneapolis: University of Minnesota Press, 1987.

—. *What Is Philosophy?* Translated by Hugh Tomlinson and Graham Burchell. New York: Columbia University Press, 1994.

Derrida, Jacques. *Specters of Marx*. Translated by Peggy Kamuf. New York: Routledge, 1994.

Derrida, Jacques and Jean Birnbaum. *Learning to Live Finally: The Last Interview*. New York: Studio Visit, 2004.

Dershowitz, Alan M. *Why Terrorism Works*. Connecticut: Yale University Press, 2002.

Downer, Anthony. "In the Event of Fire: Precarious Images, the Aesthetics of Conflict, and the Future of an Anachronism." *Ibraaz*, July 13, 2012, accessed October 4, 2012. http://www.ibraaz.org/essays/30.

Ellis, John. *Documentary: Witness and Self-Revelation*. London: Routledge, 2011.

Evans, Caroline. "Prof John Tulloch, 7/7 London Bomb Survivor, Fights to Stay in UK." *BBC News Wales*, September 2, 2012, accessed September 29, 2012. http://www.bbc.co.uk/news/uk-wales-19455691.

Felman, Shoshana. "Psychoanalysis and Education: Teaching Terminable and Interminable." In "The Pedagogical Imperative: Teaching as a Literary Genre," special issue, *Yale French Studies* 63, (1982): 21-44.

—. "In an Era of Testimony: Claude Lanzmann's *Shoah*." *Yale French Studies* 79 (1991): 39-81.

—. "Benjamin's Silence." *Critical Inquiry* 25, no.2 "Special Issue: 'Angelus Novus': Perspectives on Walter Benjamin" (1999): 201-234.

Felman, Shoshana, and Dori Laub. *Testimony: Crises of Witnessing in Literature, Psychoanalysis, and History*. New York: Routledge, 1992.

Fischer, Bernd and Tim Mehigan, eds. *Heinrich von Kleist and Modernity*. Rochester, NY: Camden House, 2011.

Fish, Stanley E. "With the Compliments of the Author: Reflections on Austin and Derrida." *Critical Inquiry* 8, no. 4 (1982): 693-721.

Formis, Barbara. "Dismantling Theatricality: Aesthetics of Bare Life." In *The Work of Giorgio Agamben: Law, Literature, Life,* edited by Justin Clemens, Nicholas Heron and Alex Murray, 181-192. Edinburgh: Edinburgh University Press, 2011.

Frances Guerin and Roger Hallas, eds. *The Image and the Witness: Trauma, Memory and Visual Culture*. London: Wallflower Press, 2007.

Freud, Sigmund. *The Uncanny*. Translated by David McLintock. New York: Penguin Books, 2003.

Friedland, Amos. "Forgiveness, Reconciliation, and the Remains of Resentment." PhD diss., New York: The New School, 2002.

Frosh, Paul and Amit Pinchevski, eds. *Media Witnessing: Testimony in the Age of Mass Communication.* Basingstoke: Palgrave Macmillan, 2009.

Frühstück, Sabine and Eyal Ben-Ari. "'Now We Show It All!' Normalization and the Management of Violence in Japan's Armed Forces." *The Journal of Japanese Studies* 28, no. 1 (Winter 2002): 1-39.

Fuchs, Thomas. "The Phenomenology of Body Memory." In *Body Memory, Metaphor and Movement*, edited by Sabine C. Koch, Thomas Fuchs, Michela Summa, and Cornelia Müller, 9-22. Amsterdam: John Benjamins Publishing, 2004.

Furedi, Frank. *Therapy Culture: Cultivating Vulnerability in an Uncertain Age*. London: Routledge, 2004.

Gailus, Andreas. *Passions of the Sign: Revolution and Language in Kant, Goethe, and Kleist.* Baltimore: The Johns Hopkins University Press, 2006.

—. "Breaking Skulls: Kleist, Hegel, and the Force of Assertion." In *Heinrich von Kleist and Modernity*, edited by Bernd Fischer and Tim Mehigan, 243-256. Rochester, NY: Camden House, 2011.

Gallop, Jane. *Thinking Through the Body, Gender and Culture*. New York: Columbia University Press, 1988.

Gibbs, Anna. "Contagious Feeling: Pauline Hanson and the Epidemiology of Affect." *The Australian Humanities Review* 24 (2001). http://www.australianhumanitiesreview.org/archive/Issue-December-2001/gibbs.html.

—. "Writing and Danger: The Intercorporeality of Affect." In *Creative Writing: Theory Beyond Practice*, edited by Nigel Krauth and Tess Brady, 157-168. Teneriffe: Post Pressed, 2006.

—. "Horrified: Embodied Vision, Media Affect And The Images From Abu Ghraib." In *Interrogating the War on Terror*, edited by Deborah Staines, 125-142. London: Cambridge Scholars Publishing, 2007.
—. "Panic! Affect Contagion, Mimesis and Suggestion in the Social Field." *Cultural Studies Review* 14, no. 2 (2008): 16.
—. "After Affect: Sympathy, Synchrony and Mimetic Communication." In *The Affect Theory Reader*, edited by Melissa Gregg and Gregory J. Seigworth, 186-205. Durham, NC: Duke University Press, 2010.
Gilman, Sander. "The Aesthetics of Blackness in Heinrich von Kleist's 'Die Verlobung in St. Domingo'." *Modern Language Notes* 90 (1975): 661-672.
Gordon, Avery F. *Ghostly Matters: Haunting and the Sociological Imagination*. Minneapolis: University of Minnesota Press, 1997.
Gregg, Melissa, and Gregory J. Seigworth, eds. *The Affect Theory Reader*. Durham, NC: Duke University Press, 2010.
—. "An Inventory of Shimmers." In *The Affect Theory Reader*, edited by Melissa Gregg and Gregory J. Seigworth, 1-25. Durham, NC: Duke University Press, 2010.
Griswold, Deirdre. *Indonesia 1965: The Second Greatest Crime of the Century*. New York: World View Publishers, 1979.
Grose, Anouchka. "In Annecy, a Child Witnesses Murder. It Can't be Sewn into 'Normal'." *The Guardian*, September 7, 2012, accessed September 26, 2012.
http://www.guardian.co.uk/commentisfree/2012/sep/07/annecy-child-witnessed-murder?INTCMP=SRCH
Günther, Kurt. "Die Konzeption von Kleists 'Die Verlobung in Santo Domingo.'" *Euphorion* 17 (1910): 68-95, 313-331.
Guyer, Paul, ed. *The Cambridge Companion to Kant's Critique of Pure Reason*. New York: Cambridge University Press, 2010.
Haidu, Peter. "The Dialectics of Unspeakability: Language, Silence, and the Narratives of Desubjectification." In *Probing the Limits of Representation: Nazism and the "Final Solution,"* edited by Saul Friedlander, 277-299. Boston: Harvard University Press, 1992.
Hallin, Daniel C. *The "Uncensored War"*. Berkeley: University of California Press, 1986.
Hanisch, Carol. "The Personal is Political." In *Notes From the Second Year: Women's Liberation: Major Writings of Radical Feminists,* edited by Shulamith Firestone and Anne Koedt. New York: Radical Feminist Publications, 1970.
Hansen, Miriam. "'With Skin and Hair': Kracauer's Theory of Film, Marseille 1940." *Critical Inquiry* 19, no. 3 (Spring 1993): 437-469.

—. "*Schindler's List* is not *Shoah*: the Second Commandment, Popular Modernism and Public Memory." *Critical Inquiry* 22 (Winter 1996): 291-312.
—. "Benjamin and Cinema: Not a One-Way Street." *Critical Inquiry* 25, no. 2 (Winter 1999): 305-343.
—. "The Mass Production of the Senses: Classical Cinema as Vernacular Modernism." In *Reinventing Film Studies,* edited by Christine Gledhill and Linda Williams, 332-350. London: Arnold, 2000.
Hardt, Michael. "Foreward." In *The Affective Turn: Theorizing the Social*, edited by Patricia Ticiento Clough, ix-xiii. Durham: Duke University Press, 2007.
Harris, Whitney. *Tyranny On Trial: The Evidence at Nuremberg*. New York: Barnes & Noble, 1954.
Herd, Judith Ann. "The Neonationalist Movement: Origins of Japanese Contemporary Music." *Perspectives of New Music* 27, no. 2 (Summer, 1989): 118-163.
Herman, Judith Lewis. *Trauma and Recovery: from Domestic Abuse to Political Terror.* London: Pandora, 1994.
High, Jeffrey. "Crisis, Denial, and Outrage: Kleist (Schiller, Kant) and the Path to the German Novella(s) of Modernity." In *Heinrich von Kleist and Modernity*, edited by Bernd Fischer and Tim Mehigan, 187-203. Rochester, NY: Camden House, 2011.
Hirsch, Marianne and Leo Spitzer. "Gendered Translations: Claude Lanzmann's *Shoah*." In *Claude Lanzmann's Shoah. Key Essays,* edited by Stuart Liebman, 175-190. Oxford: Oxford University Press, 2007.
—. "The Witness in the Archive. Holocaust Studies / Memory Studies." In *Memory. Histories, Theories, Debates,* edited by Susannah Radstone and Bill Schwartz, 396-398. New York: Fordham University Press, 2010.
Histoires d'Amérique. Directed by Chantal Akerman, 1989
Hjarvard, Stig. "From Bricks to Bytes: The Mediatization of a Global Toy Industry." In *European Culture and the Media*, edited by I. Bondebjerg and P. Golding, 43-63. Bristol: Intellect Books, 2004.
—. "The Mediatization of Religion: A Theory of the Media as Agents of Religious Change." *Northern Lights* 6 no. 1 . (2008): 9-26.
—. "The Mediatization of Society: A Theory of the Media as Agents of Social and Cultural Change." *Nordicom Review* 29, no. 2 (2008): 105-134.
Hobbes, Thomas. *Leviathan or The Matter, Forme, and Power of A Commonwealth Ecclesiasticall and Civil* (1651). Reprinted in Mentson, England: Scholar Press Limited, 1969.

Hogan, Desmond. "Kant's Copernican Turn." In *The Cambridge Companion to Kant's Critique of Pure Reason*, edited by Paul Guyer, 21-40. New York: Cambridge University Press, 2010.

Horton, Scott. "The Worst of the Worst?" *Harper's Magazine*, October 2, 2009.

Hoskins, Andrew and Ben O'Loughlin. *War and Media: The Emergence of Diffuse War*. Cambridge: Polity, 2010.

Hoskins, Andrew. *Televising War: From Vietnam to Iraq*. London: Continuum, 2004.

—. "The Mediatization of Memory." In *Save As . . . Digital Memories*, edited by Joanne Garde-Hansen, Andrew Hoskins and Anna Reading, 27–43. Palgrave Macmillan, Basingstoke, 2009.

—. "7/7 and Connective Memory: Interactional Trajectories of Remembering in Post-Scarcity Culture." *Memory Studies* 4, no. 3 (2011): 269-280.

—. *The Mediatization of Memory: Media and the End of Collective Memory*. Cambridge, MA: MIT Press, forthcoming.

Hosokawa, Shuhei. "Atomic Overtones and Primitive Undertones: Akira Ifukube's Sound Design for *Godzilla*." In *Off the Planet: Music, Sound and Science Fiction Cinema*, edited by Philip Hayward, 42-60. London: John Libbey, 2004.

Hospital, Janette Turner. *Orpheus Lost*. New York: W. W. Norton, 2007.

Hoy, David. *The Time of Our Lives: A Critical History of Temporality*. Cambridge, MA: The MIT Press, 2009.

Huff, Steven R. *Heinrich von Kleist's Poetics of Passivity*. Rochester, New York: Camden House, 2009.

Hutchings, Kimberly. *Time and World Politics: Thinking the Present*. Manchester: Manchester University Press, 2008.

Igarashi, Yoshikuni. *Bodies of Memory: Narrative of War in Postwar Japanese Culture, 1945-1970*. Princeton: Princeton University Press, 2000.

Jacobs, Carol. *Uncontainable Romanticism: Shelley, Brontë, Kleist*. Baltimore: The Johns Hopkins University Press, 1989.

Jaworski, Adam. "Introduction: An Overview." In *Silence: Interdisciplinary Perspectives,* edited by Adam Jaworski, 3-14. Berlin: Mouton de Gruyter, 1997.

Jayamanne, Laleen. *Towards the Cinema and it's Double*. Bloomington: Indiana University Press, 2001.

Jeanne Dielmann Quai de Commerce. Directed by Chantal Akerman, 1975

Johansen, Stine Liv. "The Mediatization of Children's Play." Project at the University of Copenhagen. Details, no date, accessed September 29, 2012. http://mediatization.ku.dk/publications/children/.

Jürs-Munby, Karin. "'Did you Mean Post-traumatic Theatre?': The Vicissitudes of Traumatic Memory in Contemporary Postdramatic Performance." *Performance Paradigm* 5, no. 2 (2009): 1-33.

Kaiser, Volker. "Epistemological Breakdown and Passionate Eruptions: Kleist's Die Verlobung in St. Domingo." *Studies in Romanticism* 42, no. 3 (2003): 341-367.

Kant, Immanuel. *Kritik der Urteilskraft. Werkausgabe Volume 10.* Edited by Wilhelm Weischedel. Frankfurt/Main: Suhrkamp Verlag, 1974.

—. *Critique of Pure Reason.* Translated by Norman Kemp Smith. London: MacMillan, 1978.

—. *Critique of Judgment.* Translated by Werner S. Pluhar. Indianapolis: Hackett, 1987.

—. *Prolegomena to Any Future Metaphysic that will be able to come forward as Science* in *Immanuel Kant: Philosophy of Material Nature.* Translated by James W. Ellington. Indianapolis: Hackett Publishing Copany, 1985.

Kaplan, E. Ann. *Trauma Culture: the Politics of Terror and Loss in Media and Literature.* New Brunswick, NJ: Rutgers University Press, 2005.

Kerner, Aaron. "Gojira vs. Godzilla: Catastrophic Allegories." In *Ritual and Event: Interdisciplinary Perspectives*, edited by Mark Franko, 109-124. New York: Routledge, 2007.

Kitzinger, Jenny. "Media Templates: Key Events and the (Re)construction of Meaning." *Media, Culture & Society* 22, no. 1 (2000): 61-84.

Kleist, Heinrich von. *The Marquise of O—and Other Stories.* Translated and introduction by David Luke and Nigel Reeves. New York: Penguin, 1978.

—. *Sämtliche Werke und Briefe, Münchner Ausgabe Band II: Erzählungen Prosa Gedichte Briefe.* Munich: Deutscher Taschenbuchverlag, 2011.

Koch, Gertrud. "The Aesthetic Transformation of the Image of the Unimaginable: Notes on Claude Lanzmann's '*Shoah*'." Translated by Jamie Owen Daniel and Miriam Hansen. *October* 28 (1989): 15-24.

Koestler, Arthur. *Arrival and Departure.* Harmondsworth, UK: Penguin, 1969.

Kristeva, Julia. *Powers of Horror: An Essay on Abjection.* Translated by Leon S. Roudiez. New York: Columbia University Press, 1982.

—. *Strangers to Ourselves.* Translated by Leon S. Roudiez. New York: Columbia University Press, 1991.

—. *Intimate Revolt: The Powers and Limits of Psychoanalysis*. Translated by Jeanine Herman. New York: Columbia University, 2002.

LaCapra, Dominick. *Representing the Holocaust: History, Theory, Trauma*. Ithaca, NY: Cornell University Press, 1994.

—. "Lanzmann's '*Shoah*': Here There is No Why." *Critical Inquiry* 23, no. 2 (Winter, 1997): 231-269.

—. *History and Memory after Auschwitz*. Ithaca, NY: Cornell University Press, 1998.

—. "Trauma, Absence, Loss." *Critical Inquiry* 25, no.4 (1999): 696-727.

—. *Writing History, Writing Trauma*. Baltimore: The Johns Hopkins University Press, 2001.

Lane, Richard J. *Reading Walter Benjamin: Writing Through the Catastrophe*. New York: Manchester University Press, 2005.

Lanzmann, Claude. *Shoah. The Complete Text of the Acclaimed Film*. New York: Da Capo Press, 1995.

—. *Le lièvre de Patagonie*. Paris: Gallimard, 2009

Lanzmann, Claude, Ruth Larson and David Rodowick. "Seminar With Claude Lanzmann 11 April 1990." *Yale French Studies* 79 (1991): 82-99.

Les rendez-vous d'Anna. Directed by Chantal Akerman, 1978

Levinas, Emmanuel. *Time and the Other*. Translated by Richard A. Cohen. Pittsburgh: Duquesne University Press, 1987.

Liebman, Stuart. "Introduction." In *Claude Lanzmann's Shoah. Key Essays,* edited by Stuart Liebman, 3-23. Oxford: Oxford University Press, 2007.

Lifton, Robert Jay. *Death in Life: Survivors of Hiroshima*. New York: Random House, 1967.

Limerick, Patricia Nelson. *The Legacy of Conquest: The Unbroken Past of the American West.* New York: Norton, 1987.

Livingstone, Sonia. "Foreword: Coming to Terms with 'Mediatization'." In *Mediatization: Concept, Changes, Consequences*, edited by Knut Lundby, ix-xi. New York: Peter Lang, 2009.

Lokaneeta, Jinee. "A Rose by Another Name: Legal Definitions, Sanitized Terms, and Imagery of Torture in *24*." *Law, Culture and the Humanities* 6, no. 2 (2010): 245-274.

Lorenzo-Dus, Nuria and Annie Bryan. "Dynamics of Memory: Commemorating the 2005 London Bombings in British Television News." *Memory Studies* 4, no. 3 (2011): 281-297.

Lyotard, Jean-François. *Heidegger and "the Jews"*. Translated by A. Michel and M.S. Robert. Minneapolis and London: University of Minnesota Press, 1990.

Madianou, Mirca. "News as a Looking-glass: Shame and the Symbolic Power of Mediation." *International Journal of Cultural Studies* 15, no. 1 (2011): 3-16.

Marks, Laura U. *The Skin of the Film: Intercultural Cinema, Embodiment, and the Senses.* Durham & London: Duke University Press, 2000.

Marrati, Paola. *Genesis and Trace* Stanford: Stanford University Press, 2004.

Marvin, Garry. "Wild Killing." In *Killing Animals*, edited by The Animal Studies Group, 10-29. Urbana, IL: University of Illinois Press, 2006.

Massumi, Brian. "The Autonomy of Affect." In *Deleuze: A Critical Reader*, edited by Paul Patton, 217-39. Cambridge, MA: Blackwell, 1996.

—. *Parables for the Virtual: Movement, Affect, Sensation.* Post-Contemporary Interventions. Durham: Duke University Press, 2002.

—. *Semblance and Event: Activist Philosophy and the Occurrent Arts.* Cambridge, Mass: The MIT Press, 2011.

Mazzoleni, Gianpetro and W. Schulz. "'Mediatization of Politics': A Challenge for Democracy?" *Political Communication* 16, no. 3 (1999): 247-261.

Mazzoleni, Gianpetro. "Mediatization of Politics." In *The International Encyclopedia of Communication*, edited by Woflgang Donsbach. Malden, MA: Blackwell, 2008.

McCullagh, Declan. "Congressman Wants WikiLeaks Listed as Terrorist Group." *CNET*, November 28, 2010, accessed September 26, 2012. http://news.cnet.com/8301-13578_3-20023941-38.html.

Mehigan, Tim. *Heinrich von Kleist: Writing after Kant.* Rochester, NY: Camden House, 2011.

Menninghaus, Winfried. *Disgust: Theory and History of a Strong Sensation.* Translated by Howard Eiland and Joel Golb. New York: State University of New York Press, 2003.

Merrin, William. *Baudrillard and the Media: A Critical Introduction.* Cambridge: Polity, 2005.

Miller, Philip B, ed. *An Abyss Deep Enough: Letters of Heinrich von Kleist.* New York: E.P. Dutton, 1982.

Mills, Catherine. *The Philosophy of Giorgio Agamben.* Montreal: McGill/Queen's University Press, 2008.

Moi, Toril ed. *The Kristeva Reader.* Oxford: Blackwell, 1995.

Mor, Ben. "Public Diplomacy in Grand Strategy." *Foreign Policy Analysis* 2, no. 2 (2006): 157-176.

Morrison, Toni. *Beloved.* New York: Plume, 1987.

Mottahedeh, Negar. "Bahram Bayzai." In *Life and Art: the New Iranian Cinema*, edited by Rose Issa and Sheila Whitaker, 73-82. London: National Film Theatre, 1999.

Murakami, Haruki. *South of the Border, West of the Sun*. New York: Vintage, 2000.

—. *Kafka on the Shore*. New York: Vintage, 2006.

Murray, Robin L. and Joseph K. Heumann. "Transcontinental Technologies: Telegraphs, Trains, and the Environment in *Union Pacific*, *Jesse James*, and *The Last Hunt*." In *Gunfight at the Eco-Corral: Western Cinema and the Environment*, edited by Robin L. Murray and Joseph K. Heumann, 143-173. Norman, OK: University of Oklahoma Press, 2012.

Naïr, Sami. "*Shoah*, une leçon d'humanité." In *Au sujet de Shoah: Le Film de Claude Lanzmann,* edited by Michel Deguy, 172-174. Paris: Belin, 1990.

Nash, Mark. "Experiments with the Truth: The Documentary Turn." *Anglistica* 11 no. 1-2 (2007): 33-40.

Nathanson, Donald. *Shame and Pride: Affect, Sex and the Birth of the Self.* New York and London: WW Norton, 1992.

Neilson, Brett. "Data, Zone, Territory." Position paper for *Data, Memory, Territory* 1 (2012): 16. http://digitalmediaresearch.org/wp-content/uploads/2012/11/373_UWS_Digital-Media-Research_Digest-v20-Web.pdf.

Neuman, Scott. "Clinton: WikiLeaks 'Tear At Fabric' Of Government." *NPR*, November 29, 2010, accessed September 26, 2012. http://www.npr.org/2010/11/29/131668950/white-house-aims-to-limit-wikileaks-damage.

Newman, Kim. "Japan's Bizarre Behemoth." *Sight & Sound* 20, no. 9 (September 2010): 11.

News From Home. Directed by Chantal Akerman, 1976

Nichols, Bill. *Blurred Boundaries: Questions of Meaning in Contemporary Culture.* Bloomington, Indianapolis: Indiana University Press, 1994.

—. "The Terrorist Event." In *Ritual and Event: Interdisciplinary Perspectives*, edited by Mark Franko, 93-108. New York: Routledge, 2007.

Noriega, Chon. "Godzilla and the Japanese Nightmare: When 'Them!' Is U.S." *Cinema Journal* 27, no. 1 (Autumn, 1987): 63-77.

Nuit et Brouillard. Directed by Alain Resnais, 1955.

O'Loughlin, Ben. "Commentary: The Phenomenology of the Event: Remembering the 2005 London Bombings." *Memory Studies* 4, no. 3 (2011): 328-331.

Olin, Margaret, "Lanzmann's *Shoah* and the Topography of the Holocaust Film." *Representations* 57 (1997): 1-23.

Oliver, Kelly. *Witnessing. Beyond Recognition.* Minneapolis: University of Minnesota Press, 2001.

Owens, Craig. "The Allegorical Impulse: Toward a Theory of Postmodernism." *October* 12 (Spring 1980): 67-86.

—. "The Allegorical Impulse: Toward a Theory of Postmodernism Part 2." *October* 13 (Summer, 1980): 58-80.

Peters, John Durham. "Witnessing." *Media, Culture & Society* 23, no. 6 (2001): 707-723.

Philips, James. *The Equivocation of Reason: Kleist Reading Kant.* Stanford: Stanford University Press, 2007.

Plaxton, Michael. "Justifying Absolute Prohibitions on Torture as If Consequences Mattered." In *Warrior's Dishonour: Barbarity, Morality and Torture in Modern Warfare*, edited by George Kassimeris, 205-21. Hampshire, UK: Ashgate, 2006.

Pollock, Griselda. "The Long Journey: Maternal Trauma, Tears and Kisses in a Work by Chantal Akerman." *Studies in the Maternal* 2, no. 1 (2010). www.mamsie.bbk.ac.uk.

Powell, Anna. *Deleuze and Horror Film.* Edinburgh: Edinburgh University Press, 2005.

Probyn, Eslpeth. *Blush: Faces of Shame*. Sydney: UNSW Press, 2005.

A Question of Silence. Written and directed by Marlene Gorris, 1982.

Radstone, Susannah. "Trauma Theory: Context, Politics, Ethics." *Paragraph* 30, no.1 (2007): 9-29.

Ramadanovic, Petar. "In the Future . . . On Trauma and Literature." In *Topologies of Trauma: Essays on the Limit of Knowledge and Memory,* edited by Linda Belau and Petar Ramadanovic. New York: Other Press, 2002.

Ray, Gene. "Reading the Lisbon Earthquake: Adorno, Lyotard, and the Contemporary Sublime." *The Yale Journal of Criticism* 17, no. 1 (2004): 1-18.

Reider, Noriko T. "The Appeal of 'Kaidan,' Tales of the Strange." *Asian Folklore Studies* 59, no. 2 (2000): 265-283.

—. *Japanese Demon Lore: Oni from Ancient Times to the Present*. Logan, Utah: Utah State University Press, 2010.

Rejali, Darius *Torture and Democracy*. Princeton: Princeton University Press, 2007.

Richardson, Michael. "Who Speaks? Torture and the Ethics of Voice." *TEXT* 16, no. 1 (2012). http://www.textjournal.com.au/april12/richardson.htm.

—. "Writing Torture's Remnants." In *Speaking the Unspeakable*, edited by Jeanne Clark and Catherine Collins. Oxford: ID Press, (2013).

—. "Writing Trauma: Affected in the Act." *New Writing: The International Journal for the Practice and Theory of Creative Writing* 10 (forthcoming, 2013).

Rilke, Rainer Maria. *Sonnets to Orpheus*. Translated by Stephen Cohn. New York: Routledge, 2002.

Rossiter, Ned and Soenke Zehle. "Organizing Networks: Notes on Collaborative Constitution, Translation, and the Work of Organization." *Cultural Politics* 5, no. 2 (2009): 237-264.

Rossiter, Ned. "The Informational University, the Uneven Distribution of Expertise and the Racialization of Labour." *Edu-Factory Journal* 0 (January 2010): 62-73. http://www.edu-factory.org/wp/wp-content/uploads/2011/08/Rossiter.pdf.

Rutherford, Anne. "Poetics and Politics in Garin Nugroho's *A Poet.*" *Senses of Cinema* 17 (2001). http://archive.sensesofcinema.com/contents/01/17/poet.html.

—. "The Poetics of a Potato: Documentary that Gets Under the Skin." *Metro* 137 (2003): 126-131.

—. *"What Makes a Film Tick?": Cinematic Affect, Materiality and Mimetic Innervation*. Bern: Peter Lang, 2011.

Santer, Eric. "History Beyond the Pleasure Principle: Some Thoughts on the Representation of Trauma." In *Probing the Limits of Representation Nazism and the Final Solution,* edited by Saul Friedlander, 143-154. Cambridge: Harvard University Press, 1992.

SAPFF (Sydney Asia Pacific Film Festival). Press kit for *A Poet*, 2001.

Scarry, Elaine. *The Body in Pain: The Making and Unmaking of the World*. New York: Oxford University Press, 1985.

Schefer, Raquel. "Re-constitutions. On 'Mueda, Memória e Massacre' ('Mueda, Memory and Massacre'), by Ruy Guerra." Intense Proximity, 2012. http://www.latriennale.org/en/lejournal/you-do-not-stand-one-place-watch-masquerade/re-constitutions-mueda-memoria-e-massacre.

Schmitt, Carl. *Politische Theologie*. Munich: Duncker & Humblot, 1922.

Scholem, Gershom. *Walter Benjamin: The Story of a Friendship*, translated by Harry Zohn. New York: Schocken, 1988.

Schwab, Gabriele. *Haunting Legacies: Violent Histories and Transgenerational Trauma.* New York: Columbia University Press, 2010.

Scott, D.F.S. "Heinrich von Kleist's Kant Crisis." *The Modern Language Review* 42, no. 4 (1947): 474-484.

Sedgwick, Eve Kosofsky. *Touching Feeling: Affect, Pedagogy, Performativity.* Durham & London: Duke University Press, 2003.

Sedgwick, Eve Kosofsky, and Adam Frank. "Shame in the Cybernetic Fold: Reading Silvan Tomkins." In *Shame and Its Sisters: A Silvan Tomkins Reader*, edited by Eve Kosofsky Sedgwick and Adam Frank, 1-28. Durham: Duke University Press, 1995.

Sedgwick, Eve Kosofsky, and Adam Frank, eds. *Shame and Its Sisters: A Silvan Tomkins Reader*. Durham: Duke University Press, 1995.

Selzer, Mark. *Serial Killers: Death and Life in America's Wound Culture*. New York: Routledge, 1998.

Sennett, Richard. *The Craftsman*. New Haven, CT: Yale University Press, 2008.

Shahar, Galili. "Fragments and Wounded Bodies: Kafka after Kleist." *The German Quarterly* 80, no. 4 (Fall 2007): 449-467.

Shaviro, Steven. *The Cinematic Body*. Minneapolis: Minnesota University Press, 1993.

Shepherdson, Charles. "Emotion, Affect, Drive: For Teresa Brennan." In *Living Attention: On Teresa Brennan,* edited by Alice A. Jardine, Shannon Lundeen, and Kelly Oliver, 57-78. New York: SUNY Press, 2007.

Sheridan, Mary Beth. "Hillary Clinton: WikiLeaks Release an 'Attack on International Community'." *Washington Post*, November 29, 2010, accessed September 26, 2012. http://www.washingtonpost.com/wp-dyn/content/article/2010/11/29/AR2010112903231.html.

Shoah. Directed by Claude Lanzmann, 1985.

Skoller, Jeffrey. *Shadows, Specters, Shards: Making History in Avant-Garde Film*. Minneapolis: University of Minnesota Press, 2005.

Slotkin, Richard. *The Fatal Environment: The Myth of the Frontier in the Age of Industrialization, 1800-1890*. Middletown, CT: Wesleyan University Press, 1985.

Sobchack, Vivien. *The Address of the Eye: A Phenomenology of Film Experience.* Princeton: Princeton University Press, 1992.

—. *Carnal Thoughts: Embodiment and Moving Image Culture*. Berkeley: University of California Press, 2004.

Sontag, Susan. *Styles of Radical Will.* New York: Delta Publishing, 1969.

—. *Against Interpretation, and Other Essays*. New York: Farrar, Straus and Giroux, 2001.

—. *Regarding the Pain of Others.* London: Penguin, 2003.

Spiegel Online International. "The WikiLeaks Iraq Logs: A Protocol of Barbarity." 25 October, 2010, accessed September 26, 2012. http://www.spiegel.de/international/world/the-wikileaks-iraq-logs-a-protocol-of-barbarity-a-724026-7.html.

—. "Outrage and Apologies: Washington Fights to Rebuild Battered Reputation." December 6, 2010, accessed September 26, 2012. http://www.spiegel.de/international/world/outrage-and-apologies-washington-fights-to-rebuild-battered-reputation-a-733088.html.

Spinoza. *The Ethics and Selected Letters*. Translated by Samuel Shirley. London: Hackett Publishing Company, 1982.

Spivak, Gayatri. "Can the Subaltern Speak?" In *Marxism and the Interpretation of Culture*, edited by Cary Nelson and Lawrence Grossberg, 271-313. Chicago: University of Illinois Press, 1988.

Stolen Generations. Directed by Darlene Johnson. Tapestry International Cinema, 2000.

Strömbäck, Jesper and Daniela V. Dimitrova. "Mediatization and Media Interventionism: A Comparative Analysis of Sweden and the United States." *International Journal of Press/Politics* 16, no. 1 (2011): 30-49.

Tabata, Masahide. "なぜゴジラは都市を破壊するのか" ("Why Does Godzilla Destroy Cities?") *Studies in Urban Culture* 5 (2005): 16-29.

Taussig, Michael. *Mimesis and Alterity: A Particular History of the Senses.* London and New York: Routledge, 1993.

Thompson, John. "Shifting Boundaries of Public and Private Life." *Theory, Culture & Society* 28, no. 4 (2011): 49-70.

Tomkins, Silvan and Donald Mosher. "Scripting the Macho Man: Hypermasculine Socialization and Enculturation." *Journal of Sex Research* 20, no. 1 (1988): 60-84.

Tomkins, Silvan S. *Affect, Imagery, Consciousness*. 4 vols. New York & London: Springer & Tavistock, 1963-1992.

Torchin, Leshu. *Creating the Witness: Documenting Genocide on Film, Video, and the Internet*. Minneapolis: University of Minnesota Press, 2012.

Toute une nuit. Directed by Chantal Akerman, 1982

Tulloch, John. *One Day in July: Experiencing 7/7*. London: Little, Brown, 2006.

Tulloch, John and R. Warwick Blood. *Icons of War and Terror: Media Images in an Age of International Risk*. New York and Abingdon: Routledge, 2012.

Turkle, Sherry. *Alone Together*. New York: Basic Books, 2011.

UN Committee on the Elimination of Racial Discrimination. "Concluding Observations of the Committee on the Elimination of Racial Discrimination (Australia)." United Nations, 2010. http://daccess-ods.un.org/access.nsf/Get?Open&DS=CERD/C/AUS/CO/15-17&Lang=E.

Urry, John. "The Complexity Turn." *Theory, Culture & Society* 22, no. 5 (2005): 1-14.

UWS Dissenter. http://uwsdissenter.wordpress.com/

Van Veeren, Elspeth. "Interrogating 24: Making Sense of US Counterterrorism in the Global War on Terrorism." *New Political Science* 31, no. 3 (2009): 361-384.

von Sturmer, John. "Aborigines, Representation, Necrophilia" *Art and Text* 32 (1989): 127-139.

Warlpiri Media Association. *Night Patrol (Munga Wardingki Partu).* Co-production with CAAMA, 1997.

Weineck, Silke. "Kleist and the Resurrection of the Father." *Eighteenth-Century Studies* 37, no. 1 (2003): 69-89.

Winter, Jay. "Thinking About Silence." In *Shadows of War: A Social History of Silence in the Twentieth Century,* edited by Efrat Ben-Ze'ev, Ruth Ginio and Jay Winter, 3-31. Cambridge: Cambridge University Press, 2012.

Wolfreys, Julian. *Victorian Hauntings: Spectrality, Gothic, the Uncanny and Literature*. New York: Palgrave, 2002.

Yomota, Inuhiko. "The Menace from the South Seas: Honda Ishiro's *Godzilla* (1954)." In *Japanese Cinema: Texts and Contexts*, translated by Sachiko Shikoda, edited by Alastair Phillips and Julian Stringer, 102-111. London, England: Routledge, 2007.

CONTRIBUTORS

Meera Atkinson is a writer, poet and academic. She engaged in research on the transgenerational transmission and poetics of trauma, with particular focus on the nexus between trauma and affect in familial and cultural transmission, in her PhD with the Writing and Society Research Centre at the University of Western Sydney. Her writing has appeared in many publications, including *Salon.com*, *Best Australian Stories 2007*, *Best Australian Poems 2010* and *M/C Journal,* and she has been a contributor to the Australian quarterly *Griffith REVIEW* since its beginnings.

Karyn Ball is a professor of English and Film Studies specializing in literary and cultural theory at the University of Alberta. Her articles have appeared in *Cultural Critique*, *Women in German Yearbook*, *Research in Political Economy*, *Differences*, *English Studies in Canada, New Literary History,* and *Alif.* Other publications include the edited collection, *Traumatizing Theory: The Cultural Politics of Affect in and beyond Psychoanalysis* (Other Press, 2007), and *Disciplining the Holocaust* (State University of New York Press, 2008) as well as recent chapters on Franz Kafka and Hannah Arendt. Her essay, "Hayden White's Hope, or the Politics of Prefiguration," is forthcoming in *Philosophy of History after Hayden White* edited by Robert Doran (Continuum 2013).

Jennifer L. Biddle is Senior Research Fellow in the Centre for Contemporary Art and Politics (CCAP), National Institute for Experimental Arts (NIEA), College of Fine Arts, C University of New South Wales. She conducts research with Warlpiri women in Lajamanu, and has published widely on language, affect and cultural difference; translation, art, aesthetics and the politics of interpretation; Central Desert writing and art. Her latest monograph is entitled *breasts, bodies, canvas: Aboriginal art as Experience* (2007, UNSW Press) and she is currently Australian Research Council Future Fellow for her project *Remote Avant-Garde: Experimental Indigenous Arts.*

Shoshana Felman is Woodruff Professor of Comparative Literature and French at Emory University. She specializes in 19th and 20th century

French and English literature, literature and psychoanalysis, trauma and testimony, literature and philosophy, and law and literature. Previously, she was Thomas E. Donnelly Professor of French and Comparative Literature at Yale University. Her publications include *The Juridical Unconscious: Trials and Traumas in the Twentieth Century* (2002), *What Does a Woman Want? Reading and Sexual Difference* (1993), and *Testimony: Crises of Witnessing in Literature Psychoanalysis and History* (co-authored with Dori Laub, M.D., 1992). Her work was collected in the 2007 volume *The Claims of Literature: A Shoshana Felman Reader*. In 2010 she was elected a Fellow of the American Academy of Arts and Sciences.

Anna Gibbs is Associate Professor of Communications at the University of Western Sydney and a member of the Writing & Society Research Centre. At times she has been a member of the editorial boards of *Australian Cultural Studies*, *The UTS Review*, *Cultural Studies*, and *Social Semiotics,* as well as on the board of various arts organisations. She has co-edited two collections of Australian writing, and her current research interests include affect theory, public emotion, embodiment and corporeality, psychoanalysis, and media (including writing for new media). Recent publications include 'Affect Theory and Audience' *The Handbook of Media Audiences* (ed. Virginia Nightingale, 2011) and 'After Affect' in *The Affect Theory Reader* (ed. Melissa Gregg & Greg Seigworth, 2010).

Aaron Kerner is Associate Professor in the Cinema Department at San Francisco State University. He is the author of *Torture Porn: Horror, Exploitation, and the Cinema of Sensation in the Post-9/11 Era* (forthcoming) and *Film and the Holocaust: New Perspectives on Dramas, Documentaries, and Experimental Films* (2011). He has also published on the subject of Japanese cinema in *positions: east asia cultures critique,* and the Norton reader *Film Analysis* (second edition, 2012).

Jonathan L. Knapp has worked in the film curatorial departments at Yerba Buena Center for the Arts and the Pacific Film Archive at UC Berkeley, and for a number of film festivals in the San Francisco Bay Area. He studied English literature and Film Studies at Bowdoin College and Cinema Studies at San Francisco State University. He has written about the arts, with an emphasis on film, for the *San Francisco Bay Guardian* and *Film Arts*. His present research focuses on cinematic ruins and sacred space.

Ricardo Mbarkho is an artist and Adjunct Director of the Visual Arts School of the Académie Libanaise des Beaux-Arts at the University of Balamand, Beirut, Lebanon. In his aesthetic approach, he questions a society where the breakdown of social cohabitation is maintained in a continuous struggle over power and belonging. His work has been presented at several festivals in Lebanon and internationally. He received his Art Diplomas from Ecole Nationale Supérieure des Beaux-Arts and Ecole Supérieure d'Etudes Cinématographiques, Paris, and from Institut Supérieur des Beaux-Arts, Beirut. He also completed an exchange program at Carnegie Mellon University, Pittsburgh, PA, USA. Ricardo Mbarkho is represented by Mark Hachem Gallery.

Ben O'Loughlin is Professor of International Relations and Co-Director of the New Political Communication Unit at Royal Holloway, University of London. He is co-editor of the Sage journal *Media, War & Conflict*. His books include *Radicalisation and Media: Terrorism and Connectivity in the New Media Ecology* (2011) and *War and Media: The Emergence of Diffused War* (2010). He has carried out projects on media and security for the UK's Economic and Social Research Council, Technology Strategy Board and the Centre for the Protection of National Infrastructure. He has contributed to the *New York Times*, *Guardian*, *OpenDemocracy*, *Sky News* and *Newsweek*.
Email: Ben.OLoughlin@rhul.ac.uk. Twitter: @Ben_OLoughlin

Michael Richardson completed his PhD on torture, affect and power in the war on terror with the Writing and Society Research Centre at the University of Western Sydney. Prior to commencing his doctorate he was speechwriter to Jack Layton, former Leader of the Official Opposition in Canada. His academic work has been published in *TEXT Journal*, *New Writing: The International Journal of the Theory & Practice of Creative Writing*, *Journal of Literature and Trauma Studies*, and the edited collection *Speaking the Unspeakable* (ed. Catherine Collins, 2013). He is also a novelist.

Anne Rutherford is Senior Lecturer in Cinema Studies in the School of Humanities and Communication Arts, University of Western Sydney. Her book, '*What Makes a Film Tick?': Cinematic Affect, Materiality and Mimetic Innervation* (Peter Lang 2011) examines the ways affective immersion in cinema works to engage viewers with history, memory and cultural specificity. She has published numerous essays, interviews and creative works on cinematic affect and embodiment, aesthetics, mise en scène, film sound, documentary and 'animate thought' in ethnographic photography. She has also made several short films. Her current research explores relationships between cinema and architectural space in installation work.

Magdalena Zolkos is Senior Research Fellow in the School of Humanities and Communication Arts and the University of Western Sydney. Prior to coming to Australia, she held an Izaak Walton Killam Postdoctoral Fellowship, at the University of Alberta, Canada. She is the author of *Reconciling Community and Subjective Life. Trauma Testimony as Political Theorizing in the Work of Jean Amery and Imre Kertesz* (2010), and her edited collections include *On Jean Amery: Philosophy of Catastrophe* (2011), and *State, Security, and Subject Formation* (with Anna Yeatman, 2010). She has published and taught in the fields of democratic theory, continental/critical political theory, feminism, human rights and European politics.

INDEX